faith first

Grade Two
Parish Catechist Guide

Faith First Development Team

RCL

RESOURCES FOR CHRISTIAN LIVING®

www.FaithFirst.com

"The Ad Hoc Committee to Oversee the Use of the Catechism, United States Conference of Catholic Bishops, has found the doctrinal content of this teacher manual, copyright 2006, to be in conformity with the *Catechism of the Catholic Church.*"

NIHIL OBSTAT
Reverend Robert M. Coerver
Censor Librorum

IMPRIMATUR
† Most Rev. Charles V. Grahmann
Bishop of Dallas

November 15, 2004

The Nihil Obstat and Imprimatur are official declarations that the material reviewed is free of doctrinal or moral error. No implication is contained therein that those granting the Nihil Obstat and Imprimatur agree with the contents, opinions, or statements expressed.

Send all inquiries to:
RCL • Resources for Christian Living
200 East Bethany Drive
Allen, Texas 75002-3804

Toll Free   877-275-4725
Fax   800-688-8356

Visit us at www.RCLweb.com
             www.FaithFirst.com

Printed in the United States of America

20472   ISBN 0-7829-1064-5 (Student Book)

20482   ISBN 0-7829-1076-9 (Catechist Guide)

1 2 3 4 5 6 7 8 9 10
05 06 07 08 09 10 11 12 13

ACKNOWLEDGMENTS

Scripture excerpts are taken or adapted from the *New American Bible with Revised New Testament and Psalms,* copyright © 1991, 1986, 1970, Confraternity of Christian Doctrine, Washington, D.C. Used with permission. All rights reserved. No part of the *New American Bible* may be reproduced by any means without the permission of the copyright owner.

Excerpts from the English translation of the *Roman Missal,* copyright © 1973, International Commission on English in the Liturgy, Inc. (ICEL). All rights reserved.

Excerpts from the English translation of the *Catechism of the Catholic Church* for use in the United States of America, second edition, copyright © 1997, United States Catholic Conference, Inc.—Libreria Editrice Vaticana. Used with permission.

Excerpts from *General Directory for Catechesis,* copyright © 1997, United States Conference of Catholic Bishops, Washington, D.C. Used with permission. All rights reserved. No part of this work may be reproduced or transmitted in any form without the permission in writing from the copyright holder.

Excerpts from *Sharing the Light of Faith: National Catechetical Directory for Catholics of the United States,* copyright © 1979, by the USCC; excerpts from *To Teach as Jesus Did,* copyright © 1972, by the USCC; excerpts from *Music in Catholic Worship,* copyright © 1972 Bishops' Committee on the Liturgy, USCC, Washington, D.C. Used with permission.

Excerpts from *Catechesi Tradendae: Catechesis in Our Time,* copyright © 1979, Daughters of St. Paul; excerpts from *Evangelii Nuntiandi: On Evangelization in the Modern World* copyright © 1975, Daughters of St. Paul.

Excerpts from *Paschale Solemnitatis, Concerning the Preparation and Celebration of the Easter Feasts,* copyright © 1988, Liberia Editrice Vaticana.

Excerpts from *Ceremonial of Bishops,* copyright © 1989, The Liturgical Press.

Excerpts from *Constitution on the Sacred Liturgy* (Sacrosanctum concilium) from *Vatican Council II: The Conciliar and Post Conciliar Documents,* New Revised Edition, Austin Flannery, O.P., Gen. Ed., copyright © 1975, 1986, 1992, 1996 by Costello Publishing Company, Inc. Used with Permission.

Faith First Legacy Edition Development Team

Developing a religion program requires the gifts and
talents of many individuals working together as a team.
RCL is proud to acknowledge the contributions
of these dedicated people.

Program Theology Consultants
Reverend Louis J. Cameli, S.T.D.
Reverend Robert D. Duggan, S.T.D.

Advisory Board
Judith Deckers, M.Ed.
Elaine McCarron, SCN, M.Div.
Marina Herrera, Ph.D.
Reverend Frank McNulty, S.T.D.
Reverend Ronald J. Nuzzi, Ph.D.

National Catechetical Advisor
Jacquie Jambor

Catechetical Specialist
Jo Rotunno

Contributing Writers
Student Book and Catechist Guide
Christina DeCamp
Judith Deckers
Mary Beth Jambor
Marianne K. Lenihan
Michele Norfleet

Art & Design Director
Lisa Brent

Electronic Page Makeup
Laura Fremder

Production Director
Jenna Nelson

Designers/Photo Research
Pat Bracken
Kristy O. Howard
Susan Smith

Project Editors
Patricia A. Classick
Steven M. Ellair
Ronald C. Lamping

Web Site Producers
Joseph Crisalli
Demere Henson

General Editor
Ed DeStefano

President/Publisher
Maryann Nead

Contents

Welcome to Faith First!

faith first®
Legacy Edition

Teaching the Timeless Truths of Our Catholic Faith Every Year

CREED • Trinity • God Our Father and Creator
SACRAMENTS
MORALITY
PRAYER
Saints • The Bible, the Word of God • Confirmation • Eucharist and the Mass
Mary • Baptism • Beatitudes • Jesus Christ, the Son of God
Ten Commandments • Jesus, Model of Praying • Works of Mercy
The People of God • Ways of Praying • Tradition of Prayer • Reconciliation
Liturgy • Transformation through Prayer • Making Choices
Loving Others • The Lord's Prayer • Anointing of the Sick
Virtues • Loving God • Conscience
Grace • Holy Orders • The Death and Resurrection of Jesus
Matrimony • The Holy Spirit

Faith First

The spiral learning method plus Scripture and Liturgical Year lessons make Faith First the most comprehensive program available today!

RCL
1-877-ASK-4-RCL (1-877-275-4725)

Teaching the Timeless Truths of Our Faith Every Year

Faith First is unique, effective, and comprehensive.

The *Faith First* Kindergarten through Junior High scope and sequence* is a spiral approach to learning our Catholic faith. The four pillars of the *Catechism of the Catholic Church*—Creed, Sacraments, Morality, and Prayer—are taught and developed on every grade level every year. This ensures that the beliefs of our faith are introduced to and reinforced for the young people as they grow, develop, and mature in their faith.

This educationally sound method means that each catechist will build upon and reinforce what children have learned previously in other grades. The result is age-appropriate learning on all topics of the faith.

*See the complete *Faith First* grade 2 scope and sequence chart on pages 24–27.

Each text provides:
• **Doctrine Chapters**
• **Scripture Chapters**
• **Liturgical Season Lessons**

Doctrine Chapters
While catechesis is much more than simply "teaching religion," providing children with a comprehensive understanding of our Catholic faith is essential to good catechesis. In the *Faith First* doctrine chapters, the children come to understand what we believe as Catholics and how to live out those beliefs.

Scripture Chapters

The special Scripture chapters in each unit of *Faith First* help the children come to know and understand the word of God. Each of these complete lessons has three distinctive elements:

Bible Background

The Scripture story is put into context for the children by teaching about the author, the setting, and the background of the people in the story.

Reading the Word of God

The children read or listen to a story from the Scriptures, followed by a brief summary that recalls what happened in the Scripture story.

Understanding the Word of God

This section explores the meaning of the story and helps the children see how God's love, presence, help, and Revelation continue to guide us in our daily lives.

Liturgical Season Lessons

You can teach the liturgical seasons to their fullest with the *Faith First* seasonal lessons that give the children the opportunity to celebrate and prayerfully participate in the liturgy all year long.

Advent and Christmas

Four lessons help the children joyfully prepare to celebrate the Incarnation and Christ's rebirth in our hearts at Christmas, followed by two lessons on the Christmas season.

Lent

Six lessons guide the children through Lent and help them turn their minds and hearts to God.

The Triduum and the Season of Easter

Together, you and the children journey through Holy Thursday, Good Friday, and the Easter Vigil. Then six lessons celebrate the joy of Christ's Resurrection and conclude with a lesson on the coming of the Holy Spirit at Pentecost.

FaithFirst.com

Online resources for children, catechists, and parents.

Features of the Student Book

Each chapter of Faith First has consistent features that direct learning, develop religious literacy, reinforce content, and encourage integration of faith and life.

Chapter Opener
The first page of every chapter features a photograph that illustrates in some way the focus of the chapter. This page also begins with an opening prayer and questions to assess the children's life experience and what they already know about the subject to be learned.

Faith Focus
Prepares the children for learning the content of the lesson with an introductory question.

Faith Words
Assists you in helping the children build Catholic literacy by defining and explaining important faith terms and concepts.

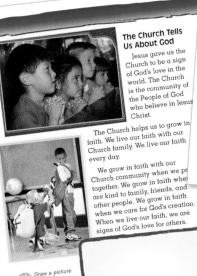

Faith-Filled People
Saints and others who have lived exemplary Catholic lives serve as models for the children.

Our Church Makes a Difference

Each chapter examines the difference the Church has made and continues to make in the lives of Christians and in the world. The children's Catholic identity is developed as they learn more about how the Church expresses its faith.

What Difference Does Faith Make in My Life?

This important step helps the children recognize that faith is not meant to be isolated or compartmentalized. Faith is meant to be lived.

We Pray

Just as we began with a prayer in the chapter opener, each chapter concludes with prayer. A variety of prayer experiences help the children grow in their appreciation of the Church's rich prayer life.

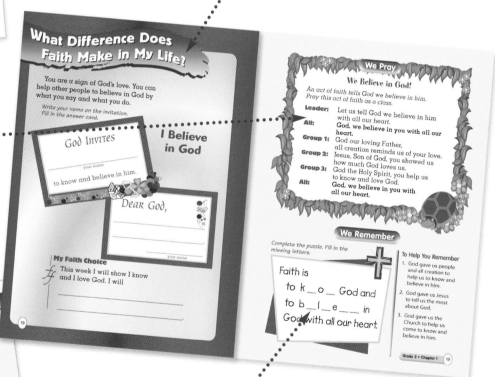

We Remember

The chapter review can be used to conclude the lesson or to begin the following week.

With My Family

Faith First offers you a way to partner with parents and help them to effectively share faith with their children. Built right into every chapter of the student book, these pages contain interesting and meaningful opportunities for making faith come alive at home.

Building Religious Literacy

Numerous resources assess the children's religious literacy in grades 1–8.

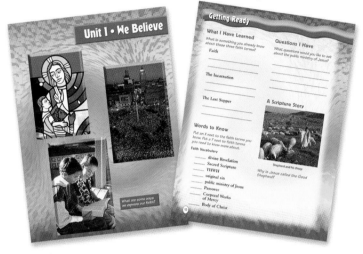

Unit Openers

Faith First unit openers are true teaching tools that
- activate prior knowledge and
- forecast unit faith themes and faith vocabulary.

Unit Reviews

A variety of strategies help the children
- reinforce key concepts and
- identify new discoveries.

Chapter Reviews

A variety of strategies help the children review key terms and concepts. (See page 9.)

Assessment Tools

A book of reproducible masters helps you create an assessment portfolio with chapter tests, unit tests, and other assessment instruments.

Online Chapter Reviews at FaithFirst.com ·····················▶

The children can study and review material from every chapter of every grade level on our Web site. The children can take an interactive test and then e-mail the results to you. It's a great interactive way to reinforce learning, and Mom and Dad can get involved too.

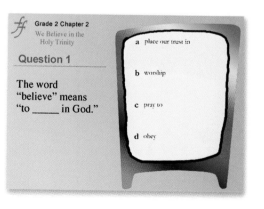

Features of the Catechist Guide

The catechist guide supports you every step of the way. Every lesson in the guide provides you with these easy-to-use resources:

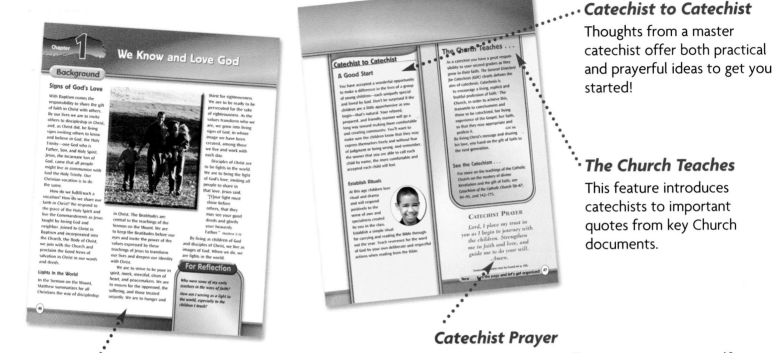

Catechist to Catechist

Thoughts from a master catechist offer both practical and prayerful ideas to get you started!

The Church Teaches

This feature introduces catechists to important quotes from key Church documents.

Background

This easy-to-read essay provides theological background on the content of the chapter. It will help you grow in your own adult understanding of our Catholic faith. Reflection questions help you connect faith concepts to your own life.

Catechist Prayer

Before you teach, you'll want to center yourself in prayer. Each chapter prayer addresses the heart of your lesson.

The **QuickStart for Catechists** on pages 17–34 and the **Faith First Legacy Edition In-Service Video** will help you get the year off to a great start.

Lesson Planner

Plan Outline

Here is your lesson plan for teaching the chapter. The plan includes a chapter focus, objectives, an outline of the lesson process, and a list of materials you will need.

Enrichment Activities

A handy list of all *Faith First* enrichment materials available for this chapter are described for you.

Online Resources

And don't forget to visit **www.FaithFirst.com** for additional chapter resources and online lesson-planning tools!

Teaching Has Never Been Easier

In Faith First you will follow this simple, effective process as you teach each lesson:

- **Engage**
- **Teach and Apply**
- **Connect**

Engage
Each chapter begins with prayer and engages the children's interest in what you will be teaching.

Teach and Apply
On every page, first you teach, then you apply.

Teach

Focus—This simple question brings the children's attention to the core content of the lesson.

Discover—These are the building blocks of your lessons and will make the core content accessible to the children.

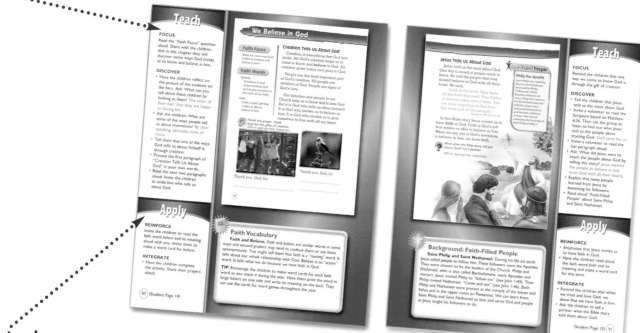

Apply

Reinforce—An easy way to reinforce learning. Answers to the questions are printed in the catechist guide.

Integrate—The children have the opportunity to integrate what they have learned into their daily lives.

Connect

Without a connection to real life, the content remains only head knowledge. This section helps the children understand how they can put their faith into action.

What Difference Does Faith Make in My Life?

At the heart of each *Faith First* lesson, the children are asked to apply what they have learned to their lives. Every child is asked to make a faith choice based on the content of the lesson.

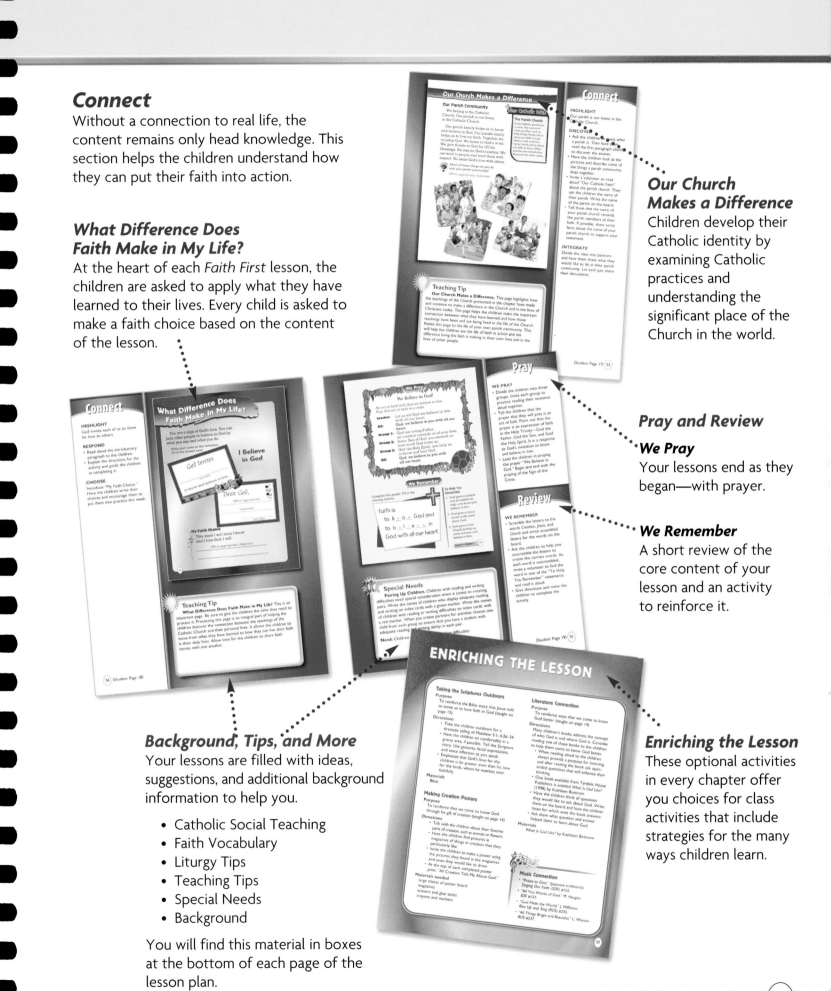

Our Church Makes a Difference

Children develop their Catholic identity by examining Catholic practices and understanding the significant place of the Church in the world.

Pray and Review

We Pray

Your lessons end as they began—with prayer.

We Remember

A short review of the core content of your lesson and an activity to reinforce it.

Enriching the Lesson

These optional activities in every chapter offer you choices for class activities that include strategies for the many ways children learn.

Background, Tips, and More

Your lessons are filled with ideas, suggestions, and additional background information to help you.

- Catholic Social Teaching
- Faith Vocabulary
- Liturgy Tips
- Teaching Tips
- Special Needs
- Background

You will find this material in boxes at the bottom of each page of the lesson plan.

Faith First Supplements

Faith First Music
For use with kindergarten and primary grades
- **Music CD**—Twelve original songs based on biblical, liturgical, and doctrinal themes.
- **Music and Prayer Celebrations**—The booklet includes complete lyrics and accompaniment for guitar and piano plus prayer celebrations.

Faith First Class Kits 1–6
Each kit contains:
- **Assessment Tools**—Use these reproducible masters to create an assessment portfolio with chapter and unit tests and other assessment instruments.
- **Additional Activities**—Enhance your lessons with time-saving reproducible activities that extend learning in class or at home.
- **Called to Prayer**—Touch the children's hearts with a variety of easy-to-use and practical prayer formats.
- **The Faith-Filled Classroom**—"Tried and true" tips from veteran catechists and Catholic school teachers.

Faith First Videos
Innovative videos bring your lessons to life with a variety of segments that reinforce and integrate faith formation.

Faith First Art & Environment Package
These colorful and inspiring resources touch the imagination and create a faith-filled learning environment. Each package contains eighteen posters, seven banners, including a Bible timeline, and pass-along cards (six packs of fifty in two designs). One package contains enough material for six classes (grades 1–6) plus a handy guide with suggested, age-appropriate uses.

Program Director's Manual
The manual includes everything the Director of Religious Education needs to implement *Faith First* in your parish, including ideas for catechist training, parent meetings, and for using *Faith First* as the foundation for catechesis in your whole parish community.

Keeping Faith First: A Resource Supporting the Whole Community of Faith
Bring together your whole parish community with this unique resource. Help parents and other adults explore the fundamental insights of our tradition, encourage them to share their stories of faith, and challenge them to be of service in the world. Plus visit **www.WholeCommunityCatechesis.com**.

Junior High

Four texts, twelve chapters each, can be used interchangeably and enable you to design up to a two-year curriculum for junior high students.

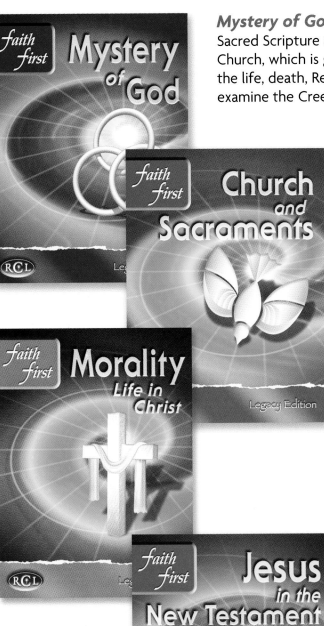

Mystery of God

Sacred Scripture and Sacred Tradition are the source of the faith of the Church, which is grounded in the fullness of Revelation that is found in the life, death, Resurrection, and Ascension of Jesus Christ. The students examine the Creed as the summary statement of our beliefs.

Church and Sacraments

The mystery of the Church unfolds as the students discover how believers take on the responsibility of continuing Christ's work on earth. The study of the sacraments centers on how they bind us together as a community of faith.

Morality: Life in Christ

As persons created in God's image, we are guided by the Ten Commandments and the Beatitudes to live a successful moral life. The principles of Catholic morality, including the social teachings of the Catholic Church, help young teens make important life choices in their daily lives.

Jesus in the New Testament

The life and message of Jesus are explored in the four Gospels with emphasis on understanding and praying the Scriptures. The students are also introduced to the writings of Saint Paul, other New Testament letters, and the Book of Revelation.

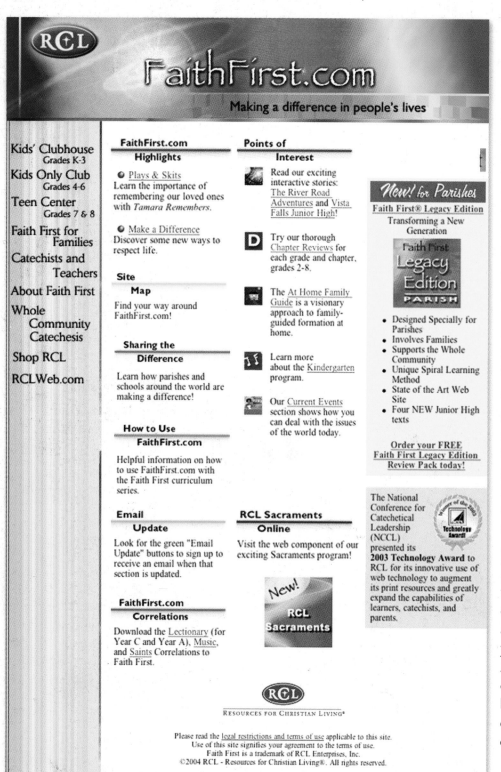

FaithFirst.com brings living and learning about faith into the twenty-first century. Catechists, children, and parents visit **FaithFirst.com** every month, resulting in over four million "hits" per month. RCL is proud to have been recognized with the Technology Award by the National Conference for Catechetical Leadership.

FaithFirst.com enables you to access practical and creative resources for all of your lessons online when and where you need them—twenty-four hours a day, seven days a week.

With **FaithFirst.com** your student books are constantly updated and expanded beyond the printed pages with learning games, chapter reviews, saints, lectionary-based lessons, contemporary issues, current events, and so much more!

FaithFirst.com encourages parents to spend time online with their children, motivates children to want to learn more about their faith, and empowers you with the latest resources. And remember, every minute a child spends at **FaithFirst.com** brings faith into the home and extends your lessons beyond class time.

QuickStart for Catechists

An Interactive Workshop on the Catechetical Ministry

Welcome to Faith First!

You have agreed to serve your parish this year as a *Faith First* catechist. *Faith First* invites you, the children, their families, and the whole faith community to discover the difference that Catholic faith can make.

Faith is rooted in God's call to all people, fully revealed in Jesus Christ, guided by the Holy Spirit. *Faith First* is rooted in five principles:

- **Faith is a gift from God. It is also our free response to all that God has revealed to us.**

- **Faith includes not only an intellectual understanding of doctrine but also a conversion of heart.**

- **Faith grows and develops throughout life.**

- **Faith is lived in community.**

- **Faith-filled people look at their actions and the world differently. All life changes when seen through the eyes of faith.**

As you begin this workshop, take a few moments to reflect on your personal faith.

> **For Reflection**
>
> *In what ways do I live my Catholic faith day by day?*
>
> *Who has been a strong influence in my life of faith?*

What Is a Catechist?

You have chosen to be a catechist! You are joining a long line of dedicated believers stretching back through the ages who have answered God's call to share their faith with others. Like them, you have been touched by your experience of Jesus Christ and are unable to keep the good news to yourself.

As important as your role is, it is not the most important one in the faith formation of your learners. That role is reserved for their parents; your role is to support them. You assist in their children's faith formation by making more explicit the teachings of the Catholic Church and helping the children celebrate their faith and apply its teachings to their lives.

Catechists echo the word of God to others to deepen their understanding and lead them to deeper conversion of mind and heart to God. You may be a little daunted by this definition, and wonder if you are up to the challenge. Relax! Your fears were faced by our ancestors in faith— Moses, Jeremiah, Peter, and Mary. But with God's help, they did great things. You will too!

Over twenty-five years ago, *Sharing the Light of Faith: National Catechetical Directory for Catholics of the United States* identified six important qualities of the ideal catechist. Some you already have and others you will develop along the way. Remember, it takes time to develop all these qualities. As you grow in your commitment to this ministry of the word, you'll find that you are doing what all good catechists do—learning by doing. These six qualities are described on the next page.

Qualities of Catechists

1. **You are responding to a call from the Lord** expressed through your local parish. You have agreed not only to catechize others but to continue growing in your own faith and your knowledge of Sacred Scripture and Tradition.

2. **You are a witness to the Gospel** message of Jesus Christ as taught by his Church. You believe in this message and in its power to change the lives of all who believe in it.

3. **You are committed to the Church** and try to express the teachings of the Catholic Church as clearly as you can. You constantly test your own understanding of your faith against the Church's wisdom.

4. **You build a faith community among your learners** because you have experienced its power and importance in your own life. You encourage your learners to gather at the Eucharist, "the source and summit of the Christian life" (*Dogmatic Constitution on the Catholic Church* 11), and to live lives of forgiveness, reconciliation, and peacemaking.

5. **You are a servant of the Church,** seeking out the needs of others and teaching your learners to do the same. You model for your learners what it means to be a follower of Jesus.

6. **You are willing to acquire the basic skills and abilities** needed to conduct effective catechetical sessions.

For Reflection

Place a star next to the qualities that are your greatest strengths. Place a check next to the ones you want to work on this year. Discuss your assessment with another catechist and with your program DRE or coordinator, who can help you develop a growth plan for the coming year.

What Is My Task?

[T]he definitive aim of catechesis is to put people not only in touch but in communion [and] intimacy, with Jesus Christ.

CATECHESIS IN OUR TIME 5

Catechists do a lot of different things. First and most important of all, you are a model for children of what it means to be a disciple of Jesus Christ. That doesn't mean that you are perfect. It means that you remember the children are watching you to learn what it means to be a Catholic. So you try your best to look, act, and sound like one. Of course, at various times you also will make short presentations, tell stories, facilitate dialogue and activities, and lead prayer.

The *General Directory for Catechesis* identifies six important tasks of catechesis (*GDC* 85–87). Reflect on the list on the next page and assess your abilities in each of these areas before you begin the year.

Tasks of Catechesis

1. **Promoting knowledge of the faith.** Catechists introduce their learners to all that has been revealed through Jesus Christ by initiating them gradually into the whole truth revealed through Scripture and Tradition. Your *Faith First* student text and catechist guide will show you what to teach this year.

2. **Liturgical education.** As a catechist you help children understand the Church's sacramental life and give them an experience of the signs, symbols, gestures, prayers, and creeds of the Church. The weekly and seasonal *Faith First* prayer experiences will give you many examples.

3. **Moral formation.** Moral catechesis involves both the announcement of the good news through your proclamation of the Gospel call to moral living and your presentation of what the Church's Tradition teaches about this message. *Faith First* will help you with the best language and strategies to use.

4. **Teaching to pray.** As you teach the Our Father, the prayer that Jesus taught, you will introduce children ever more deeply to the forms of prayer that it includes: adoration, praise, thanksgiving, intercession, and petition and expression of sorrow for sins, all expressed with the intimacy that comes from knowing we are children of God. *Faith First* will provide you with a wide variety of prayer experiences and also offer you a complete unit exploring the prayer life of the Church, especially the Our Father.

5. **Education for community life.** You are leading children into a way of life that you are already experiencing. You invite them to join a loving community of faith, to live simply and humbly, to care for the poor and alienated, to forgive as they wish to be forgiven, and to join in common prayer. Your classroom will become a weekly experience of Christian community for the children.

6. **Missionary initiation.** Catechesis prepares children to live the Gospel in daily life and to work to prepare the way for the coming of the kingdom of God. *Faith First* is filled with suggestions for outreach activities and service projects to build in children a sense of the Church's mission.

> **For Reflection**
>
> *For which task of catechesis do you feel most qualified? Which seems most daunting?*
>
> *Share with another catechist what strengths and concerns you bring to the catechetical vocation.*

> **For Further Study**
>
> *See* Echoes of Faith "Roles of the Catechist" *module.*

Teaching Others to Pray

Liturgical formation . . . must explain what the Christian liturgy is, and what the sacraments are. It must also however, offer an experience of the different kinds of celebration and it must make symbols, gestures, etc., known and loved. GENERAL DIRECTORY FOR CATECHESIS 87

Prayer is listening with openness to God's word, and responding in faith, hope, and love. Our response involves a willingness to spend time with God, to ponder the words of Scripture, to discern God's message to us, and to respond with our whole selves—body, mind, and heart.

Worship is simply the prayer of the Church. We gather together to lay our lives before God the Father, to praise him and give thanks for the gift of his love, and to join with his Son in offering our lives for his service. That is why the **Catechism of the Catholic Church** refers to liturgy as "the participation of the People of God in the work of God" (*CCC* 1069). Liturgical celebrations weave together signs and symbols drawn from our human experience—words and actions, singing and music, and sacred images. An artful blending of these elements produces a worship experience that can evoke for us the mystery of God and lead us to a fruitful response.

As children experience such gestures as signing, anointing, blessing, and kneeling within the intimacy of your classroom setting, you will be preparing them to participate more fully in the worship of the whole community. Just as you have certain ways of praying with which you are most comfortable, you'll find that children have their preferences too. The many approaches that are included will provide a true school of prayer for your learners.

How *Faith First* Will Help You

- Beginning and closing prayer experiences in every lesson
- A rich variety of prayer experiences using the signs, symbols, and gestures of the Church's liturgy whenever appropriate
- An exposition of the rich variety of the Church's Tradition of prayer, liturgy, and sacraments
- Full instructions on how to lead each prayer experience

For Reflection

How do you create opportunities in your daily life to hear the voice of God speaking to you?

What forms of prayer will you most enjoy leading for your learners?

For Further Study

See Echoes of Faith "Prayer and Spirituality" *and* "Liturgy and Sacraments" *modules.*

The Faith First Approach

Faith First lessons are built upon the three foundations: the **word of God** clearly expressed, **worship and prayer**, and the **call to service** for the reign of God.

Each *Faith First* lesson teaches as Jesus did:

- **Engage**
  Learners reflect on life experiences and recall prior knowledge about faith concepts.

- **Teach and Apply**
  On each content page, we first teach, then we apply. We teach the story of faith and challenge learners to assimilate concepts and apply them to what they already know.

- **Connect**
  Two pages, *Our Church Makes a Difference* and *What Difference Does Faith Make in My Life?*, help connect lesson concepts to the Church's life and to the lives of the learners.

A Spiral Approach

Faith First uses a spiral approach to curriculum development that incorporates doctrine, Scripture, and liturgy.

Doctrine
- Each year in grades 1–6, *Faith First* offers four units correlating to the four pillars, or sections, of the *Catechism of the Catholic Church:*
  - We Believe (Creed),
  - We Worship (Liturgy and Sacraments),
  - We Live (Morality), and
  - We Pray (Prayer and Spirituality).

- We repeat key concepts each year on the Teach and Apply pages. Core content is introduced in primary grades, then developed and reinforced in middle and upper grades.

Scripture

Sacred Scripture in each lesson and special Scripture chapters in each unit deepen understanding and challenge children to live the biblical message.

Liturgy
- Weekly prayer experiences introduce children to the rich and varied tradition of the Church's prayer and worship.

- Twenty-two special seasonal lessons help the children and their families explore and celebrate seasonal feasts and seasons of the Church's year.

On the next four pages, you will see a detailed outline of what you will be teaching this year. Study the outline of the grade 2 content on the scope and sequence chart, then respond to the reflection questions below.

For Reflection

What topics do you feel most comfortable teaching this year?

What topics would you like to learn more about?

For Further Study

The five Echoes of Faith "Theology" *modules*—"I Believe/We Believe" (Creed), "Liturgy and Sacraments," "Catholic Morality," "Prayer and Spirituality," *and* "Introduction to the Scriptures"—*will offer you an excellent introduction to the main themes of Catholic teaching.*

Scope and Sequence (Grade 2)

Unit 1 We Believe (Creed)

CHAPTER 1 — WE KNOW AND LOVE GOD

Faith Concepts: Divine Revelation, creation, Jesus, the Church, belief, faith

Sacred Scripture: Psalm 96:1, Matthew 6:25 (Jesus invites us to have faith in God)

Faith Vocabulary: Believe, faith

Faith-Filled People: Saint Philip the Apostle

Our Catholic Faith: The parish church

Our Church Makes a Difference: Our parish community

Prayer: An act of faith

Catechism of the Catholic Church (*CCC*): 50–67, 84–85, and 142–175

CHAPTER 2 — WE BELIEVE IN THE HOLY TRINITY

Faith Concepts: Holy Trinity; God the Father, Creator; our soul; God the Son, Son of God; God the Holy Spirit, received at Baptism, helper

Sacred Scripture: Luke 11:13 (promise of the Holy Spirit), Matthew 22:37–39 (God's law of love)

Faith Vocabulary: Holy Trinity, soul

Faith-Filled People: Saint Patrick

Our Catholic Faith: Sign of the Cross

Our Church Makes a Difference: Sign of the Cross

Prayer: Signing ourselves with a cross

CCC: 232–260

CHAPTER 3 — GOD IS OUR FATHER

Faith Concepts: Attributes of God: Creator, Almighty, Father

Sacred Scripture: Genesis 1:1, 7–12, 16, 20–21, 24–25, 31 (story of creation)

Faith Vocabulary: Creator, Almighty

Faith-Filled People: Saint Bonaventure

Our Catholic Faith: Lord's Prayer

Our Church Makes a Difference: School creation project

Prayer: Our Father

CCC: 268–274, 279–314, 325–349

CHAPTER 4 — PRAISING GOD: A SCRIPTURE STORY

Faith Concepts: Psalms, Psalm 148, kinds of psalms

Sacred Scripture: Psalm 33:3, 5; Psalm 148:2–3, 9–13 (psalms of praise)

Faith Vocabulary: Psalms, prayer of praise

Our Catholic Faith: Responsorial Psalm

Our Church Makes a Difference: Saint Francis's "The Canticle of the Sun"

Prayer: Psalm 147

CCC: 1156–1158, 2623–2643, 2700–2704

CHAPTER 5 — JESUS IS THE SON OF GOD

Faith Concepts: Covenant, Noah, Abraham, Moses, birth of Jesus, Saint Joseph, ministry of Jesus

Sacred Scripture: Isaiah 9:5; Luke 2:5–7 (Jesus is born); Matthew 14:13, 15–17, 19–20 (Jesus feeds a crowd)

Faith Vocabulary: Covenant, Jesus Christ

Faith-Filled People: Blessed Virgin Mary

Our Catholic Faith: Works of Mercy

Our Church Makes a Difference: Ways the Church cares for people

Prayer: The Angelus

CCC: 51–67, 456–560

CHAPTER 6 — JOHN THE BAPTIST: A SCRIPTURE STORY

Faith Concepts: Work of John the Baptist, Elizabeth and Zechariah, John the prophet, ways we prepare for Jesus

Sacred Scripture: Psalm 111:2, 9; Matthew 3:2–3, 6 and John 1:29, 34 (preaching of John the Baptist)

Faith Vocabulary: Prophet

Our Catholic Faith: Ambo

Our Church Makes a Difference: Bible readings at Mass

Prayer: Come, Lord Jesus

CCC: 64, 522–524, 702, 717–720, 849–856, 2581–2584

CHAPTER 7 — JESUS IS OUR SAVIOR

Faith Concepts: Jesus Christ the Savior, sent by the Father, the name *Jesus,* Jesus shows his love, the Crucifixion, the Resurrection

Sacred Scripture: Psalm 119:41; Matthew 1:20–23 (the angel's announcement to Joseph); Luke 23:33–34, 44, 46 (the Crucifixion); Luke 24:4, 6, 9, 11–12 (the Resurrection)

Faith Vocabulary: Crucifixion, Resurrection

Faith-Filled People: Mary Magdalene

Our Catholic Faith: The crucifix

Our Church Makes a Difference: The Easter candle

Prayer: Acclamation at Mass

CCC: 422–451, 456–478, 599–655

CHAPTER 8 — THE TRAVELER ON THE ROAD TO EMMAUS: A SCRIPTURE STORY

Faith Concepts: Apostles, first Christians, Gospels, the New Testament, Emmaus story, Jesus is alive in a new way, breaking of bread

Sacred Scripture: Matthew 28:20; Luke 24:15–16, 28–31 (the traveler to Emmaus)

Faith Vocabulary: Apostles, Gospels

Our Catholic Faith: Altar bread

Our Church Makes a Difference: Consecrated bread, Body of Christ

Prayer: Meditation

CCC: 610–611, 1356–1405

CHAPTER 9 — THE HOLY SPIRIT

Faith Concepts: Promise of the Holy Spirit, fulfillment of the promise, Ascension, Pentecost, Holy Spirit first received at Baptism, Holy Spirit always with us, our helper

Sacred Scripture: Psalm 104:30; Luke 24:49 (Jesus' promise to send the Holy Spirit); Acts of the Apostles 2:1–4, 14, 22 (Pentecost)

Faith Vocabulary: Ascension, Pentecost

Faith-Filled People: Saint Luke the Evangelist

Our Catholic Faith: Celebrations of the Church

Our Church Makes a Difference: The work of the Church

Prayer: Prayer to the Holy Spirit

CCC: 687–741

CHAPTER 10 — THE CHURCH

Faith Concepts: People of God; Catholic Church; pope's and bishops' roles; Body of Christ; Communion of Saints; Mary, the Mother of God, of the Church, and of all

Sacred Scripture: Psalm 33:12, Matthew 28:19–20 (Jesus' commission to the Apostles)

Faith Vocabulary: Body of Christ, Communion of Saints

Faith-Filled People: The faithful

Our Catholic Faith: Patron saints

Our Church Makes a Difference: The Church honors Mary and the saints

Prayer: Litany of the Saints

CCC: 751–776, 781–801, 874–993

Unit 2 We Worship (Liturgy and Sacraments)

CHAPTER 11 — WE WORSHIP GOD

Faith Concepts: Words and actions of Jesus, Jairus's faith, words and actions of the Church, worship, the seven sacraments

Sacred Scripture: Psalm 67:4; Mark 5:22–24, 38, 41–42 (Jairus's daughter)

Faith Vocabulary: Worship, sacraments

Faith-Filled People: Saint Mark the Evangelist

Our Catholic Faith: Sacramentals

Our Church Makes a Difference: Sacrament words and actions

Prayer: Using actions in prayer

Catechism of the Catholic Church (*CCC*): 1066–1118

CHAPTER 12 — WE CELEBRATE BAPTISM AND CONFIRMATION

Faith Concepts: Sacraments of Christian Initiation; Sacraments of Baptism and Confirmation, their words and actions

Sacred Scripture: Psalm 36:10

Faith Vocabulary: Baptism, Confirmation

Faith-Filled People: Cornelius the Roman soldier

Our Catholic Faith: Baptismal candle

Our Church Makes a Difference: A multiethnic Lenten celebration

Prayer: Prayer of adoration

CCC: 1210–1274, 1285–1314

CHAPTER 13 — THE FORGIVING FATHER: A SCRIPTURE STORY

Faith Concepts: Jesus the teacher, use of parables, forgiveness, mercy and love, sin

Sacred Scripture: Psalm 130:4, 7; Luke 15:12–13, 16–18, 20–24 (the Forgiving Father)

Faith Vocabulary: Parable

Our Catholic Faith: Act of Contrition

Our Church Makes a Difference: Saint John Vianney

Prayer: Lord, have mercy

CCC: 545–546, 587–590, 976–983, 1439, 1465, 1846–1848

CHAPTER 14 — GOD'S FORGIVING LOVE

Faith Concepts: Making choices, sin, forgiveness, reconciliation, sacrament of Reconciliation

Sacred Scripture: Psalm 51:3, 10

Faith Vocabulary: Sin, Reconciliation

Faith-Filled People: Zacchaeus

Our Catholic Faith: Gift of peace

Our Church Makes a Difference: Saint Dominic Savio

Prayer: Praying with Scripture

CCC: 1420–1484

CHAPTER 15 — WE GATHER FOR MASS

Faith Concepts: Praising and thanking God, Introductory Rites, Liturgy of the Word

Sacred Scripture: Psalm 147:1

Faith Vocabulary: Mass, Liturgy of the Word

Faith-Filled People: The assembly

Our Catholic Faith: The sanctuary

Our Church Makes a Difference: Processions at Mass

Prayer: Prayer of the Faithful

CCC: 1322–1332, 1345–1349

CHAPTER 16 — THE LAST SUPPER: A SCRIPTURE STORY

Faith Concepts: Passover, the Last Supper, the Eucharist

Sacred Scripture: Psalm 150:1–2, Luke 22:17–20

Faith Vocabulary: Last Supper

Our Catholic Faith: Washing of feet

Our Church Makes a Difference: Saint Francis breadline

Prayer: Response: Blessed be God

CCC: 1333–1344

CHAPTER 17 — WE GIVE THANKS TO GOD

Faith Concepts: Liturgy of the Eucharist, preparation of the Gifts, Eucharistic Prayer, Holy Communion

Sacred Scripture: Psalm 92:2

Faith Vocabulary: Eucharist, Liturgy of the Eucharist

Faith-Filled People: Saint Pius X

Our Catholic Faith: Holy Sacrifice

Our Church Makes a Difference: Concluding Rites of Mass

Prayer: Lamb of God

CCC: 1345–1405

Scope and Sequence (continued)

Unit 3 We Live (Christian Morality)

CHAPTER 18 — WE ARE GOD'S CHILDREN

Faith Concepts: Honoring God; Jesus and the children; Jesus is the way, the truth, and the life; gift of grace

Sacred Scripture: Psalm 18:2, John 14:6 (Jesus is the way, the truth, and the life)

Faith Vocabulary: Honor, grace

Faith-Filled People: Saint Teresa of Avila

Our Catholic Faith: Fruits of the Holy Spirit

Our Church Makes a Difference: Saint Thérèse of Lisieux

Prayer: A blessing prayer

CCC: 1699–1756, 1996–2016

CHAPTER 19 — THE GREAT COMMANDMENT: A SCRIPTURE STORY

Faith Concepts: Jesus teaches in the Temple, Great Commandment

Sacred Scripture: Psalm 1:2, Matthew 22:37–40 (Great Commandment)

Faith Vocabulary: Temple in Jerusalem, Great Commandment

Our Catholic Faith: Mission cross

Our Church Makes a Difference: Missionaries

Prayer: An Act of Love

CCC: 2052–2055, 2083, 2196

CHAPTER 20 — THE TEN COMMANDMENTS

Faith Concepts: First three Commandments: love for God; Fourth through Tenth Commandments: love for others

Sacred Scripture: Psalm 25:5

Faith Vocabulary: Commandments, Ten Commandments

Faith-Filled People: Saint John Bosco

Our Catholic Faith: Almsgiving

Our Church Makes a Difference: Saint Vincent de Paul

Prayer: Sign Prayer to the Holy Spirit

CCC: 2083–2550

CHAPTER 21 — PROVERBS: A SCRIPTURE STORY

Faith Concepts: Proverbs, wise choices, Book of Proverbs, living as children of God

Sacred Scripture: Psalm 19:9, 119:33–34; Proverbs 3:5, 16:3

Faith Vocabulary: Proverbs, wise choices

Our Catholic Faith: Bishop's motto

Our Church Makes a Difference: Christian sayings

Prayer: Asking the Lord's guidance

CCC: 1830–1832, 2568–2589, 2653–2654

CHAPTER 22 — WE MAKE CHOICES

Faith Concepts: Making choices, heaven, consequences of choices, gift of conscience

Sacred Scripture: Psalm 40:9, Sirach 15:14–15 (God's gift of free choice)

Faith Vocabulary: Consequences, conscience

Faith-Filled People: Saint Philip Neri

Our Catholic Faith: Examination of conscience

Our Church Makes a Difference: Morning and night prayers

Prayer: Prayer of Saint Francis

CCC: 1716–1724, 1730–1738, 1776–1794

CHAPTER 23 — WE SHARE IN GOD'S LIFE

Faith Concepts: Sanctifying grace, choosing to live a holy life, mortal sin, venial sin, Reconciliation, forgiveness

Sacred Scripture: Psalm 57:3, Galatians 3:26 (adoption through faith), Luke 6:37 (forgiveness)

Faith Vocabulary: Sanctifying grace

Faith-Filled People: Saint Monica

Our Catholic Faith: Religious medals

Our Church Makes a Difference: Saint Catherine of Siena

Prayer: Hail Mary

CCC: 1846–1869, 1996–2016

CHAPTER 24 — WE TALK WITH GOD

Faith Concepts: Prayer, talking and listening to God, times and places to pray

Sacred Scripture: Psalm 113:3

Faith Vocabulary: Prayer

Faith-Filled People: Maria von Trapp

Our Catholic Faith: Family prayer

Our Church Makes a Difference: Blessed Kateri Tekakwitha

Prayer: Spending time with God

CCC: 2559–2616, 2697–2719

CHAPTER 25 — JESUS TEACHES US TO PRAY: A SCRIPTURE STORY

Faith Concepts: Jesus and prayer; Our Father, Lord's Prayer

Sacred Scripture: Psalm 95:1, 23:1, 3; Matthew 6:9–13

Faith Vocabulary: Lord's Prayer

Our Catholic Faith: Daily prayer

Our Church Makes a Difference: People of prayer in the Church

Prayer: Psalm 23

CCC: 2598–2615, 2746–2751, 2759

CHAPTER 26 — THE OUR FATHER

Faith Concepts: Learning about and praying the Our Father

Sacred Scripture: Psalm 136:1

Faith Vocabulary: Kingdom of God

Faith-Filled People: Saint Benedict

Our Catholic Faith: Vocation

Our Church Makes a Difference: Family of God

Prayer: Go Forth

CCC: 2777–2856

We Celebrate the Liturgical Seasons

The Liturgical Year
The seasons of the Church's year.

Ordinary Time
The Church celebrates our faith all year long. We listen to and reflect on the Gospels.

The Season of Advent
First Week: We get ready to welcome Jesus.
Second Week: God promises a special leader.
Third Week: We hope and trust in God.
Fourth Week: Jesus was born in Bethlehem.

The Season of Christmas
Christmas: Angels announced the birth of Jesus to the shepherds. **Epiphany:** The Magi.

The Season of Lent
First Week: Our Lenten sacrifices show our love for God and others. **Second Week:** Jesus is the vine and we are the branches. **Third Week:** We pray the Stations of the Cross. **Fourth Week:** We share our time and talents with others. **Fifth Week:** We remember that Jesus forgives us again and again.

Holy Week
Palm Sunday of the Lord's Passion: Palm Sunday is the first day of Holy Week. **Triduum/Holy Thursday:** We remember all Jesus did at the Last Supper. **Triduum/Good Friday:** We listen to the story of Jesus' suffering and death and honor the cross. **Triduum/Easter:** We celebrate that we share in the new life of the Risen Jesus.

The Season of Easter
Second Week: We are Easter people because we share the joy of Easter with one another. **Third Week:** On the Sunday after Jesus died, three women discovered that God had raised Jesus from the dead. **Fourth Week:** Peter the Apostle told many people of Jesus' death and Resurrection. **Fifth Week:** The early Christians shared meals and prayed together. **Sixth Week:** Jesus told his disciples to invite others to become his followers. **Seventh Week:** Throughout the day all over the world the Church gathers to pray the Liturgy of the Hours. **Pentecost:** The Holy Spirit came to the disciples.

Catholic Prayers and Practices

Sign of the Cross • Glory Prayer • Lord's Prayer • Hail Mary • Act of Contrition • Apostles' Creed • Nicene Creed • Prayer to the Holy Spirit • A Vocation Prayer • Morning Prayer • Evening Prayer • Grace Before Meals • Grace After Meals • Rosary • The Great Commandment • Jesus' Commandment • The Ten Commandments • The Seven Sacraments

Who Are My Second Graders?

Catechesis based on different age groups is an essential task of the Christian community.
GENERAL DIRECTORY FOR CATECHESIS 171

You and your second graders can have an exciting and meaningful year together. Change is happening almost moment to moment for children of this age. As a child becomes seven, some of their earlier exuberance may be replaced with fears and worries as they place high expectations on themselves. Second graders have a sense of wonder and vivid imaginations. They love to create, build, and investigate the world around them.

Growing as Catholics

Second graders are moving from a very self-absorbed stage of development to one based on concrete operational thinking. During this time of transition, they can become increasingly sensitive to how their actions affect others. At this time they can develop worries about their own abilities and imperfections and fears that they will not be liked. They need adults in their lives who will help them to experience God's love for them as they are. They need to have opportunities to celebrate their special God-given gifts and talents in a supportive and caring community.

For Reflection

• *What do you recall about yourself as a seven-year-old? What experiences did you have? What did you enjoy doing?*

• *What will be the most enjoyable aspects of serving as a catechist to seven-year-olds? What will be most challenging?*

For Further Study

See Echoes of Faith "Introduction to the Learner" *module.*

Physical Characteristics

- Increased control of fine and gross motor skills
- Becomes very engrossed in an activity
- May have difficulty copying from the board
- Attention span no more than seven minutes

Cognitive/Learning Skills

- Learns best through touch, exploration, and movement
- Thought processes may be very intent and concentrated
- Likes to try to solve problems independently
- Has very high expectations of self and others

Relationships

- May be more silent, self-conscious, worried or moody than ever before
- Family very important and a source of pride
- Play with friends more harmonious than at earlier ages
- May prefer to play only with members of their own gender
- Emotionally involved with teacher and wants very much to be liked by him or her

Religious Growth

- Growing sense of right and wrong based on fairness
- Developing interest in peers can foster an understanding of community
- Enjoys hearing and telling stories from the Bible
- Interprets stories literally and cannot derive symbolic meaning
- Natural sense of wonder fosters sensitivity to the sacred
- Enjoys ceremony and ritual actions such as processions, liturgical gestures, and blessings
- Comfortable with formal and spontaneous prayer
- Awareness of Church limited to experience at home and in the parish
- Imagines God as a human person

How Do Children Learn?

Many Gifts, One Lord

There are different kinds of spiritual gifts but the same Spirit; there are different forms of service but the same Lord.

1 CORINTHIANS 12:4–5

How do you prefer to learn new things? Do you like to attend a lecture or watch one on TV? Do you like to read novels or see movies and reflect on the life messages they hold? When you cook, do you follow a recipe or learn through trial and error? Do you just want the facts, or do you like open-ended questions with lots of possibilities? The way in which you answer these questions tells a lot about how you prefer to learn and express yourself. You may prefer to learn by listening, by seeing, by imagining, or by doing. Children, as well, have preferred ways of learning that educators call learning styles.

But there is another way to think about learning. Learning preferences may reflect only our "comfort zones." According to a popular theory, each of us is born with at least eight different ways of processing and responding to new information. A well-known theorist, Howard Gardner, calls them "multiple intelligences." You might think of them as eight different ways of

being smart. All of us possess each of these kinds of "smart" in one degree or another. The particular combination that we have is one of the things that makes each of us unique. One or several of them is probably dominant in each of us.

Some children learn and express their ideas best through words, others by thinking things out or putting them in categories, and still others learn by using their bodies. Some learn and express themselves best when things are presented in a musical or rhythmic way. Some are best at writing and quiet, self-directed activities, others at group activity or sharing. Still others learn best through their contact with nature, through field trips, or by nurturing plants and animals.

In religious formation, as in classroom education, attention to the variety of gifts among the children will help them grow in an understanding of their faith and deepen their relationship with God. *Faith First* presents you with many different strategies to honor the gifts that already exist in your learners and to encourage them to express themselves in new ways. Here are some activities that support the different ways that children can learn about and express their relationship with God and one another.

Language- and Music-Related Activities

- Researching word meanings
- Word games and puzzles
- Reading and Bible search activities
- Storytelling and journal writing
- Learning hymns and Mass responses
- Writing prayers or songs
- Using background music for activities

Object-Related Activities

- Learning "how many?" of different categories: sacraments, Apostles, and so on
- Celebrating Church seasons
- "You are there" activities placing oneself in the action of a Bible story
- Using maps and models
- Graphic organizers to display information visually
- Posters and "designing" activities
- Crafts and classroom dramas
- Using gestures with songs and prayers
- Expressing response through dance
- Nurturing plants and animals
- Creating gardens or nature areas on parish grounds

Person-Related Activities

- Cooperative group learning activities
- Peer tutoring and sharing
- Teaching other students
- Games and simulations
- Quiet prayer times
- Writing and drawing in journals
- Creating autobiographies
- Self-assessment activities

For Reflection

What kinds of activities did you enjoy most as a child?

What kinds of activities are you most comfortable leading? What is a new kind of activity you would be willing to try with the children?

For Further Study

The Echoes of Faith "Methods for Grades 1 and 2" *module demonstrates a variety of classroom activities that you will enjoy leading.*

When he saw the crowds, he went up the mountain, and after he had sat down, his disciples came to him. He began to teach them. MATTHEW 5:1–2

Through the centuries, good catechists have taught outdoors under trees, in churches, and in public places. Jesus taught seated on hillsides, walking along roads, and at dinner tables. Twenty-first-century catechists in the United States most often teach in classrooms, in homes, or in parish halls or meeting rooms. No matter how simple your space, here are some things you can do to improve the environment for good catechesis.

- **Your Prayer Center.** This is the heart of your catechetical space. You will gather the children in the prayer center each week when you pray with them. If others use your catechetical space during the

week, you may wish to carry your prayer center materials in a box or plastic crate. Here are some suggestions:

- Cover the table with an attractive cloth that matches the color of the liturgical season.

- Place a crucifix at the highest point in the prayer center.

- Place a candle on the surface as a sign of the light of faith. (Light the candle only during the prayer service. Use an electric candle if fire regulations require it.)

- Enthrone an open Bible on the table. The opening lesson in your student book includes a prayer service for enthroning the Bible on the first day of class.

- Place a plant or other objects in the prayer center to symbolize the lesson themes.

- **Your Teaching Space.** Before your first class, visit your teaching space and evaluate its strengths and limitations. Learn the answers to these questions:

  - Is your space shared with a Catholic school teacher? If so, meet with him or her and try to build a spirit of cooperation.

  - Are chairs, desks, and tables of an appropriate size? See if it is permissible to move them. If the floor is uncarpeted, consider a stack of carpet squares to provide alternative seating for storytelling and sharing activities.

  - Can you adjust lighting and temperature for comfort?

  - Does the room have a chalkboard, a dry-erase board, or newsprint? Will you need to provide chalk or markers?

  - Find out if you will be allowed to tape or staple posters or other materials to walls or bulletin boards. Can you leave materials from week to week, or must you remove them after each class?

  - What electronic media equipment is available? Take some time to learn how to use any unfamiliar items.

- **Supplies.** Most catechists say that the most convenient way to carry their weekly supplies is in a plastic crate. Here is a checklist of typical supplies:

  - Catechist guide
  - Materials for prayer center
  - Special art supplies for scheduled activities
  - Visual aids, either packaged or those you have created
  - Your own chalk, eraser, markers, scissors, extra pencils
  - Copies of handouts, markers and pencils for children

For Reflection

What can I do to create a climate for prayer in my teaching space?

How can I make my teaching space an inviting climate for catechesis?

For Further Study

The Echoes of Faith "Getting Started as a Catechist" *module offers wonderful and varied ideas for creating an inviting teaching space and an attractive prayer center.*

Resource Bibliography

Church Documents

Abbot, Walter M., S.J., gen. ed. *The Documents of Vatican II.* New York: Herder and Herder, 1966.

Congregation for the Clergy. *General Directory for Catechesis.* Vatican City: Libreria Editrice Vaticana, 1997.

Connell, Martin, ed. *The Catechetical Documents: A Parish Resource.* Chicago: Liturgy Training Publications, 1996.

A Family Perspective in Church and Society: Tenth Anniversary Edition. Washington, D.C.: United States Catholic Conference, 1998.

Go and Make Disciples: A National Plan and Strategy for Catholic Evangelization in the United States. Washington, D.C.: National Conference of Catholic Bishops, 1999.

Hoffman, Elizabeth, ed. *The Liturgy Documents,* Volume 1. Chicago: Liturgy Training Publications, 1991.

Lysik, David A., ed. *The Bible Documents.* Chicago: Liturgy Training Publications, 2001.

———. *The Liturgy Documents,* Volume 2. Chicago: Liturgy Training Publications, 1999.

National Conference of Catholic Bishops, *Sharing the Light of Faith: National Catechetical Directory for Catholics of the United States.* Washington, D.C.: USCC, 1979.

Our Hearts Were Burning Within Us: A Pastoral Plan for Adult Faith Formation in the United States. Washington, D.C.: United States Catholic Conference, 1999.

Pope John Paul II. *Redemptoris Missio* (The Mission of the Redeemer).

Sharing Catholic Social Teaching: Challenges and Directions. Washington, D.C.: United States Catholic Conference, 1998.

Trouvé, Marianne Lorraine, ed. *Mother of the Christ, Mother of the Church: Papal Documents on the Blessed Virgin Mary.* Boston: Pauline Books, 2001.

Theological Resources

Bokenkotter, Thomas. *A Concise History of the Catholic Church.* New York: Doubleday, 2004.

Cameli, Louis J. *Going to God Together: A Spirituality of Communion.* Notre Dame, Ind.: Ave Maria Press, 2002.

Groome, Thomas H. *What Makes Us Catholic: Eight Gifts for Life.* San Francisco: HarperSanFrancisco, 2003.

Himes, Michael J. *The Mystery of Faith: An Introduction to Catholicism.* Cincinnati, Ohio: St. Anthony Messenger Press, 2004.

Huebsch, Bill. *The General Directory for Catechesis in Plain English.* Mystic, Conn.: Twenty-third Publications, 2001.

McKenzie, John, S.J. *Dictionary of the Bible.* New York: Macmillan, 1965. (Reprint edition: Touchstone Books, 1995.)

Catechetical Resources

Akin, Terri and Dianne Schilling. *Everybody Wins! 100 Games Children Should Play.* Jalmar Press. (Available through Pro-Ed., Inc., Austin, Tex.)

Armstrong, Thomas. *Multiple Intelligences in the Classroom.* Virginia: ASCD, 1994.

Campbell, Anne, Kathryn Waite, and Anne Mikelonis. *Creative Crafts for All Seasons: Projects That Help Kids Learn.* Allen, Tex.: RCL · Resources for Christian Living, 1999.

Campbell, Anne, et. al. *The Faith-filled Classroom: Top 10 Ideas That Really Work.* Allen, Tex.: RCL · Resources for Christian Living, 1999.

Cavaletti, Sofia, et. al. *The Religious Potential of the Child: Experiencing Scripture and Liturgy with Young Children.* Chicago: Liturgy Training Publications, 1993.

Coles, Robert, Ph.D. *The Spiritual Life of Children.* Boston: Houghton-Mifflin, 1990.

Costello, Gwen. *School Year Activities for Religion Classes.* Mystic, Conn.: Twenty-third Publications, 2000.

Cronin, Gaynell Bordes. *Friend Jesus: Prayers for Children (Guiding Children into Daily Prayer).* Cincinnati: St. Anthony Messenger Press, 1999.

Drew, Naomi. *Learning the Skills of Peacemaking: A K–6 Activity Guide on Resolving Conflict, Communicating, Cooperating.* Jalmar Press. (Available through Pro-Ed, Inc., Austin, Tex.)

Dues, Greg. *Catholic Customs & Traditions: A popular guide.* Mystic, Conn.: Twenty-third Publications, 1990.

Duggan, Robert. *Teaching Kids the Basics of Liturgy: Making Rituals More Meaningful.* Allen, Tex.: RCL · Resources for Christian Living, 1999.

Florian, Amy. *Sign & Symbol, Word and Song.* Notre Dame, Ind.: Ave Maria Press, 2001.

Gallagher, Maureen. *The Art of Catechesis: What You Need to Be, Know, and Do.* Mahwah, N.J.: Paulist Press, 1998.

Gardner, Howard. *Intelligence Reframed: Multiple Intelligences for the 21st Century.* New York: Basic Books, 2000.

Gargiulo, Barbara. *How Do I Talk to God? Prayers for the School Year.* Allen, Tex.: RCL · Resources for Christian Living, 1999.

Gather Comprehensive. Chicago: GIA Publications, 1994.

Huebsch, Bill. *A Handbook for Success in Whole Community Catechesis.* Mystic, Conn.: Twenty-third Publications, 2004.

———. *Whole Community Catechesis in Plain English.* Mystic, Conn.: Twenty-third Publications, 2002.

Jambor, Mary Beth. *Helping Kids Live Their Faith: Service Projects That Make a Difference.* Allen, Tex.: RCL•Resources for Christian Living, 1999.

MacDonald, Margaret Read. *The Storyteller's Start-up Book.* Little Rock, Ark.: August House Publishers, 1993.

Malone, Peter with Sr. Rose Pacatte. *Lights, Camera . . . Faith! A Movie Lectionary. Cycle A.* Boston: Pauline Books and Media, 2001. (Cycles B and C also available.)

Mazer, Peter. *School Year, Church Year: Activities and Decorations for the Classroom.* Chicago: Liturgy Training Publications, 2001.

McGrath, Eileen, Ph.D. *Kids Get Stressed Too: Understanding What's Going On and How to Help.* Allen, Tex.: RCL · Resources for Christian Living, 1999.

Mongoven, Anne Marie. *The Prophetic Voice in Catechesis.* Mahwah, N.J.: Paulist Press, 2000.

Neuberger, Anne. *Stories of Saints through the Centuries.* Mystic, Conn.: Twenty-third Publications, 1999.

Palomares, Susanna. *Lessons in Tolerance and Diversity.* Jalmar Press. (Available through Pro-Ed, Inc., Austin, Tex.)

Rise Up and Sing. Portland, Ore.: Oregon Catholic Press, 2000.

Rotunno, Jo McClure. *Heritage of Faith: A Framework for Whole Community Catechesis.* Mystic, Conn,: Twenty-third Publications, 2004.

Singing Our Faith: A Hymnal for Young Catholics. Chicago: GIA Publications, 2001. (Accompaniment book also available.)

Vasiloff, Barbara C. *Teaching Self-Discipline to Children: 15 Essential Skills.* Mystic, Conn.: Twenty-third Publications, 2003.

faith first

Legacy Edition
PARISH

Grade Two

RESOURCES FOR CHRISTIAN LIVING®

www.FaithFirst.com

"The Ad Hoc Committee to Oversee the Use of the Catechism, United States Conference of Catholic Bishops, has found this catechetical series, copyright 2006, to be in conformity with the *Catechism of the Catholic Church.*"

NIHIL OBSTAT
Reverend Robert M. Coerver
Censor Librorum
IMPRIMATUR
† Most Rev. Charles V. Grahmann
Bishop of Dallas
September 1, 2004

The Nihil Obstat and Imprimatur are official declarations that the material reviewed is free of doctrinal or moral error. No implication is contained therein that those granting the Nihil Obstat and Imprimatur agree with the contents, opinions, or statements expressed.

Send all inquiries to:
RCL • Resources for Christian Living
200 East Bethany Drive
Allen, Texas 75002-3804

Toll Free 877-275-4725
Fax   800-688-8356

Visit us at www.RCLweb.com
             www.FaithFirst.com

Printed in the United States of America

20472   ISBN 0-7829-1064-5 (Student Book)
20482   ISBN 0-7829-1076-9 (Catechist Guide)

1 2 3 4 5 6 7 8 9 10
05 06 07 08 09 10 11

ACKNOWLEDGMENTS
Scripture excerpts are taken or adapted from the *New American Bible with Revised New Testament and Psalms,* copyright © 1991, 1986, 1970, Confraternity of Christian Doctrine, Washington, DC. Used with permission. All rights reserved. No part of the *New American Bible* may be reproduced by any means without the permission of the copyright owner.

Excerpts are taken or adapted from the English translation of *Rite of Baptism for Children* © 1969, International Committee on English in the Liturgy, Inc. (ICEL); the English translation of *The Roman Missal* © 1973, ICEL; the English translation of *Rite of Confirmation, Second Edition* © 1975, ICEL; the English translation of the Act of Contrition from *Rite of Penance* © 1974, ICEL; excerpts from the English translation of *A Book of Prayers* © 1982, ICEL; excerpts from the English translation of *Book of Blessings* © 1988, ICEL. All rights reserved.

Excerpts are taken from the English translation of The Nicene Creed, Apostles' Creed, and *Gloria Patri* by the International Consultation on English Texts (ICET). All rights reserved.

Photograph and Illustration Credits appear on page 304.

2

Faith First Legacy Edition Development Team

Developing a religion program requires the gifts and talents of many individuals working together as a team. RCL is proud to acknowledge the contributions of these dedicated people.

Program Theology Consultants
Reverend Louis J. Cameli, S.T.D.
Reverend Robert D. Duggan, S.T.D.

Advisory Board
Judith Deckers, M.Ed.
Elaine McCarron, SCN, M.Div.
Marina Herrera, Ph.D.
Reverend Frank McNulty, S.T.D.
Reverend Ronald J. Nuzzi, Ph.D.

National Catechetical Advisor
Jacquie Jambor

Catechetical Specialist
Jo Rotunno

Contributing Writers
Student Book and Catechist Guide
Christina DeCamp
Judith Deckers
Mary Beth Jambor
Marianne K. Lenihan
Michele Norfleet

Art & Design Director
Lisa Brent

Electronic Page Makeup
Laura Fremder

Production Director
Jenna Nelson

Designers/Photo Research
Pat Bracken
Kristy O. Howard
Susan Smith

Project Editors
Patricia A. Classick
Steven M. Ellair
Ronald C. Lamping

Web Site Producers
Joseph Crisalli
Demere Henson

General Editor
Ed DeStefano

President/Publisher
Maryann Nead

3

Contents

5

We Celebrate: The Liturgical Seasons

6

We Pray

Dear God,
We think second grade will be lots of fun. There will be lots to do and learn. We will learn more about you, about Jesus, and about your Church. Help us to listen well, to take part in activities, and to do our best to love you and others each day. Amen.

Welcome to Faith First!

A Quick Look at Me

Make a nametag to tell others about yourself.

- In the middle, write in large letters what you like to be called.
- In each corner, write or draw these four things about yourself.
  1. A favorite story
  2. Something I like to do with my family
  3. My favorite holiday
  4. Something I do well

7

Teaching Tip

Getting to Know Your Children. This opening session provides you with the first opportunity to discover the talents and gifts of your children. It is only a beginning. Each week talk with the children about the exciting moments in their young lives and the fun things they do with their family and friends. It is important to affirm each child every session. Make this one of your goals.

TO THE CATECHIST

Creating an inviting environment is an important part of everything you do with young children. Before your first meeting, prepare name tags for the children. Greet each child as they arrive. This will help them feel safe and ready to learn. This first session provides the opportunity for you to get to know the children. By setting realistic expectations, introducing them to their new books, and creating an atmosphere of prayer and hospitality, the children will know they are welcome.

INVITE

- Have the children hold hands and pray the opening prayer after you.
- Give each child a name tag.
- Ask the children to open their books to page 7 and write what they like to be called on their name tags.
- Have the children draw four things about themselves listed in the "A Quick Look at Me" activity. Allow them time to complete their name tags.
- Ask the children to share some of the things they wrote about or drew about themselves.

- Introduce the book and allow the children to look through it and find a favorite picture.
- Have them share their favorite picture with the child beside them.
- Tell the children that they will now join with a partner to complete the activity on pages 8 and 9. Let them know that you will help them.
- Read to the group the "We Believe" activity. Have them turn to page 62 and find the name *Jesus*. Have everyone write the name *Jesus* in the first box in the "New Things to Learn" activity.
- Have the children read the question and clue in the "We Worship" activity and turn to page 131 to find the word described by the clue.
- Ask volunteers to share their discovery.
- Have everyone write the word *Alleluia* in the second box on page 8.

New Things to Learn

This year we will learn many new things about God. We will learn more about Jesus and about how to celebrate with our Church family.

Play this game with a partner to begin to learn new things. As you come to each lily pad, write the answer to the question.

1.

Jesus

Start

1. We Believe

Jesus is God's own Son. He is the Savior of the world.

Write the word that means "God saves."

Clue: Look on page 62.

2.

Alleluia

2. We Worship

At Mass we listen to God's word and give thanks to him.

What is a word we sing before the Gospel at Mass?

Clue: Look on page 131.

8

Teaching Tip

Setting Expectations. The children will be curious about what they will be doing during the sessions. They will also want and need to know what you expect of them. There are many ways to set expectations. One way is to create signs using the colors red, yellow, and green. Whenever you put up the red sign the children know they need to stop and be quiet. The yellow sign reminds them that they are learning something new and need to listen. The green sign means it is all right to talk with one another about the questions or activity. Use the signs more as a reminder when the children seem to be losing focus.

4. We Pray

The Our Father is the prayer of the whole Church.

What is another name for the Our Father?

Clue: Look on page 220.

4.

Lord's Prayer

Finish

3. We Live

God shares his life with us and helps us to live as his children.

What is the name of the gift that makes us God's children?

Clue: Look on page 198.

3.

sanctifying grace

9

DISCOVER AND INVOLVE

- Work with the children on the "We Live" activity, read the question, and help them find the bold-faced term on page 198. Then have the children write the term *sanctifying grace* in box three on page 9 in their books.
- Ask the children to share with their partner one way they can live as a child of God.
- Have the children focus on the "We Pray" activity and read the question.
- Have them turn to page 220 and discover another name for the Our Father.
- Give them time to write *Lord's Prayer* in the final blank space on page 9 in their books.
- Choose volunteers to read each question and share what answer they have written in the box. This will help you make sure everyone has the correct answers.

Teaching Tip

Knowing Your Learners. Remember that everything you do with the children helps you get to know them a little more. You will have many opportunities during the sessions to get to know their learning styles and their talents and gifts. Observing each of the children working in the total group, in small groups, or with a partner will help you plan your lessons and meet the needs of all the children.

- Invite the children to prepare for prayer. Reverently hold a Bible slightly above your head and lead them in procession to the prayer space.
- Teach the children to echo, or repeat after you, the parts of the prayer marked "All."
- After a moment of silence, pray the prayer. Use a hand gesture to invite the children to join in when you want them to echo their parts of the prayer.
- After the prayer, place the Bible on the prayer table and reverence it by slightly bowing your head. Invite each child to come forward and do the same.
- Thank the children for being good learners and remind them to have a fun week.

How Great Is Your Name!

LEADER: We gather to praise your name, O LORD.

ALL: O LORD, how great is your name.

LEADER: LORD, when I see the moon and all the stars you put in place, I wonder how you can remember us.

ALL: O LORD, how great is your name.

LEADER: But you made us little less than angels, You made us shepherds of all you made.

ALL: O LORD, how great is your name.
Based on Psalm 8:2, 4–7, 10

Come forward and bow before the Bible.

10

Teaching Tip

Creating a Prayer Space. Having a prayer space that is decorated in a special way will help the children realize the importance of prayer. Display the Bible in your prayer space in such a way that shows its importance. Talk about respecting the Bible. Always hold the Bible reverently when you proclaim God's word. Before you pray together, allow a moment of quiet time and share with the group that God is with them.

A Catechist's Prayer

Gracious God, I ask for your blessing as I begin this year as a catechist. I wonder if I am up to the task. Yet I am inspired by my ancestors in faith who also were surprised by God.

Give me the **courage** of Abraham and Sarah, who did not hesitate when God called them to a new land. With them as my models, surely I can face a class of energetic children once a week!

Let me be a **liberator** like Moses, setting children free from their fears and giving them the hope that comes from believing in a Provident God.

Give me the **wisdom** of Samuel to listen more than I speak. Remind me to allow the moments of silence that permit children to reflect on you.

Give me the **patience** of Job, so that when the children get beyond me, or my best-laid plans fall flat, I can believe that the next week will be better.

Give me the **justice** of Amos, so that I will challenge the children to take up the work of building your kingdom of justice and peace here on earth.

Give me the **faith** of Joseph, so that I can be a model of faith to the children in my care. Let the children learn what faith is, not only from the definition I teach them, but from the witness of my life.

Give me the **humility** of Mary, so that I will remember that you are the source of any good I do. Help me create a loving, fair, and secure environment for the sharing of faith, as Mary and Joseph did for the child Jesus.

Give me the **hospitality** of Martha and Mary, joyfully welcoming the children each week. Help me remember to be, like Mary, a prayerful person who listens to your will for me. But like Martha, help me also to do the practical work that ensures a successful session.

Give me the **enthusiasm** of Mary Magdalene, first witness to the Resurrection. Help me enter my classroom each week with the same passion to share the good news of the Risen Lord.

Above all, let me never waver in my **respect** for the dignity of each child that you have entrusted to my care. Let me teach as your Son did, listening to them, and allowing them to grow in the ways that are best for them.

With your **love**, the example of your Son, and the power of the Holy Spirit, I think I am ready to begin!

Amen.

Unit 1 Opener

The unit opener pages are designed to assess, through a variety of questioning techniques, the children's prior knowledge about the key faith concepts presented in the unit. Processing these pages should not take more than ten or fifteen minutes.

USING ILLUSTRATIONS

Pictures help stimulate the religious imaginations of the children. The first page of the unit opener contains pictures that illustrate some of the important concepts in the unit.

- Invite the children to look at and think about the pictures.
- Have the children describe what each picture says to them.
- Invite the children to share a response to the question.

Unit 1 • We Believe

What does the Church ask us to believe?

11

Teaching Tip

Importance of Prior Knowledge. Most of the children come to their religion class with prior faith knowledge and experiences. You will want to draw on their experiences to help them build new understandings of their faith. By starting with the children's knowledge you show them that you respect and value their thinking. There are many techniques to assess prior knowledge. Pictures, questions, the use of vocabulary, and Scripture stories have been incorporated on these pages to encourage the children to share what they already know.

Getting Ready

What I Have Learned

What is something you already know about these three faith words?

God the Father

_____Responses will vary._____

_____

The Bible

_____Responses will vary._____

_____

The People of God

_____Responses will vary._____

_____

Words to Know

Put an X next to the faith words you know. Put a ? next to the faith words you need to know more about.

Faith Words

_____ believe

_____ faith

_____ Holy Trinity

_____ Creator

_____ Gospels

_____ Pentecost

(12)

A Question I Have

What question would you like to ask about the Holy Trinity?

_____Responses will vary._____

_____

A Scripture Story

John the Baptist

What do you know about John the Baptist?

Responses will vary.

GETTING READY

The "Getting Ready" page engages the children in sharing prior knowledge and aids you in planning your lessons to meet their needs.

What I Have Learned

- Read to the children the concepts and ask volunteers to share ideas they know about each concept.

Words to Know

Read each faith term to the group. Have them put a check next to the terms they know and a question mark next to the ones they may need to learn more about.

A Question I Have

- Invite the children to ask questions about the Holy Trinity.
- Write their questions on a chart.

A Scripture Story

The story of John the Baptist is one of the Scripture stories in this unit. Have the children look at the picture and answer the question.

We Know and Love God

Background

Signs of God's Love

With Baptism comes the responsibility to share the gift of faith in Christ with others. By our lives we are to invite others to discipleship in Christ, and, as Christ did, be living signs inviting others to know and believe in God, the Holy Trinity—one God who is Father, Son, and Holy Spirit. Jesus, the Incarnate Son of God, came that all people might live in communion with God the Holy Trinity. Our Christian vocation is to do the same.

How do we fulfill such a vocation? How do we share our faith in Christ? We respond to the grace of the Holy Spirit and live the Commandments as Jesus taught by loving God and neighbor. Joined to Christ in Baptism and incorporated into the Church, the Body of Christ, we join with the Church and proclaim the Good News of salvation in Christ in our words and deeds.

Lights in the World

In the Sermon on the Mount, Matthew summarizes for all Christians the way of discipleship

in Christ. The Beatitudes are central to the teachings of the Sermon on the Mount. We are to keep the Beatitudes before our eyes and invite the power of the values expressed by these teachings of Jesus to transform our lives and deepen our identity with Christ.

We are to strive to be poor in spirit, meek, merciful, clean of heart, and peacemakers. We are to mourn for the oppressed, the suffering, and those treated unjustly. We are to hunger and

thirst for righteousness. We are to be ready to be persecuted for the sake of righteousness. As the values transform who we are, we grow into living signs of God, in whose image we have been created, among those we live and work with each day.

Disciples of Christ are to be lights in the world. We are to bring the light of God's love, inviting all people to share in that love. Jesus said,

"[Y]our light must shine before others, that they may see your good deeds and glorify your heavenly Father." MATTHEW 5:16

By living as children of God and disciples of Christ, we live as images of God. When we do, we are lights in the world.

For Reflection

Who were some of my early teachers in the ways of faith?

How am I serving as a light to the world, especially to the children I teach?

Catechist to Catechist

A Good Start

You have accepted a wonderful opportunity to make a difference in the lives of a group of young children—each uniquely special and loved by God. Don't be surprised if the children are a little apprehensive as you begin—that's natural. Your relaxed, prepared, and friendly manner will go a long way toward making them comfortable and creating community. You will want to make sure the children know that they may express themselves freely and without fear of judgment or being wrong. And remember, the sooner that you are able to call each child by name, the more comfortable and accepted each child will feel.

Establish Rituals

At this age children love ritual and drama and will respond positively to the sense of awe and specialness created by you in the class.  Establish a simple ritual for carrying and reading the Bible throughout the year. Teach reverence for the word of God by your own deliberate and respectful actions when reading from the Bible.

The Church Teaches . . .

As a catechist you have a great responsibility to your second graders as they grow in their faith. The *General Directory for Catechesis (GDC)* clearly defines the aim of catechesis. Catechesis is

to encourage a living, explicit and fruitful profession of faith.[1] The Church, in order to achieve this, transmits to catechumens and those to be catechized, her living experience of the Gospel, her faith, so that they may appropriate and profess it. GDC 66

By living Christ's message and sharing his love, you hand on the gift of faith to the next generation.

See the Catechism . . .

For more on the teachings of the Catholic Church on the mystery of divine Revelation and the gift of faith, see *Catechism of the Catholic Church* 50–67, 84–95, and 142–175.

CATECHIST PRAYER

Lord, I place my trust in you as I begin to journey with the children. Strengthen me in faith and love, and guide me to do your will. Amen.

Footnote references may be found on p. 456.

LESSON PLANNER

Engage

Page 13
Focus
To help the children get to know each other and explore their books

Opening Prayer

Discussion
Getting to know people is fun. God wants us to get to know him.

Teach and Apply

Pages 14–16
Focus
To discover that creation, Jesus, and the Church tell us about God

Presentation
Read, discuss, and summarize content.

Scripture
Matthew 6:26

Activities
• Finish the prayer.
• Listen to the Bible story about trusting in God.
• Draw a picture of someone who tells us about God.

Faith-Filled People
Saint Philip the Apostle

Connect

Pages 17–18
Focus
To demonstrate ways we show God we believe in him

Our Church Makes a Difference
Discover that our parish community helps us know God.

Our Catholic Faith
The Parish Church

What Difference Does Faith Make?
Activity
An invitation to believe in God
Faith Choice
Name a way to show love for God this week.

We Pray

Page 19
Prayer Form
An act of faith
Prayer
Choose a leader. Introduce the prayer and pray together.

We Remember

Review
• Complete the puzzle activity.
• Read "To Help You Remember" statements aloud.
Preview
Highlight features of the "With My Family" page.

Materials

• pens or pencils
• crayons or markers
• index cards

Enriching the Session

Blackline Masters
Additional Activities booklet:
Chapter 1
Coloring the signs of God's love
Drawing God taking care of you
Assessment Tools booklet:
Chapter 1 Test

Faith First **Grade 2 Video**
Segment 1: "Bible Songs"
Segment 6: "The Lost Sheep"

Enriching the Lesson (CG page 57)
Taking the Scriptures Outdoors
Making Creation Posters
Literature Connection

Music Connection (CG page 57)

www.FaithFirst.com

We update the *Faith First* Web site weekly. Check each week for new content and features. Here are some places to begin:

Catechists and Teachers
• Current Events
• Chapter Downloads
• Catechist Prayer

Faith First **for Families**
• Bible Stories
• Make a Difference

Kids' Clubhouse
• *Faith First* Activities
• Chapter Reviews
• Games
• Saints

Don't Forget! You can make lesson planning a breeze—check out the **Online Lesson Planner.**

We Know and Love God

We Pray

Sing to God, all creation.

Based on Psalm 96:1

O God, all your creation praises you. We ask you to bless us and to help us love you. **Amen.**

How do you get to know more about your friends?

Getting to know people is fun. God wants us to get to know him too. God tells us about himself in many ways.

What are some ways you have come to know God?

13

PRAY

- Quiet the children by asking them to look at the photo on the page. Remind the children that the rainbow is a symbol of God's love and that he is with us as we pray.
- Begin by praying the Sign of the Cross together.
- Choose a volunteer to read the Psalm verse.
- Pray the opening prayer together and conclude with the Sign of the Cross.

DISCOVER

- **Purpose:** To discover what the children may already know about knowing and loving God
- Ask the children how they get to know people.
- Tell them that God wants them to get to know him, and that there are many ways to learn about God.
- Ask the children how they have learned about God. Accept all appropriate answers.

Liturgy Tip

The chatter of our busy lives can drown out the voice of the Lord. If we take some quiet time we can hear God speaking to us in prayer, through people, and through the environment around us. Using a single ring of a bell or a drum beat is a beautiful way to remind children to quiet themselves for prayer. Urge children to listen for God's word to them as they pray.

Teach

FOCUS

Read the "Faith Focus" question aloud. Share with the children that in this chapter they will discover some ways God invites us to know and believe in him.

DISCOVER

- Have the children reflect on the picture of the students on the bars. Ask: What can you tell about these children by looking at them? The color of their hair; that they are happy or having fun.
- Ask the children: What are some of the ways people tell us about themselves? By their speaking, attitudes, tone of voice.
- Tell them that one of the ways God tells us about himself is through creation.
- Present the first paragraph of "Creation Tells Us About God" in your own words.
- Read the next two paragraphs aloud. Invite the children to underline who tells us about God.

Apply

REINFORCE

Invite the children to read the faith word *believe* and its meaning aloud with you. Invite them to make a word card for *believe*.

INTEGRATE

- Have the children complete the activity. Share their prayers aloud.

We Believe in God

Faith Focus

What are some ways God invites us to know and believe in him?

Faith Words

believe
To believe in God means to know God and to give ourselves to him with all our heart.

faith
Faith is God's gift that makes us able to believe in him.

Creation Tells Us About God

Creation is everything that God has made. All God's creation helps us to come to know and **believe** in God. All creation gives honor and glory to God.

People are the most important part of God's creation. All people are children of God. People are signs of God's love.

Our families and people in our Church help us to know and to love God. But it is God who tells us about himself. It is God who invites us to believe in him. It is God who invites us to give ourselves to him with all our heart.

ACTIVITY *Finish the prayer. Thank God for the gifts of creation.* Affirm appropriate responses.

Thank you, God, for

_____.

Thank you, God, for

_____

_____.

14

Faith Vocabulary

Faith and Believe. *Faith* and *believe* are similar words in some ways and second graders may tend to confuse them or use them synonymously. You might tell them that faith is a "naming" word. It tells about our whole relationship with God. Believe is an "action" word. It tells what we do because we have faith in God.

TIP: Encourage the children to make word cards for each faith word as you teach it during the year. Have them print the word in large letters on one side and write its meaning on the back. They can use the cards for word games throughout the year.

Jesus Tells Us About God

Jesus told us the most about God. One day a crowd of people came to Jesus. He told the people that they should believe in God with all their heart. He said,

"Look at the birds. They have all the food they need. Your Father in heaven takes care of them. You are more important to God than the birds and all the animals."

Based on Matthew 6:26

In this Bible story Jesus invites us to have **faith** in God. Faith is God's gift that makes us able to believe in him. When we say yes to God's invitation to believe in him, we have faith.

 What does the Bible story tell you about God? Tell a partner.

Affirm appropriate responses.

Faith-Filled People

Philip the Apostle

Saint Philip was called by Jesus to be his follower. Jesus said to Philip, "Follow me." Philip became a follower of Jesus. Philip then went to his friend Nathanael and told him about Jesus. Nathanael believed too and became a follower of Jesus. The Church celebrates the feast day of Saint Philip on May 3.

15

Background: Faith-Filled People

Saint Philip and Saint Nathanael. During his life on earth Jesus called people to follow him. These followers were the Apostles. They were chosen to be the leaders of the Church. Philip and Nathanael, who is also called Bartholomew, were Apostles and martyrs. Jesus invited Philip to "follow me" (see John 1:43). Then Philip invited Nathanael, "Come and see" (see John 1:46). Both Philip and Nathanael were present at the miracle of the loaves and fishes and in the upper room on Pentecost. We can learn from Saint Philip and Saint Nathanael to love and serve God and people as Jesus taught his followers to do.

Teach

FOCUS

Remind the children that one way we come to know God is through the gift of creation.

DISCOVER

- Tell the children that Jesus told us the most about God.
- Invite a volunteer to read the Scripture based on Matthew 6:26. Then ask the group to listen to find out what Jesus said to the people about trusting God. God cares for us.
- Invite a volunteer to read the last paragraph aloud.
- Ask: What did Jesus want to teach the people about God by telling this story? Jesus wanted the people to believe in and trust God with all their hearts.
- Explain that many people learned from Jesus by becoming his followers.
- Read aloud "Faith-Filled People" about Saint Philip and Saint Nathanael.

Apply

REINFORCE

- Emphasize that Jesus invites us to have faith in God.
- Have the children read aloud the faith word *faith* and its meaning and make a word card for this term.

INTEGRATE

- Remind the children that when we trust and love God, we show that we have faith in him.
- Ask the children to tell a partner what the Bible story told them about God.

(Student Page 15) 51

Teach

FOCUS

Remind the children that Jesus tells us the most about God. Tell them they are going to learn another way we learn about God.

DISCOVER

- Write the word *Church* on the board. Invite the children to share words that say something about the Church. Jot their words around the word *Church,* creating a word map.
- Read the opening paragraph to the children. Ask them to listen for words that tell what the Church is. Ask for their responses, and add these concepts to the word map.
- Have the children read the last paragraphs silently to find out how the Church helps us grow in our faith.

Apply

REINFORCE

Invite volunteers to read a sentence from the text that tells us how we grow in faith in our community.

INTEGRATE

- Explain the activity directions and give the children sufficient time to complete the activity.
- Ask volunteers to share their drawings and tell how the people in their drawings tell them about God.

The Church Tells Us About God

Jesus gave us the Church to be a sign of God's love in the world. The Church is the community of the People of God who believe in Jesus Christ.

The Church helps us to grow in faith. We live our faith with our Church family. We live our faith every day.

We grow in faith with our Church community when we pray together. We grow in faith when we are kind to family, friends, and other people. We grow in faith when we care for God's creation. When we live our faith, we are signs of God's love for others.

ACTIVITY Draw a picture of someone who tells you about God.

Responses will vary.

(16)

Teaching Tip

Learning Styles and Behavior. Be aware that some children are uncomfortable reading aloud. Give them opportunities to participate in other ways. Many of the children may need visual aids to assist them in learning. You might want to start a picture file and add to it as the year goes on. In addition to having varied learning styles, second graders also have varied personalities and behaviors. Encourage the children who are shy, while giving positive attention to those who will demand it. Accept no behaviors that are rude, unkind, or potentially dangerous.

Our Church Makes a Difference

Our Parish Community

We belong to the Catholic Church. Our parish is our home in the Catholic Church.

Our parish family helps us to know and believe in God. Our parish family helps us to live our faith. Together we worship God. We listen to God's word. We give thanks to God for all his blessings. We care for God's creation. We are kind to people and treat them with respect. We share God's love with others.

Our Catholic Faith

The Parish Church

Every Catholic parish has a name. The names of some parishes, such as Holy Trinity Parish, tell us about our faith in God. Others, such as Divine Savior Parish, tell us about our faith in Jesus. Other parishes are named after Mary and the other saints.

QUESTION *Which of these things do you do with your parish community?*

Affirm appropriate responses.

17

HIGHLIGHT

Our parish is our home in the Catholic Church.

DISCOVER

- Ask the children to guess what a parish is. Then have them read the first paragraph silently to discover the answer.
- Have the children look at the pictures and describe some of the things a parish community does together.
- Invite a volunteer to read aloud "Our Catholic Faith" about the parish church. Then ask the children the name of their parish. Write the name of the parish on the board.
- Tell them that the name of your parish church reminds the parish members of their faith. If possible, share some facts about the name of your parish church to support your statement.

INTEGRATE

Divide the class into partners and have them share what they would like to do in their parish community. Let each pair share their discussions.

Teaching Tip

Our Church Makes a Difference. This page highlights how the teachings of the Church presented in the chapter have made and continue to make a difference in the Church and in the lives of Christians today. This page helps the children make the important connection between what they have learned and how those teachings have been and are being lived in the life of the Church. Relate this page to the life of your own parish community. This will help the children see the life of faith in action and the difference living the faith is making in their own lives and in the lives of other people.

Connect

HIGHLIGHT

God invites each of us to show his love to others.

RESPOND

- Read aloud the introductory paragraph to the children.
- Explain the directions for the activity and guide the children in completing it.

CHOOSE

Introduce "My Faith Choice." Have the children write their choices and encourage them to put them into practice this week.

What Difference Does Faith Make in My Life?

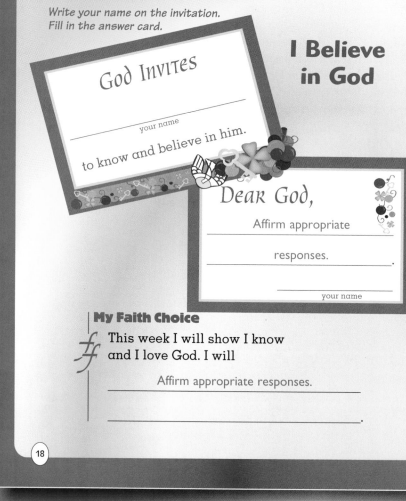

You are a sign of God's love. You can help other people to believe in God by what you say and what you do.

Write your name on the invitation. Fill in the answer card.

I Believe in God

God Invites

_____
your name

to know and believe in him.

Dear God,

Affirm appropriate

responses.

_____
your name

My Faith Choice

This week I will show I know and I love God. I will

Affirm appropriate responses.

_____

_____

18

Teaching Tip

What Difference Does Faith Make in My Life? This is an important page. Be sure to give the children the time they need to process it. Processing this page is an integral part of helping the children discover the connection between the teachings of the Catholic Church and their personal lives. It allows the children to move from what they have learned to how they can live their faith in their daily lives. Allow time for the children to share faith stories with one another.

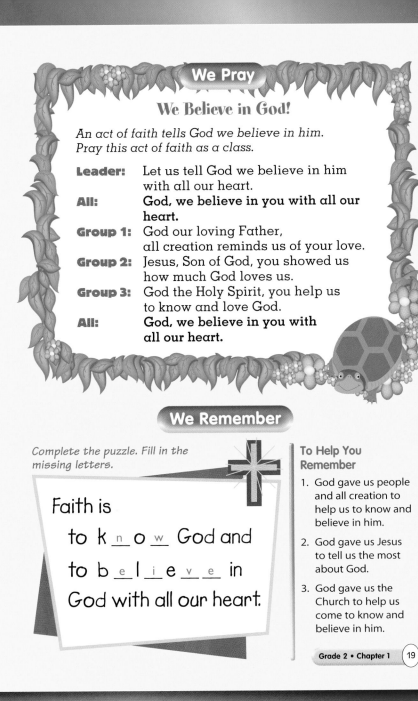

We Pray

We Believe in God!

An act of faith tells God we believe in him.
Pray this act of faith as a class.

Leader: Let us tell God we believe in him with all our heart.

All: **God, we believe in you with all our heart.**

Group 1: God our loving Father, all creation reminds us of your love.

Group 2: Jesus, Son of God, you showed us how much God loves us.

Group 3: God the Holy Spirit, you help us to know and love God.

All: **God, we believe in you with all our heart.**

We Remember

Complete the puzzle. Fill in the missing letters.

Faith is
to k _n_ o _w_ God and
to b _e_ l _i_ e _v_ e in
God with all our heart.

To Help You Remember

1. God gave us people and all creation to help us to know and believe in him.

2. God gave us Jesus to tell us the most about God.

3. God gave us the Church to help us come to know and believe in him.

Grade 2 • Chapter 1　(19)

WE PRAY

- Divide the children into three groups. Invite each group to practice reading their sentence aloud together.

- Tell the children that the prayer that they will pray is an act of faith. Point out that the prayer is an expression of faith in the Holy Trinity—God the Father, God the Son, and God the Holy Spirit. It is a response to God's invitation to know and believe in him.

- Lead the children in praying the prayer "We Believe in God." Begin and end with the praying of the Sign of the Cross.

Review

WE REMEMBER

- Scramble the letters to the words *Creation*, *Jesus*, and *Church* and write scrambled letters for the words on the board.

- Ask the children to help you unscramble the letters to create the correct words. As each word is unscrambled, invite a volunteer to find the word in one of the "To Help You Remember" statements and read it aloud.

- Give directions and invite the children to complete the activity.

Special Needs

Pairing Up Children. Children with reading and writing difficulties need special consideration when it comes to creating pairs. Write the names of children who display adequate reading and writing on index cards with a green marker. Write the names of children with reading or writing difficulties on index cards with a red marker. When you create partners for activities choose one child from each group to ensure that you have a student with adequate reading and writing ability in each pair.

Need: Children with reading and writing difficulties

At Home

ENCOURAGE

Have the children carefully tear out pages 19 and 20 along the perforation. Encourage the children to share the pages with their families and to do the activities together. If they did not complete the review activity on page 19 by the end of the session, emphasize that they can complete it with their families.

VISIT FAITHFIRST.COM

• Share with the children the many activities on the *Faith First* Web site.

• Encourage the children to visit **www.FaithFirst.com.**

With My Family

This Week . . .

In chapter 1, "We Know and Love God," your child learned that God reveals himself to us and invites us to believe in him. All creation helps us come to know and believe in God. Our families and people in our Church help us come to know and believe in God. Jesus told us the most about God. He invites us to have faith in God. Faith is God's gift that makes us able to believe in him. Jesus Christ is the greatest sign of God's love. We grow in faith and live our faith every day.

For more on the teachings of the Catholic Church on the mystery of divine Revelation and the gift of faith, see *Catechism of the Catholic Church* paragraph numbers 50–67, 84–95, and 142–175.

Sharing God's Word

Read the Bible story in Matthew 6:26–34 about Jesus inviting the people to have faith in God or read the adaptation of the story on page 15. Emphasize that in this Bible story Jesus invites us to have faith in God.

Praying

In this chapter your child learned to pray an act of faith. Read and pray together the prayer on page 19.

Making a Difference

Choose one of the following activities to do as a family or design a similar activity of your own.

• All of creation is a sign of God's love. Take a walk outdoors. Look at all the wonderful things that God has created. Talk about what these things tell us about God.

• Name some of the people who help you come to know and believe in God. Write down their names. When you have finished, have each family member write a note of thanks to one person on the list.

• Learn more about the ways your parish helps you grow in faith. Thank God for your parish.

For more ideas on ways your family can live your faith, visit the "Faith First for Families" page at **www.FaithFirst.com**. You will find the "About Your Child" helpful as your child begins a new year.

20

Before Moving On . . .

As you finish today's lesson, reflect on the following question before moving on to the next chapter.

What more can I do to make sure everyone is involved in class activities?

Evaluate

Take a few moments to evaluate this week's lesson.
I feel (circle one) about this week's lesson.

    a. very pleased

    b. OK

    c. disappointed

The activity the children enjoyed most was . . .

The concept that was most difficult to teach was . . .

because . . .

Something I would like to do differently is . . .

ENRICHING THE LESSON

Taking the Scriptures Outdoors

Purpose

To reinforce the Bible story that Jesus told to invite us to have faith in God (taught on page 15)

Directions

- Take the children outdoors for a dramatic telling of Matthew 5:1; 6:26–34.
- Have the children sit comfortably in a grassy area, if possible. Tell the Scripture story. Use gestures, facial expressions, and voice inflection as you speak.
- Emphasize that God's love for the children is far greater even than his love for the birds, whom he watches over faithfully.

Materials

Bible

Making Creation Posters

Purpose

To reinforce that we come to know God through his gift of creation (taught on page 14)

Directions

- Talk with the children about their favorite parts of creation, such as animals or flowers.
- Have the children find pictures in magazines of things in creation that they particularly like.
- Invite the children to make a poster using the pictures they found in the magazines and ones they would like to draw.
- At the top of each completed poster print: "All Creation Tells Me About God."

Materials needed

large sheets of poster board
magazines
scissors and glue sticks
crayons and markers

Literature Connection

Purpose

To reinforce ways that we come to know God better (taught on page 14)

Directions

Many children's books address the concept of who God is and where God is. Consider reading one of these books to the children to help them come to know God better.

- When reading aloud to the children always provide a purpose for listening, and after reading the book ask open-ended questions that will enhance their thinking.
- One book available from Tyndale House Publishers is entitled *What Is God Like?* (1998) by Kathleen Bostrom.
- Have the children think of questions they would like to ask about God. Write them on the board and have the children listen for which ones the book answers.
- Ask them what question and answer helped them to learn about God.

Materials

What Is God Like? by Kathleen Bostrom

Music Connection

- "Praise to God," (Japanese traditional). *Singing Our Faith (SOF)* #155.
- "All You Works of God," M. Haugen. *SOF* #157.
- "God Made the World," J. Miffleton. *Rise Up and Sing (RUS)* #235.
- "All Things Bright and Beautiful," L. Wasson. *RUS* #237.

We Believe in the Holy Trinity

Background

The Mystery of God

When we make the Sign of the Cross, we pray, "In the name of the Father, and of the Son, and of the Holy Spirit." We don't pray, "In the names of . . ." The plural word, *names,* would imply three Gods. By using the singular, we confess there is one God in three distinct divine Persons: "the almighty Father, his only Son, and the Holy Spirit: the Most Holy Trinity" (*Catechism of the Catholic Church* 233).

The Holy Trinity is the central mystery of Christian life and faith. This truth about God is something that we would never be able to know about him unless he revealed it to us.

Before his Passover, Jesus told the disciples that they would not be alone in their ministry. The Holy Spirit would come to them and remain with them. The Father would send the Holy Spirit to them in Jesus' name. Just as the Holy Spirit spoke through the prophets, he will now accompany, teach, and guide Jesus' disciples. That means us!

The Mystery of God with Us

As disciples of Christ we are never alone. At Baptism, we were joined to Jesus, received the gift of the Holy Spirit, and became adopted children of God the Father. By virtue of our Baptism, the Trinity dwells with us and within us for the entirety of our lives on earth.

We hope to see face to face and be with the Trinity forever in heaven after we die.

The Holy Trinity is our constant source of enlightenment and blessing. The grace of our Lord Jesus Christ and the love of God the Father and the fellowship of the Holy Spirit are with us.

In the trials of our lives on earth, as we attempt to live as followers of Christ, we believe and trust that it is the Father who draws us and the Holy Spirit who moves us to live our new lives in Christ, the Incarnate Son of God. Joined to Christ in Baptism, we have been sanctified by the grace of God. We are temples of the living triune God. As Jesus promised,

> "Whoever loves me will keep my word, and my Father will love him, and we will come to him and make our dwelling with him." *JOHN 14:23*

In our journey toward a life of eternal communion with God, we pray with Blessed Elizabeth of the Trinity:

> "O my God, Trinity, whom I adore, help me forget myself entirely so to establish myself in you. . . . may each minute bring me more deeply into your mystery!"

For Reflection

How do I relate and pray to each Person of the Holy Trinity?

How has my faith in and awareness of the Holy Trinity dwelling within me shaped my life?

Catechist to Catechist

As You Begin

As you begin this second session, you and the children have already begun the process of getting to know one another. If you are gathering at the end of a long school day, know that the children may be tired. If your sessions are on the weekend, the children may be anxious to get back to weekend activities. In other words, seven- and eight-year-olds will just be themselves. Be patient with them and with yourself.

Begin with Prayer

Remember to begin each session with prayer. It will not only remind the children of God's presence in their lives, but will also have a  calming effect on both you and them. During this session take the opportunity to re-teach the Sign of the Cross. Tell the children that they are now old enough to understand this beautiful prayer and its importance to us as Christians. Then begin and end this session by praying the Sign of the Cross slowly and prayerfully.

The Church Teaches . . .

The *General Directory for Catechesis* tells us that

"every mode of presentation must always be christocentric-trinitarian: 'Through Christ to the Father in the Holy Spirit.'[1] 'If catechesis lacks these three elements or neglects their close relationship, the Christian message can certainly lose its proper character'"[2] (*GDC* 100).

This is why the mystery of the Trinity is introduced early in *Faith First,* helping the children to center themselves in a Trinitarian faith.

See the Catechism . . .

For more on the teachings of the Catholic Church on the mystery of the Trinity, see *Catechism of the Catholic Church* 232–260.

CATECHIST PRAYER

Father, help me share love with your children. Jesus, be my guide as I use your example to teach about our Father. Holy Spirit, be my inspiration as I help these little ones know and live their faith. Amen.

Footnote references may be found on p. 456.

LESSON PLANNER

Focus

Focus To discover what Jesus told us about who God is

Engage

Page 21
Focus
To help the children identify what the Sign of the Cross tells us about the mystery of God

Opening Prayer

Discussion
Involve the children in a discussion of solving mysteries.

Teach and Apply

Pages 22–24
Focus
To know and believe there is one God in three Persons—the Father, the Son, and the Holy Spirit

Presentation
Read, discuss, and summarize content.
Scripture
Matthew 22:37–39
Activities
- Use the words *Abba* and *Father* when you pray.
- Learn to sign Jesus' message about loving God.
- Color the words in the banner.

Faith-Filled People
Saint Patrick

Connect

Pages 25–26
Focus
To discover ways the Catholic Church shows we believe in the Holy Trinity

Our Church Makes a Difference
We pray the Sign of the Cross.
Our Catholic Faith
Sign of the Cross

What Difference Does Faith Make?
Activity
Telling people about the Holy Trinity
Faith Choice
Name a way to tell others about the Holy Trinity this week.

We Pray

Page 27
Prayer
Blessing
Prayer
Choose a leader and pray "Signing Ourselves" together.

We Remember

Review
- Complete the sentence activity.
- Read the "To Help You Remember" statements aloud.
Preview
Preview the "With My Family" page.

Materials

- pens or pencils
- crayons or markers

Enriching the Session

Blackline Masters
Additional Activities booklet:
  Chapter 2
  Praying the Sign of the Cross
  Drawing yourself in the picture
Assessment Tools booklet:
  Chapter 2 Test
Faith First **Grade 2 Video**
  Segment 1: Bible songs
Enriching the Lesson (CG page 69)
  Illustrating the Holy Trinity
  Living as Children of God
  Learning about the Trinity with Music

Music Connection (CG page 69)

www.FaithFirst.com

We update the *Faith First* Web site weekly. Check each week for new content and features. Here are some places to begin:

Catechists and Teachers
- Current Events
- Chapter Downloads
- Catechist Prayer

Faith First **for Families**
- Bible Stories
- Saints
- Make a Difference

Kids' Clubhouse
- *Faith First* Activities
- Chapter Reviews
- Games

Don't Forget! You can make lesson planning a breeze—check out the **Online Lesson Planner.**

We Believe in the Holy Trinity

Stained-glass window showing the Church's belief in the Holy Trinity (21)

We Pray

Jesus prayed, "Father, give them the Holy Spirit."
Based on Luke 11:13

Glory to the Father, and to the Son, and to the Holy Spirit. Amen.

Do you like to solve mysteries?

The Church teaches us about the mystery of God. We can never understand completely the mystery of God.

What mystery about God does the Sign of the Cross tell us about?

Engage

PRAY
- Ask the children to quiet themselves for prayer. Remind them that Jesus is with us as we pray.
- Pray the Sign of the Cross together.
- Choose a volunteer to read the Scripture verse based on Luke 11:13.
- Invite the children to echo each phrase of the Glory Prayer after you.

DISCOVER
Purpose: To discover what the children may already know about the Holy Trinity
- Ask the children if they like to solve mysteries.
- Invite the children to reflect on the stained-glass window. Ask a volunteer to guess what mystery the image represents.
- Have a volunteer read the introductory paragraph.
- Tell the children that they are going to learn a mystery about God.

✟ Liturgy Tip

Blessing Prayers. Catechists and parents have the right and privilege of imparting blessings by virtue of their Baptism. Blessings might include such ritual actions as sprinkling with water or tracing a cross on the person(s) being blessed. Blessings within classroom prayer services should include a proclamation of the word of God, a praise of God's goodness, and a petition for his help. When laypeople impart blessings, they join their hands when imparting the blessing, rather then extending them over the persons being blessed. You can find complete guidelines for imparting blessings in the *Book of Blessings* (Study Edition), prepared by the International Commission on English in the Liturgy. Collegeville, MN: The Liturgical Press, 1989.

Teach

Read the "Faith Focus" question to the children. Share with the children that in this chapter they will learn about the Holy Trinity.

DISCOVER

- Write the word *Trinity* on the board. Tell the children to listen for this word as you read aloud the introductory paragraph.
- Have a volunteer read aloud the faith word *Holy Trinity* and its meaning.
- Remind the children that the Holy Trinity is a mystery of faith that we cannot fully understand. We believe it because God has revealed it.
- Ask volunteers to read the next two paragraphs. Ask what they learned about the people God created.

Apply

REINFORCE

Emphasize that the Holy Trinity is one God in three Persons. Have the children make word cards for *Holy Trinity* and *soul*.

INTEGRATE

- Have the children share what they think a good father does for his children. Loves and cares for them, wants them to be happy, provides a home.
- Tell them that God the Father loves us even more than a good father does.
- Have the children complete the activity.

One God in Three Persons

Faith Focus

What did Jesus tell us about who God is?

Faith Words

Holy Trinity
The Holy Trinity is one God in three Persons—God the Father, God the Son, and God the Holy Spirit.

soul
Our soul is that part of us that lives forever.

God the Father

Jesus told us there is only one God who is God the Father, God the Son, and God the Holy Spirit. We call the one God in three Persons the **Holy Trinity.** The word *trinity* means "three in one."

God the Father is the first Person of the Holy Trinity. In the Apostles' Creed we pray,

"I believe in God the Father almighty, creator of heaven and earth."

God the Father created everyone and everything out of love. He created all people in his image and likeness. He created each person with a body and a **soul.** Our soul is that part of us that lives forever. God the Father loves us and cares for us. He creates us to be happy with him now and forever in heaven.

ACTIVITY Jesus used the word Abba when he prayed to God the Father. Write the words Abba and Father on the lines. Use the words when you pray.

Abba _____

Father _____

22

Teaching Tip

Highlighting Faith. Children this age are fascinated with highlighters. Supply highlighters for the children to share. Each week have the children highlight important faith statements in the lesson. This will make occasional reviews easier to facilitate.

God the Son

God the Son is the second Person of the Holy Trinity. At Mass we pray,

"We believe in one Lord,
Jesus Christ,
the only Son of God."

God the Father sent his Son to be one of us and live with us. Jesus is the Son of God. Jesus told us to call God our Father. He taught us that we are children of God. We are to live as children of God. Jesus said,

"Love God with all your heart. Love other people as much as you love yourself." Based on Matthew 22:37–39

Faith-Filled People

Patrick

Saint Patrick was a bishop. There is a story about Saint Patrick that tells us that he showed people a shamrock to help them learn about the Trinity. The Church celebrates the feast day of Saint Patrick on March 17.

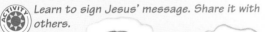
ACTIVITY Learn to sign Jesus' message. Share it with others.

Love   God   with

all   your   heart. (23)

Background: Faith-Filled People

Saint Patrick. As a young boy Saint Patrick (389–461) was taken from his father's farm in Britain and made a slave in Ireland. There he tended sheep and was terribly isolated and lonely. His loneliness led him to a deep experience of prayer. Patrick finally escaped from slavery and returned to Britain. He became a priest and returned to Ireland as a missionary. He traveled throughout Ireland and introduced thousands of Irish people to Christianity.

Teach

FOCUS

Remind the children that God the Father is the first Person of the Holy Trinity. Tell the children that now they are going to learn more about the second Person of the Holy Trinity, Jesus, the Son of God.

DISCOVER

- Tell the children some things about a friend of yours. Teach the children that they know some things about your friend because you told them.
- Explain that Jesus does the very same thing. He tells us about God the Father.
- Read "God the Son" and ask the children to listen for who Jesus is and what he told us about God the Father.
- Invite volunteers to respond at the end of the reading.

Apply

REINFORCE

- Read aloud "Faith-Filled People." Tell the children about Saint Patrick.
- Draw an image of a shamrock on the board and label the first leaf *Father,* the second leaf *Son,* and the third leaf *Holy Spirit* to demonstrate how Saint Patrick used the shamrock to teach people about the Trinity.

INTEGRATE

Teach the children to sign Jesus' message.

Teach

FOCUS

Remind the children that God the Father sent his only Son, the second Person of the Holy Trinity, to be one of us. Jesus is the Son of God who became one of us. Then point out that Jesus told us about the third Person of the Holy Trinity, the Holy Spirit.

DISCOVER

- Ask the children what they know about the Holy Spirit.
- Have the group follow along as volunteers read aloud "God the Holy Spirit."
- Ask the group to underline what Jesus told us about the Holy Spirit.

Apply

REINFORCE

- Ask volunteers to read what they have underlined.
- Emphasize that the Holy Spirit helps us live as children of God.

INTEGRATE

- Invite the children to color the banner.
- Ask each child to turn to a partner and name one way they can show their love for others.

God the Holy Spirit

God the Holy Spirit is the third Person of the Holy Trinity. At Mass we pray,

"We believe in the Holy Spirit,
the Lord, the giver of life."

Jesus told us about the Holy Spirit. He told the disciples, "The Father in heaven will send you the Holy Spirit" (based on Luke 11:13). We first receive the gift of the Holy Spirit at Baptism. The priest or deacon says, "I baptize you in the name of the Father, and of the Son, and of the Holy Spirit." This shows that we share in the life of the Holy Trinity.

God sends us the Holy Spirit to help us to know and love God better. The Holy Spirit helps us to live as children of God.

ACTIVITY Color the words in the rainbow banner. Thank God for telling you who he is.

God is Father, Son, and Holy Spirit.

24

Teaching Tip

Preparing to Celebrate. Your computer may come in handy for designing a banner similar to the banner on this page. Outline a banner and have the children color it in and decorate the letters. Hang it in a place where it is visible for the closing prayer experience.

Our Church Makes a Difference

The Sign of the Cross

Catholics often pray the Sign of the Cross. We pray,
"In the name of the Father, and of the Son, and of the Holy Spirit. Amen."

As we say the words of the prayer, we bless ourselves. We touch our forehead, our shoulders, and our chest over our heart. We remember that we are baptized. We belong to God's family. We are to love God and all people as Jesus taught.

When do you pray the Sign of the Cross?

Affirm appropriate responses.

Our Catholic Faith

Sign of the Cross

We pray the Sign of the Cross at Mass. We begin Mass by blessing ourselves as we say the words. Before we listen to the Gospel we make a small Sign of the Cross on our forehead, on our lips, and over our heart. At the end of Mass, the priest makes the Sign of the Cross over the people and asks God to bless them.

25

Background: Catholic Traditions

Prayer Before the Gospel. Explain to the children that before the Gospel reading is proclaimed at Mass, they may have noticed their family members and other parishioners marking themselves with three small signs of the cross—on their foreheads, on their lips, and over their hearts. Explain that as a sign of respect for God's word in the Gospel, many Catholics sign themselves three times and pray that God's word will stay within their minds, on their lips, and in their hearts.

HIGHLIGHT

Remind the children that there is one God in three Persons.

DISCOVER

- Tell the children that at the beginning of every class, they show their belief in the Holy Trinity. Ask volunteers how they show that belief. By praying the Sign of the Cross.
- Review with the children the correct way to pray the Sign of the Cross.
- Invite students to look at three photos of people making the Sign of the Cross. (Note: The baseball player is Erubiel Durazo of the St. Louis Cardinals.)
- Ask: How is the Sign of the Cross a prayer to the Holy Trinity? When we make and pray the Sign of the Cross we pray to God the Father, God the Son, and God the Holy Spirit.

INTEGRATE

- Talk with the children about other times when they and their families make the Sign of the Cross.
- Ask the children to read "Our Catholic Faith" silently.
- Encourage them to pray the Sign of the Cross every day.

Connect

Remind the children that God wants everyone to know who he is.

RESPOND

- Read aloud the introductory paragraph.
- Remind the children about Saint Patrick and the shamrock.
- Explain the activity and have the children complete it.
- Invite volunteers to share what they have drawn or written.

CHOOSE

- Present "My Faith Choice."
- Help the children brainstorm ideas to complete their faith choices.
- Encourage the children to keep their faith choices in the week ahead.

What Difference Does Faith Make in My Life?

God loves people so much. He wants everyone to know who he is.

Saint Patrick used a shamrock to help people come to know the Holy Trinity. On each leaf of the shamrock, draw or write what you can tell others about the Holy Trinity.

Father

Holy Spirit

Son

Responses will vary.

My Faith Choice

ff I will tell others about the Holy Trinity this week. I will say

Affirm appropriate responses.

_____

_____.

26

Teaching Tip

Providing Visuals. Many children have never seen an actual shamrock. Shamrock plants are readily available in supermarkets, or you or a friend may have one at home. If possible, bring one in for the children to see. Place it on your prayer table during today's lesson.

We Pray

Signing Ourselves

The Church uses many gestures, or actions, to help us to pray. Signing ourselves with a cross is one of the gestures the Church uses.

Leader: Come forward one at a time. I will make a small sign of the cross on your forehead and say, *"(Name), you belong to Christ."* Then sign yourself and say, *"I belong to Christ."*

(Name), you belong to Christ.

Child: **I belong to Christ.**

We Remember

Complete the sentences. Use the words in the word box.

> one   three   Trinity

1. We believe in the Holy _Trinity_ .

2. There is _one_ God in _three_ Persons.

To Help You Remember

1. There is one God in three Persons. We call this the Holy Trinity.

2. God the Father is the first Person of the Holy Trinity.

3. God the Son is the second Person of the Holy Trinity.

4. God the Holy Spirit is the third Person of the Holy Trinity.

Grade 2 • Chapter 2   27

WE PRAY

- Gather the children in the prayer center.
- Explain the order of prayer.
- Lead the ritual prayer experience. Be sure to look the children in their eyes as you gently sign each of them.

WE REMEMBER

- Create three overlapping images on the board, such as triangles or circles. Write the words *Holy Trinity* over the organizer. Write the words *Father*, *Son*, and *Holy Spirit* in each of the three spaces.
- Ask the children to help you label the images properly as the first, second, and third Persons of the Holy Trinity.
- Explain the directions for the "We Remember" review activity. Have volunteers share their responses as a final review.

Special Needs

Providing Reading Assistance. For each sentence in the "We Remember" activity, tell the children how many letters are present in the expected answer. This will help them narrow down the choices and select the appropriate response more successfully.

Need: Children with reading deficits

At Home

ENCOURAGE

Have the children carefully tear out pages 27 and 28 along the perforation. Encourage the children to share the pages with their families and to do the activities together. If they did not complete the review activity on page 27 by the end of the session, emphasize that they can complete it with their families.

VISIT FAITHFIRST.COM

- Share with the children the many activities on the *Faith First* Web site.
- Encourage the children to visit **www.FaithFirst.com.**

Before Moving On . . .

As you finish today's lesson, reflect on the following question before moving on to the next chapter.

Which children seem to work especially well together?

2 With My Family

This Week . . .

In chapter 2, "We Believe in the Holy Trinity," your child learned about the mystery of the Holy Trinity—the mystery of one God in three divine Persons: Father, Son, and Holy Spirit. We could never have come to know this wonderful truth about the identity of God on our own. Out of love, God revealed this about himself to us in Jesus Christ. The belief in the mystery of the Trinity is at the heart of the Church's living faith.

For more on the teachings of the Catholic Church on the mystery of the Trinity, see *Catechism of the Catholic Church* paragraph numbers 232–260.

Sharing God's Word

Read together John 14:26 in which Jesus promised the disciples that the Holy Spirit would come to them. Emphasize that there is one God who is Father, Son, and Holy Spirit.

Praying

In this chapter your child was signed with a cross. Use the prayer on page 27 and have family members sign one another with a cross in the morning or in the evening at bedtime.

Making a Difference

Choose one of the following activities to do as a family or design a similar activity of your own.

- The Sign of the Cross helps us remember and express our faith in the Holy Trinity. Encourage your child to make the Sign of the Cross each time you pray.
- Create a Holy Trinity banner. Make three headings: Father, Son, and Holy Spirit. Under each heading write down what you know about each Person of the Holy Trinity or draw a symbol for each Person of the Trinity.
- Choose one way your family can reflect the love of the Holy Trinity to your neighbors or relatives.

For more ideas on ways your family can live your faith, visit the "Faith First for Families" page at **www.FaithFirst.com.** Click on "Games" and make learning fun for your child.

✔ Evaluate

Take a few moments to evaluate this week's lesson. I feel (circle one) about this week's lesson.

    a. very pleased
    b. OK
    c. disappointed

The activity the children enjoyed most was . . .

The concept that was most difficult to teach was . . .

because . . .

Something I would like to do differently is . . .

ENRICHING THE LESSON

Illustrating the Holy Trinity

Purpose

To reinforce that the Holy Trinity is one God in three Persons – God the Father, God the Son, and God the Holy Spirit (taught on page 22)

Directions

- Provide the children with heavy paper that has been folded into three sections.
- Then have them write *Father* at the top of the first section, *Son* at the top of the middle section, and *Holy Spirit* at the top of the third section.
- Challenge the children to write as many things as they can remember about each of the three Persons of the Trinity.
- Have the children decorate their lists with crayons or markers.
- Invite the children to take their lists home and share them with their families.

Materials

construction paper
crayons or markers

Living as Children of God

Purpose

To reinforce the teaching that we are children of God (taught on pages 22 and 24)

Directions

- Brainstorm with the children ways we show we are living as children of God.
- In small groups have the children create a scenario showing second graders living as children of God.
- Have the groups present their role plays and have the other children give them a silent cheer for their good work which is another way of living as children of God.

Materials

Learning About the Trinity with Music

Purpose

To reinforce some of the things the children have learned about the Holy Trinity (taught on pages 22–24)

Directions

- Sing this song to the tune of "Row, Row, Row Your Boat" to help the children recall some of the things they learned about the Holy Trinity.

    One, two, three Persons,
    In the Trinity.
    Father, Son, and Spirit
    God is one in three.

    God is our Father,
    Jesus is his Son,
    God the Holy Spirit,
    God is three in one.

- Practice the song several times and invite them to sing the song for their family.

Materials

You might want to copy the song for the children to sing with their families.

Music Connection

- "Praise to the Trinity," R. Glover. *Singing Our Faith (SOF)* #161.
- "Walking By Faith," D. Haas. *(SOF)* #179.
- "One Lord," S. Soper. *Rise Up and Sing (RUS)* #81.
- "We Believe, We Believe in God," C. Landry. *(RUS)* #279.

God Is Our Father

Background

Love God with Your Whole Heart

Belief in God is the starting point of faith. Everything in our lives as Christians, as disciples of the Incarnate Son of God, refers back to the simple words of faith, "I believe in God." All the articles in the Apostles' Creed, all the works and wonders of Jesus Christ, the creation and progress of humanity speak of God.

The Old Testament reads like a record book of God's involvement with his people. Jesus most fully reveals God, inviting us to place our faith, hope, and love for God above all else.

God, Abba, Father

We are not invited to believe and love a God who is unfeeling, capricious, or distant. We are invited to believe in God, who is Abba, our loving, caring, ever-present, unconditionally merciful Father. The Bible is a moving testimony to God the Father, who lavishes upon us his kindness, grace, goodness, and unending love.

The works of God in Sacred Scripture reveal that he is always faithful and true, reliable and loyal. If we turn to him, we will

not be disappointed. His love will never leave us (see Isaiah 54:10). There are enormous consequences to trusting and loving God. Here are just a few:

1. In a rapidly changing world, defying us to adapt, there is one constant: God, "with whom there is no alteration or shadow caused by change" (James 1:17). When everything else is taken from us, God will always remain.

2. God values us as sons and daughters and tends to our needs. We will never be orphans; we need never fear abandonment.

3. God always guides everything back to his will. "God cares for

all, from the least things to the great events of the world and its history" (*Catechism of the Catholic Church* 303).

4. The greatness and goodness of God are inexhaustible. Our quest for God can be a source of endless discovery and delight.

5. Since everything we are and have comes from God, we can transform our lives into an act of thanksgiving.

6. God created all people in his image and likeness. Thus, we can look upon our neighbors and see their true dignity and worth.

7. In times of trouble, God is with us. With Saint Teresa of Jesus we pray:

> Let nothing trouble you,
> Let nothing frighten you.
> Everything passes;
> God never changes.
> Patience obtains all.
> Whoever has God
> Wants for nothing.
> God alone is enough.

For Reflection

How is God working in my life?

When do I give my whole heart to God? What are the consequences?

Catechist to Catechist

Awe and Wonder

Seven- and eight-year-olds are still very much in awe of God's creation. The beauty of creation stimulates the religious imagination for children. Be sure to nurture the wonderful curiosity of these young people. Encourage them to observe their world more clearly, see the beauty of creation, and give thanks and praise to God.

Images for God

Another thing to remember is that children this age often find images a wonderful aid in learning. The following is one way to help convey the message of God the Father's unconditional love for them. Have the children imagine all of the people in their lives who love and care for them. Have them imagine all these people rolled up into one. Tell them that all these people are a small sign of God the Father's love for them.

The Church Teaches . . .

The *General Directory for Catechesis* reminds us,

> The Christian knows that every human event—indeed all reality—is marked by the creative activity of God which communicates goodness to all beings (*GDC* 16).

That is why every *Faith First* chapter begins by helping the child to situate the lesson concepts in their own life experience. As each child learns to reflect on their life experiences, they can begin to see the hand of the Almighty Creator at work. Through continued catechesis, a child can grow to recognize God's revelation in his or her daily life.

See the Catechism . . .

For more on the teachings of the Catholic Church on the mystery of God the Creator and Father, see *Catechism of the Catholic Church* 268–274, 279–314, and 325–349.

CATECHIST PRAYER

Father,
sometimes in the hurrying
of my days, I forget to notice
the wonders with which you
have surrounded me. Awaken
once again in me that sense
of awe that I possessed as a child
and help me to be thankful.
Amen.

Footnote references may be found on p. 456.

LESSON PLANNER

Engage

Page 29
Focus
To help the children identify what they know about creation

Opening Prayer

Discussion
The Bible teaches us that God is our Father and Creator.

Teach and Apply

Pages 30–32
Focus
To appreciate that God created everyone and everything out of love without any help

Presentation
Read, discuss, and summarize content.
Scripture
Genesis 1:1–31
Activities
- Listen to the story of creation from the Bible.
- Circle the words that tell about God.
- Draw a picture of what the Our Father brings to mind.

Connect

Pages 25–26
Focus
To describe ways the Church and its members honor God the Father and Creator

Our Church Makes a Difference
Saint Augustine's Garden
Our Catholic Faith
The Lord's Prayer

What Difference Does Faith Make?
Activity
Draw a picture that includes the gifts of God's creation.
Faith Choice
Name a way to show the love God our Creator and Father has for us.

We Pray

Page 35
Prayer Form
The Our Father
Prayer
Choose a leader. Introduce the prayer, and then pray it together.

We Remember

Review
- Complete the crossword puzzle.
- Read the "To Help You Remember" statements aloud.

Preview
Preview the "With My Family" page.

Materials

- pens or pencils
- crayons or markers
- index cards

Enriching the Session

Blackline Masters
Additional Activities booklet:
Chapter 3
Writing a creation poem
Making a tree of life
Assessment Tools booklet:
Chapter 3 Test

Faith First **Grade 2 Video**
Segment 1: "Bible Songs"

Enriching the Lesson (CG page 81)
Echo Reading
Taking Part in a Nature Project
Sharing a Story

Music Connection (CG page 81)

www.FaithFirst.com

We update the *Faith First* Web site weekly. Check each week for new content and features. Here are some places to begin:

Catechists and Teachers
- Current Events
- Chapter Downloads
- Catechist Prayer

Faith First **for Families**
- Bible Stories
- Saints
- Make a Difference

Kids' Clubhouse
- *Faith First* Activities
- Chapter Reviews
- Games

Don't Forget! You can make lesson planning a breeze—check out the **Online Lesson Planner.**

God Is Our Father

We Pray

Come, see
everything God
has done for us.
Based on Psalm 66:5

**God our Father,
bless us with
your gifts of
faith, hope, and
love.**   **Amen.**

*How do family
members show their
trust in one another?*

The Bible and our
Church teach us that
God is our Father.
We believe in him
and trust him.

*What have you
learned about God
our Father?*

(29)

PRAY

- Ask the children to quiet themselves for prayer. Remind them that Jesus is with us as we pray.
- Pray the Sign of the Cross together.
- Choose a volunteer to read Psalm 66:5.
- Lead the opening prayer, and invite the children to echo each phrase after you.

DISCOVER

Purpose: To discover what the children may already know about God the Father

- Have the children look at the picture. Ask who made the sky and the planets. Remind them that God created the whole world.
- Ask the children to share how family members show trust in one another. Read the opening paragraph.
- Invite responses to the question on the bottom of the page.

Liturgy Tip

Signing Prayer. The more children repeat something, the more it becomes a part of them. Last week they learned American Sign Language signs for "Love God with all your heart." Take a moment before you pray the opening prayer to go over these signs. Then you can make the signing part of your prayer. The more movement and gestures you are able to incorporate into their prayers, the more meaningful they will be to the children. A good resource is *Religious Signing: A Comprehensive Guide for All Faiths* (Elaine Castello, Ph.D., New York: Bantam, 1997).

Teach

FOCUS

Read the "Faith Focus" question aloud. Tell the children that in this chapter they will learn why we call God our Father.

DISCOVER

- Read the first paragraph of "God the Creator."
- Ask the children to now read the first paragraph silently and look for a sentence that tells them something new about God. God is the Creator.
- Proclaim the Scripture story of creation based on Genesis 1:1–31.
- Ask the children to recall some of the wonderful things God made. Ask them what God thought of the things he had made. They were good.

Apply

REINFORCE

- Ask a volunteer to read the definition for *Creator* in the "Faith Words." Have them create a word card for *Creator*.
- Have the children examine the photos on the page. Ask volunteers to describe other pictures that might show that God's creation is good. Pictures of babies, trees, forests, or mountains.

INTEGRATE

Ask the children which part of God's creation in the Bible story they are most thankful for. Accept all answers.

God Our Creator and Father

Faith Focus

Why do we call God our Father?

Faith Words

Creator
God alone is the Creator. God has made everyone and everything out of love and without any help.

almighty
God alone is almighty. This means that only God has the power to do everything.

God the Creator

You are getting to know more and more about God. God the Father is the **Creator**. He made everyone and everything out of love and without any help. He made the creatures we can see and the angels we cannot see.

God tells us the story of creation. It is the first story in the Bible.

In the beginning God created the heavens and the earth. He made the sun, the other stars, and the moon. He made the sky, the earth, and the sea.

God made plants, trees, and flowers. He made all the fish and the birds. He made all the animals and other creatures that live on the land. Then God created people in his image and likeness.

God looked at all that he had created. He saw that it was very good. Based on Genesis 1:1, 7–12, 16, 20–21, 24–25, 27, 31

What does creation tell you about God the Creator? Affirm appropriate responses.

Catholic Social Teaching

Care for God's Creation. We show our respect for God the Creator by caring for all that he created. Caring for creation is, in fact, a requirement of Christian faith. First of all, we are called by God to show respect for all people, since we are all created in his image. This is the foundation of our human dignity. We are to be stewards of the earth as well. Christians must measure every choice by the impact it has on human life and on the environment.

Tips: Draw a ladder on poster board. Label the ladder from top to bottom with these words: *God, angels, humans, animals,* and *plants.* Invite the children to cut out magazine pictures of God's creation. Have the children paste the pictures on the corresponding places on the ladder.

30

God the Almighty

We can learn about God when we look at creation. We see how much God loves us.

As we get to know God more, we learn that God is **almighty.** This means that only God has the power to do everything.

God tells us that he does everything out of love. God is always good and loving. We believe in and love God the Father with all our heart. We show God and others our trust and love for him.

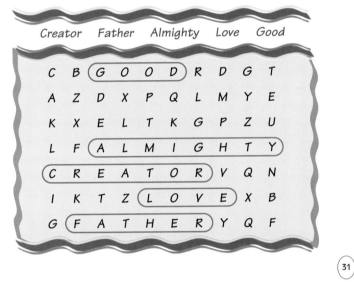

Find and circle the words that tell about God. What does each word tell you about God? Affirm appropriate responses to the question.

Creator   Father   Almighty   Love   Good

(31)

Faith-Filled People

Bonaventure

Saint Bonaventure looked at creation and came to know and love God. He said that creation was like a mirror. Whenever he looked at creation, he saw a good and loving God. The Church celebrates the feast day of Saint Bonaventure on July 15.

Background: Faith-Filled People

Saint Bonaventure. Saint Bonaventure (1221–1274) was a great theologian, preacher, and leader. His writings are filled with love and prayer. He was a person of compassion, virtue, and deep prayer. The words and actions of Saint Bonaventure are based on loving God with one's whole mind, heart, and soul. The Church honors him as a Doctor of the Church, which means he is an accomplished teacher. The feast of Saint Bonaventure is celebrated on July 15. Legend tells us that Saint Bonaventure received his name when, in response to the pleading of his mother, Saint Francis of Assisi prayed for his recovery from a dangerous illness, and foreseeing the future greatness of the boy cried, *"O Buona ventura"*— O good fortune!

Teach

FOCUS

Remind the children that creation is a sign of God's love. Tell them they are now going to discover why God could make all things.

DISCOVER

- Invite volunteers to name people they know who can do many things well.
- Tell the children that only God can do everything because he is almighty. This means he has the power to do everything. And God does everything out of love.
- Ask the children to read the third paragraph to learn what we believe about God. Ask volunteers to share what they learn.

Apply

REINFORCE

- Ask a child to read the definition of the faith word *almighty.*
- Have the children read "Faith-Filled People" together to learn about Saint Bonaventure.

INTEGRATE

Explain the activity and allow the children time to complete it. Invite volunteers to share what each word tells them about God.

Teach

FOCUS

Remind the children that God the Father does everything out of love. Then tell them they are going to learn more about a time that Jesus taught his disciples about God the Father.

DISCOVER

- Ask the children: Who do you go to when you need to know something?
- Jesus' friends asked him to teach them how to pray.
- Invite a volunteer to read the Bible verse. Ask them what Jesus taught them to pray.
- Ask the children to read the next paragraph silently to discover what Jesus taught us about God our Father. Accept all appropriate responses that reflect concepts in the last paragraph on student page 32.

Apply

REINFORCE

- Read "Our Catholic Faith" on page 33 and ask the children to listen for why we also call the Our Father the Lord's Prayer.
- Invite volunteers to share ways their family members care for them.

INTEGRATE

- Discuss the activity question on page 32 with the group and have them complete the activity.
- Invite children to share their drawings with a friend.

God Our Father

Jesus told us the most about God. One day Jesus' friends asked him to teach them to pray. He taught them to pray,

"Our Father in heaven hallowed be your name."
Matthew 6:9

Jesus taught that God the Father is our Father. He loves and cares for us. He knows what we need before we ask for it. God always does what is best for us. We are to believe in him and trust him.

ACTIVITY When you pray the Our Father, what picture comes to your mind? Draw it here.

Responses will vary.

Affirm appropriate responses.

32

Special Needs

Developing and Understanding Vocabulary. Show the children smaller parts of difficult words. Write the word *almighty* on a large index card and display it on the board. Highlight the word *mighty* and ask volunteers to explain or demonstrate the meaning of the word. Explain that the word *almighty* means that God has the power to do all things. Give students a piece of drawing paper. On one side ask them to write the word *almighty*. On the other side ask them to draw a picture of something from creation, such as a mountain, that reminds them that God is almighty.

Need: Children with learning difficulties

Our Church Makes a Difference

Saint Augustine's Garden

The children of Saint Augustine's School honor God the Father and Creator in a special way. They grow vegetables and food in a garden at Saint Augustine's School.

They plant the seeds. They harvest their crops. They wash and bag the fruits and vegetables, and take the food to a food bank.

As they work in the garden, the children feel close to God. They show their love for God and people when they take care of creation.

QUESTION *How do you and your friends care for creation?*
Affirm appropriate responses.

Our Catholic Faith

The Lord's Prayer

The Our Father is the prayer of all Christians. It is called the Our Father because these are the first words of the prayer. The Our Father is also called the Lord's Prayer because Jesus our Lord gave this prayer to the Church.

33

HIGHLIGHT
Remind the children that we show our love for God when we take care of creation.

DISCOVER
- Ask the children if they ever worked in a garden.
- Tell the children the story of Saint Augustine's School's garden.
- Ask how the schoolchildren were caring for creation.
  Helping plants to grow; helping to feed hungry people.

INTEGRATE
Divide the class into pairs and let them share how they care for creation.

Teaching Tip

Visual Summaries. You may wish to help children understand the outcome of Saint Augustine's School's garden project by drawing a visual summary for them. Draw a timeline on the board. Invite them to help you mark the key events: planting seeds, watering plants, harvesting crops, packaging vegetables, delivering to food bank, giving to people in need, people enjoying a good meal. This will give them a good image of the big effects of small actions done for the love of God and others.

Connect

HIGHLIGHT

Help the children recall that God created everyone and everything out of love and that his love for us will last forever.

RESPOND

- Explain the directions to the activity "Gifts of God's Creation."
- Give the children sufficient time to complete the activity.

CHOOSE

- Invite the children to read silently "My Faith Choice," think about it, and write their idea.
- Encourage the children to put their choice into practice this week.

What Difference Does Faith Make in My Life?

God created everyone and everything out of love. God shares the gift of his love with you every day.

Draw yourself with the gifts of God's creation. Be sure to include other people.

Gifts of God's Creation

Responses will vary.

My Faith Choice

This week I will show my love for others. I will

Affirm appropriate responses.

_____

34

Teaching Tip

Providing Options. Be sure to help the children brainstorm ideas for their drawings to stimulate their imaginations before they do the activity. If time allows, you may wish to give the children other options as well. For example, you can suggest that they mime the object they are thinking of, and invite the class to guess what they are. This can be a lot of fun if they choose a gift of creation such as a tree, a mountain, or a river.

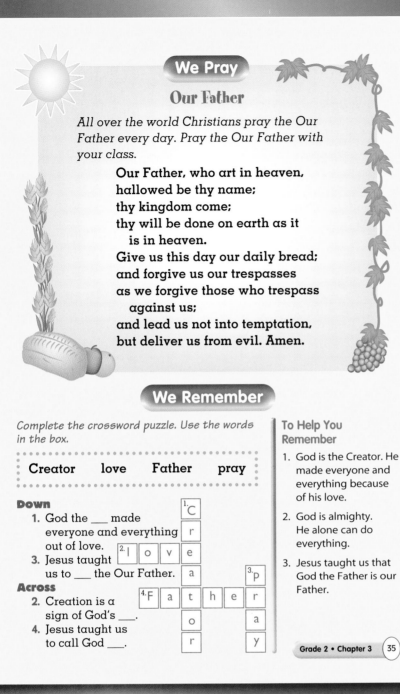

We Pray

Our Father

All over the world Christians pray the Our Father every day. Pray the Our Father with your class.

Our Father, who art in heaven,
hallowed be thy name;
thy kingdom come;
thy will be done on earth as it
is in heaven.
Give us this day our daily bread;
and forgive us our trespasses
as we forgive those who trespass
against us;
and lead us not into temptation,
but deliver us from evil. Amen.

We Remember

Complete the crossword puzzle. Use the words in the box.

| Creator | love | Father | pray |

Down
1. God the ___ made everyone and everything out of love.
3. Jesus taught us to ___ the Our Father.

Across
2. Creation is a sign of God's ___.
4. Jesus taught us to call God ___.

To Help You Remember

1. God is the Creator. He made everyone and everything because of his love.

2. God is almighty. He alone can do everything.

3. Jesus taught us that God the Father is our Father.

Grade 2 • Chapter 3 35

WE PRAY

- Gather the children in the prayer center. Remind them of the *orans* prayer position, with hands raised, palms up. Invite them to use this posture as you pray together.
- Pray the Our Father together.

Review

WE REMEMBER

- Write these three words on the board: *Creator, almighty, Father*. Invite the children to share a sentence using the words.
- Introduce the activity and allow time to complete it.
- Review the "To Help You Remember" sentences.

✝ Liturgy Tip

Spontaneous Prayer. Children have the ability to be honest and candid and say what they are thinking. What a wonderful thing it would be to turn these thoughts and words into prayer. This is an excellent time to build the habit of spontaneous prayer. Most children are not yet too inhibited to share their thoughts and feelings openly.

At Home

ENCOURAGE

Have the children carefully tear out pages 35 and 36 along the perforation. Encourage the children to share the pages with their families and to do the activities together. If they did not complete the review activity on page 35 by the end of the session, emphasize that they can complete it with their families.

VISIT FAITHFIRST.COM

• Share with the children the many activities on the *Faith First* Web site.

• Encourage the children to visit **www.FaithFirst.com.**

3 With My Family

This Week . . .

In chapter 3, "God Is Our Father," your child learned more about the faith of the Catholic Church. We profess the faith of the Church in God the Father each Sunday at Mass. We pray, "We believe in God the Father almighty, maker of heaven and earth." The Our Father, or Lord's Prayer, is the prayer of all Christians. The Church prays it every day. Each time we gather and celebrate Mass, we pray the Our Father as we begin our preparation to share in Holy Communion.

For more on the teachings of the Catholic Church on the mystery of God as Creator and Father, see *Catechism of the Catholic Church* paragraph numbers 268–274, 279–314, and 325–349.

Sharing God's Word

Read together the Bible story in Matthew 6:9–13 about Jesus teaching his friends how to pray or read the adaptation of the story on page 32. Emphasize that Jesus taught us to pray the Our Father.

Praying

In this chapter your child prayed the Our Father. Read and pray together the prayer on page 35.

Making a Difference

Choose one of the following activities to do as a family or design a similar activity of your own.

• Draw a creation mural. Write "God the Creator" at the top of the mural. Decorate the mural with pictures of things God created.

• When people work in a garden, they are caring for God's creation. Choose one thing you can do together this week to care for creation.

• Pray the Our Father often this week. When you take part in Mass this week, join in praying aloud or singing the Our Father with the rest of the assembly.

For more ideas on ways your family can live your faith, visit the "Faith First for Families" page at **www.FaithFirst.com**. Click on "Make a Difference" for ideas on how your family can share your faith in God with others.

36

Before Moving On . . .

As you finish today's lesson, reflect on the following question before moving on to the next chapter.

What children could use more praise from me?

Evaluate

Take a few moments to evaluate this week's lesson.
I feel (circle one) about this week's lesson.

a. very pleased
b. OK
c. disappointed

The activity the children enjoyed most was . . .

The concept that was most difficult to teach was . . .

because . . .

Something I would like to do differently is . . .

ENRICHING THE LESSON

Echo Reading

Purpose

To reinforce the story of creation (taught on page 30)

Directions

Retell the biblical account of creation by reading aloud Genesis 1:1–31.

- Add gestures for the various works of creation to reinforce concepts. Invite the children to echo each gesture after you. For example:

  In the beginning God created the heavens and the earth.
  [Raise arms slowly, cross wrists overhead, and bring arms down slowly.]
  Then he said, "Let there be plants and trees."
  [Move hands down to floor and then raise hands overhead.]

- Invite the children to retell the story using the gestures.

Materials
Bible

Taking Part in a Nature Project

Purpose

To reinforce the teaching about our responsibility to care for creation (taught on pages 30 and 33)

Directions

Children love to be outdoors and have a natural love for nature and all that it holds.

- Brainstorm with the children several projects they can do to take care of creation.
- Have the children agree on a project that they can do as a group.
- Have the children write a note to themselves to remind them to work on their project.

Materials
paper
pencils

Literature Connection

Purpose

To reinforce that we can learn about God when we look at creation (taught on page 31)

Directions

A wonderful book that will reinforce the children's sense of the depth and breadth of God's love is *Old Turtle* by Douglas Wood. (Pfeifer-Hamilton, Publishers, 1992).

- Tell the children that in the book each part of creation is insisting that God is most like the qualities that it possesses.
- Have them predict what the wind might say and ask them to listen to see if they were correct.
- When you have finished reading the story you might invite the children to make small movements with each part of creation, such as blow like the breeze, move their hands like fish, and so on, and retell the story.
- An open-ended question might be, "Why did the people finally listen?"

Materials
Old Turtle, by Douglas Wood

Music Connection

- "We Believe," C. Walker. *Rise Up and Sing (RUS)* #91.
- "Let There Be Peace on Earth," S. Miller / J. Jackson. *(RUS)* #22.
- "All Grownups, All Children," P.J. Shelly. *Singing Our Faith,* #147.
- "All You Works of God," M. Haugen. *(RUS)* #157.

Praising God
A Scripture Story

Background

Outbursts of the Human Heart

The Psalms are a prayer legacy from the people of the Old Covenant to those of us living in the new and everlasting Covenant, established in Jesus Christ. Over many centuries the Psalms were collected into the five books of the Psalter (or "Praises") and have been handed down to us as a master work of prayer.

The Psalms, while originating in the communities of the Holy Land and the Diaspora, have a universal appeal to all peoples of faith because they express the deepest desires of the human heart for God. The Psalms are hymns, outbursts of praise, wails of sorrow, and chants of thanksgiving.

[W]hether individual or communal, whether royal chants, songs of pilgrimage, or wisdom-meditations, the Psalms are a mirror of God's marvelous deeds in the history of his people, as well as reflections of the human experiences of the Psalmist.
CATECHISM OF THE CATHOLIC CHURCH 2588

An Unrivaled Prayer Book

The Psalms can be for Christians an unrivaled prayer book. Though the Psalms may deal with past events, they still possess wisdom for us today. Their depth and simplicity express the human spirit reaching out to God. Their words of praise and thanksgiving can be exclaimed by people of every era. Through the Holy Spirit's inspiration, they teach the People of God, generation after generation, how to pray.

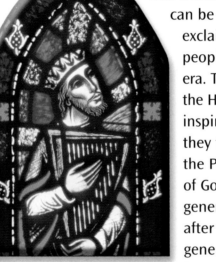

The Psalms teach us about praying spontaneously. They tell of a burning desire within us to be with God. They give words to our anguish when we have fallen victim to betrayal or abuse or temptations. The Psalms give unparalleled expression to the awe we feel in God's creation. They offer us encouragement to place our trust in God, who is always loving and faithful.

What is more pleasing than a psalm? David expresses it well: "Praise the Lord, for a psalm is good: let there be praise of our God with gladness and grace!" Yes, a psalm is a blessing on the lips of the people, praise of God, the assembly's homage, a general acclamation, a word that speaks for all, the voice of the Church, a confession of faith in song.
SAINT AMBROSE, NARRATION ON PSALM 1

The Church continues to honor and be nourished by the Psalms. Just as the Israelites prayed the Psalms during the great feasts at Jerusalem, the Catholic Church proclaims the ancient praises during the Mass and throughout each and every day in the Liturgy of the Hours. The Liturgy of the Word continues the tradition of chanting the Psalms as a way to worship our God and Redeemer.

For Reflection

How might I include my favorite Psalm or Psalms in my daily prayers?

When I pray my favorite Psalm how does it deepen my communion with God? How does its wisdom inspire me?

Catechist to Catechist

Song Prayers

During this session show the children how to find the Psalms in the Bible. Talk to them about how the Psalms are songs of prayer and how we too use songs to pray to God. You may have heard that when we sing we pray twice. It certainly involves an added dimension to prayer when those in the assembly join their voices in a common prayer. Since singing is one aspect of community celebration, encourage the children to join in singing with the assembly at Mass.

Song Prayers

The children are old enough now to begin to follow the words to songs in the hymnals in church. Take a little time to help the children  develop the skill of finding the song numbers when they are announced and then following along from verse to chorus. The hymn suggestions at the end of each chapter of *Faith First* are all taken from hymnals commonly used in Catholic parishes.

The Church Teaches . . .

The *General Directory for Catechesis* states:

> The historical character of the Christian message requires that catechesis attend to . . . presentation of salvation history by means of Biblical catechesis so as to make known the "deeds and the words" with which God has revealed himself to man. **GDC 108**

For this reason, *Faith First* incorporates special Scripture chapters into every unit and includes Bible verses and stories throughout the text.

See the Catechism . . .

For more on the teachings of the Catholic Church on the Psalms, singing, music, and Christian prayer, see *Catechism of the Catholic Church* 1156–1158, 2623–2643, and 2700–2704.

CATECHIST PRAYER

My God, I will praise you in the daytime and in the night. I will praise you on my good days and on my not-so-good days. Amen.

LESSON PLANNER

Engage

Page 21
Focus
> To help the children express ways they praise God

Opening Prayer

Discussion
> Sometimes we use music and singing to praise God.

Teach and Apply

Pages 22–24
Focus
> To discover that the Psalms are prayer-songs found in the Bible

Presentation
> Read, discuss, and summarize content.

Scripture
- Psalm 148:2–3, 9–13
- Psalm 147:1

Activities
- Draw pictures about creation.
- Meditate on your favorite part of creation.
- Clap to the rhythm of the words as you pray aloud.

Connect

Pages 25–26
Focus
> To explain that the Church sings hymns and Psalms of praise to God

Our Church Makes a Difference
> Become familiar with a song Saint Francis of Assisi loved to sing.

Our Catholic Faith
Responsorial Psalm

What Difference Does Faith Make?
Activity
> Create a CD cover for a favorite hymn that you sing at Mass.

Faith Choice
> Name something you can sing to God about this week.

We Pray

Page 27
Prayer
> Psalm of praise
Prayer
> Choose a leader and then pray the Psalm together.

We Remember

Review
- Complete the sentence activity.
- Read the "To Help You Remember" statements aloud.

Preview
> Preview the "With My Family" page.

Materials

- crayons or markers
- missalette or parish worship aid for upcoming Sunday

Enriching the Session

Blackline Masters
Additional Activities booklet:
> Chapter 4
> > Solving a code
> > Seeing the beauty and wonder in creation

Assessment Tools booklet:
> Chapter 4 Test

Enriching the Lesson (CG page 93)
> Preparing for Liturgy
> Making a Class Psalter
> Literature Connection

Music Connection (CG page 93)

www.FaithFirst.com

We update the *Faith First* Web site weekly. Check each week for new content and features. Here are some places to begin:

Catechists and Teachers
- Current Events
- Chapter Downloads
- Catechist Prayer

***Faith First* for Families**
- Bible Stories
- Saints
- Make a Difference

Kids' Clubhouse
- *Faith First* Activities
- Chapter Reviews
- Games

Don't Forget! You can make lesson planning a breeze—check out the **Online Lesson Planner.**

Praising God
A Scripture Story

4

We Pray

Sing to God for all
the good things
of the earth.
Based on Psalm 33:3, 5

**Blessed are you,
God the Creator.
Everything good
comes from you!
Amen.**

*What are some
ways you show
others how you feel?*

Sometimes we use
more than words to
tell others how we
think and feel.
Sometimes we use
music and singing
to praise and give
thanks to God.

*When do you use
music and singing
to praise God?*

(37)

PRAY

- Ask the children to quiet themselves for prayer. Remind them that Jesus is with us as we pray.
- Pray the Sign of the Cross together.
- Choose a volunteer to read the Psalm verses.
- Lead the opening prayer and invite the children to echo each phrase after you.

DISCOVER

Purpose: To discover what the children already know about ways to praise God

- Ask the children to look at the picture and suggest what the children might be doing. Singing, praying
- Read aloud the introductory paragraph and invite responses to the question on the bottom of the page. Accept all appropriate responses.

Background: Scripture

Scripture Chapters. In each *Faith First* Scripture chapter there are three distinctive elements that bring the Bible stories to life. First, the "Bible Background" section puts the Scripture story in a context the children can understand. They learn about the author, the setting, and the background of the people in the story. Second, in "Reading the Word of God," the word of God is proclaimed. Third, in "Understanding the Word of God," the children explore the meaning and relevance of God's message. The chapter concludes with a reflection on the significance of the Scripture message for the Church and for their own lives.

Teach

FOCUS

Ask a child to read aloud the "Faith Focus" question. Tell the children that in this lesson they will learn about a special type of prayer-song found in the Bible.

DISCOVER

- Invite the children to name different ways they communicate with one another.
- If the children do not name singing or music, be sure to tell them we can communicate through song. Then point out that we can use music and sing our prayers.
- Have the children read "We Sing to God" silently and find the name we give to the prayer-songs found in the Bible. Psalms
- Tell the children that the Book of Psalms is in the Old Testament. Open the Bible to Psalm 148 and put it in the prayer area, if you have not already done so.

Apply

REINFORCE

Read "Faith Words" together. Tell the children that some of the Psalms are prayers of praise. Have the children make word cards for the two terms.

INTEGRATE

- Explain the directions for the "Give Praise to God" activity and have the children complete it.
- Invite volunteers to share their drawings with the group.

Bible Background

Faith Focus

Why do we pray the Psalms?

Faith Words

psalms
Psalms are songs of prayer.

prayer of praise
A prayer of praise gives honor to God for his great love and kindness.

We Sing to God

People pray in many ways. People pray alone and with others. People pray aloud and they pray silently. Sometimes people sing their prayers.

The Bible has many prayers that God's people sang. These prayers are called **psalms**. They are found in the Book of Psalms in the Old Testament. There are 150 psalms in the Book of Psalms.

God's people prayed many kinds of psalms. Some of the Psalms they prayed are **prayers of praise**. They honor God for his great love and his kindness.

ACTIVITY Draw a picture about creation that helps you to praise God.

Give Praise to God

Responses will vary.

38

Liturgy Tip

Praying the Psalms Today. Explain to the children that the Psalms the Church prays are ancient Jewish prayers often prayed through song. Tell the children that Jesus prayed the Psalms often and from memory. These same Psalms are prayed today both by the Jewish people and by Christians.

Reading the Word of God

We Praise God

Psalm 148 is a psalm of praise. The beautiful words of this psalm almost make music. Listen for the sound of the words as we pray,

Praise God, all you angels.
Praise him, sun and moon;
    give praise, all shining stars.
Praise the LORD, you mountains
    and hills.
Praise God, all animals
    that live on the land and that live
    in the water.
All people, young and old, lift up
    your hearts.
All praise the name of God.

Based on Psalm 148:2–3, 9–13

ACTIVITY *Look at the picture you drew on page 38. Close your eyes. See your favorite part of creation. Hear the sounds of creation. Quietly praise God in your heart.*

39

Teaching Tip

Invite a Leader of Song to Visit. Invite one of your parish's leaders of song to class to speak to the children about the Psalms and how the Church prays them each day. Of course, it would also be a wonderful experience for the children to be led by your guest in singing some of the more familiar Responsorial Psalms used at Sunday liturgy. Above all, invite your guest to make the visit an enjoyable and lively interactive session with the children.

Teach

FOCUS
Remind the children that only some of the Psalms are prayers of praise.

DISCOVER
- Introduce "We Praise God." Tell the group that they are going to pray aloud a prayer of praise.
- Have the children listen for the rhythm of the words as you pray Psalm 148 aloud together.
- Ask the children to look at the illustration to help them uncover what Psalm 148 praises God for. Creation

Apply

REINFORCE
- Ask the children to name parts of creation for which they would most like to praise God.
- Invite volunteers to read aloud their favorite line from Psalm 148.

INTEGRATE
- Explain the directions for the praying activity. You might play a recording of an appropriate piece of background music during this activity.
- Invite the children to say to themselves, "Praise to you, O God," at the conclusion of their prayers.

Teach

FOCUS

Remind the children that we prayed Psalm 148 to *praise* God. Point out to the children that there are several different kinds of psalms.

DISCOVER

- Summarize "The Psalms" for the children in your own words.
- Explain that the writers of the Psalms wrote psalms that people could pray when they were happy or sad or needed forgiveness or to tell God that they loved him.

Apply

REINFORCE

- Write the words *sad*, *sorry*, and *asking* on the board.
- Have the children work with partners to make up short prayers that fall into these categories.
- Ask volunteers to share their prayers.

INTEGRATE

Introduce the hand-clapping activity. Have the children practice reading the words first without clapping to get a sense of the rhythm. Then have the group say the words aloud together while clapping. Point out that they will clap on the words that have a picture of hands under them.

Understanding the Word of God

The Psalms

The writers of the Psalms wrote many kinds of psalms. They wrote some psalms for people to pray when they are happy. They wrote other psalms for people to pray when they are sad.

There are also psalms for people to pray when they want to ask God's help or forgiveness. There are other psalms to help people tell God they love him. Some psalms, such as Psalm 148, help people to praise God for everything he does for them.

ACTIVITY *Clap your hands as you pray aloud the lyrics of this song.*

God Is Always with Us

God is with us day to day.

God is with us when we play.

God is with us when we pray.

God, I love you in every way.

(40)

Teaching Tip

All children have ways that they can best express their learning. Some prefer writing, others prefer drawing, and others using their voices. Some children actually express their learning best through music and rhythm. Today's clapping activity will appeal to children who have a musical or rhythmic "intelligence."

Our Church Makes a Difference

Christians Sing to God

Saint Francis of Assisi loved to sing about God. He sang a song that Christians still sing today. It is called "The Canticle of the Sun." Here is part of the song Saint Francis sang.

Be praised, my Lord,
    with all your creatures,
    especially Brother Sun!
Be praised, my Lord,
    for Sister Moon and Stars!
    They are bright and lovely and fair.
Be praised, my Lord,
    for Brother Wind, and for Air and
    Weather, cloudy and clear.

Today we can listen to Christian songs on CDs and on the radio. Christian singers sing of God's love and goodness. Many of their songs remind us to live as Jesus taught us.

 Pretend you are a Christian singer. What would you sing about? Share your ideas with a partner. Responses will vary.

Our Catholic Faith

Responsorial Psalm

Every day the Church prays the Psalms. After the first reading at Mass, the cantor, or song leader, leads us in singing or praying a psalm aloud.

41

Background: Scripture

Responsorial Psalms. The Hebrew word for Psalms is *Tehilliam*. The root of this word means "praise." The Psalms are a remarkable collection of poems in praise of God. They are poems that reflect a variety of human experiences. The words of the Psalms are powerful and sincere and able to be spoken or sung by all of us. At Mass, the assembly sings the Psalms during the Liturgy of the Word. Led by the cantor, or leader of song, we pray the Responsorial Psalm together.

Connect

HIGHLIGHT

Remind the children that Christians today sing the Psalms to sing of God's love and goodness.

DISCOVER

- Ask the children what they know about Saint Francis of Assisi. Tell them that Saint Francis lived many hundreds of years after the writers of the Psalms. He wrote a singing prayer that Christians still sing today.
- Ask the children to read the first paragraph of "Christians Sing to God" and underline the name of this song. The Canticle of the Sun. Explain that *canticle* is another word for song.
- Have the children read aloud the words from Saint Francis's "The Canticle of the Sun" with you.
- Ask the children if they know any other songs we sing at church.
- Present "Our Catholic Faith," about the Responsorial Psalm used at Mass.
- Have the Responsorial Psalm for next Sunday available and share it with the children.

INTEGRATE

- Tell the children that being a Christian singer and writer of songs is a wonderful gift from God.
- Present the activity and encourage volunteers to share their responses with the group.
- You might ask volunteers who enjoy singing to make up verses for their songs and sing them to the class. Invite them to work in pairs to help them overcome shyness.

Connect

HIGHLIGHT

Remind the children that the writers of the Psalms and Saint Francis of Assisi were all filled with God's love and used music to praise him.

RESPOND

- Name some of the hymns sung at your parish's Sunday liturgies and have the children name their favorite hymn. Write the titles of the hymns on the board. Note: The children will probably not know the hymns by name. Ask them to sing a line they remember from the hymn.
- Ask the children to read the directions and complete the CD activity. Invite the children to share their CD covers with one another.

CHOOSE

Present "My Faith Choice." Have the children write their choice and encourage them to put their choice into practice this week.

What Difference Does Faith Make in My Life?

God's love filled the hearts of the writers of the Psalms and Saint Francis of Assisi. God's love fills your heart too.

Each Sunday at Mass you join with your parish in singing to God. Create a cover for a CD for one of your favorite hymns.

Responses will vary.

My Faith Choice

This week I will lift up my heart in song to God. I will sing about

Affirm appropriate responses.

42

Teaching Tip

Including All Children. You will find that not all children in your class know many hymns, and perhaps none at all. Bring a CD of liturgical hymns to class and invite the children to listen to several examples and choose a favorite. Explain the lyrics as well. Then invite them to complete the page activity.

We Pray

Praying a Psalm

The Church prays the Psalms every day. Join with the Church and pray this verse of Psalm 147.

Leader: Let us give praise to God.

All: **How good to celebrate our God in song.**

Leader: God is kind and good.

All: **How good to celebrate our God in song.**

Psalm 147:1

We Remember

Read each sentence. Color the ◯ next to each correct sentence.

- ● Psalms tell God how good he is.
- ● Psalms help us to tell God we love and trust him.
- ● Catholics pray the Psalms at Mass.

To Help You Remember

1. Psalms are prayers we sing.
2. Some of the Psalms give praise and thanks to God.
3. Some of the Psalms help us to pray for other people and for ourselves.

Grade 2 • Chapter 4   43

Pray

WE PRAY

- Gather the children in the prayer center.
- Practice the Psalm response.
- Pray together.

Review

WE REMEMBER

- Read aloud the "To Help You Remember" statements, and have the children complete the "We Remember" activity. Give the children time to complete it. Have them check their answers with a partner.

Teaching Tip

Young Children and the Bible. Although children at age seven or eight might have difficulty reading the Bible, that does not mean that they should not page through a Bible and become familiar with it. Explain the difference between the Bible and books of Bible stories, often called children's Bibles. Make sure they know that Bible storybooks are great for now, but that they are not Bibles. At this same time, reinforce reverence for the Bible by the way it is handled by you and the children during your sessions. Always enthrone a Bible on your prayer table and use it during prayer. Keep it open to the Scripture passage being taught or prayed in class.

At Home

ENCOURAGE

Have the children carefully tear out pages 43 and 44 along the perforation. Encourage the children to share the pages with their families and to do the activities together. If they did not complete the review activity on page 43 by the end of the session, emphasize that they can complete it with their families.

VISIT FAITHFIRST.COM

- Share with the children the many activities on the *Faith First* Web site.
- Encourage the children to visit **www.FaithFirst.com.**

---

4 With My Family

This Week . . .

In chapter 4, "Praising God: A Scripture Story," your child learned about the Psalms. Praying the Psalms is a key form of Christian prayer. The Psalms have been prayed since Jesus' time as the public prayer of the Church. There are 150 psalms in the Book of Psalms, which is found in the Old Testament. Psalms express our prayer in many forms. Some of the Psalms bless and give adoration to God. Others give thanks to God for his love and kindness. Others are prayers asking God for help and forgiveness. Others praise God for the good things he has done for us and has given us.

For more on the teachings of the Catholic Church on the Psalms, singing and music, and Christian prayer, see *Catechism of the Catholic Church* paragraph numbers 1156–1158, 2623–2643, and 2700–2704.

Sharing God's Word

Read together Psalm 148 or the adaptation of the verses from Psalm 148 on page 39. Emphasize that the Psalms are prayers and that Psalm 148 is a prayer to God, praising him for all creation.

Praying

In this chapter your child prayed a prayer using Psalm 147:1. Read and pray together the prayer on page 43.

Making a Difference

Choose one of the following activities to do as a family or design a similar activity of your own.

- Ask each family member to share a favorite song that praises God. Choose one that you can all sing together. Sing it at dinnertime this week.

- Make a book illustrating Psalm 148. Adaptations of verses from Psalm 148 are on page 39.

- There are some excellent contemporary Christian music groups that perform powerful praise music. Search the Internet or a local music store to find something your child likes. Listen to this music with your child.

> For more ideas on ways your family can live your faith, visit the "Faith First for Families" page at **www.FaithFirst.com.** Click on "Family Prayer" for a prayer you can pray as a family this week.

44

Before Moving On . . .

As you finish today's lesson, reflect on the following question before moving on to the next chapter.

Am I providing enough time to discuss the children's questions?

✓ Evaluate

Take a few moments to evaluate this week's lesson.
I feel (circle one) about this week's lesson.

    a. very pleased
    b. OK
    c. disappointed

The activity the children enjoyed most was . . .

The concept that was most difficult to teach was . . .

because . . .

Something I would like to do differently is . . .

ENRICHING THE LESSON

Preparing for Liturgy

Purpose

To reinforce the teaching about the Responsorial Psalm prayed at Mass (taught on page 40)

Directions

- Share with the children the Responsorial Psalm for the upcoming Sunday liturgy.
- Invite the children to listen as you sing or pray the Psalm refrain.
- Practice praying a Responsorial Psalm. Then lead the class in praying it. Sing the Responsorial Psalm if possible.

Materials

Sunday missalette or worship aid

Making a Class Psalter

Purpose

To reinforce the children's praying of different kinds of psalms (taught on pages 38 and 40)

Directions

Explain to the children that a book containing the Psalms is called a Psalter.

- Invite the children to create a Psalter by adding decorations to pages on which you, in advance, have printed short Psalm verses. Make sure you use Psalm verses that are appropriate for the children in your group.
- Have the children create and decorate a cover using the title "Our Book of Psalms."

Materials

Bible
construction paper
crayons or markers

Literature Connection

Purpose

To reinforce the children's understanding of the different kinds of Psalms (taught on page 40)

Directions

- Use *My Tall Book of Psalms* written by Donna Huisjen (Zondervan, 1999) to introduce the children to the variety of Psalms.
- Consider reading one or more of the Psalms from this book as part of your opening prayer each week. In this book the children hear the rhythmic beauty of the Psalms.
- Invite the children to design a prayer card using one of their favorite psalms. Remind them to pray the psalm frequently.
- Two other books the children might enjoy on the Psalms are *Praise the Lord, My Soul: Psalm 104 for Children* by Christopher L. Webber (Morehouse, 2002) and *Shout for Joy & Sing! Psalm 65 for Children* by Christopher L. Webber (Morehouse, 2003).

Materials

one or both of the suggested books

Music Connection

- "Psalm 147: Happy Are All," R. Glover. *Singing Our Faith (SOF)* #54.
- "Canticle of the Sun," M. Haugen. *(SOF)* #145.
- "Let Us Sing," C. Landry. *Rise Up and Sing (RUS)* #192.
- "The Wonders I See," B. Farrell. *(RUS)* #296.

Jesus Is the Son of God

Background

The Mystery of Love

The mystery of the Incarnation—the Son of God, the second Person of the Holy Trinity, taking on flesh and becoming fully human while remaining divine—is a mystery of divine love beyond the comprehension of the human mind and heart. What kind of life on earth did the Incarnate Son of God, Jesus, live?

Jesus could have been a monarch so splendid that he would make Louis XIV blush with envy, a warrior of unrivaled courage. He could have been whoever and whatever he wanted to be. And who did this Incarnate Son of God, the Holy One of God, choose to become? Instead of ruling by regal pomp or power, the Son of God chose to identify himself by humility, servanthood, and suffering. God's own word to us could not have more clearly revealed this:

> Who, though he was in the
> form of God, . . .
> he emptied himself, . . .
> becoming obedient to death,
>   even death on a cross.
> PHILIPPIANS 2:6, 7, 8

In Jesus of Nazareth, the only Son of God took on the life most common to humans, that of power-lessness, obedience, and poverty. By doing so he showed us how the human condition could be trans-formed into the kingdom of God.

Jesus, the Incarnate Son of God, is the Christ. The English word *Christ* is from the Greek word *Kristos*, which is the Greek translation of the Hebrew *masch* (Messiah), a word meaning "anointed." Jesus Christ, anointed by the Holy Spirit to be Priest, Prophet, and King, established a kingdom that would last forever. The true meaning of Christ's kingship was revealed only after his Crucifixion, death, Resurrection, and glorious Ascension. By his Paschal Mystery, Christ effectively destroyed death's power and gave people the promise of eternal life. He freed people from the tragic death-bearing consequences of sin and opened the way to new and everlasting life.

In Jesus we have the promise of life in the kingdom of God. He invites us to a life of holiness—to a life of everlasting communion with God the Father, Son, and Holy Spirit.

The Way of Jesus

Jesus is the truth, the life, and the way (see John 14:6). Like Jesus, we are to trust in the Father, who we address and know as *Abba*. In childlike surrender, we trust in the providential care of our heavenly Father, who knows our needs.

We seek first the kingdom, and then all we need will be ours

as well (see Matthew 6:33). To those who think that wealth, power, and fame are the paths, or way, to happiness, Jesus proclaims that happiness resides in the poor in spirit and in those struggling to achieve peace and goodness (see Matthew 5:3, 9). By his poverty, the Incarnate Son of God shows us how to transform the privations and sufferings that may come our way.

For Reflection

Who is Jesus for me?

How willing am I to give all for love of God and neighbor?

Catechist to Catechist

The Heart of Christmas

This chapter tells the Christmas story. Get out those bathrobes, pillowcases, and towels. Nothing makes a story come alive more quickly for seven- and eight-year-olds than acting out the Gospel accounts of the Nativity. Enlist the help of parents and set up a video camera. The script in this chapter is short so you could even have two or three casts. Save the video and show it just before Christmas. The actors and actresses will be delighted!

Jesus' Presence with Us

As we celebrate the birth of Christ, we need to remind ourselves that Jesus is present with us whenever we gather in his name. Remind the children that he is uniquely present in every celebration of the Eucharist during which the bread and wine through the words of the priest and power of the Holy Spirit become the Body and Blood of Christ. Celebrate with the children that Jesus' presence with us is the real and true reason for our happiness. It gives us the hope that we live out and carry into the hearts of the children we teach. Through this lesson help the children realize that the gift of Jesus' presence is with us, and this is cause for joy.

The Church Teaches . . .

The *General Directory for Catechesis* states:

> The relationship between the Christian message and human experience is not a simple methodological question. It springs from the very end of catechesis, which seeks to put the human person in communion with Jesus Christ. . . . Catechesis operates through this identity of human experience between Jesus the Master and his disciple and teaches us to think like him, to act like him, to love like him.[1]   *GDC* 116

As you interact with the children during your sessions with them, be aware that the children come to know Jesus through the experience of being loved and loving others.

See the Catechism . . .

For more on the teachings of the Catholic Church on the Covenant and the mystery of the Incarnation, see *Catechism of the Catholic Church* 51–67 and 456–560.

CATECHIST PRAYER

*Jesus, you are
my Savior—willing to give
all so that I may live. Amen.*

Footnote references may be found on p. 456.

LESSON PLANNER

Focus — To discover how Jesus reveals God's love and mercy

Engage

Page 45
Focus

To help the children recall the story of the birth of Jesus

Opening Prayer

Discussion

What does your family do to celebrate Christmas?

Teach and Apply

Pages 46–48
Focus

To identify Jesus as true God and true man

Presentation
- Read, discuss, and summarize content.

Scripture
- Isaiah 9:2, 6
- Matthew 14:13–20

Activities
- What might the shepherds have said?
- Describe the action in the pictures.

Faith-Filled People
The Blessed Virgin Mary

Connect

Pages 49–50
Focus

To describe ways the Church cares for people

Our Church Makes a Difference
Discover that treating others as Jesus did builds a world of kindness.

Our Catholic Faith
The Homily

What Difference Does Faith Make?
Activity
Write a story about people caring for others.

Faith Choice
Name a way to live as a sign of God's love and mercy this week.

We Pray

Page 51
Prayer Form
Prayer of praise

Prayer
Choose a leader, and then pray the Angelus together.

We Remember

Review
- Complete the words to finish the sentences.
- Read the "To Help You Remember" statements aloud.

Preview
Preview the "With My Family" page.

Materials

pens or pencils

Enriching the Session

Blackline Masters
Additional Activities booklet:
   Chapter 5
   Making a caring card
   Completing a picture of the Nativity
Assessment Tools booklet:
   Chapter 5 Test

Enriching the Lesson (CG page 105)
Pantomiming a Scripture Story
Making Headlines
Literature Connection

Music Connection (CG page 105)

www.FaithFirst.com

We update the *Faith First* Web site weekly. Check each week for new content and features. Here are some places to begin:

Catechists and Teachers
- Current Events
- Chapter Downloads
- Catechist Prayer

Faith First for Families
- Bible Stories
- Saints
- Make a Difference

Kids' Clubhouse
- *Faith First* Activities
- Chapter Reviews
- Games

Don't Forget! You can make lesson planning a breeze—check out the **Online Lesson Planner.**

Jesus Is the Son of God

5

We Pray

Rejoice, the Prince
of Peace is born.
Based on Isaiah 9:5

God our Father,
thank you
for sending us
Jesus, your Son.
Amen.

*How does your
family celebrate
Christmas?*

*Each year at
Christmas we
remember that God
fulfilled a special
promise.*

*What promise do
we celebrate at
Christmas?*

Statues from a
Christmas crèche

45

PRAY

- Ask the children to quiet themselves for prayer. Remind them that Jesus is with us as we pray.
- Pray the Sign of the Cross together.
- Proclaim Isaiah 9:5.
- Lead the opening prayer, and invite the children to echo each phrase after you.
- Close the prayer with the praying of the Sign of the Cross.

DISCOVER

Purpose: To discover what the children may already know about the birth of Jesus, the Son of God

- Invite the children to identify the people in the picture. Then have the children tell what they know about Christmas.
- Ask volunteers to share how their family celebrates Christmas.
- Read the introductory paragraph. Ask the children what special promise God made that we celebrate at Christmas. God's promise to send the Savior.

Background: Scripture

Set the scene for the story of the Nativity by helping the children gain some sense of the land in which Jesus lived. Explain that Jesus lived in Palestine, a land that today includes Israel and the West Bank. In the time of Jesus, the land was ruled by the Roman Empire. The people who lived in Palestine had to do what the Romans told them to do. Once when the Romans wanted to count all the people living in Palestine, Mary and Joseph had to make a trip to Bethlehem, the hometown of Joseph's family. When Mary and Joseph arrived in Bethlehem, there was no place for them to stay. An innkeeper let them stay in his stable, or barn. It was there, among the animals, that Jesus was born.

Teach

FOCUS

Ask a volunteer to read aloud the "Faith Focus" question. Tell the children they are going to learn more about a special promise God kept by sending his Son, Jesus, to us.

DISCOVER

- Talk with the children about making and keeping promises. Point out that some promises are easy to keep, while others are very difficult.
- Have the children follow along as you read "God Keeps His Promise" to find out how God kept his promise. He sent his Son Jesus Christ to become one of us. Jesus Christ is true God and true man. He is the second Person of the Holy Trinity.

Apply

REINFORCE

- Write on the board:
  _____ is the Son of God.
  _____ is the second Person of the Holy Trinity.
  _____ is true God and true man.
- Invite volunteers to fill in the blank in each sentence.
- Together read the "Faith Words" *Covenant* and *Jesus Christ* and their meanings. Have the children make word cards for both faith words.

INTEGRATE

Invite the children to answer the question on the bottom of the page with a partner.

God's Special Promise

Faith Focus

How does Jesus show us God's love and mercy?

Faith Words

Covenant
The Covenant is God's promise always to love and be kind to his people.

Jesus Christ
Jesus Christ is the Son of God. He is the second Person of the Holy Trinity who became one of us. He is true God and true man.

God Keeps His Promise

The Bible tells us about a promise God made to his people. We call this promise the **Covenant**. This promise shows that God always loves and is kind to people.

God's Covenant with people began at creation. Our first parents broke the promises they made to God. They sinned. We call this sin original sin.

God made the Covenant again with Noah and with Abraham and with Moses. God's people still sometimes broke the Covenant. When God's people broke their part of the Covenant, God promised to send someone to make God and people friends again.

God kept his promise. He sent **Jesus Christ.** Jesus Christ is the Son of God. He is the new and everlasting Covenant. He is the second Person of the Holy Trinity who became one of us. Jesus is true God and true man.

QUESTION *What does the Covenant tell about God and God's love?*

Affirm appropriate responses.

46

FAITH WORDS

Faith Vocabulary

Covenant. The word *covenant* is about promises. A covenant is a promise entered into by two people or groups. Each person or group pledges to be loyal to their promise holding up their end of the bargain. Remind the children that while God's people often broke the Covenant they made with God, he always kept his part of the Covenant. Tell them that God's promise to love us will never be broken.

Jesus Is Born

The Bible tells us about the birth of Jesus. We call this story the Nativity. Act out this play about the Nativity.

Narrator Just before Jesus' birth, Joseph and Mary traveled to Bethlehem. Mary and Joseph stopped to find a room at an inn.

Action Joseph knocks on the door of the inn. The innkeeper opens the door.

Joseph Do you have a room for my wife and me?

Innkeeper There are no rooms left. You may stay in the stable.

Narrator Mary and Joseph went to the stable. Jesus was born there.
Based on Luke 2:5–7

Faith-Filled People

The Blessed Virgin Mary

The Blessed Virgin Mary is the mother of Jesus, the Son of God. The Church celebrates and honors Mary as the Mother of God on January 1.

Glory to God!

Shepherds' Words

"We have good news of great joy. The

Savior has been born in Bethlehem."

My Words

Responses will vary.

Activity The Bible tells us that angels told shepherds about the birth of Jesus. Write the words of joy the shepherds might have said. Write your own words of joy.

47

Background: Faith-Filled People

The Blessed Virgin Mary. Mary is honored with many titles that express the Church's faith in her. Many of these titles are named in the Litany of the Blessed Virgin Mary. The Gospel of John refers to Mary as the "Mother of Jesus." Luke's Gospel honors Mary as God's favored one (Luke 1:28) who was full of grace from the very beginning of her existence. The Gospel accounts name Mary to be the Mother of the Son of God. Mary is truly the Mother of God because she is the mother of Jesus, the eternal Son of God.

Teach

FOCUS

Remind the children that God kept his promise to send someone to make him and people friends again. Jesus is the new and everlasting Covenant.

DISCOVER

- Write the word *Nativity* on the board and tell the children that *Nativity* is the name we give the Bible story of the birth of Jesus.
- Choose volunteers to take the parts of Narrator, Joseph, and Innkeeper. The rest of the group can be the people of the village. If there are enough students in your group, divide the class into several acting groups.
- Allow the volunteers a few minutes to practice reading and acting out their parts. Encourage them to create their own dialogue.
- When the volunteers are ready, have them perform the play.

Apply

REINFORCE

- Ask volunteers to retell the Nativity story in their own words.
- Ask a volunteer to read "Faith-Filled People."

INTEGRATE

- Have the children work with partners to complete the activity, "Glory to God." Invite volunteers to share their responses.

Teach

FOCUS

Remind the children of the meaning of the word *Nativity*. Tell them that when Jesus grew up he traveled from place to place and taught about God's mercy and love.

DISCOVER

- Ask the children how their families show love and care for them. Using kind words, feeding and clothing them, teaching them.
- Ask the children to listen for why Jesus fed the crowd as you proclaim the Scripture based on Matthew 14:13, 15–17, 19–20. Jesus showed the people God's love when he gave them food.
- Invite the children to tell what this story teaches us about God's love and mercy. God cares about his people and wants all to know he loves us.

Apply

REINFORCE

Remind the children that Jesus used loving actions as well as words to teach people about God's mercy and love.

INTEGRATE

Ask several volunteers to answer the question at the bottom of the page. Discuss with the children how each of them can be a sign of God's love when they are kind to others.

God Cares for All People

The Bible tells us that when Jesus grew up, he traveled from place to place. He taught about God's mercy and love. The word *mercy* means "great kindness." Read this Bible story about God's mercy.

People followed Jesus from the towns. As nighttime came, Jesus saw that the people were hungry. The disciples had only two fish and five loaves of bread to feed all the people. Jesus took the food, looked to heaven, and blessed the food. Then he gave the food to his disciples to give to the people. Everyone had enough to eat. There was even food left over.

Based on Matthew 14:13, 15–17, 19–20

 How do you show kindness to others? Share how you are a sign of God's love when you are kind to people.

Affirm appropriate responses.

48

Background: Scripture

Kindness, or Mercy. The Hebrew word in the Bible that we translate into English as *mercy* is *hesed*. This Hebrew word is often connected to the Covenant God entered into with his people. It is used to describe the unconditional kindness with which God reaches out to his people. Such is the mercy or kindness that we petition for when we pray, "Lord, have mercy." Such is the kindness and mercy that we are to offer to one another, especially those who "trespass against us."

Our Church Makes a Difference

Build a World of Kindness

The Church teaches people about God's mercy when the Church cares for people. The Church cares for people in many ways.

We help people build and repair homes. We take care of people who are sick. We share our clothes with people who cannot buy clothes. We give food and water to people who are hungry and thirsty.

When we do these and other kind things, we treat others as Jesus did. We treat others as God does. We do works of mercy. We help build a world of kindness and love.

Our Catholic Faith

Works of Mercy

The Church teaches us the works of mercy. The works of mercy are ways to be kind and loving to people as Jesus was.

 *Write how the people in these pictures are sharing God's love.*

Affirm appropriate responses.
_____

Affirm appropriate responses.
_____

Affirm appropriate responses.
_____

49

Teaching Tip

Jesus Is Our Gift Too. One of your tasks as a catechist is to help the children understand and appreciate that Jesus is a gift to us too. People two thousand years ago were lucky enough to walk, talk, and celebrate with Jesus. Today we too can walk, talk, and celebrate with Jesus who is always present with us in a different way than he was when he lived on earth. Help the children recognize how close Jesus is to each one of them when we celebrate the Eucharist and the other sacraments, when we pray, and when we read the Bible. Point out that Jesus taught that when we do the works of mercy we are following him (see Matthew 25:31–46).

Connect

HIGHLIGHT

Point out that Jesus taught about God's mercy and love. Tell the children that the Church has some special ways to show people God's mercy and love as Jesus did.

DISCOVER

- Ask the children to listen for ways the Church cares for people as volunteers read "Build a World of Kindness."
- Have the children name these ways and list them on the board. Explain that these are some of the caring acts that the Church calls works of mercy.
- Invite a volunteer to read "Our Catholic Faith" to learn more about the works of mercy.

INTEGRATE

- Direct the children's attention to the three pictures on page 49 and have the children choose phrases from the list on the board to create titles for each picture. Have the children share the titles that they gave to the pictures.
- Conclude the activity by asking volunteers to share a work of mercy they have done.

Connect

HIGHLIGHT

Remind the children that Jesus is the greatest sign of God's love and mercy. The Holy Spirit, the third Person of the Holy Trinity, helps us to live as signs of God's love and mercy.

RESPOND

- Share a story you have heard or read about recently in which people cared for others as Jesus did.
- Have the children describe what is happening in the three illustrations on page 50.
- Introduce the activity and give clear directions for each part. Invite the children to complete their outlines and then write their stories. Ask several volunteers to share their completed stories with the class.

CHOOSE

- Invite the children to read silently "My Faith Choice."
- Encourage them to write their faith choices and put them into practice this week.

What Difference Does Faith Make in My Life?

Jesus is the greatest sign of God's love and mercy. You are a follower of Jesus. The Holy Spirit helps you to live as a sign of God's love and mercy.

You hear stories about people caring for others. Write a story about one of these pictures. Share your story with a partner.

Responses will vary. Affirm appropriate responses.

Story title _____

Where did it happen? _____

When did it happen? _____

Who was there? _____

_____

What happened? _____

_____

My Faith Choice

This week I will live as a sign of God's love and mercy. I will

Affirm appropriate responses.

_____

_____ .

50

Teaching Tip

Writing Stories. The outline in today's activity can be a starting point for several other activities as time allows. The children can use these outlines to tell a fuller story using the "intelligence" or way that they best express their learning. For example, children who express themselves best through drawing might create a storyboard showing a beginning, middle, and end for their stories. Children who prefer writing can create a narrative for their stories. Children who express themselves well through movement can work with others to create skits. Try to offer children opportunities for more than one kind of activity in each week's lesson.

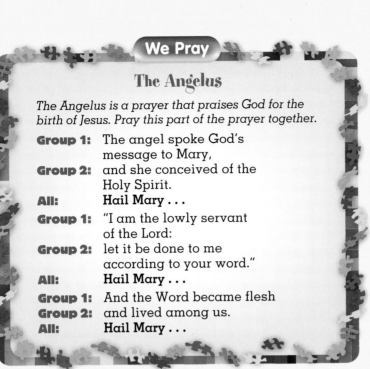

We Pray

The Angelus

The Angelus is a prayer that praises God for the birth of Jesus. Pray this part of the prayer together.

Group 1: The angel spoke God's message to Mary,

Group 2: and she conceived of the Holy Spirit.

All: **Hail Mary . . .**

Group 1: "I am the lowly servant of the Lord:

Group 2: let it be done to me according to your word."

All: **Hail Mary . . .**

Group 1: And the Word became flesh

Group 2: and lived among us.

All: **Hail Mary . . .**

We Remember

Add letters to complete the words in the sentences.

1. M <u>a</u> <u>r</u> <u>y</u> is the mother of Jesus.

2. <u>J</u> <u>e</u> s <u>u</u> <u>s</u> is the Son of God.

3. Jesus showed us God's love and <u>M</u> <u>e</u> r <u>c</u> y.

To Help You Remember

1. The Covenant is a sign of God's love and mercy.
2. The birth of Jesus Christ, the Son of God, is a sign of God's love and mercy.
3. Everything Jesus said and did shows us God's love and mercy.

Liturgy Tip

Praying Antiphonally. The Angelus, as the Liturgy of the Hours, is often prayed as an antiphon—the prayers are said or sung with one person or group starting a line and another completing it. As you divide the class for the praying of the Angelus it would be helpful to choose a volunteer to be a prayer leader for each group. Ask the leaders to stand facing the groups and gesture when it is time for their peers to recite the response.

Pray

WE PRAY

- Make sure that you write the words of the Hail Mary on the board or on poster board for the children to use during the praying of the prayer.
- Tell the children that they are going to pray the Angelus, a very old prayer of the Church. Point out that the name *Angelus* comes from a word in the first line of the prayer. Ask them what the word is. Angel.
- Practice their responses to the prayer. Point out that each one is different. Tell them that after each response, they will pray the Hail Mary together. You will recite the first part, and they will finish the prayer.
- Gather the children in the prayer area and pray the Angelus together.

Review

WE REMEMBER

- Write the words *love* and *mercy* on the board. Ask the children to brainstorm three things they have learned about God's love and mercy for his people. Read the "To Help You Remember" statements aloud and ask the children to compare the statements with their answers. Affirm all appropriate responses.
- Give instructions for the "We Remember" activity and allow time for the children to complete it. Ask all to share their work with a partner.

At Home

Have the children carefully tear out pages 51 and 52 along the perforation. Encourage the children to share the pages with their families and to do the activities together. If they did not complete the review activity on page 51 by the end of the session, emphasize that they can complete it with their families.

VISIT FAITHFIRST.COM

- Share with the children the many activities on the *Faith First* Web site.
- Encourage the children to visit **www.FaithFirst.com.**

---

5 With My Family

This Week . . .

In chapter 5, "Jesus Is the Son of God," your child learned about the Covenant that God entered into with his people. The Covenant is a sign of God's love and mercy. The Covenant was first made with people at creation. When Adam and Eve sinned and broke the Covenant, God promised to send someone to renew the Covenant. God fulfilled his promise by sending the Son of God, Jesus Christ, who became man and lived among us. Jesus Christ is true God and true man. He is the new and everlasting Covenant.

For more on the teachings of the Catholic Church on the Covenant and the mystery of the Incarnation, see *Catechism of the Catholic Church* paragraph numbers 51–67 and 456–560.

52

Sharing God's Word

Read together the Bible story in Luke 2:1–14 about Jesus' birth or read the play about the Nativity on page 47. Emphasize that Jesus Christ is the Son of God.

Praying

In this chapter your child prayed part of the Angelus. Read and pray together the prayer on page 51.

Making a Difference

Choose one of the following activities to do as a family or design a similar activity of your own.

- Read together the Bible story on page 48, which is about Jesus feeding the people. Talk about how the hungry people must have felt when they realized that Jesus gave everyone more than enough to eat.
- Everything Jesus did was a sign of God's love. Choose to do one thing together this week to live as signs of God's love.
- Jesus told people over and over again about God's love for them. Look around your home for something that reminds you of God's love.

For more ideas on ways your family can live your faith, visit the "Faith First for Families" page at **www.FaithFirst.com.** You will find the "Contemporary Issues" page helpful this week.

✓ Evaluate

Take a few moments to evaluate this week's lesson.
I feel (circle one) about this week's lesson.

    a. very pleased
    b. OK
    c. disappointed

The activity the children enjoyed most was . . .

The concept that was most difficult to teach was . . .

because . . .

Something I would like to do differently is . . .

Before Moving On . . .

As you finish today's lesson, reflect on the following question before moving on to the next chapter.

How much quiet time do I allow for the children to think about the concepts I am presenting?

ENRICHING THE LESSON

Pantomiming a Scripture Story

Purpose

To reinforce the children's understanding of Matthew 14:13–20 (taught on page 48)

Directions

- Involve the children in a Scripture pantomime of Matthew 14:13–20. The following will help you begin:

    People followed Jesus from the towns.
    Walk in place; put hand over eyes and point to someone up ahead.)

    As nighttime came, Jesus saw that people were hungry.
    (Raise arms above head and pull down the darkness; then hold stomach as if hungry.)

    The disciples had only two fish and five loaves of bread to feed all the people.
    (Raise two fingers, then five fingers on the other hand; point to people all around you.)

- Divide the class into several groups and teach each group gestures for one part of the story. When the children are ready, place the groups in the correct sequence and have them pantomime the Scripture story as you read it aloud.

Materials

Bible

Making Headlines

Purpose

To reinforce the children's living of Jesus' teaching about God's mercy (taught on page 48)

Directions

- Brainstorm with the children ways that they show kindness to one another in the classroom. Tell them you will be observing the ways they care for others.
- As you observe the children showing care for one another affirm those behaviors immediately and make a note of them.

- Start a mini-newspaper. Elicit the help of an aide or parent to type up the short descriptions of kindness you see in the children each week.
- Include the stories of kindness in the "newspaper" and send copies of the newspaper home with the children.

Materials

copies of "newspaper" for parents

Literature Connection

Purpose

To reinforce the teaching about kindness (taught on page 49)

Directions

Mrs. Katz and Tush by Patricia Polacco (Dragonfly Books, 1994) illustrates how kindness leads to friendship. This book describes the relationship between a young African-American and Mrs. Katz, a Jewish widow.

- Brainstorm with the children ways they could make someone who is lonely feel happy.
- Have the children listen for how Lionel makes Mrs. Katz happy as you read the story.
- In partners have the children retell all the acts of kindness they heard in the story.

Materials

Mrs. Katz and Tush by Patricia Polacco

Music Connection

- "Good News," H. Olson. *Singing Our Faith (SOF)* #162.
- "Jesus in the Morning," (African-American folk song). *SOF* #168.
- "Jesus' Hands Were Kind Hands," (Old French melody). *SOF* #170.

John the Baptist
A Scripture Story

Background

The Son of Elizabeth and Zechariah

John the Baptist was the herald of and the immediate forerunner to Christ. He preached good tidings to the afflicted, healing for the brokenhearted, liberty to captives, and release from the prisons that entrap so many of us. By his preaching of conversion to God, John, the son of Elizabeth and Zechariah, made ready "a people fit for the Lord" (Luke 1:17).

Sacred Scripture provides us a portrait of Saint John the Baptist. John was one of the first among the children of Israel to recognize the Christ, God's Anointed One. When Mary visited Elizabeth, John the unborn infant in Elizabeth's womb leaped in recognition of the infant Jesus in Mary's womb. Zechariah, upon naming the child John, ecstatically prophesied:

"And you, child, will be
called prophet of the
Most High,
for you will go before the
Lord to prepare his
ways." LUKE 1:76

The Herald of the Lord!

Luke's Gospel tells us that "the word of God came to John . . . for the forgiveness of sins"

(Luke 3:2–3). John's preaching and baptizing attracted a great deal of attention—so much so that some wondered if *he* was the Messiah. When asked if he were the Messiah, John replied,

"I baptize with water; but there is one among you whom you do not recognize, the one who is coming after me, whose sandal strap I am not worthy to untie."
JOHN 1:26–27

When John saw Jesus coming toward him, he exclaimed, "Behold, the Lamb of God, who takes away the sin of the world" (John 1:29). Jesus replied by asking John to baptize him. There at the Jordan River, after Jesus was baptized, the heavens opened, the Spirit of God

descended like a dove upon Jesus, and a voice from the heavens proclaimed, "This is my beloved Son, with whom I am well pleased" (Matthew 3:17).

John the Baptist was a witness to Christ, allowing his life and ministry to serve that of Jesus'. We also are to witness to Christ and be his heralds as John was. John gave us a simple spiritual blueprint of how we are to be heralds of Christ when he said, "He must increase; I must decrease" (John 3:30). John's willingness to be a voice of consolation and truth inspires us to be witnesses of Christ, the Light of the world.

Jesus said that John was no mere reed swayed by the wind or one given to wearing fine clothing (see Matthew 11:7). Saint John the Baptist was the last of the prophets and he was martyred because of his commitment to fulfilling the work God chose him to do.

For Reflection

How does my work as a catechist compare with Saint John the Baptist's work of heralding the Lord?

How can I decrease and Christ increase as I share the Good News of Christ with others?

Catechist to Catechist

Witness Our Faith

Saint John the Baptist lived a life drastically removed from the majority of the people of his day. Some people must have been attracted to him simply out of curiosity. Is it really so much different today? Are not the ones who live and preach the Good News today out of step with some of today's cultures and passions?

Commitment to Gospel Values

Christian heroes, such as Saint John the Baptist, are difficult for many people of our day and age to understand because of their total commitment to their faith  in God. The children see around them a widespread lack of commitment to God and to the values of the Gospel. Today's youngsters—and oldsters—need to look at John the Baptist as an example of putting their priorities in order and then living by them. The children you serve must be given sufficient reason to choose to place service to God and others at the top of their lists.

The Church Teaches . . .

The *General Directory for Catechesis* states:

Catechesis transmits the content of the word of God . . . whereby the Church possesses it, interiorizes it and lives it. . . . Both Sacred Scripture and the Catechism of the Catholic Church must . . . become true vehicles of the content of God's word.   *GDC* 128

As the children prepare for Jesus, the "Lamb of God who takes away the sin of the world," they must learn the importance of listening to Jesus and living as he taught.

See the Catechism . . .

For more on the teachings of the Catholic Church on Saint John the Baptist, the prophets, and the Church's mission of evangelization, see *Catechism of the Catholic Church* 64, 522–524, 702, 717–720, 849–856, and 2581–2584.

CATECHIST PRAYER

Lord Jesus, help me to prepare my mind, heart, and soul to be ready to receive your message in whatever way you choose to bring it to me. Amen.

LESSON PLANNER

Engage

Page 53
Focus
To help the children identify how to get ready for someone special

Opening Prayer

Discussion
What does your family do to get ready when visitors are coming?

Teach and Apply

Pages 54–56
Focus
To introduce the children to John the Baptist and his example of how to get ready for Jesus

Presentation
Read, discuss, and summarize content.
Scripture
• Psalm 111:2, 9
• Matthew 3:2–6, 13
• John 1:29, 34
Activities
• Work the maze.
• Listen to the Bible story of John the Baptist's message.
• Complete the writing activity about preparing for Jesus.

Connect

Pages 57–58
Focus
To identify how the Church comes to know God's love and mercy at Mass

Our Church Makes a Difference
Discover the importance of listening to God's word at Mass.
Our Catholic Faith
Ambo

What Difference Does Faith Make?
Activity
Telling people about Jesus.
Faith Choice
Decide what to tell others about Jesus.

We Pray

Page 59
Prayer Form
Prayer of petition
Prayer
Choose a leader. Introduce the prayer, and then pray together.

We Remember

Review
• Complete the scrambled letters activity.
• Read the "To Help You Remember" statements aloud.
Preview
Preview the "With My Family" page.

Materials

pens or pencils

Enriching the Session

Blackline Masters
Additional Activities booklet:
Chapter 6
Choosing the good choices
Making good choices
Assessment Tools booklet:
Chapter 6 Test
Enriching the Lesson (*CG* page 117)
Singing About John the Baptist
Proclaiming God's Word
Literature Connection
Music Connection (*CG* page 117)

www.FaithFirst.com

We update the *Faith First* Web site weekly. Check each week for new content and features. Here are some places to begin:

Catechists and Teachers
• Current Events
• Chapter Downloads
• Catechist Prayer

Faith First **for Families**
• Bible Stories
• Saints
• Make a Difference

Kids' Clubhouse
• *Faith First* Activities
• Chapter Reviews
• Games

Don't Forget! You can make lesson planning a breeze—check out the **Online Lesson Planner.**

John the Baptist
A Scripture Story

6

We Pray

Blessed be God,
who has come to
save his people.
Based on Psalm 111:2, 9

**Lord our God,
speak to us.
Help us to know
you.   Amen.**

*What does your
family do to get
ready when visitors
are coming?*

The Bible has many
stories of people
who helped others
get ready for Jesus.

*Why were the
people of the Bible
waiting for Jesus?*

53

Liturgy Tip

Proclaiming the Gospel. Proclaiming the Bible provides an excellent opportunity to instruct the children in the posture and responses we use during Mass. Have the children stand when the Gospel is being read aloud.

> Reader: "A reading from the Holy Gospel according to . . ."
> Response: "Glory to you, Lord."
> Reader: Reads Gospel. "The gospel of the Lord."
> Response: "Praise to you, Lord Jesus Christ."

Engage

PRAY

- Ask the children to quiet themselves for prayer. Remind them that Jesus is with us as we pray.
- Read Psalm 111:2, 9 aloud.
- Lead the opening prayer and invite the children to echo each phrase after you. Respond "Amen" together.
- Close with the Sign of the Cross.

DISCOVER

Purpose: To discover what the children may already know about God's people's need for a special leader

- Invite volunteers to share what their families do to get ready when visitors are coming.
- Ask the children to describe what the family in the photograph is doing together. Reading the Bible together.
- Tell the children that the Bible tells many stories of people getting ready for Jesus.
- Ask: Why were the people waiting for Jesus? Tell the children they will learn the answer in this chapter.

Teach

FOCUS

Ask a volunteer to read aloud the "Faith Focus" question. Share with the children that in this chapter they will learn about John the Baptist. Point out that John the Baptist gave the people a special message about Jesus.

DISCOVER

- Ask the children who in their families are the best at giving advice. Accept all appropriate answers.
- Tell the children that before Jesus came, God sent his prophets. Point out the "Faith Word" *prophet* and present its meaning. Explain that some of the prophets helped God's people get ready for Jesus.
- Ask the children to read the first paragraph of "The Work of John the Baptist" silently to find out the name of one of these prophets. John the Baptist.

Apply

REINFORCE

Remind the children that Saint John the Baptist helped people get ready for Jesus.

INTEGRATE

Have the children complete the maze to help the people find John the Baptist. Ask the children to think about a question they might ask him about Jesus.

Bible Background

Faith Focus

What did John the Baptist tell the people?

Faith Words

prophet
A prophet in the Bible is a person who God chose to speak in his name.

The Work of John the Baptist

There are stories in the Bible about people who helped others get ready for Jesus. John the Baptist was one of those people. John was the son of Elizabeth and Zechariah.

ACTIVITY *Pretend you are one of the people in the group. You are looking for John the Baptist. Follow the maze and lead the people to John. What question would you ask John when you reach him?* Affirm appropriate responses.

54

Teaching Tip

Sunday Liturgy. This is an important year for the children to understand their responsibility to join with other Catholics each week to celebrate the Eucharist. Point out how many people traveled to a distant place in the desert to hear John the Baptist teach about God and to baptize them. Acknowledge that while it is sometimes difficult to get to Mass each weekend, it is our responsibility and obligation as Catholics to take part in Mass on Sundays and holy days of obligation unless there is a serious reason, such as being sick, that prevents us from doing it.

Reading the Word of God

John Gets the People Ready

Many people believed John was a **prophet.** A prophet is a person God chooses to speak in his name. God chose John the Baptist to tell the people that Jesus was the Savior he had promised to send. Many people came to John the Baptist to listen to his message. John told the people,

"Someone will soon be coming. You must get ready for him. Sin no more." Some of the people told John, "We are sorry for our sins." John told them, "You need to ask God for forgiveness." John invited them into the river and he baptized them.

One day Jesus came to John. John baptized Jesus. He told the people, "This is the One God promised to send. He is the Son of God."
Based on Matthew 3:2–3, 5–6 and John 1:29, 34

QUESTION *What is one thing you can do to help someone come to know Jesus better?*
Affirm appropriate responses.

55

Catholic Social Teaching

Life and Dignity of the Human Person. All human life is sacred. This is the source of our fundamental dignity as a human person. Here are some of the Catholic Church's teachings that flow from this principle: Direct abortion, euthanasia, suicide, and assisted suicide are inherently evil; human cloning and genetic engineering threaten the uniqueness of each human life; the death penalty can seldom if ever be justified; war should be a last resort in the resolution of differences (see *CCC* 2258–2317).

Tips: Establish respect for one another's views within your classroom. Help the children listen to one another and not to interrupt one another until they are finished presenting their point of view.

Teach

FOCUS
Remind the children that God chose Saint John the Baptist to give the people a special message.

DISCOVER
- Invite the children to close their books and listen for John's message as you read "John Gets the People Ready."
- Ask: What did John tell the people? Jesus was the Savior God had promised to send. What did John tell the people to do to get ready for Jesus? Sin no more. You need to ask God for forgiveness.
- Have the children read the words aloud that John said to the people when Jesus came to be baptized.

Apply

REINFORCE
Emphasize that a prophet is a person God chooses to speak in his name. Have the children make a word card for *prophet.*

INTEGRATE
Share with the children that many people today have not heard about Jesus. Have the children name some things they might do to help people know Jesus better. List their ideas on the board.

Teach

FOCUS

Remind the children that Saint John the Baptist told the people to prepare for Jesus by sinning no more. Point out that even though Jesus has already come, we have to prepare ourselves over and over to welcome him into our lives.

DISCOVER

- Invite the children to share how they and their families prepare to welcome visitors to their homes.
- Explain that we also must prepare to welcome Jesus into our lives.
- Have the children read "We Prepare for Jesus" to find out how we get ready for Jesus.

Apply

REINFORCE

Ask the children where they listen to God's word. At Mass, at home, in religion class. Accept other appropriate responses.

INTEGRATE

- Have the children look at the two illustrations and talk about how the children are welcoming Jesus into their lives. The boy is reading the Bible. The girl is living as Jesus taught by helping the boy. Accept other appropriate responses.
- Help the children brainstorm other ways that they can welcome Jesus into their lives.
- Have the children complete the writing activity.

Understanding the Word of God

We Prepare for Jesus

The people listened to John and began to prepare to welcome Jesus. We also need to prepare ourselves to welcome Jesus into our lives.

We prepare for Jesus by listening to God's word and by praying. When we do, we come to know Jesus better. We learn to love God above all else. We try to live as God's children.

ACTIVITY *Write what you could do this week to prepare to welcome Jesus into your life.*

Responses will vary.

Affirm appropriate response.

56

Special Needs

Providing Writing Assistance. Children with writing or spelling difficulties may have difficulty doing the activity on this page. Allow these children to tell you what they will do to prepare to welcome Jesus. Then help them write their responses.

Need: Children with writing and spelling deficits

Our Church Makes a Difference

We Hear God's Word at Mass

When we listen to the Bible readings at Mass, we are listening to God. At Mass on Sunday a member of the parish community proclaims the first two readings. We call the people who do this readers, or lectors. The deacon or priest proclaims the Gospel.

After the Gospel is proclaimed, the priest or deacon preaches a homily. This helps us to understand God's word to us. We learn more and more about God and his mercy and love. We learn to share God's love and mercy with people.

QUESTION *What is one thing you have learned about Jesus at Mass?*
Affirm appropriate responses.

Our Catholic Faith

Ambo

The Church proclaims God's word at every Mass. The ambo is the place in the church where God's word is proclaimed. This place is also called the lectern. The ambo, or lectern, is often made of the same material as the altar.

57

Background: Our Catholic Faith

The word *ambo* is a word of Greek origin signifying a mountain or elevation. Ambos are believed to have taken their origin from the raised platform from which the Jewish rabbis read the Scriptures. In the early churches and basilicas an ambo was an elevated desk or pulpit where the Gospel and Epistle were chanted or read, and many kinds of communications were made to the assembly. Today, the ambo is near the altar in the sanctuary.

Connect

HIGHLIGHT

Remind the children that we must all prepare to welcome Jesus into our lives. Tell them they are going to learn how we do this at Mass.

DISCOVER

- Ask the children to share some things they have noticed when the Bible readings are proclaimed at Mass. Then have the children read "We Hear God's Word at Mass" silently and underline or highlight the words *readers, lectors, deacon, priest,* and *homily.* Ask volunteers to read the sentences that tell what these people do at Mass.
- Remind the children that we also pray aloud or sing a Psalm prayer during the Sunday readings between the first and second readings.
- Read aloud "Our Catholic Faith" and emphasize that the ambo is the place in church where God's word is proclaimed. Encourage the children to look for the ambo when they are in church.

INTEGRATE

- Encourage the children to share with one another one thing they have learned about Jesus at Mass.
- Remind the children that when we hear the Scriptures proclaimed at Mass we are learning about Jesus as the people did from Saint John the Baptist.

Connect

HIGHLIGHT

Remind the children that they are called to help others know about Jesus as Saint John the Baptist did.

RESPOND

- Point out that the Holy Spirit helps us tell others about Jesus.
- Have the children look at the "Telling People About Jesus" activity as you read and explain the directions to them.
- Invite the children to write their responses. Call on volunteers to share their responses.

CHOOSE

- Have the children read "My Faith Choice" silently and write their faith choices.
- Encourage everyone to put their faith choices into practice this week.

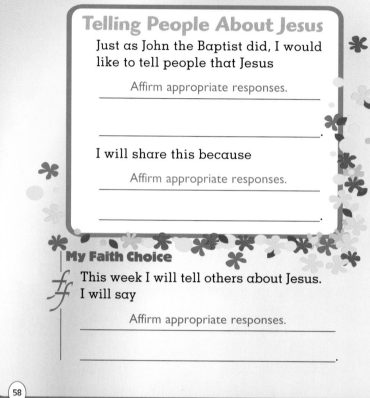

What Difference Does Faith Make in My Life?

You can help others come to know more and more about Jesus as John the Baptist did. The Holy Spirit helps you to tell others about Jesus.

Write one thing about Jesus that you would like to tell a friend or someone in your family. Tell why you want to share that message with them.

Telling People About Jesus

Just as John the Baptist did, I would like to tell people that Jesus

Affirm appropriate responses.

_____

_____.

I will share this because

Affirm appropriate responses.

_____

_____.

My Faith Choice

This week I will tell others about Jesus. I will say

Affirm appropriate responses.

_____

_____.

58

Background: Doctrine

The Church exists to evangelize and catechesis is a "remarkable moment in the process of evangelization" (GDC 63). Catechists have the ministry to join with the Church and to announce the Good News of Jesus, to invite the children to open their lives to Jesus and to grow in intimacy with him. Achieving this goal "demands of the community a great fidelity to the action of the Holy Spirit, the constant nourishment of the Body and Blood of Christ and continuing education in the faith, listening all the time to the word" (GDC 70).

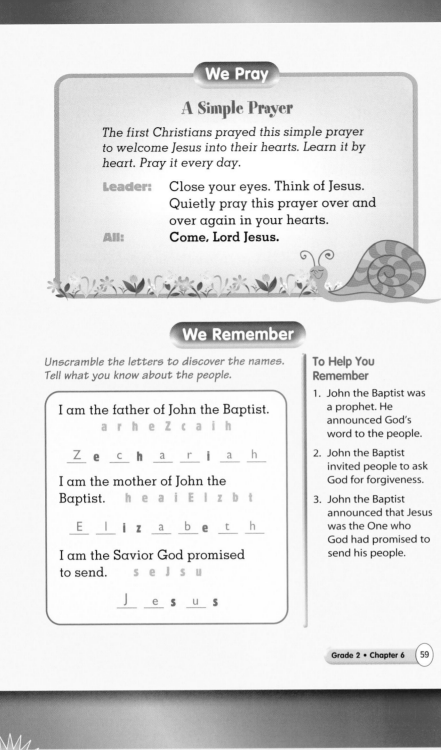

We Pray

A Simple Prayer

The first Christians prayed this simple prayer to welcome Jesus into their hearts. Learn it by heart. Pray it every day.

Leader: Close your eyes. Think of Jesus. Quietly pray this prayer over and over again in your hearts.

All: **Come, Lord Jesus.**

We Remember

Unscramble the letters to discover the names. Tell what you know about the people.

I am the father of John the Baptist.
a r h e Z c a i h

Z e c h a r i a h

I am the mother of John the Baptist. h e a i E l z b t

E l i z a b e t h

I am the Savior God promised to send. s e J s u

J e s u s

To Help You Remember

1. John the Baptist was a prophet. He announced God's word to the people.

2. John the Baptist invited people to ask God for forgiveness.

3. John the Baptist announced that Jesus was the One who God had promised to send his people.

Grade 2 • Chapter 6 59

Teaching Tip

God's Messengers. There are many people today who do the kind of work Saint John the Baptist did, namely, they tell us about Jesus and teach us to prepare our hearts to receive Jesus. Talk with the children about who these people are—priests, sisters, teachers, moms and dads, grandparents, and many others. Discuss what they do—share God's message, tell people what God wants, and show people how they should act. Explain that we need to listen to these special people and follow their examples of how to love and obey God. Remind the children that they too can be God's messengers to others.

Pray

WE PRAY

- Tell the children that today we are praying a very brief, simple prayer that the early Church prayed. Read the prayer, "Come, Lord Jesus," aloud to the class. Have everyone echo the words after you.
- Gather the children in the prayer center and invite them to sit on the floor. Light a candle if permissible and play soft music.
- Lead the children in prayer as described in the text.

Review

WE REMEMBER

- Draw a simple stick figure drawing of Saint John the Baptist on the board. Write his name underneath the drawing.
- Remind the children that Saint John the Baptist was a prophet. Then ask the children to review with a partner the things that Saint John the Baptist told the people about Jesus. Invite several sets of partners to come up and act out one of the things they remember.
- Conclude by reading aloud together the "To Help You Remember" statements.
- Explain the directions and invite the children to complete the scrambled letters activity. Tell the children to use the text to check their answers.

At Home

ENCOURAGE

Have the children carefully tear out pages 59 and 60 along the perforation. Encourage the children to share the pages with their families and to do the activities together. If they did not complete the review activity on page 59 by the end of the session, emphasize that they can complete it with their families.

VISIT FAITHFIRST.COM

- Share with the children the many activities on the *Faith First* Web site.
- Encourage the children to visit **www.FaithFirst.com.**

Before Moving On . . .

As you finish today's lesson, reflect on the following question before moving on to the next chapter.

What have I learned about the different gifts and talents of the children?

---

6 With My Family

This Week . . .

In chapter 6, "John the Baptist: A Scripture Story," your child learned about John the Baptist. John the Baptist was the last of the prophets who prepared the way for the Lord Jesus. John prepared the way of the Lord by his preaching and his baptizing. He pointed to Jesus as the Savior of the world. As John the Baptist did, all Christians are to make Jesus known to others and invite them to become followers of Jesus.

For more on the teachings of the Catholic Church on John the Baptist, the prophets, and the Church's mission of evangelization, see *Catechism of the Catholic Church* paragraph numbers 64, 522–524, 702, 717–720, 849–856, and 2581–2584.

Sharing God's Word

Read together the Bible stories in Matthew 3:1–6, 13–17 and John 1:29–34 about John the Baptist or read the adaptation of the stories on page 55. Emphasize that John the Baptist helped people prepare for the coming of Jesus.

Praying

In this chapter your child prayed an invocation, or a short prayer that is said over and over. Read and pray together the prayer on page 59.

Making a Difference

Choose one of the following activities to do as a family or design a similar activity of your own.

- Talk about what John the Baptist told people about Jesus. Invite each family member to share what they would tell others about Jesus.

- John the Baptist was different from most other people of his time. Talk about how every person is different and unique. Each person is a wonderful work of God's creation.

- Reading Bible stories helps us listen to God. Read the story about John the Baptist as a family one more time. Draw a picture of what you heard.

For more ideas on ways your family can live your faith, visit the "Faith First for Families" page at **www.FaithFirst.com**. Check out "Bible Stories." Read and discuss the Bible story as a family this week.

Evaluate

Take a few moments to evaluate this week's lesson.
I feel (circle one) about this week's lesson.

a. very pleased
b. OK
c. disappointed

The activity the children enjoyed most was . . .

The concept that was most difficult to teach was . . .

because . . .

Something I would like to do differently is . . .

ENRICHING THE LESSON

Singing About John the Baptist

Purpose

To reinforce the Scripture story about Saint John the Baptist (taught on page 55)

Directions

Invite the children to sing the following song to the tune of "Mary Had a Little Lamb." Copy the words of the song for the children. You can help them make up additional verses.

> John the Baptist announced to all
> Announced to all, announced to all,
> John the Baptist announced to all
> That Jesus was God's Son.
>
> God the Father has sent his Son,
> Has sent his Son, has sent his Son,
> God the Father has sent his Son,
> This was John's big news.

Materials

copies of the song

Proclaiming God's Word

Purpose

To reinforce the teaching about the Sunday readings (taught on page 57)

Directions

- Prepare several short Gospel readings. Provide each child with a paper on which you have printed in large type the words of one of the readings. Underline words that should be emphasized.
- Ask the children to read the reading on their paper silently and rehearse it quietly.
- Invite volunteers to stand one at a time at the prayer center and proclaim their reading. At the conclusion, have them raise the paper higher as if it were the Book of the Gospels and say, "The Gospel of the Lord."

- Invite the class to stand for the reading and respond, "Praise to you, Lord Jesus Christ."

Materials

sheets of paper printed with Gospel readings

Literature Connection

Purpose

To reinforce the concept of *prophet* (taught on pages 54–55)

Directions

- To help the children discover contemporary figures who speak God's words of justice to others, share with the children the book *Harvesting Hope: The Story of Cesar Chavez*, by Kathleen Krull (Harcourt Brace, 2003). This beautifully illustrated book traces the story of Cesar Chavez from his childhood in Arizona to his successful protest in defense of migrant farm workers.
- After reading the story aloud, discuss with the children the hardships Cesar endured in his childhood, his love for his family, and his desire to help others have a better life.

Materials

Harvesting Hope: The Story of Cesar Chavez, by Kathleen Krull

Music Connection

- "Prepare the Way," P. Inwood. *Rise Up and Sing (RUS)* #98.
- "Watch for Messiah," (Yiddish traditional), arr. W. Wold. *Singing Our Faith (SOF)* #100.
- "Advent Gathering: Make Ready the Way/ Come, O Lord," D. Haas. *SOF* #102.
- "Stay Awake, Be Ready," J. Berthier. *SOF* #103.

Jesus Is Our Savior

Background

Jesus the Savior

As soon as Jesus' public ministry began, he attracted the distrust and enmity of some religious and political leaders. Jesus expelled demons, forgave sins by his own powers, healed on the Sabbath, and interpreted the Law of Moses in a new way.

Some people interpreted these actions of Jesus to be the works of a false prophet and a man possessed by an evil spirit. A few judged Jesus to be guilty of blasphemy, a man who falsely claimed to be God (see John 10:33). A claim, under the Jewish law, was worthy of death. Many came to understand that Jesus is truly the Son of God (see John 1:14).

The Hope of Resurrection and New Life for All

The suffering and death of Jesus are at the heart of God's plan of salvation in Christ that had been prefigured in Isaiah's prophecy about the suffering Servant (see Isaiah 52:13–53:12; Acts 8:32–35). Jesus gave "his life as a ransom for many" (Matthew 20:28). Jesus died for everyone without exception. The Church states clearly: "There is not, never has been, and never will be a single human being for whom

Christ did not suffer" (*Council of Quiercy* 853).

If the death of Jesus on the cross had been the end of the story of his life and work, he might have become just an inspirational footnote in history. But the life and work of Jesus did not did end on the cross. Jesus was raised from the dead to new and glorified life. The Resurrection was, in a sense, the Father's seal of approval on his Son, Jesus, and the work he was sent to do.

Christ's Resurrection both fulfills the promises of the Old Testament and is our promise of new and glorified life. It is the divine assurance that Christ has conquered death and sin, and that they no longer have power over human life. Christ's Resurrection is the divine promise that we, like Christ, shall live forever. Death has lost its sting!

The Resurrection is the source of our own future resurrection, which we profess in the Apostles' Creed: "I believe in . . . the resurrection of the body." By Adam's sin, we all die. By the death and Resurrection of Christ, we receive the power to die to sin and are given the gift of new life in Christ. The Risen Christ lives in us. We no longer live for ourselves but for him who has died for our sake (see 2 Corinthians 5:15).

For Reflection

What does being baptized into Christ's death and Resurrection mean for me?

How do I live no longer for myself but for him who has died for me—and for all people?

Catechist to Catechist

Jesus' Death and Resurrection

Catholic children are familiar with the crucifix, candles, and other symbols of Christianity. Asked where they would see a crucifix and candles, they would readily reply, "In church!" They are now at an age where they can begin to comprehend the basic tenets of our faith that the crucifix and candles symbolize.

True God and True Man

Since most of the children you are teaching this year will soon receive the sacraments of Reconciliation and Eucharist, it is important for them to  understand that Jesus is true God and true man. Jesus is the Son of God who became a man and died for each one of us. Jesus suffered and died for all people of all time. Three days later Jesus was raised from the dead. Because of Jesus' Resurrection, we too will live forever. The Easter candle reminds us of Jesus' Resurrection. Remind the children that we are to love one another—all people—as Jesus commanded us to do.

The Church Teaches . . .

In his encyclical on *Catechesis in Our Time* (*CT*), Pope John Paul II reminds us that:

at the heart of catechesis we find, in essence, a Person, the Person of Jesus of Nazareth, "the only Son from the Father, . . . full of grace and truth."[1]   *CT* 5

It is important that catechists introduce their students to the Person of Jesus so that they may develop a personal relationship with him and grow in intimacy with him.

See the Catechism . . .

For more on the teachings of the Catholic Church on the mystery of Jesus Christ and God's loving plan of salvation, see *Catechism of the Catholic Church* 422–451, 456–478, and 599–655.

CATECHIST PRAYER

Jesus,
the depth of your love
for me is overpowering.
You gave your life for me.
May my life lead others
to discover your
unconditional love.
Amen.

Footnote references may be found on p. 456.

LESSON PLANNER

Focus   **To discover that Jesus Christ is the Savior of all people**

Engage

Page 61
Focus
To help the children express what they know about Jesus' death and Resurrection

Opening Prayer

Discussion
God wants to save us from our sins.

Teach and Apply

Pages 62–64
Focus
To identify Jesus Christ as the Savior of the world

Presentation
Read, discuss, and summarize content.
Scripture
• Psalm 119:41
• Matthew 1:20–23
• Luke 23:33–34, 44–46
Activities
• Color the name *Jesus*.
• Answer the question.
• Connect the dots.
Faith-Filled People
Mary Magdalene

Connect

Pages 65–66
Focus
To explain the Church's use of candles

Our Church Makes a Difference
Discover why we light the Easter candle.

Our Catholic Faith
The Crucifix

What Difference Does Faith Make?
Activity
Design a bookmark to remember Jesus' love.

Faith Choice
Name a way to share the story of God's love with others this week.

We Pray

Page 67
Prayer
Prayer of praise
Prayer
Choose a leader. Introduce the prayer, and then pray the acclamation together.

We Remember

Review
• Complete the sentences.
• Read the "To Help You Remember" statements aloud.
Preview
Preview the "With My Family" page.

Materials

pens or pencils

crayons or markers

Enriching the Session

Blackline Masters
Additional Activities booklet:
Chapter 7
Completing the sentences
Numbering the pictures in order
Assessment Tools booklet:
Chapter 7 Test
Enriching the Lesson (CG page 129)
Making Story Cards
Designing a Parish Bulletin Board
Literature Connection
Music Connection (CG page 129)

www.FaithFirst.com

We update the *Faith First* Web site weekly. Check each week for new content and features. Here are some places to begin:

Catechists and Teachers
• Current Events
• Chapter Downloads
• Catechist Prayers

Faith First for Families
• Bible Stories
• Saints
• Make a Difference

Kids' Clubhouse
• *Faith First* Activities
• Chapter Reviews
• Games

Don't Forget! You can make lesson planning a breeze—check out the **Online Lesson Planner.**

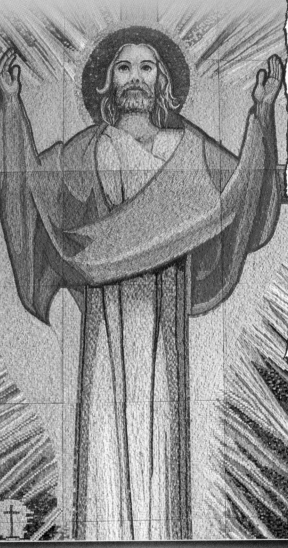

Jesus Is Our Savior

7

We Pray

LORD, out of love, you promised to save us.
Based on Psalm 119:41

Jesus, you are the Savior of the world.

Amen.

Who in your community helps people who are in danger?

A firefighter might save someone from a burning house. God sent his only Son to save us from our sins.

What did Jesus do to save us from our sins?

The Risen Jesus

61

PRAY

- Have the children quiet themselves for prayer. Remind them that Jesus is with us when we gather to pray.
- Proclaim the Psalm verse.
- Lead the praying of the opening prayer and have the children echo each phrase after you. All say "Amen" together.

DISCOVER

Purpose: To discover what the children may already know about Jesus' Crucifixion and Resurrection.

- Ask the children who they know who has saved someone from danger. Let them share their stories.
- Present the opening paragraph in your own words.
- Have the children describe what they see in the picture. Possible answers: Jesus; the Risen Jesus. Accept and affirm all appropriate responses.
- Invite volunteers to respond to the question under the paragraph.

Liturgy Tip

Contemplative prayer is a form of prayer that helps us place ourselves in God's presence by focusing on an image or words. In our churches and our homes there are many beautiful examples of Christian art and devotion that can assist us in this type of prayer. Children at this age can be very impressed by the artwork and religious images around them. Expose the children to the closeness of God by giving them the opportunity to focus on these images briefly and in silence. You can begin with the image of the Risen Jesus on this page.

Teach

FOCUS

Ask a child to read aloud the "Faith Focus" question. Share with the children that in this chapter they will discover why Jesus is the Savior of all people.

DISCOVER

- Ask the children how they show their families that they love them.
- Present the opening paragraph of "God Sends the Savior" in your own words.
- Ask a volunteer to read again the opening Psalm verse based on Psalm 119:41.
- Tell the children that now they are going to hear how God kept his promise to send the Savior to his people. Ask the children to close their books and listen as you proclaim the Scripture based on Matthew 1:20–23.
- Present the last paragraph in your own words.

Apply

REINFORCE

- Ask the children to look for the angel's message to Joseph in the Scripture passage and to underline it.

INTEGRATE

- Have the children color the name *Jesus.*
- Invite the children to pray silently a brief prayer of thanksgiving for the gift of Jesus.

God Fulfills His Promise

Faith Focus

Why do we call Jesus Christ the Savior of all people?

Faith Words

Crucifixion
The Crucifixion is the death of Jesus on a cross.

Resurrection
The Resurrection is God's raising Jesus from the dead to new life.

God Sends the Savior

God promised to send his people a savior. A savior is a person who sets people free. God the Father sent his Son, Jesus, to be the Savior of the world. Read this Bible story. It is the announcement that the time had come when God would fulfill his promise to send the Savior.

An angel came to Joseph before Jesus was born. The angel said to Joseph, "Mary, your wife, will give birth to a son. You are to give him the name Jesus. He will save his people from their sins. All this will happen to fulfill God's promises."

Based on Matthew 1:20–23

The name *Jesus* means "God saves." Jesus died on the cross to free us from our sins. God's forgiveness is a sign of his mercy and love.

ACTIVITY Color the name Jesus. Say a prayer thanking Jesus for his love.

JESUS

62

Teaching Tip

Symbols of Jesus. Ask the children if they know any signs or symbols the Catholic Church uses to represent Jesus. Most will think of a cross or crucifix. Remind them of the fish symbol that is used so often today. Tell the children that in the early Church Christians often had to meet secretly. When they did they sometimes drew a fish to identify themselves as followers of Jesus. Have the children look at the front of their books. Remind them that the bread and wine are symbols for Jesus too. These remind us that the Eucharist is the Body and Blood of Christ.

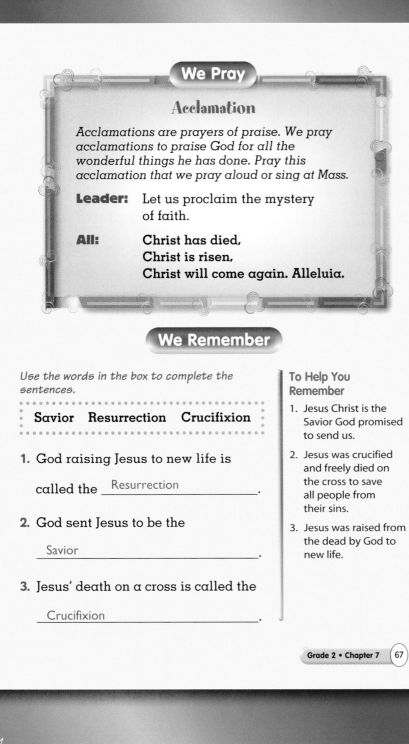

We Pray

Acclamation

Acclamations are prayers of praise. We pray acclamations to praise God for all the wonderful things he has done. Pray this acclamation that we pray aloud or sing at Mass.

Leader: Let us proclaim the mystery of faith.

All: Christ has died,
Christ is risen,
Christ will come again. Alleluia.

We Remember

Use the words in the box to complete the sentences.

    Savior   Resurrection   Crucifixion

1. God raising Jesus to new life is

   called the <u>Resurrection</u>.

2. God sent Jesus to be the

   <u>Savior</u>.

3. Jesus' death on a cross is called the

   <u>Crucifixion</u>.

To Help You Remember

1. Jesus Christ is the Savior God promised to send us.

2. Jesus was crucified and freely died on the cross to save all people from their sins.

3. Jesus was raised from the dead by God to new life.

Grade 2 • Chapter 7 (67)

WE PRAY

- Gather the children in the prayer center. Tell them that today they are going to pray a special prayer called an acclamation. Use the prayer introduction to explain about acclamations.
- Practice the acclamation together.
- Lead the class in prayer.

Review

WE REMEMBER

- Ask the children to look at the acclamation they just prayed. Ask volunteers to tell you how they would explain part of the acclamation to someone. Invite the children to use "To Help You Remember" to explain the acclamation.
- Introduce the "We Remember" activity and allow time for the children to complete it. Invite the children to check their answers with a partner.

Background: Liturgy

The Memorial Acclamation. The acclamation that follows the Consecration at Mass is called the Memorial Acclamation. In addition to the acclamation that is used for the prayer in this lesson, there are three other forms of the Memorial Acclamation. They are:

Dying you destroyed our death, / rising you restored our life. / Lord, Jesus, come in glory.

When we eat this bread and drink this cup, / we proclaim your death, Lord Jesus, / until you come in glory.

Lord, by your cross and Resurrection / you have set us free. / You are the Savior of the world.

At Home

Have the children carefully tear out pages 67 and 68 along the perforation. Encourage the children to share the pages with their families and to do the activities together. If they did not complete the review activity on page 67 by the end of the session, emphasize that they can complete it with their families.

VISIT FAITHFIRST.COM

- Share with the children the many activities on the *Faith First* Web site.
- Encourage the children to visit **www.FaithFirst.com.**

Before Moving On . . .

As you finish today's lesson, reflect on the following question before moving on to the next chapter.

How well am I allowing the students to use their talents in the various class activities?

---

7 With My Family

This Week . . .

In chapter 7, "Jesus Is Our Savior," your child learned that Jesus is the Savior of all people. Our salvation flows from God's initiative of love and mercy. Because God loves us, he sent the Son of God who freely died to free all people from sin. We call this saving event the Crucifixion. God raised Jesus from the dead to a new and glorified life. We call this event the Resurrection. We too shall live after we die. God invites us to live an eternal life of happiness with him and with Mary and all the saints.

For more on the teachings of the Catholic Church on the mystery of Jesus Christ and God's loving plan of salvation, see *Catechism of the Catholic Church* paragraph numbers 422–451, 456–478, and 599–655.

Sharing God's Word

Read the Bible story about the angel who came to Joseph before Jesus was born. You can find this story on page 62 or in Matthew 1:20–23. Emphasize that the angel came to announce that the time had come for God to fulfill his promises.

Praying

In this chapter your child learned to pray a memorial acclamation. Read and pray together the prayer on page 67.

Making a Difference

Choose one of the following activities to do as a family or design a similar activity of your own.

- The crucifix reminds us of God's love for us. Talk about how your family reminds each other about God's love.

- When you go to Mass this week, pay close attention to the Memorial Acclamation. Use the acclamation you sang at Mass for family prayer at home.

- The lighted Easter candle is the most important candle our Church uses. We use other candles too. All lighted candles remind us that the Risen Jesus is always with us. This week when you go to Mass, notice where you see lighted candles used in your parish.

> For more ideas on ways your family can live your faith, visit the "Faith First for Families" page at **www.FaithFirst.com**. You will find the "Contemporary Issues" page helpful this week.

68

Evaluate

Take a few moments to evaluate this week's lesson.
I feel (circle one) about this week's lesson.

a. very pleased
b. OK
c. disappointed

The activity the children enjoyed most was . . .

The concept that was most difficult to teach was . . .

because . . .

Something I would like to do differently is . . .

ENRICHING THE LESSON

Making Story Cards

Purpose

To reinforce the story of the Crucifixion and the Resurrection (taught on pages 63 and 64)

Directions

- Provide the children with heavy tagboard folded in half so that it stands up.
- Have the children draw images and write words about the Crucifixion on one side and images and words about the Resurrection on the other.
- Invite the children to use their pictures to tell their families about Jesus. Suggest that they display them at home.

Materials

tagboard
crayons or markers

Designing a Parish Bulletin Board

Purpose

To reinforce the children's knowledge about Jesus, the Savior (taught on page 62)

Directions

One way to strengthen the children's participation in parish life is to create a parish bulletin board. The bulletin board will show the entire parish what the children are learning.

- Discuss with the children the kinds of things they might want to tell the parish about what they have learned about Jesus, the Savior of the world.
- In partners have the children draw what they have learned. Their drawings might illustrate the crucifix, the Risen Jesus, and so on.
- Have the children decide on a title for the bulletin board and display their pictures on the board. Place the bulletin board where parishioners can enjoy it.

Materials

corkboard for the bulletin board
construction paper
crayons
push pins

Literature Connection

Purpose

To reinforce the story of the birth and death of Jesus (taught on pages 62 and 63)

Directions

The children will enjoy hearing *The Legend of the Three Trees* by Catherine McCafferty (Tommy Nelson Publishers, 2001). In this lovely picture book, three trees are cut down, but each is remade into an object that plays a part in the life of Jesus.

- The story reinforces themes of sacrifice and how death leads to new life. (This story is told by a second grade catechist in the *Echoes of Faith* module "Methods for Grades 1 and 2.")
- Tell the story and invite the children to share which tree they think had the biggest job of all.
- Ask what it must have felt like to play the role that each tree played.

Materials

The Legend of the Three Trees by Catherine McCafferty

Music Connection

- "Memorial Acclamation A," M. Haugen. *Singing Our Faith (SOF)* #73.
- "Dust and Ashes," D. Haugen. *SOF* #120.
- "O How Good Is Christ the Lord," (Puerto Rican traditional), arr. R. Batastini. *SOF* #124.
- "Jesus Is with Us," O. Alstott. *SOF* #274.

The Traveler on the Road to Emmaus A Scripture Story

Background

The Mysterious Traveler

The Resurrection narrative of the disciples going to Emmaus is among those most often retold. Imagine you are one of the two disciples of Jesus returning to Emmaus three days after the death and burial of Jesus. You are downcast and confused. You had hoped that Jesus the Nazarene was the one to redeem Israel. You are devastated by his execution, by the certainty of his death. You are confused, bewildered, and, at the same time, astounded to hear that some women from your group not only had found his tomb empty, but had reported they had seen "a vision of angels who announced that he was alive" (Luke 24:23).

A traveler whom you do not recognize to be Jesus joins you for your journey. You discuss the events of the last few days with him. Then this traveler gives you history's greatest Scripture lesson. He begins with Moses and all the prophets and proceeds to interpret the meaning of the final days of Jesus' life.

At this point, you are nearing Emmaus. You really do not want this mysterious traveler to leave and continue on his journey. So,

you urge him to stay with you since it is nearly nightfall. He accepts your hospitality, and while you are in the middle of dinner, he takes bread, says a blessing, breaks it, and shares it with you. With those simple gestures, you recognize that this mysterious traveler is the Lord, who is alive as the women reported. He then vanishes from your sight.

Always in Our Midst Too!

This wonderful and often told Gospel story serves as a foretelling of what Jesus will do for all of his followers. Jesus is always in our midst too. He travels life with us as our companion.

When we are most confused or downhearted, Jesus is there, accompanying us on our journey. He is with us in the word of God, Sacred Scripture, to help us understand the mysteries of his life and death—and our own life and death. He is uniquely present in the Eucharist. When we bless and break the bread of hospitality and charity for others, we again encounter Christ in those whom we serve (see Matthew 25:31–40).

The disciples on the road to Emmaus were not, at first, able to recognize their Risen Savior and Lord. His real body now possessed "the new properties of a glorious body: not limited by space and time but able to be present how and when he wills"[1] (*Catechism of the Catholic Church* 645). Christ who dwells in a heavenly realm now abides with his Father and intercedes for us. We believe and trust that he is ever present among us too!

For Reflection

When am I most often aware of Christ's presence with me? At those moments, do I talk with him in prayer?

When has my faith in Christ's presence with me given me courage and hope?

Catechist to Catechist

Breaking Bread

Second graders often start the year looking forward to and preparing for their First Holy Communion. Capitalize on this anticipation and excitement and use this story of the disciples on the road to Emmaus as a natural time of preparation for their first reception of the Eucharist.

Unleavened Bread

To really get into the presentation of the Emmaus story, consider baking some homemade unleavened bread. You might enlist some parents to bring fresh-baked  unleavened bread to the session for the children to enjoy as you have them act out the Emmaus story on page 71 of their books. Remind the children that they too are disciples and that each time they take part in Mass they will have the opportunity to recognize Jesus "in the breaking of bread."

The Church Teaches . . .

The Gospels are the living memories of Christ and his Church. The *General Directory for Catechesis* points out:
Catechetics forms part of that "memory" of the Church which vividly maintains the presence of the Lord among us.[1] Use of memory, therefore, forms a constitutive aspect of the pedagogy of the faith since the beginning of Christianity.[2] *GDC* 154
Therefore, the stories, sayings, and prayers of Jesus are good subjects for young children to begin to memorize.

See the Catechism . . .

For more on the teachings of the Catholic Church on the mystery of Christ's presence with the Church, see *Catechism of the Catholic Church* 610–611 and 1356–1405.

CATECHIST PRAYER

Lord, the disciples recognized you in the breaking of bread. Give me a greater appreciation of your gift of the Eucharist so that I may help the children also know you, present in the Eucharist. Amen.

Footnote references may be found on p. 456.

LESSON PLANNER

Focus To discover what the disciples traveling on the road to Emmaus did after Jesus was raised from the dead

Engage

Page 69
Focus
To help the children describe Gospel stories they remember about people sharing meals with Jesus

Opening Prayer

Discussion
After Jesus died, the disciples missed him.

Teach and Apply

Pages 70–72
Focus
To introduce the children to the Gospel story of Emmaus as a story about the Eucharist

Presentation
Read, discuss, and summarize content.
Scripture
• Matthew 28:20
• Luke 24:15–31
Activities
• Think of a Gospel story about Jesus and make a storyboard about that story.
• Complete the word search of Old Testament words.
• Identify when the priest breaks the consecrated bread at Mass.

Connect

Pages 73–74
Focus
To describe how we recognize Jesus at Mass

Our Church Makes a Difference
At Mass the priest breaks and shares the consecrated bread, the Body of Christ.
Our Catholic Identity
Altar Bread and Wine

What Difference Does Faith Make?
Activity
Identify some people who help us know Jesus is with us.
Faith Choice
Identify a way to be a sign that Jesus is with us this week.

We Pray

Page 75
Prayer Form
Meditation
Prayer
Introduce the meditation and guide the children through the steps.

We Remember

Review
• Complete the ordering activity.
• Check "To Help You Remember" statements aloud against the text.
Preview
Preview the "With My Family" page.

Materials

pens or pencils

Enriching the Session

Blackline Masters
Additional Activities booklet:
  Chapter 8
    Making a recipe for friendship
    Putting the events of the Emmaus story in order
Assessment Tools booklet:
  Chapter 8 Test
Enriching the Lesson (CG page 141)
Role-playing the Emmaus Story
Sharing Bread at Family Meals
Literature Connection
Music Connection (CG page 141)

www.FaithFirst.com

We update the *Faith First* Web site weekly. Check each week for new content and features. Here are some places to begin:

Catechists and Teachers
• Current Events
• Chapter Downloads
• Catechist Prayer

Faith First for Families
• Bible Stories
• Saints
• Make a Difference

Kids' Clubhouse
• *Faith First* Activities
• Chapter Reviews
• Games

Don't Forget! You can make lesson planning a breeze—check out the **Online Lesson Planner.**

The Traveler on the Road to Emmaus

A Scripture Story

8

We Pray

"I am with you always."

Matthew 28:20

Holy Spirit, help us to share the good news of Jesus' Resurrection. Amen.

When have you missed someone who went away?

After Jesus died, the disciples missed him very much. Three days later, they saw him again!

Why did the disciples get to see Jesus again?

The Risen Jesus with two disciples on the road to Emmaus

69

PRAY

- Have the children quiet themselves for prayer. Remind them that Jesus is with us when we gather to pray.
- Proclaim Matthew 28:20 together.
- Invite the children to echo each phrase of the opening prayer after you, and lead in praying the prayer. Conclude by saying "Amen" together.

DISCOVER

Purpose: To discover what the children may know about the post-Resurrection appearances of the Risen Jesus

- Ask the children when they may have missed someone in their families who went away.
- Read the introductory paragraph and invite responses to the question. Ask the children to read the title of this chapter and connect the title with the picture. Ask them what they think this Gospel story will be about.

Teaching Tip

Sharing Meals. Be sure to incorporate into your discussions with the children the importance of sharing meals and mealtimes with their families and friends. Encourage the children to pray before and after meals to acknowledge that God is the source of all our material and spiritual blessings. Placing an emphasis on shared meals and praying before and after meals this year also helps second graders to realize the significance of the most important shared meal of all—the Holy Eucharist.

Teach

FOCUS

Ask a volunteer to read the "Faith Focus" question. Connect the question to the picture on page 69 and share with the children that they are going to learn about this Gospel story.

DISCOVER

- Present "The Four Gospels" in your own words. Ask the children to underline the words that tell the meaning of the word *gospel*. Good news.
- Show the children the location of the four Gospels in the Bible. Remind them that the Gospels tell us about Jesus.
- Open the Bible to the Gospel of Matthew. Hand the Bible reverently to each child. As they are holding it, ask a volunteer what Gospel stories are the most important stories in the New Testament. The most important stories in the New Testament are the Gospel stories of the suffering, death, and Resurrection of Jesus Christ.

Apply

REINFORCE

Have the children read aloud the "Faith Words" and their meanings. Have them make word cards for *Apostles* and *Gospels*.

INTEGRATE

Ask the children to read the directions for the activity and draw their stories in the box. Have them tell their stories to a partner.

Bible Background

Faith Focus

What does the Gospel story about walking to the village of Emmaus teach us?

Faith Words

Apostles
The Apostles were the disciples who Jesus chose and sent to preach the Gospel to the whole world in his name.

Gospels
The Gospels are the first four books in the New Testament.

The Four Gospels

The Church shares the faith stories that the **Apostles** and the first Christians told about Jesus. These stories are found in the four **Gospels.** The word *gospel* means "good news." The Gospels share the good news about Jesus with the world.

The Gospels are the first four books in the New Testament. The New Testament is the second main part of the Bible. The most important stories in the New Testament are the Gospel stories of the suffering, death, and Resurrection of Jesus Christ.

In these boxes draw a Bible story you know about Jesus. Share it with a partner and your family.

Affirm appropriate responses.

70

Faith Vocabulary

Gospels. The word *gospel* comes from the Greek word *evangelion* and means "good news" or "glad tidings." There are four Gospels in the New Testament. They are written by the four Evangelists, Saint Matthew, Saint Mark, Saint Luke, and Saint John. The word *evangelist* is also from the Greek word *evangelion*, and means "messenger of good tidings."

Reading the Word of God

The Traveler to Emmaus

Two of Jesus' disciples were walking to the village of Emmaus. It was three days after Jesus died and was buried. The Gospel of Luke tells what happened.

The Risen Jesus began to walk along with them. They did not recognize Jesus. When they came close to Emmaus, they invited Jesus to stay with them. They sat down for a meal and Jesus took the bread. He thanked and blessed God, broke the bread, and shared it with them. Suddenly, the disciples recognized that the traveler who had been with them was the Risen Jesus.

Based on Luke 24:15–16, 28–31

This Gospel story shares that the Risen Jesus is alive in a new way. He is always with us.

QUESTION *When does the Church break and share bread?* At Mass. Accept other appropriate wording of responses.

(71)

(Student Page 71) 135

Teaching Tip

Storytelling. Practice telling this Scripture story aloud. Think of ways to make the characters come alive. Use props and visuals in your presentation, such as bread. You might walk along as you share the beginning part of the story and sit for the part about the meal. Acting out gestures will capture the children's imaginations and keep their attention focused.

Teach

FOCUS
Remind the children that the four Gospels contain the stories the early Church told about Jesus. Point out that one of those Gospel stories tells us about a meal Jesus shared with two disciples after he was raised from the dead.

DISCOVER
- Tell the children to listen attentively as you proclaim the Gospel story of Emmaus based on Luke 24:15–16, 28–31.
- Ask the children when the disciples recognized Jesus. When Jesus thanked and blessed God, broke the bread, and shared it with them.
- Ask volunteers why they think the disciples recognized Jesus when he broke bread with them. This is what Jesus had done at the Last Supper.

Apply

REINFORCE
Invite several children to mime the Scripture story as you proclaim it a second time.

INTEGRATE
Ask the children how this story helps them understand what happens at Mass. At Mass the priest breaks the Eucharist bread that we receive in Holy Communion. Accept other appropriate responses.

Teach

FOCUS

Share with the children that there are similarities between the Emmaus story and what happens at Mass.

DISCOVER

- Point out to the children that the early Church used the words *the breaking of bread* for the Eucharist.
- Have three volunteers read aloud "The Breaking of Bread." Ask the class to listen to discover the connection between the Emmaus story and the Mass.

Apply

REINFORCE

Have volunteers share what Bible stories about breaking bread tell us about God. God is always with us. He always cares for us.

INTEGRATE

- Ask the children to study the pictures about how bread was made in Jesus' time and compare the steps with what modern bakers do today when they make bread.
- Ask the children to tell when the priest breaks the consecrated bread at Mass. Before we receive Holy Communion.

Understanding the Word of God

The Breaking of Bread

Bread was very important to the early Christians. Look at these pictures to see how bread was made.

1. Cutting the wheat

2. Grinding the wheat

The two disciples recognized the Risen Jesus when he broke bread and shared it with them. This was what Jesus also did at the Last Supper. The Last Supper is the last meal Jesus ate with his disciples before he died.

The early Christians used the words "the breaking of bread" for the Eucharist. Jesus is with us in a most special way when we celebrate the Eucharist. The bread and wine become the Body and Blood of Christ. We receive Jesus in Holy Communion.

Bible stories about breaking and sharing bread remind us that God is always with his people. God always takes care of his people.

QUESTION *When does the priest break the consecrated bread at Mass? Clue: Turn to page 294.* During the Communion Rite before we receive Holy Communion.

3. Kneading the bread dough

4. Baking the bread

72

Background: Doctrine

Breaking Bread. The meal is the center of many family events and traditions. We gather together to nourish our bodies, our minds, and our spirits through the company of family and friends. The same was true in Jesus' time. The evening meal was often the center of the day. It was the event around which all other actions took place. The Eucharist is the center of the Christian life. Everything we do centers around the Eucharist. Everything leads to it and flows from it (see *Catechism of the Catholic Church* 1324 and 1327).

Our Church Makes a Difference

The Bread of Life

At Mass the priest breaks and shares the consecrated bread, the Body of Christ. As the priest breaks the bread, he prays aloud, "Lamb of God, you take away the sins of the world." Jesus Christ is the Lamb of God. He is the Savior of the world.

The breaking of the consecrated bread at Mass shows that we all share one Bread, Jesus, the Bread of Life. Receiving Jesus, the Bread of Life, in Holy Communion joins us more closely to him and to one another. We receive the grace to live as followers of Jesus. We live as Jesus taught and help people in need.

QUESTION *What is one way your parish helps people in need?*
Affirm appropriate responses.

Our Catholic Faith

Altar Bread

The bread we use at Mass is unleavened bread made from wheat. Unleavened bread is made without yeast. Yeast is used to make bread dough rise. The wine we use for Mass is always made from grapes.

73

Background: Sacred Scripture

Jesus, the Bread of Life. In John 6:22–59 we read Jesus' "Bread of Life" discourse. John tells us that after the miracle of the multiplication of the loaves and fishes (John 6:1–15), the disciples crossed the Sea of Tiberias and the crowds followed them. The next day Jesus addressed the crowds and, after dialoguing with them about the Exodus story of the Israelites eating manna in the desert, he declared that he, Jesus, was the true bread from heaven, saying, "I am the bread of life; whoever comes to me will never hunger, and whoever believes in me will never thirst" (John 6:32, 35). As time allows, share this wonderful story with the children. If there is not sufficient time to share it with the children, prayerfully read and reflect on it yourself.

Connect

HIGHLIGHT
Share with the children that we receive Jesus, the Bread of Life, in Holy Communion.

DISCOVER
- Present "The Bread of Life" in your own words.
- Ask a volunteer to find the answer to the question: What does the breaking of bread at Mass show? It shows that we all share in the one Bread, the Body of Christ.
- Invite a volunteer to read "Our Catholic Faith" to learn more about the bread we use at Mass.

INTEGRATE
- Invite the children to share how Holy Communion helps us live as followers of Jesus. It joins us more closely to Jesus and one another, gives us grace, and gives us strength to help people in need.
- Read the closing question aloud and invite volunteers to name ways they know their parish helps people in need.

Connect

(Student Page 74)

HIGHLIGHT

Remind the children that the Eucharist is the Body and Blood of Christ. Jesus gives himself to us in the Eucharist. Then present the introductory paragraph.

RESPOND

• Introduce the "I Am Always With You" activity and have the children write about someone who helps them know Jesus is with them.

• After completing the activity have volunteers share their responses.

CHOOSE

• Have the children read "My Faith Choice" and write their responses.

• Encourage everyone to put their choices into practice this week.

What Difference Does Faith Make in My Life?

At Mass we receive the Body and Blood of Christ. Jesus, the Bread of Life, shares himself with us. The Holy Spirit invites you to share your talents with others.

Who are some of the people who help you to know that Jesus is with you? Write their names and tell what they do.

"I Am Always With You"

Name	What They Do
	Responses will vary.

My Faith Choice

This week I will be a sign that Jesus is always with us. I will

Affirm appropriate responses.

74

Catholic Social Teaching

Option for the Poor and Vulnerable. An inordinate and self-centered attachment to wealth and possessions is contrary to living as a disciple of Christ. The Catholic Church teaches this very principle: We are obligated to share our possessions. We are to be detached from them and to work together for the elimination of the inequitable distribution of material and spiritual goods among peoples. Working to meet the needs of the poor and the vulnerable must be a priority.

TIPS: Invite the children to compose Mass petitions for the poor and needy. Invite them to participate in parish food drives.

We Pray

"I Am Always with You"

Meditation is a type of prayer. In a meditation we use our imagination. We ask the Holy Spirit to teach us to live as Jesus taught.

1. Close your eyes. Remember that the Holy Spirit lives within you.

2. Pretend that you are one of the disciples in this Bible story.

3. Listen to Luke 24:13–31.

4. Ask the Holy Spirit to help you tell others about Jesus.

We Remember

Number the sentences in the order the events take place in the Gospel story.

___2___ The disciples invited Jesus to share a meal with them.

___3___ Jesus blessed, broke, and shared the bread with them.

___I___ Jesus met two disciples on their way to Emmaus.

___4___ The disciples recognized the Risen Jesus.

To Help You Remember

1. The four Gospels share with us the teachings and life of Jesus.

2. The most important stories in the Gospels are about the death and Resurrection of Jesus.

3. At Mass the bread and wine become the Body and Blood of Jesus. He is really with us.

Pray

WE PRAY

- Gather the children in the prayer center and have them sit quietly on the floor in a circle.
- Introduce the prayer by telling the children that today's prayer is a prayer of meditation. Then read to the children the introductory paragraph to the prayer. Tell them that they are going to meditate together on the Emmaus story.
- Lead the children in the meditation.

Review

WE REMEMBER

- Create word games with the three "To Help You Remember" statements that will reinforce the children's grasp of the key faith concepts of the lesson. For example, turn the faith statements into false statements by changing a key word. Call on volunteers to supply the correct word for each statement.
- Invite the children to complete the "We Remember" activity. Then have volunteers take turns telling the Emmaus story using these sentences as a guide.

Special Needs

Using Manipulatives. Cut sentence strips of appropriate length from lightweight poster board. You can also purchase ready-made sentence strip paper at a teacher supply store. Write the four Emmaus-story sentences from the "We Remember" section on the sentence strips. Attach tape to each strip and secure to the board. Allow students to arrange the sentences into correct sequence by moving the strips. When they have arranged them they can number them on the board and then copy the correct numbers into their workbooks.

Need: All young learners; children with visual difficulties

At Home

Have the children carefully tear out pages 75 and 76 along the perforation. Encourage the children to share the pages with their families and to do the activities together. If they did not complete the review activity on page 75 by the end of the session, emphasize that they can complete it with their families.

VISIT FAITHFIRST.COM

• Share with the children the many activities on the *Faith First* Web site.

• Encourage the children to visit **www.FaithFirst.com.**

 With My Family

This Week . . .

In chapter 8, "The Traveler on the Road to Emmaus: A Scripture Story," your child learned that our Church shares the faith stories that the Apostles and the first Christians told about Jesus. These stories are found in the four Gospels. The Gospel story of two disciples walking to Emmaus shares that Jesus was raised from the dead and is alive in a new way. Jesus is with us in a unique way at Mass. At Mass the bread and wine become the Body and Blood of Christ. We receive Jesus, the Bread of Life, in Holy Communion.

For more on the teachings of the Catholic Church on the mystery of Christ's presence with the Church, see *Catechism of the Catholic Church* paragraph numbers 610–611 and 1356–1405.

Sharing God's Word

Read together the Bible story in Luke 24:13–31 about the disciples who were walking to the village of Emmaus or read the adaptation of the story on page 71. Emphasize that at Mass the bread and wine become the Body and Blood of Christ and Jesus is really with us.

Praying

In this chapter your child prayed a meditation prayer. Pray together the meditation on page 75.

Making a Difference

Choose one of the following activities to do as a family or design a similar activity of your own.

• Look on the Internet or at your public library for pictures of the Holy Land. Look for the village of Emmaus and the city of Jerusalem. Talk about what it might have been like to walk from Jerusalem to Emmaus.

• The Bible story in this chapter reminds us how important it is for us to share meals together. Talk about ways your family can make everyday meals together special.

• Make a loaf of homemade bread and eat it together. Talk about how the disciples recognized the Risen Jesus when he broke the bread and shared it with them. Relate this story to the celebration of the Eucharist.

> For more ideas on ways your family can live your faith, visit the "Faith First for Families" page at **www.FaithFirst.com.** This week you will find it useful to visit "Questions Kids Ask" and discuss the question.

76

Evaluate

Take a few moments to evaluate this week's lesson.
I feel (circle one) about this week's lesson.

    a. very pleased

    b. OK

    c. disappointed

The activity the children enjoyed most was . . .

The concept that was most difficult to teach was . . .

because . . .

Something I would like to do differently is . . .

Before Moving On . . .

As you finish today's lesson, reflect on the following question before moving on to the next chapter.

What have I done to bring a spirit of Christian joy into my classroom?

ENRICHING THE LESSON

Role-playing the Emmaus Story

Purpose

To reinforce the story of "The Traveler to Emmaus" (taught on page 71)

Directions

- Invite the children to role-play the story to reinforce the story of "The Traveler to Emmaus."
- Choose children to play each of the story parts. Include more children by adding travelers passing by and meal servers for the place where the disciples and Jesus dine.
- Give the children simple props such as bread, cups, and walking sticks to enhance the action.
- Invite the children to act out the story using their own words.

Materials

simple props

Sharing Bread at Family Meals

Purpose

To reinforce an understanding of the Emmaus story about breaking and sharing bread (taught on page 72)

Directions

- Send home with each child a small loaf of unleavened bread, such as pita bread. Attach a label to each loaf with the following directions:

Family Bread

- Place this bread in a place of honor on your meal table. At the beginning of your family meal, pass the loaf to each person.
- Invite each person to break off a piece of bread. When every family member has a piece of bread in hand, pray this prayer:

Jesus, you are the Bread of Life. You come to us in many ways each day. May we recognize you in every person and in every event of our lives. Amen.

Materials

loaves or pieces of unleavened bread
plastic wrap
ribbon to tie label on bread
labels prepared in advance

Literature Connection

Purpose

To reinforce the background to the teaching about bread as a source of nourishment in many cultures (taught on page 73)

Directions

Ann Morris' book called *Bread, Bread, Bread* (William Morrow & Company, 1993) has beautiful illustrations of different kinds of bread and of people making bread. It tells how and why we eat bread.

- Bring samples of various kinds of bread and allow the children to taste them.
- Be sure to ask families about food allergies before you offer to let the children taste different kinds of breads. If you have any children in your group who have bread allergies, have the parents send a bread substitute so this child will not feel left out.

Materials

Bread, Bread, Bread by Ann Morris
samples of different kinds of bread

Music Connection

- "Sing Alleluia," J. Vogt. *Rise Up and Sing* #246.
- "When Jesus Saw the Fishermen," R. L. Van Oss. *Singing Our Faith (SOF)* #165.
- "Two By Two," J. Berthier. *SOF* #188.
- "Bring Forth the Kingdom," M. Haugen. *SOF* #192.

The Holy Spirit

The Gift of the Holy Spirit

The Holy Spirit is the third divine Person of the Holy Trinity, distinct from the Father and the Son. Of the same substance with the Father and the Son, the Holy Spirit is inseparable from them. The Holy Spirit always works with the Father and the Son. He was there at creation. He was there at the beginning of God's plan of salvation. He will be at its completion.

On the day of Pentecost, the work of the Church began with the outpouring of the Holy Spirit upon the disciples.

To fulfill this divine plan, Jesus Christ founded the Church, built on the Apostles. He gave them the Holy Spirit from the Father and sent them to preach the Gospel to the whole world[1]. . . .

As the Church lives the Gospel she is continually made fruitful by the Holy

Spirit. The Spirit causes her to grow constantly in her understanding of the Gospel, prompts her and sustains the task of proclaiming the Gospel in every corner of the world.[2]
GENERAL DIRECTORY FOR CATECHESIS 43

The outpouring of the Holy Spirit never ceases to guide the Church and make present the mission of Christ in the world until the end of time.

Through the Power of the Spirit

When we were baptized, we received the Holy Spirit, the Sanctifier. The sign of water in Baptism signifies the new birth given to us by the Holy Spirit (see John 3:4–5). The sign of anointing symbolizes our union with Christ, Priest, Prophet, and King. The sign of fire signifies the transforming power given to the Church by the Holy Spirit to keep the flame of faith in Christ alive in the world until the end of time.

In a world that often seems to prize greed and selfishness, the Holy Spirit is at work in the life of the Church and in the lives of all the baptized, bringing "love, joy, peace, patience, kindness, generosity, faithfulness, gentleness, self-control" (Galatians 5:22–23) to the world.

For Reflection

When do I converse in prayer with the Holy Spirit who dwells within me?

How has the Holy Spirit been my advocate and guide in living the gift of new life in Christ?

Catechist to Catechist

Come, Holy Spirit

Seven- and eight-year-olds are trying to understand the world around them. As they do so, they soon discover that there are some things they cannot understand. In the Church they have learned about God the Father and Creator, Jesus the Incarnate Son of God and the Savior, and the Holy Spirit the Sanctifier. They have done this by their participation in the celebrations of the Church and by listening to stories of our faith.

The Holy Spirit's Work

This session provides the children with an opportunity to learn more about the Holy Spirit. Their faith in the Holy Spirit will be deepened as they discover more about the Spirit's work in helping them learn to live as Christians. The prayer life of children this age is just beginning to be personal. Share with them that the Holy Spirit will help them as they, more and more, pray in their own words.

The Church Teaches . . .

The *General Directory for Catechesis* tells us:

> The Christian faith is, above all, conversion to Jesus Christ,[1] full and sincere adherence to his person and the decision to walk in his footsteps. This "Yes" . . . is possible only by means of the action of the Holy Spirit.[2] *GDC* 53 and 54

This chapter helps the children deepen their knowledge of and faith in the Holy Spirit, who is ever present to them, guiding them to live their Baptism.

See the Catechism . . .

For more on the teachings of the Catholic Church on the mystery of the Holy Spirit, see *Catechism of the Catholic Church* 687–741.

CATECHIST PRAYER

*Spirit of God,
as an adult I have experienced
your assistance in my life.
May I continue to be aware of
your ever-present love and guidance.
Help these young children to
understand that you will always
surround them with that same love.
Amen.*

Footnote references may be found on p. 456.

LESSON PLANNER

FOCUS To discover what the New Testament tells us about the Holy Spirit

Engage

Page 77
Focus

To help the children recall what they remember about the Holy Spirit as our helper

Opening Prayer

Discussion

When have we needed help from others?

Teach and Apply

Pages 78–80
Focus

To discover that the Holy Spirit, the third Person of the Blessed Trinity, is always with us

Presentation

Read, discuss, and summarize content.

Scripture

- Psalm 104:30
- Luke 24:49
- Acts of the Apostles 2:2–11 and 32

Activities

- Decorate a postcard.
- Write a short prayer to the Holy Spirit.

Faith-Filled People

Saint Luke the Evangelist

Connect

Pages 81–82
Focus

To discover what the Church and its members remember when they celebrate Pentecost

Our Church Makes a Difference

The work of the Church began on Pentecost.

Our Catholic Identity

Celebrations of the Church

What Difference Does Faith Make?

Activity

Write about or draw one talent you have.

Faith Choice

Identify a way to share God's love with other people this week.

We Pray

Page 83

Prayer Form

Prayer of petition

Prayer

Divide the children into two groups. Choose a leader and pray the "Prayer to the Holy Spirit" together.

We Remember

Review

- Complete the matching activity.
- Review the "To Help You Remember" statements.

Preview

Preview the "With My Family" page.

Materials

- index cards
- pencils
- crayons or markers

Enriching the Session

Blackline Masters

Additional Activities booklet:
  Chapter 9
    Birthday celebration
    Color the children of God
Assessment Tools booklet:
  Chapter 9 Test

Enriching the Lesson (CG page 153)

Making a Holy Spirit Display
Making a Holy Spirit Collage
Literature Connection

Music Connection (CG page 153)

www.FaithFirst.com

We update the *Faith First* Web site weekly. Check each week for new content and features. Here are some places to begin:

Catechists and Teachers
- Current Events
- Chapter Downloads
- Catechist Prayer

Faith First for Families
- Bible Stories
- Saints
- Make a Difference

Kids' Clubhouse
- *Faith First* Activities
- Chapter Reviews
- Games

Don't Forget! You can make lesson planning a breeze—check out the **Online Lesson Planner.**

The Holy Spirit

9

We Pray

Lord God, send us
your Spirit,
and renew all the
earth.
Based on Psalm 104:30

**Come, Holy
Spirit, fill our
hearts with your
love. Amen.**

*What are some
times when you
have needed help
from others?*

Every Christian
needs help to live
as a follower of
Jesus. Jesus sent
the Holy Spirit to
help us.

*What do you
know about the
Holy Spirit?*

77

PRAY

- Have the children quiet themselves for prayer. Remind them that Jesus is with us when we gather to pray.
- Pray the Scripture verse based on Psalm 104:30 together.
- Lead the opening prayer. Invite the children to echo each phrase after you.
- Close the prayer with the Sign of the Cross.

DISCOVER

Purpose: To discover what the children may already know about the role of the Holy Spirit.

- Ask the children to name times when they have needed help from others. Read the introductory paragraph to them.
- Invite the children to tell why they think this picture was chosen for this chapter.
- Ask volunteers to share what they know about the Holy Spirit.

Teaching Tip

Admitting Needs. Children of seven or eight are trying to experience their first taste of independence. At times it is difficult for them to admit they need the help of others. When asked if they need help, they may say no, convinced that they can take care of themselves. Remind them that we all rely on the help of others.

Teach

FOCUS

Ask a volunteer to read aloud the "Faith Focus" question. Remind the children that the Holy Spirit is the third Person of the Holy Trinity. Tell the children that now they are going to learn more about the Holy Spirit.

DISCOVER

- Ask the children to read silently "The Promise of the Holy Spirit" to find out when Jesus made the promise that the Father would send the Holy Spirit. Before he returned to his Father in heaven.

- Ask: What do we call Jesus' return to his Father? The Ascension. Print the word Ascension on the board.

REINFORCE

Have the children make a word card for Ascension.

INTEGRATE

Have the children complete the "Sharing the Promise" activity about the Holy Spirit. Have them share their postcard with a partner.

God's Gift of Love

Faith Focus

What does the New Testament tell us about the Holy Spirit?

Faith Words

Ascension
The Ascension is the return of the Risen Jesus to his Father in heaven forty days after the Resurrection.

Pentecost
Pentecost is the day the Holy Spirit came to the disciples of Jesus, fifty days after the Resurrection.

The Promise of the Holy Spirit

Jesus promised that the Father would send the Holy Spirit to be our helper. The Holy Spirit is the third Person of the Holy Trinity.

Jesus made this promise before he returned to his Father in heaven. We call the return of the Risen Jesus to his Father in heaven the **Ascension**. This happened forty days after the Resurrection. Jesus said,

"I am sending the promise of my Father to you. It is the gift of the Holy Spirit." Based on Luke 24:49

The Holy Spirit is always with us.

ACTIVITY *Decorate this postcard. Share Jesus' promise with your family and friends.*

Sharing the Promise

Responses will vary.

Affirm appropriate responses.

78

Background: Catholic Tradition

Pentecost. Pentecost celebrates the descent of the Holy Spirit on the Apostles in tongues resembling fire. The feast of Pentecost has been a Christian feast since the first century. The name *Pentecost* is derived from the Greek word meaning "fifty," and the feast of Pentecost occurs fifty days after Easter, much as the Jewish harvest feast of Pentecost occurred fifty days after Passover. Originally, Pentecost simply marked the end of the Easter season. Traditions surrounding Pentecost vary around the world. In Italy, many churches release rose petals from the ceiling to resemble tongues of fire. In France, trumpets blow to recall the roar of the wind as the Holy Spirit descended upon the disciples in the upper room in Jerusalem.

Pentecost

Jesus' promise came true fifty days after the Resurrection. The day that the Holy Spirit came to the Apostles is called **Pentecost.** This is what the Bible tells us happened.

After Jesus returned to his Father, the disciples and Mary, the mother of Jesus, were praying together in a room. Suddenly, a big sound filled the house. It was the sound of a strong wind. Small flames settled over each disciple's head. The disciples were all filled with the Holy Spirit. Peter and the disciples then left the house. They went to tell others about Jesus.

Based on Acts of the Apostles 2:1–4, 14, 22

We first receive the gift of the Holy Spirit at Baptism. The Holy Spirit helps us tell others about Jesus as Peter did.

QUESTION What is one thing you want to tell someone about Jesus?

Responses will vary.

Faith-Filled People

Luke the Evangelist

Saint Luke sometimes traveled from place to place with Saint Paul to preach the Gospel. Saint Luke is one of the four Evangelists, or "tellers of the Gospel." Saint Luke also wrote the Acts of the Apostles. The story of Pentecost is told in the Acts of the Apostles. The Church celebrates the feast day of Saint Luke on October 18.

79

Background: Faith-Filled People

Saint Luke the Evangelist. The word *evangelist* means "one who announces the Good News." Saint Luke the Evangelist wrote one of the four Gospels as well as the Acts of the Apostles. His account of the Gospel takes us from the announcement of the birth of John the Baptist to the Ascension of Jesus. The Acts of the Apostles tells us what happened in the early Church after the Ascension. Saint Luke traveled with Saint Paul when he preached the Gospel and stayed with him when he was in prison. Throughout his life, Saint Luke showed great concern for the poor and needy. He is the patron saint of physicians and painters. The feast of Saint Luke is celebrated on October 18.

FOCUS

Remind the children that God the Father and his Son, Jesus, sent the Holy Spirit to help us live as children of God and followers of Jesus. Tell the children they will now discover when the Holy Spirit came to the Apostles as Jesus promised.

DISCOVER

- Write the word *Pentecost* on the board. Explain that Jesus' promise came true when the Holy Spirit came to the Apostles on Pentecost.
- Have the children close their eyes and imagine they are with Mary and the disciples.
- Proclaim the Pentecost story based on Acts of the Apostles 2:1–4, 14, 22.
- Invite the children to open their eyes and share the thoughts and feelings they had as they listened.
- Ask a volunteer to read "Faith-Filled People" about Saint Luke.

Apply

REINFORCE

Ask a volunteer to read the definition of *Pentecost* in "Faith Words." Have the children make a word card for *Pentecost.*

INTEGRATE

Ask the children to name one thing they could tell someone about Jesus. Have volunteers share their responses.

Teach

FOCUS

Remind the children that the Holy Spirit came to the Apostles on Pentecost. Tell them they are going to learn some of the things the Holy Spirit does to help us live as followers of Jesus.

DISCOVER

- Remind the children that the Holy Spirit, the third Person of the Holy Trinity, helps us believe and trust in God our Father and in Jesus Christ, who is the Son of God.
- Invite the children to work with a partner. Tell them to take turns reading "The Holy Spirit Is Always with Us" and to find two other things the Holy Spirit helps us to do. Teaches us how to follow Jesus and to pray.

Apply

REINFORCE

Remind the children that prayer is talking and listening to God. The Holy Spirit helps us to pray.

INTEGRATE

- Invite the children to write a short prayer to the Holy Spirit using their own words.
- Encourage the children to pray their prayers this week with their families.

The Holy Spirit Is Always with Us

The Holy Spirit helps us to believe and trust in God the Father and in Jesus Christ. The Holy Spirit helps us to live as children of God and followers of Jesus.

The Holy Spirit helps us to pray. When we pray, the Holy Spirit helps us to pray the way Jesus taught us. We tell God our Father what is in our thoughts and in our hearts. We ask the Holy Spirit to teach us and help us to live as children of God.

ACTIVITY *Write a short prayer to the Holy Spirit. Use your own words.*

Praying to the Holy Spirit

Come, Holy Spirit, help me to

_____ Responses will vary. _____ .

Come, Holy Spirit, teach me to

_____ Responses will vary. _____ .

Liturgy Tip

Liturgical Music. Help the children develop a repertoire of simple church hymns and responses. The simple Taize chant "Veni, Sancte Spiritu" would be appropriate to learn at this time. It is a simple one-note chant that the children can repeat over and over as a centering prayer or as a quieting activity before a classroom prayer experience. The "Music Connection" at the end of each chapter suggests other appropriate selections of hymns for young children related to each chapter theme.

Our Church Makes a Difference

The Work of the Church

Saint Peter and the other disciples received the gift of the Holy Spirit on Pentecost. The work of the Church began. Each year the Church celebrates Pentecost. We sing special songs and say special prayers. The vestments at Mass are red. Sometimes red banners hang in our parish churches.

We remember what happened on the first Pentecost. Peter told people from many countries about Jesus. Many people became followers of Jesus. This was the beginning of the Church.

 How do you see the people of your parish telling others about Jesus?

Affirm appropriate responses.

Our Catholic Faith

Celebrations of the Church

The Church celebrates the solemnity of Pentecost each year. The most important of the Church's celebrations are called solemnities. Easter is the greatest solemnity of the Church. Other days are called feasts or memorials.

I AM WITH YOU ALWAYS

81

Teaching Tip

Making a T-chart. A simple T-chart can help the children visualize similarities or differences. For the "Integrate" activity on this page you could draw a large "T" on the board to create two columns. Head one side *Birthdays* and the other side *Pentecost*. Brainstorm with the children ways that the two experiences are the same. Be careful that the children's responses really do indicate similarities; otherwise the activity will be confusing. For example, candles are a part of both celebrations. The church is decorated with banners, just as we usually decorate for birthday parties. However, playing party games would not be a similarity.

Connect

HIGHLIGHT

Ask the children to recall what happened on Pentecost. Tell the children that Pentecost is one of the great celebrations of the Church's year.

DISCOVER

- Have the children read to find out how the Church celebrates Pentecost. Singing special songs; praying special prayers; using red vestments and red banners.
- Tell them that the work of the Church began on Pentecost.
- Write the word *solemnity* on the board. Remind the children that something that is solemn is very important. Ask them why they think Easter is the greatest solemnity. Because it is the day of Jesus' Resurrection.
- Present "Our Catholic Faith" about celebrations of the Church.

INTEGRATE

- Ask the children how their birthday celebrations and the Church's celebration of Pentecost are alike and different.
- Ask the children to help you brainstorm ways the people of your parish tell others about Jesus as the disciples did on Pentecost.

Connect

HIGHLIGHT

Tell the children that the Holy Spirit, the third Person of the Holy Trinity, gives us special gifts to help us share the gift of God's love with other people.

RESPOND

- Talk with the children about how the talents given them by the Holy Spirit help them to live as Jesus, the Son of God, taught.
- Give the children time to do the activity. When they are finished, let them share what their talent is and how they will use it.

CHOOSE

Invite the children to read "My Faith Choice" and write their choices. Encourage them to put their choices into practice this week.

What Difference Does Faith Make in My Life?

The Holy Spirit gives you special gifts called talents. These gifts help you to know God's love. They help you to share the gift of God's love with people.

A flame of fire is one symbol the Church uses for the Holy Spirit. In the flame, write or draw one talent you have. Use that talent to share the gift of God's love with others.

Sharing the Gift of God's Love

Responses will vary.

Affirm appropriate responses.

My Faith Choice

This week I will share the gift of God's love with other people. I will

Affirm appropriate responses.

_____

_____

82

Teaching Tip

Doing Our Best. Remember that children need varying lengths of time for given tasks. Children with disabilities may need more time to do certain things. Some children may rush through activities, wanting and needing to be the first child finished. Explain that doing our best work should always be our goal, no matter how much time that might take.

We Pray

Prayer to the Holy Spirit

The Holy Spirit teaches us to pray and to live as children of God. Pray this prayer to the Holy Spirit together.

Leader: Let us pray to the Holy Spirit.

Group 1: Come, Holy Spirit,
fill the hearts of your faithful,

Group 2: and kindle in them
the fire of your love.

Group 1: Send forth your Spirit
and they shall be created.

Group 2: And you will renew
the face of the earth. Amen.

We Remember

Match each word with its correct meaning.

Words

b **1.** Pentecost

d **2.** Ascension

a **3.** Jesus

c **4.** Holy Spirit

Meanings

a. the One who asked the Father to send the Holy Spirit

b. the day the work of the Church began

c. the third Person of the Holy Trinity

d. the return of the Risen Jesus to his Father in heaven

To Help You Remember

1. Before he returned to his Father in heaven, Jesus promised that the Father would send the Holy Spirit.

2. The Holy Spirit came to the disciples on Pentecost.

3. The Holy Spirit is our helper and teacher.

Grade 2 • Chapter 9 · 83

Teaching Tip

The Power of the Holy Spirit. Unfortunately, too many young children live in situations that cause them fear. Events in the daily news can also create anxiety for them. Remind them that the Holy Spirit helped Saint Peter and the other Apostles and disciples to follow Jesus and be courageous enough to preach and live the Gospel. Knowing this may encourage the children to turn to the Holy Spirit when they too need the courage to make good decisions and do the things they know God wants them to do. When they experience the temptation to make a selfish choice, the Holy Spirit will help them. Encourage them to memorize the simple beginning of today's prayer: "Come, Holy Spirit, fill the hearts of your faithful," and to pray it at the beginning of each day.

Pray

WE PRAY

- Invite the children to bring their books and gather in the prayer center. Divide the children into two groups.
- Tell the children that they are going to pray one of the Church's best-known prayers to the Holy Spirit. Encourage the children to learn this prayer by heart.
- Point out the meaning of the word *kindle* that might be unfamiliar to them. *Kindle* means to prepare a fire in such a way that it will burn quickly and easily.
- Lead the "Prayer to the Holy Spirit."

Review

WE REMEMBER

Write a word bank on the board with the words *Holy Spirit, Pentecost,* and *Father.* Turn each of the "To Help You Remember" statements into a question to which one of these words provides the answer. Ask volunteers to guess the right word; invite them to come up and erase or cross out the word they used.

At Home

ENCOURAGE

Have the children carefully tear out pages 83 and 84 along the perforation. Encourage the children to share the pages with their families and to do the activities together. If they did not complete the review activity on page 83 by the end of the session, emphasize that they can complete it with their families.

VISIT FAITHFIRST.COM

- Share with the children the many activities on the *Faith First* Web site.
- Encourage the children to visit **www.FaithFirst.com.**

Before Moving On . . .

As you finish today's lesson, reflect on the following question before moving on to the next chapter.

What opportunities have I provided for the children to tell personal faith stories?

---

9 With My Family

This Week . . .

In chapter 9, "The Holy Spirit," your child learned about the Holy Spirit, the third Person of the Holy Trinity. The Father and Jesus sent us the Holy Spirit to be our helper and teacher. The Holy Spirit is the source of all the Church does. The Holy Spirit helps the whole Church learn what Jesus taught. The Holy Spirit helps all the baptized to pray and to live as children of God and followers of Christ.

For more on the teaching of the Catholic Church on the mystery of the Holy Spirit, see *Catechism of the Catholic Church* paragraph numbers 687–741.

Sharing God's Word

Read the Bible story in Acts 2:1–11, 22 about Pentecost or read the adaptation of the story on page 79. Emphasize that the Holy Spirit came to the disciples on Pentecost.

Praying

In this chapter your child prayed to the Holy Spirit. Read and pray together the prayer on page 83.

Making a Difference

Choose one of the following activities to do as a family or design a similar activity of your own.

- The Holy Spirit is our helper. Talk about ways you can help one another. Have each family member choose one thing they will do this week to be a helper.
- Make a banner with the words "Come, Holy Spirit." Decorate the banner and display it where it can remind everyone that the Holy Spirit is always with you as your helper.
- Use the prayer to the Holy Spirit on page 83 as your family prayer before meals or bedtime this week. Talk about how your family can call on the Holy Spirit to help your family grow as a Christian family.

For more ideas on ways your family can live your faith, visit the "Faith First for Families" page at **www.FaithFirst.com.** This week take the time to read an article from "Just for Parents."

84

Evaluate

Take a few moments to evaluate this week's lesson.
I feel (circle one) about this week's lesson.

    a. very pleased

    b. OK

    c. disappointed

The activity the children enjoyed most was . . .

The concept that was most difficult to teach was . . .

because . . .

Something I would like to do differently is . . .

ENRICHING THE LESSON

Making a Holy Spirit Display

Purpose
To reinforce that the Holy Spirit helps us to live as followers of Jesus (taught on page 80)

Directions
- Brainstorm with the children ways they could show that the love of the Holy Spirit is burning in their hearts.
- Have them write their names on one side of a flame made of colored construction paper and on the other side write their intentions.
- Tape the flames to a bulletin board display entitled "Come, Holy Spirit" or onto a piece of poster board.

Materials
construction paper and tape
pens or pencils
poster board or mural paper

Making a Holy Spirit Collage

Purpose
To reinforce that the Holy Spirit gives us gifts to use our talents to help others (taught on page 82)

Directions
Remind the children that we can see the Holy Spirit through actions of other people. Have the children make collages that show people using their talents to help others.
- Divide the children into groups of three. Have them look through magazines and newspapers for appropriate pictures.
- Have the children glue their pictures to a piece of art paper that you have labeled with the title "Holy Spirit People."
- Ask each group to describe their collage for the class.

Materials
art paper
magazines and newspapers
glue sticks

Literature Connection

Purpose
To reinforce the concept of the coming of the Holy Spirit on Pentecost (taught in chapter 9)

Directions
Use the picture book *Gilberto and the Wind* by Marie Hall (Puffin Books, 1978) to help the children unlock the concept of the Holy Spirit. In this perennial favorite, a young Brazilian boy learns about the wind by seeing its effects.
- Tell the story to the children, giving the group time to see all the pictures.
- Discuss the story by asking the children to name all the things the wind does. Point out that the wind moves, that it has power, and that it changes things.
- Point out that the Holy Spirit is like that. The Holy Spirit is with us, even though the Spirit cannot be seen. We can see the Holy Spirit through our good actions and those of others.

Materials
Gilberto and the Wind by Marie Hall

Music Connection
- "God Is a Part of My Life," by C. Landry. *Rise Up and Sing (RUS)* #185.
- "Send Us Your Spirit," by D. Haas. *Singing Our Faith (SOF)* #171.
- "Spirit-Friend" (Gonja folk song), acc. M. Haugen. *SOF* #177.
- "If You Believe and I Believe" (Zimbabwean traditional), arr. J. Bell. *SOF* #258.

The Church

Background

The People of God

Have you ever yearned for a community that transcends national boundaries, ethnic groupings, religious affiliation, or cultural background? Have you ever wished for a community that is dedicated to charity and caring, family-like support and loving-kindness? God has called such a community together in the name of Jesus, his Incarnate Son. As God first called the Israelites to be his people, he gathers a new People of God in Jesus, the new and everlasting Covenant.

The Church is the new People of God. The vocation of all members of the Church is to be salt of the earth and light of the world (see Matthew 5:13–16). In our families and workplaces and communities, our mission is to live Jesus' message of hope and love.

The Church is both the means and the goal of God's plan: prefigured in creation, prepared for in the Old Covenant, founded by the words and actions of Jesus Christ, fulfilled by his redeeming cross and his Resurrection, the Church has been manifested as the mystery of salvation by the outpouring of the Holy Spirit.

CATECHISM OF THE CATHOLIC CHURCH 778

The Body of Christ

The new People of God, or the Church, is the Body of Christ. Not only have we been gathered in his name, but we are one in him. When Saint Joan of Arc was put on trial, her judges asked about her beliefs in the Church. She replied: "About Jesus Christ and the Church, I simply know they're just one thing, and we shouldn't complicate the matter."

Christ and the Church make up the "whole Christ." Christ is the Head of the Church, his Body, and we are her members. We are one with Christ himself. Christ is present in us, uniting our sorrows with his Passover, helping us grow strong in him.

Mary shows us best what it means to be a member of the Body of Christ. She had unquestioning faith in God the Father and in her Son and opened her heart to the working of the Holy Spirit. When the darkness of Jesus' death clouded the disciples' vision, Mary gave them hope. Just as Mary stood at the foot of her Son's cross, she stands by us in our trials and suffering. She is our mother. She is the mother of the Church. United with Christ, the Head of the Church, her heart beats with our hearts. Her prayers join our prayers.

For Reflection

How does my being a member of the People of God affect my relationships with other people?

In what concrete and practical ways am I, a member of the Body of Christ, the Church, a sign of Christ present in the world?

Catechist to Catechist

Belonging

This is the age when the children will begin to feel more a part of the Church community. In addition to the fact that most of them will be receiving the Eucharist for the first time this year, they are now able to read and thus participate more fully in the responses and the singing at Mass. They have grown to better understand the concept of being part of the Church and helping one another.

Living Reminders of Jesus

Seven- and eight-year-olds are ready spiritually to become more active members of the Church. They have grown in their belief that God is

working in their lives. They see God as Someone whom they can love and with whom they can communicate. Their prayers are simple and beautifully honest and heartfelt. They bring an enthusiasm to the community and to its celebrations that reminds us that we are all members of the Body of Christ with unique and special gifts and talents to share.

The Church Teaches . . .

The *General Directory for Catechesis* reminds us:

Catechesis is an essentially ecclesial act.[1] The true subject of catechesis is the Church which, continuing the mission of Jesus the Master and, therefore animated by the Holy Spirit, is sent to be the teacher of the faith.   *GDC* 78

That is why *Faith First* puts much emphasis on the actions and mission of the Body of Christ, the Church.

See the Catechism . . .

For more on the teachings of the Catholic Church on Mary and the mystery of the Church, see *Catechism of the Catholic Church* 751–776, 781–801, and 874–993.

CATECHIST PRAYER

Lord, help me set my priorities by what is important in your sight. Let me always use the talents you have given me to join with the whole Church in doing your work.
Amen.

Footnote references may be found on p. 456.

LESSON PLANNER

Focus
To identify that the Church is the People of God, the Body of Christ, and the Communion of Saints

Engage

Page 85
Focus
To help the children identify the Church as a group we belong to

Pray Together
Discuss
We belong to many groups.

Teach and Apply

Pages 86–88
Focus
To discover what it means to say that the Church is the People of God, the Body of Christ, and the Communion of Saints

Presentation
Read, discuss, and summarize content.
Scripture
Psalm 33:12
Matthew 28:19–20
Activities
Say a prayer for your bishop.
Identify followers of Jesus.
Complete the Hail Mary.
Faith-Filled People
The Faithful

Connect

Pages 89–90
Focus
To appreciate that every member of the Church is important

Our Church Makes a Difference
Discover why and how the Church honors Mary and the saints.
Our Catholic Faith
Patron Saints

What Difference Does Faith Make?
Activity
Write about or draw something we can do as members of the Church.
Faith Choice
Choose one way to live as a member of the Church this week.

We Pray

Page 91
Prayer Form
Litany
Prayer
Introduce the prayer, and then pray the Litany of the Saints together.

We Remember

Review
• Mark the sentences that are true.
• Read the "To Help You Remember" statements aloud.
Preview
Preview the "With My Family" page.

Materials

pens and pencils

Enriching the Session

Blackline Masters
Additional Activities booklet:
Chapter 10
Drawing a picture to honor Mary
Inviting people to follow Jesus
Assessment Tools booklet:
Chapter 10 Test
Unit 1 Review
Faith First **Grade 2 Video**
Segment 2: "Mrs. Pockets' Story"
Segment 6: The Visual Bible™/ "Call of the First Disciples"
Enriching the Lesson (CG page 165)
A Helping Hands Mural
Creating Hand Gestures
Literature Connection
Music Connection (CG page 165)

www.FaithFirst.com

We update the *Faith First* Web site weekly. Check each week for new content and features. Here are some places to begin:

Catechists and Teachers
• Current Events
• Chapter Downloads
• Catechist Prayer

Faith First **for Families**
• Bible Stories
• Saints
• Make a Difference

Kids' Clubhouse
• *Faith First* Activities
• Chapter Reviews
• Games

Don't Forget! You can make lesson planning a breeze—check out the **Online Lesson Planner.**

The Church

We Pray

Blessed are those who God has chosen to be his own people.

Based on Psalm 33:12

Father, thank you for calling us to be your Church. Amen.

What groups do you belong to?

We belong to many groups. We belong to our families. We belong to a school. We belong to the Catholic Church.

Who belongs to the Catholic Church?

85

PRAY

- Have the children quiet themselves for prayer. Remind them that Jesus is with us as we pray.
- Begin with the Sign of the Cross.
- Invite a volunteer to read the Psalm verse based on Psalm 33:12.
- Pray the opening prayer together.
- Close the prayer with the Sign of the Cross.

DISCOVER

Purpose: To discover the children's knowledge and experience of the Church

- Have the children name a group they belong to and to share a good experience they have had in that group.
- Present the introductory paragraph and invite responses to the question "Who belongs to the Catholic Church?"

Background: Doctrine

The People of God. The Vatican II document on the Church described the Church as the new People of God. It teaches that grace is given to all the baptized and forms us into the new People of God. All people are called to belong to the People of God. As the People of God we are called to lives of love, and failure to put love into practice is a rejection of salvation itself (see *Dogmatic Constitution on the Church* [Lumen gentium], chapter 2).

Teach

Ask a volunteer to read the "Faith Focus" question. Share with the children that in this chapter they will learn more about the Church.

DISCOVER

- Explain that we belong to the Catholic Church. Invite the children to talk about some of the best things about belonging to the Church.
- Have the children follow along as you read aloud "The People of God."
- Ask them to listen for the name of the Church we belong to. Catholic Church.
- Ask a volunteer to read aloud a sentence that tells about the new People of God.
- Explain that the pope and bishops are the leaders of the Church. They take the place of the Apostles who were the leaders of the Church chosen by Jesus.

Apply

REINFORCE

Remind the children that the Holy Spirit invites all people to become disciples of Jesus. Ask a volunteer to read aloud the Scripture passage.

INTEGRATE

Lead the children in a short prayer asking the Holy Spirit to guide them.

Names for the Church

Faith Focus

What is the Church?

Faith Words

Body of Christ
The Church is the Body of Christ. Jesus Christ is the Head of the Church and all the baptized are its members.

Communion of Saints
The Church is the Communion of Saints. It is the communion of all the faithful followers of Jesus on earth and those who have died.

 Find out the name of your bishop. Say a prayer asking the Holy Spirit to help him serve the Church, the People of God.

The People of God

God sent Jesus to all people. Jesus told the Apostles to invite all people to become his followers. He said,

"Make all people to be my disciples. Baptize them and teach them all I taught you."
Based on Matthew 28:19–20

The Holy Spirit invites all people from every race and nation to become disciples of Jesus. The Church is the new People of God.

We are members of the Catholic Church. We become members of the Church at Baptism. God's people in the Catholic Church share the same faith and sacraments. We share the same leadership and help of the pope and the bishops. The pope and the bishops take the place of the Apostles in the Church today.

86

Teaching Tip

Teaching Difficult Concepts. Help the children distinguish between the whole Catholic Church (the Church led by the pope), their diocese (led by their bishop), and their parish (led by their pastor). To help make it clearer, draw a big circle on the board. Label it "The Catholic Church." Then draw a smaller circle within the larger circle. Label this "Diocese." Draw an even smaller circle within the diocese circle and label it "Our Parish." Take a few moments to review the circles and what they stand for. Help the children recognize the differences among the three communities of the Church.

The Body of Christ

The New Testament tells us the Church is the **Body of Christ.** The words "Body of Christ" help us to understand what the Church is.

All the parts of our body make up one body. Our eyes are different from our ears. Our brain is different from our heart. Every part of our body has something different and important to do.

The Church is the one Body of Christ. Jesus Christ is the Head of the Church. All the baptized are its members. All the members of the Church have something different and important to do. The Holy Spirit gives all members of the Church the grace to live as followers of Jesus.

On the lines under each picture write how the people are living as followers of Jesus.

Faith-Filled People

The Faithful

The members of the Church are called the faithful. Some members of the Church are bishops, priests, and deacons. Others are religious brothers and sisters. Others are married men and women. Others do not marry and remain single. Every member of the Church contributes in their own way to the work of the Church.

Responses will vary.

Affirm appropriate responses.

87

Background: Faith-Filled People

The Faithful. The vocation of bishops, priests, and deacons is to preach the Gospel, shepherd the faithful in unity, and celebrate divine worship. The vocation of laymen and laywomen is to give the light of Christ to the world wherever they live by the example of their lifestyle, prayer, and work. The vocation of religious men and religious women is to consecrate their entire lives to God by serving his people. All the People of God are called to live holy lives.

Teach

FOCUS

Remind the children that the Church is the new People of God who follow Jesus. Tell them they are going to learn a new way of naming the people who belong to the Church.

DISCOVER

- Talk with the children about how our eyes and ears, our hearts, and our brains are different but each has an important job to do in our bodies.
- Have the children follow along as you read the last paragraph on page 87.
- Invite volunteers to explain in their own words that the Church is the Body of Christ. Commend them on their good listening skills.
- Present "Faith-Filled People" about the faithful. Remind the children that all members of the Church are called to contribute in their own way to the work of the Church.

Apply

REINFORCE

- Ask a volunteer to read aloud the definition of *Body of Christ* in "Faith Words."
- Ask the children to make a word card for this word.

INTEGRATE

Direct the children to look at the pictures and suggest how the people in the pictures are living as followers of Jesus. Then ask them to write what they can do.

Teach

FOCUS

We know now that the Church is the People of God and the Body of Christ. Tell the children they are going to learn another name for the Church.

DISCOVER

Invite a volunteer to read aloud the first paragraph to discover who the Communion of Saints includes.

Apply

REINFORCE

- Have the children turn back to page 86 and read the definition of *Communion of Saints* in "Faith Words." Have them make a word card for this word.
- Ask the children who they know who belongs to the Communion of Saints. Affirm all appropriate responses.

INTEGRATE

Tell the children that Mary is the greatest saint of heaven. Discuss ways that families sometimes show their love for Mary. Use this opportunity to review the Hail Mary by completing the activity. Encourage the children to pray the Hail Mary several times every day.

The Communion of Saints

The Church is the **Communion of Saints**. The Church includes all the followers of Jesus who live on earth. It also includes all the saints in heaven. Saints are those who love God and others with their whole heart.

Mary is the greatest saint. She is the mother of Jesus, the Son of God. She is the Mother of God. Jesus told us that Mary is the mother of all his followers too. Mary is the mother of the Church.

ACTIVITY *Write the name Mary on the blank lines. Honor Mary as the Mother of God and as your mother. Pray the Hail Mary.*

The Hail Mary

Hail _____ Mary _____, full of grace,

the Lord is with you!

Blessed are you among women,

and blessed is the fruit of your womb, Jesus.

Holy _____ Mary _____, Mother of God,

pray for us sinners,

now and at the hour of our death. Amen.

88

Background: Doctrine

Mary, Our Mother. Mary is the greatest saint. Millions of girls are given her name at birth. Thousands of churches are dedicated to her. Popular devotions to Mary span the centuries. Her exceptional faith inspires us. When we pray the Hail Mary, we honor Mary because she is "full of grace." Mary shared in God's life and love in a unique way. God the Father chose her to be the mother of his Son, Jesus. Mary is the Mother of God. Have the children slowly recite the Hail Mary, pausing on the phrase "full of grace." Ask the children: What is grace? Emphasize that grace is both sharing in God's life and love and the help he gives us to live holy lives.

Honoring Mary and the Saints

Mary

The Church honors Mary and the saints. This means that we have a special love for Mary and all the saints who now live with God in heaven.

The Church shows our love of Mary and the saints in many ways. We name certain days to honor them. We pray to Mary and the saints. We create statues of Mary and the other saints. Statues remind us of these people who are dear to us. We paint pictures and write songs about saints.

All these things help us to love God and other people with our whole heart. They help us to live as saints.

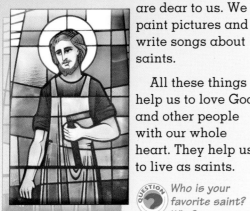
Saint Joseph

Our Catholic Faith

Patron Saints

Patron saints pray for us and help us to live as followers of Jesus. Parish churches, students, other groups of people, and even countries have patron saints.

Saint Anne and Mary

QUESTION *Who is your favorite saint? Why?*

Responses will vary.
Affirm appropriate responses.

89

HIGHLIGHT

Share with the children that they are going to learn how the Church honors Mary and the saints.

DISCOVER

- Ask the children to share what they know about Mary.
- Invite them to read the first paragraph to find out why the Church honors Mary and the saints.
- Invite volunteers to read the next two paragraphs to discover how the Church honors Mary and the saints.
- Present "Our Catholic Faith" about patron saints. Tell the children that a patron saint is someone who prays for us and our needs. Point out that we all have a patron saint for whom we were named at Baptism.

INTEGRATE

Share with the children about your favorite saint and the reason why that saint is your favorite. Ask the children about favorite saints they may know about.

Teaching Tip

Images of Mary. Explain to the children that no one knows what Mary actually looked like since she lived long before cameras were invented. Although it might have been possible that someone drew Mary's image, it is not very likely. The paintings and sculptures we have of Mary are the expressions of the artists' and sculptors' love of Mary. Invite the children to use their imaginations to create pictures of Mary. Emphasize that they can picture Mary any way they want as long as their drawings show reverence for her as the mother of Jesus. When the children have completed their drawings, post them in an area where others can enjoy them.

Connect

Remind the children that each member of the Church is important.

RESPOND

- Explain the directions for the activity to the children.
- Give them time to complete the activity and let them share their work with a partner.

CHOOSE

Have the children read "My Faith Choice" and write their decisions. Encourage them to put their choices into practice this week.

What Difference Does Faith Make in My Life?

You are an important member of the Church. The Holy Spirit helps you to be a follower of Jesus.

Write or draw something you can do together with the Church. Live your faith in God and Jesus.

I Am a Member of the Church

Responses will vary.

Affirm appropriate responses.

My Faith Choice

This week I will live as a member of the Church. I will

Affirm appropriate responses.

_____

_____

90

Teaching Tip

Church Leaders and Helpers. When talking about the gifts and talents we use for God's work, take the time to talk with the children about the work of priests, religious brothers and sisters, missionaries, and other parish ministers. Consider inviting one of these ministers to speak to the children about the kind of work he or she does for God. Encourage the children to ask any questions they may have.

We Pray

The Litany of the Saints

A litany is one kind of prayer the Church prays. When we pray a litany, we repeat one part over and over again. Here is part of the Litany of the Saints.

Leader	All
Holy Mary, Mother of God	pray for us.
Saint Joseph	pray for us.
Saint John the Baptist	pray for us.
Saint Mary Magdalene	pray for us.
Saint Anne	pray for us.
Saint Agnes	pray for us.
Saint Francis of Assisi	pray for us.
Saint Teresa of Avila	pray for us.
All holy men and women	pray for us.

We Remember

Color the box to mark the sentences that are true.

- ■ Jesus gave us the Church.

- ■ Jesus told the disciples to invite all people to become his disciples.

- ■ Jesus Christ is the Head of the Church.

- ■ Mary is the greatest saint of the Church.

To Help You Remember

1. The Church is the People of God who follow Jesus Christ.
2. The Church is the Body of Christ.
3. The Church is the Communion of Saints.

Pray

WE PRAY

- Gather the children in the prayer center. Remind them of the structure of a litany.
- Tell the children that this litany calls upon some of the well-known saints of the Church and invites them to pray for us.
- Practice the response.
- Lead the children in praying "The Litany of the Saints."

Review

WE REMEMBER

- Draw a circle on the board and write the word *Church* inside it.
- Using the "To Help You Remember" statements, help the children recall three phrases that describe the people who belong to the Church.
- Have the children complete the review activity by marking the sentences that are true.

Teaching Tip

Reviewing Faith Choices. As you complete this first unit have the children think about the faith choices they made in the chapters. Have them identify those choices they have successfully implemented. Invite volunteers to share success stories. Include everyone who wants to share his or her story. Affirm everyone for striving to put their choices into practice.

At Home

ENCOURAGE

Have the children carefully tear out pages 91 and 92 along the perforation. Encourage the children to share the pages with their families and to do the activities together. If they have not completed the review activity on page 91 by the end of the session, emphasize that they can complete it with their families.

VISIT FAITHFIRST.COM

- Share with the children the many activities on the *Faith First* Web site.
- Encourage the children to visit **www.FaithFirst.com.**

Before Moving On . . .

As you finish today's lesson, reflect on the following question before moving on to the next chapter.

How well have I modeled affirming comments and behaviors that I would like the children to use with one another?

---

10 With My Family

This Week . . .

In chapter 10, "The Church," your child learned about the Church. The Church is the community of people God gathers together in Christ. The Church is the People of God, the Body of Christ, and the Communion of Saints. Mary is the greatest saint and the mother of the Church. All of the baptized have important roles to play in the work of the Church.

For more on the teachings of the Catholic Church on Mary and the mystery of the Church, see *Catechism of the Catholic Church* paragraph numbers 751–776, 781–801, and 874–993.

Sharing God's Word

Read together the Bible story in Matthew 28:19–20 about Jesus commanding the Apostles to make disciples of all people or read the adaptation of the story on page 86. Emphasize that the Church today continues the work Jesus gave to the first disciples.

Praying

In this chapter your child prayed part of the Litany of the Saints. Read and pray together the prayer on page 91.

Making a Difference

Choose one of the following activities to do as a family or design a similar activity of your own.

- The Church is called the Body of Christ. Every member of the Church has an important role in doing the work of the Church. Talk about how your family lives as members of the Body of Christ and takes part in the work of the Church.

- Jesus invites all of us to be his followers. If Jesus were to spend a day with your family, what would you want to do and why? Be sure to let everyone share their ideas.

- Mary is the mother of the Church. Use the Hail Mary on page 88 as your family prayer this week. Pray it before meals or bedtime.

For more ideas on ways your family can live your faith, visit the "Faith First for Families" page at **www.FaithFirst.com.** Click on "Saints" and discover other faith-filled people of the Church.

92

Evaluate

Take a few moments to evaluate this week's lesson.
I feel (circle one) about this week's lesson.

a. very pleased
b. OK
c. disappointed

The activity the children enjoyed most was . . .

The concept that was most difficult to teach was . . .

because . . .

Something I would like to do differently is . . .

Catechist to Catechist

Our Church Home

When taking part in Mass and other Church celebrations, we should feel at home and able to participate easily and comfortably. To do this we need to understand what is happening and what is expected of us. Teaching children the basic words and actions of Catholic worship will allow them to celebrate with joy rather than watch with anxiety.

The Language of the People

One of the characteristics of Catholic worship is the constancy of the words and actions from day to day and from place to place. As we attend different Catholic churches to  worship, we need to accept and appreciate the small differences, legitimately recognized by the Church, that "manifest the catholicity of the Church, because they signify and communicate the same mystery of Christ" (*Catechism of the Catholic Church* 1208).

The Church Teaches . . .

The *General Directory for Catechesis* places great importance on liturgical formation.

> Liturgical formation . . . must explain what the Christian liturgy is, and what the sacraments are. It must also however, offer an experience of the different kinds of celebration and it must make symbols, gestures, etc. known and loved. *GDC* 87

That is why *Faith First* includes liturgical celebrations and prayer experiences as a regular part of its curriculum.

See the Catechism . . .

For more on the teachings of the Catholic Church on worship and the sacraments, see *Catechism of the Catholic Church* 1066–1186.

CATECHIST PRAYER

Lord, I know the children will learn much more from what I do than what I say. So please, Lord, guide me to be a good example. Amen.

Footnote references on these two pages may be found on p. 456.

LESSON PLANNER

Engage

Page 97
Focus
To help the children recall how the Church celebrates

Opening Prayer

Discussion
Where have you had some of your best celebrations?

Teach and Apply

Pages 98–100
Focus
To appreciate that the Church uses words and actions in the seven sacraments

Presentation
Read, discuss, and summarize content.
Scripture
• Psalm 67:4
• Mark 5:22–24, 39, 41–42
Activities
• Draw or write about something Jesus said or did.
• Identify the actions in the pictures as celebrations of the Church.
• Identify the sacraments that you have already received.
Faith-Filled People
Saint Mark the Evangelist

Connect

Pages 101–102
Focus
To discover some of the words and actions the Church uses to worship God

Our Church Makes a Difference
Identify some words and actions the Church uses in celebration of the sacraments.
Our Catholic Faith
Sacramentals

What Difference Does Faith Make?
Activity
Finish the prayer and pray it with actions.
Faith Choice
Pray using both words and actions.

We Pray

Page 103
Prayer Form
Prayer of praise and thanksgiving
Prayer
Introduce the prayer. Choose a leader. Hold hands, and then pray together.

We Remember

Review
• Complete the sentences.
• Read the "To Help You Remember" statements aloud.
Preview
Preview the "With My Family" page.

Materials

• pens or pencils
• crayons or markers

Enriching the Session

Blackline Masters
Additional Activities booklet:
Chapter 11
Growing as a child of God
Sharing feelings about a miracle
Assessment Tools booklet:
Chapter 11 Test
Faith First **Grade 2 Video**
Segment 4: Bible Songs
Enriching the Lesson (CG page 181)
Retelling a Scripture Story
Preparing a Skit
Making a Booklet
Music Connection (CG page 181)

www.FaithFirst.com

We update the *Faith First* Web site weekly. Check each week for new content and features. Here are some places to begin:

Catechists and Teachers
• Current Events
• Chapter Downloads
• Catechist Prayer

Faith First **for Families**
• Bible Stories
• Saints
• Make a Difference

Kids' Clubhouse
• *Faith First* Activities
• Chapter Reviews
• Games

Don't Forget! You can make lesson planning a breeze—check out the **Online Lesson Planner.**

We Worship God

11

We Pray

Our LORD and God, may all people praise you.

Based on Psalm 67:4

God our loving Father, we worship you in the name of Jesus Christ.   Amen.

What are some of the things you do and say when you celebrate?

We celebrate special times in our lives. Catholics gather to celebrate our love for God and one another. We use special words and actions.

What are some of the words and actions the Church uses in its celebrations?

97

Teaching About Prayer and Worship

Point out that the formal prayers of the Church that we pray are not the only way of showing God our love and gratefulness. We give glory and praise to God by the way we act each day toward others and use the talents he has given us.

PRAY

- Have the children quiet themselves for prayer.
- Pray the Sign of the Cross together.
- Read Psalm 67:4 and invite the children to echo each phrase after you.
- Lead the opening prayer and invite all to pray it with you
- Conclude by praying the Sign of the Cross together.

DISCOVER

Purpose: To discover what the children already know about the celebrations of the Catholic Church

- Ask the children to share some of the things they say and do when they celebrate a special occasion.
- Have volunteers share what they think is happening in the picture. The people and the priest are greeting one another before or after Mass. Affirm all appropriate responses.
- Ask the children to share the kinds of celebrations they have been to at church.

Teach

FOCUS

Ask a volunteer to read the "Faith Focus" question on page 98 aloud. Tell the children they are going to learn more about words and actions Jesus used.

DISCOVER

- Explain that the Scripture story of Jesus and Jairus' daughter is one example of how Jesus used words and actions to do his saving work.
- Read the story of Jairus' daughter.
- Ask what action Jesus used to make the little girl better. He took the girl's hand. What words did Jesus say? "Little girl, I say to you, arise!"
- Point out that the words and actions of Jesus were signs of God's love.

Apply

REINFORCE

Write three sentences on the board that tell the beginning, the middle, and the end of the story. Ask volunteers to put the sentences in order.

INTEGRATE

- Invite the children to read the directions for the activity and then complete the activity on their own.
- Have the children share their work with a friend.

The Church Worships God

Faith Focus

How does our Church worship God?

Faith Words

worship
Worship means to honor and love God above all else.

sacraments
The sacraments are the seven signs of God's love for us that Jesus gave the Church. We share in God's love when we celebrate the sacraments.

Words and Actions of Jesus

Jesus used words and actions to show God's love for us. One time Jairus came to Jesus. Jairus was a religious leader who had great faith in God. Jairus asked Jesus to help his daughter who was very sick. Read what happened next.

Jesus and his disciples followed Jairus to his house. Jesus entered the house and went over to the daughter of Jairus. Jesus took her by the hand and said, "Little girl, I say to you, arise!" The girl got up immediately and walked around.
Based on Mark 5:22–24, 38, 41–42

People came to believe in Jesus. They came to believe that Jesus is the Son of God.

 In the box draw or write about something Jesus did or said. Tell how it helps us to believe and trust in God.

Responses will vary.

98

Teaching Tip

Challenging Questions. Children sometimes ask challenging questions. It is perfectly all right to tell the children you aren't sure of an answer but that you will be glad to find out the answer for them. This models what they themselves will often have to do in life. After you find the answer, share your findings with the children and explain where you found it, such as from your pastor or religious education director, the *Catechism of the Catholic Church*, the *Catholic Encyclopedia*, and so on. Make sure all print sources have the Nihil Obstat and Imprimatur, which affirm that the materials are free of doctrinal or moral error.

The Church Uses Words and Actions

God loves us very much. One way we show our love for God is to **worship** him. We use words and actions to worship God. We honor and love God above all else. Our words and actions tell God we believe in him, hope in him, and love him.

When we worship God, we listen to God. We give adoration to God and praise him. We pray aloud and we sing. We stand and sit and walk in procession.

QUESTION *Which of these pictures do you recognize as celebrations of the Church? Tell what is happening in each picture.*
All pictures are Church celebrations: from top to bottom, they show the sacrament of Reconciliation, the Mass, and Holy Communion at Mass.

99

Background: Faith-Filled People

Saint Mark. Around the year A.D. 60, Mark wrote a vivid account of the life and death of Jesus. He wrote in Greek for the Gentiles who converted to Christianity. During that time the Church was enduring great persecution. The key points of Mark's Gospel are an attempt to understand the humanity of Jesus and his suffering and death. Tradition says that Mark died as a martyr in Alexandria, Egypt. The symbol of Mark's Gospel is a winged lion. The lion is a desert animal that symbolizes the regal power of Christ. The feast of Saint Mark is celebrated on April 25.

Teach

FOCUS
Tell the children they are going to learn about some of the words and actions the Church uses to worship God.

DISCOVER
- Ask the children to name some ways they show that they love their families. Answers will vary.
- Tell the children that their answers included both words and actions. Explain that the Church uses words and actions to worship God.
- Write the word *worship* on the board. Ask children to recall different ways that we worship God. Jot their answers on the board. Have them read the last paragraph silently to check their answers.
- Read "Faith-Filled People" about Saint Mark to the children.

Apply

REINFORCE
Summarize the main points of the text about worship. Invite the children to read aloud the word *worship* in "Faith Words" and its meaning. Have the children make a word card for this term.

INTEGRATE
Invite the children to do the activity at the bottom of the page. Ask several volunteers to share their ideas.

Teach

FOCUS

Remind the children that Jesus' words and actions show us God's love. Point out that the Church celebrates seven special signs of God's love. These seven signs of God's love are called the sacraments.

DISCOVER

- Invite volunteers to share their understanding of what the sacraments are.
- Explain that Jesus is really present with us when we celebrate the sacraments.
- Have volunteers read the description of each sacrament.
- Ask the children to name the sacraments they have already celebrated.

Apply

REINFORCE

Ask a volunteer to turn to page 98 and read the definition of *sacraments* in "Faith Words." Have them make a word card for this term.

INTEGRATE

- Have the children look again at the boxes on this page that describe the sacraments.
- Invite them to place a check mark in the boxes for the sacraments they have already celebrated.

The Seven Sacraments

Jesus gave the Church a special way to worship. He gave the Church the seven **sacraments.** The seven sacraments are signs of God's love for us. Jesus is really present with us when we celebrate the sacraments. The Holy Spirit helps us to celebrate the sacraments. When we celebrate the sacraments, we share in God's love.

ACTIVITY *Place a ✔ in the box next to the sacraments you have received or have seen others receive.* Responses will vary.

☐ **Baptism**
We are joined to Jesus and become a part of his Church.

☐ **Confirmation**
The Holy Spirit helps us to live as children of God.

☐ **Eucharist**
We receive the Body and Blood of Jesus.

☐ **Reconciliation**
We receive God's gift of forgiveness and peace.

☐ **Anointing of the Sick**
We receive God's healing strength when we are sick or dying.

☐ **Holy Orders**
A baptized man is called by God to serve the Church as a bishop, priest, or deacon.

☐ **Matrimony**
A baptized man and a baptized woman make a lifelong promise to love and respect each other.

100

Teaching Tip

One way we can help the children grow to know God's love for them is by praying a prayer of blessing for them. Remind the children that the priest at the end of Masses asks God to bless us. Before dismissing the children, pray this prayer of blessing with your hands folded together:

> The Lord bless you and keep you!
> The Lord let his face shine upon you, and be gracious to you!
> The Lord look upon you kindly and give you peace!

End the blessing by tracing a cross on each child's head.

Our Church Makes a Difference

Sacrament Words and Actions

The Church uses certain words and actions when we celebrate the sacraments. These words and actions help us to understand what is happening.

We are baptized with water. We are blessed with oil. We offer and share bread and wine. We bless and receive blessings. We make promises.

All the words and actions we use in the sacraments show that God is sharing his love with us. They help us to give thanks and praise to God for all he has done for us.

QUESTION *What words and actions do you use to worship God?* Affirm appropriate responses.

Our Catholic Faith

Sacramentals

The Church uses objects and blessings, words and actions to help us worship God. These are called sacramentals. Holy water is one of the sacramentals the Church gives us. We bless ourselves with holy water. This reminds us of Baptism and that we are children of God.

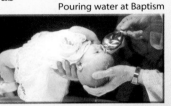
Pouring water at Baptism

Bringing up bread and wine at Eucharist

Anointing with oil at Confirmation

101

HIGHLIGHT

Point out that the Church uses special words and actions in the celebration of the sacraments.

DISCOVER

- Invite volunteers to read "Sacrament Words and Actions." Ask the children to listen for actions that help us worship God.
- Present "Our Catholic Faith" about sacramentals.
- Place rosaries, crucifixes, and holy water in the prayer area as examples of sacramentals. Tell the children that blessings are sacramentals too.

INTEGRATE

Encourage the children to think of a way that they use one of the sacramentals that you placed in the prayer center. Example: When they use holy water to bless themselves, they recall their Baptism and their faith in the Holy Trinity.

Teaching Tip

The use of sacramentals at home is not as widespread as it was in the past. For example, holy water fonts at the doorways of rooms, crucifixes on display, and the rosary prayed together every evening or once a week were more common. Display and use the sacramentals the Church has given us during your sessions. Especially use the sacramentals that are used in the liturgical celebrations of the Church.

Connect

HIGHLIGHT

Our words and actions can be a sign that helps others come to know God's love.

RESPOND

- Present the opening paragraph in your own words.
- Discuss "Praying with Actions" and invite the children to finish each line of the prayer.
- When everyone is finished, have them practice the actions and use them as they pray together.

CHOOSE

Have the children read "My Faith Choice" and write their decisions. Encourage them to put their choices into practice this week.

Your words and actions can be signs of God's love. Your words and actions can help people believe and trust in God's love.

We use many different actions when we pray. Finish each line of the prayer. Pray your prayer with the actions. Responses will vary.

Praying with Actions

With hands outstretched I ask you, God, for

_____.

With bowed head I thank you, God, for

_____.

With folded hands I praise you, God, for

_____.

With hands raised high, I show my love for you, O God! Amen.

My Faith Choice

This week I will pray using both words and actions. I will say my prayer

☐ in the morning. ☐ after school.

☐ at dinnertime. ☐ at bedtime.

102

✝ Liturgy Tip

Gestures in Prayer. When we pray, we use gestures that express our reverence toward God. Special meaning is given to our prayers when we use such gestures as folded hands, bowing, and genuflecting. Have the children name gestures they use when they pray. List them on the board and add some of your own. Then have the children tell when or with what prayers they use gestures. Write their responses next to the gestures on the list.

We Pray

We Pray as God's Family

Holding hands when we pray shows we believe we belong to the family of God. Form a circle, hold hands, and pray this prayer.

Leader: Let us pray together as God's family. We are your children, God. We love you.

All: **We love you, God.**

Leader: We are your children, God.

All: **Thank you, God, for your blessings.**

We Remember

Complete the sentences, using the words below.

sacraments	actions	love

To Help You Remember

1. We worship God by using words and actions.
2. We worship God when we celebrate the sacraments.
3. The Holy Spirit helps us to celebrate the sacraments and worship God.

1. The words and actions of Jesus helped people to know God's

_____ love _____.

2. We share in God's love when we

celebrate the _____ sacraments _____.

3. The Church uses words and

_____ actions _____ to worship God.

Grade 2 • Chapter 11 (103)

✝ Liturgy Tip

Children's Participation in Prayer. Children can take on various roles in prayer. Children can serve as prayer leaders from time to time. Be sure to prepare them for their role. Let them know a week ahead of time, or at least at the beginning of class, so they have time to rehearse their lines. Teach them simple gestures such as raising a hand to indicate to others when they are to join in a response. Other children can take the part of readers of Scripture passages. Children can also be divided into groups to make different prayer responses.

Pray

WE PRAY

- Gather the children in the prayer center. Remind them that we are a community of faith when we pray together.
- Tell them that as a sign that we are a community of faith we will stand, form a circle, and hold hands as we pray.
- Point out the responses to the children and rehearse them.
- Lead the prayer.

Review

WE REMEMBER

- On separate paper strips, write the words *worship, celebrate,* and *Holy Spirit.* Prepare enough strips so that there is one for every child. Hand one of the strips to each child.
- Write the three "To Help You Remember" statements on the board, leaving out the key words on the strips.
- Read each statement aloud, leaving out the key words.
- Invite each child who has the missing word to come to the front of the room and hold up the strips for all to see.
- Have the rest of the class say the word and then read the complete sentence together.
- Explain the review activity and allow time for all to finish.

At Home

ENCOURAGE

Have the children carefully tear out pages 103 and 104 along the perforation. Encourage the children to share the pages with their families and to do the activities together. If they did not complete the review activity on page 103 by the end of the session, emphasize that they can complete it with their families.

VISIT FAITHFIRST.COM

- Share with the children the many activities on the *Faith First* Web site.
- Encourage the children to visit **www.FaithFirst.com.**

---

11 With My Family

This Week . . .

In chapter 11, "We Worship God," your child learned about worshiping God. By listening to and thinking about the Gospel story of Jairus's daughter (Mark 5:41–42), your child discovered that the words and actions of Jesus helped people come to believe and trust in God and in God's love for us. The Church uses special words and actions to celebrate the sacraments. Through the celebration of the sacraments we worship God and we are made sharers in the life and love of God.

For more on the teaching of the Catholic Church on worship and the sacraments, see *Catechism of the Catholic Church* paragraph numbers 1066–1186.

Sharing God's Word

Read together the Bible story in Mark 5:41–42 about Jesus healing the daughter of Jairus or read the adaptation of the story on page 98. Emphasize that Jesus healed people to show them God's love.

Praying

In this chapter your child prayed using the gesture of holding hands. Read and pray together the prayer on page 103.

Making a Difference

Choose one of the following activities to do as a family or design a similar activity of your own.

- Talk about the sacraments that each family member has received. What words and actions do you remember from the celebration of each sacrament? Discuss the meaning of those words and actions.
- Name the people in your parish who are signs of God's love for your family. Tell how they are signs of God's love.
- Body language and gestures help us pray. This week hold hands when you pray as a family. Remember that you all belong to God's family as well as your family.

For more ideas on ways your family can live your faith, visit the "Faith First for Families" page at **www.FaithFirst.com.** Click on "Games" and make learning fun for your child.

104

Evaluate

Take a few moments to evaluate this week's lesson.
I feel (circle one) about this week's lesson.

    a. very pleased
    b. OK
    c. disappointed

The activity the children enjoyed most was . . .

The concept that was most difficult to teach was . . .

because . . .

Something I would like to do differently is . . .

Before Moving On . . .

As you finish today's lesson, reflect on the following question before moving on to the next chapter.

What do I do to encourage and affirm the sense of humor I see in some of the children?

ENRICHING THE LESSON

Retelling Scripture Stories

Purpose

To reinforce the story of Jairus's daughter (taught on page 98)

Directions

Young children enjoy a variety of ways to retell Scripture stories.

- Divide the class into groups of three. Ask one child to be Jairus, another Jesus, and the third Jairus's daughter.
- Allow each group to practice retelling the story using their person.
- Have the groups present their retellings. After each presentation have the children give a silent cheer for each group.

Materials

Preparing Skits About Trust

Purpose

To reinforce that through our words and actions we show our love for God (taught on page 99)

Directions

Remind the children that our words and actions in everything we do show our love for God.

- Brainstorm with the children all the different activities they do during the week. Make a list of these on the board.
- In partners, have the children prepare a skit demonstrating how through the words and actions of one of these activities they show their love for God.
- Have the children present their skits and discuss other ways they can show their love for God.

Materials

Making a Sacrament Booklet

Purpose

To reinforce the words and actions of the sacraments (taught on page 101).

Directions

To prepare for this activity take four pieces of construction paper and staple them together on the short side. Make one booklet for each child.

- Pass out the booklets and have the children write *My Sacrament Booklet* in the center of the top cover sheet. Have them print their names in the corner.
- Have the children write the names of the seven sacraments on the back of the cover sheet. Tell them they can turn to page 101 to recall the names of the sacraments.
- Invite the children to look on page 101 in their books and draw something they know about one of the sacraments.
- Remind the children that as they work through the chapters in Unit 2 they will write and draw many more words and actions in their booklets.
- Collect the sacrament booklets and store them for the children.

Materials

booklets for each child
pencils, crayons or markers

Music Connection

- "Take the Word of God with You," C. Walker. *Rise Up and Sing (RUS)* #187.
- "Jesus' Hands Were Kind Hands," (Old French melody). *Singing Our Faith (SOF)* #170.
- "Friends, All Gather 'Round," J. Doucet/ C. Landry. *SOF* #233.
- "We Come to Your Table," C. Landry. *SOF* #237.

We Celebrate Baptism and Confirmation

Background

Baptism

The sacraments are rich in importance and inspiration for Catholics. They accompany us through all the stages and transitions in our lives. Baptism is the gateway to all the other sacraments. Baptism joins us to Christ and incorporates us into the Church. We receive the gift of the Holy Spirit, new life in Christ, and become adopted sons and daughters of God the Father. Through Baptism we are made sharers in the divine plan of salvation. Original sin and all personal sins are forgiven. An indelible sign, or character, is marked on the soul of the newly baptized, identifying us as belonging to Christ forever.

The most expressive way to be baptized is by triple immersion into the sacred water. Three times we enter into the water and rise from it to new life. This signifies our baptism into the death and Resurrection of Christ. However, from its earliest days, the Church has also used the rite of a triple pouring of water over the head as an expression of a person's being baptized. In both Baptism by immersion and by the pouring of water, the celebrant baptizes as Christ commanded, "In the name of the Father, and of the Son, and of the Holy Spirit" (see Matthew 28:19).

You might ask, "Is Baptism by water the only form of Baptism? Does a person have to be baptized in water to be saved?" The answer is no. A person who truly desires to be baptized and does not have the opportunity to receive the sacrament can be saved through the baptism of desire. The Church also teaches that those who have not come to know and believe in Christ and who sincerely seek God and strive to lead a virtuous life can be saved even though they have not been baptized. God loves all people and desires all to live in communion with him forever.

Confirmation

Confirmation perfects the graces of Baptism. Sealed with the gift of the Holy Spirit in Confirmation, the baptized are united more firmly to Christ and the Church and strengthened with the gifts of the Holy Spirit. We are confirmed to be faithful witnesses to the word planted in us at Baptism. (See *Catechism of the Catholic Church* 1302–1305.) As Baptism does, Confirmation seals our souls with a spiritual mark and thus can only be received once.

Baptism and Confirmation are ordered to participation in the Eucharist, which is the third Sacrament of Christian Initiation. Eucharist unites us most fully with Christ and the members of the Body of Christ, the Church. (See *Catechism of the Catholic Church* 1275.)

For Reflection

When I reflect on my initiation into Christ and the Church, what is my most vivid memory?

What does this memory say to me about my identity?

Catechist to Catechist

Belonging to God's Family

Most of the children in your group probably were baptized as infants and have no recollection of their Baptism. Some may have experienced the Baptism of family members or have been present at a parish baptismal celebration. It is important to help the children understand just how they became Catholics.

Sacraments of Christian Initiation

To belong, to be a part of something, to be welcomed, are all human cravings that last a lifetime. In the sacraments of Baptism and Confirmation and the Eucharist we are joined to Christ and are initiated into the Church. As the children come to better understand the Sacraments of Christian Initiation, they will be able to respond in a more complete way to the graces of these sacraments.

The Church Teaches . . .

Sharing the Light of Faith: National Catechical Directory for Catechesis (1974) states:

> [C]atechesis has the task of preparing individuals and communities for knowing, active, and fruitful liturgical and sacramental celebration. . . . The liturgy and sacraments are the supreme celebration of the paschal mystery. They express the sanctification of human life . . . [and] accomplish the saving acts which they symbolize.　　*NCD* 44

This year the children will grow in their awareness and understanding of the sacraments and gain a deeper appreciation for the celebrations of the Catholic Church.

See the Catechism . . .

For more on the teachings of the Catholic Church on the sacraments of Baptism and Confirmation, see *Catechism of the Catholic Church* 1210–1274 and 1285–1314.

CATECHIST PRAYER

Lord, I am so blessed to have been received into the Catholic Church. I have the sacraments to celebrate your presence in my life. May my life itself be a daily thank-you for these blessings. Amen.

LESSON PLANNER

Focus To recognize Baptism and Confirmation as two sacraments of welcome in which we receive the gift of the Holy Spirit

Engage

Page 105
Focus
To help the children express what they know about the sacraments of Baptism and Confirmation

Opening Prayer

Discussion
When a person is baptized, it is a happy day for our Church family.

Teach and Apply

Pages 106–108
Focus
To recognize Baptism and Confirmation as two of the three Sacraments of Christian Initiation

Presentation
Read, discuss, and summarize content.
Scripture
• Psalm 36:10
Activities
• Complete the prayer.
• Describe the actions in the pictures.
• Complete the word puzzle.
Faith-Filled People
Cornelius

Connect

Pages 109–110
Focus
To describe ways the Church shares in God's love

Our Church Makes a Difference
Discover the special way some young children share God's love with other people.
Our Catholic Faith
Baptismal candle

What Difference Does Faith Make?
Activity
Write words on the path that tell about living a holy life.
Faith Choice
Identify a way to live a holy life this week.

We Pray

Page 111
Prayer Form
Prayer of praise and blessing
Prayer
Choose a leader, and then pray together.

We Remember

Review
• Complete the word search activity.
• Read the "To Help You Remember" statements aloud.
Preview
Highlight features of the "With My Family" page.

Materials

pens or pencils

Enriching the Session

Blackline Masters
Additional Activities booklet:
Chapter 12
Interviewing someone about Baptism
Illustrating your Baptism
Assessment Tools booklet:
Chapter 12 Test
Enriching the Lesson (CG page 193)
Welcoming the Newly Baptized
Staging a Baptism Role Play
Lights for the World
Music Connection (CG page 193)

www.FaithFirst.com

We update the *Faith First* Web site weekly. Check each week for new content and features. Here are some places to begin:

Catechists and Teachers
• Current Events
• Chapter Downloads
• Catechist Prayer
Faith First for Families
• Bible Stories
• Saints
• Make a Difference
Kids' Clubhouse
• *Faith First* Activities
• Chapter Reviews
• Games

Don't Forget! You can make lesson planning a breeze—check out the **Online Lesson Planner.**

We Celebrate Baptism and Confirmation

We Pray

LORD, you are the fountain of life.
Based on Psalm 36:10

Praise to you, almighty God. You created water to give us life. **Amen.**

Why is it a happy time for a family to welcome a new baby?

When someone is baptized, the person becomes a member of the Church. It is a happy day for our Church family.

What do you see and hear at Baptism?

(105)

PRAY

- Have the children quiet themselves for prayer. Remind them that Jesus is with us when we gather to pray.
- Pray the Sign of the Cross together.
- Proclaim the Psalm verse.
- Lead the opening prayer, having the children echo each phrase after you.
- Conclude by praying the Sign of the Cross.

DISCOVER

Purpose: To discover what the children may already know about the sacraments of Baptism and Confirmation

- Ask the children to describe what is happening in the picture. A young boy is being baptized.
- Point out that not all people are baptized when they are infants.
- Summarize the introductory paragraph. Ask the second question and talk with the children about Baptism.

Teaching Tip

Baptismal Stories. Send home a short note asking the parents to show their child their baptismal garment and candle and photos of the special day if they have photos. Ask families to tell their child about his or her Baptism: Who was there? What was the priest's or deacon's name? Who were the godparents? Was there a family celebration afterward? The more the children know about their own Baptism, the easier it is for them to identify with the Catholic Church's teaching on Baptism. More importantly, it will help the children come to know God's love and their family's love for them.

Teach

FOCUS

- Ask a volunteer to read the "Faith Focus" question aloud.
- Share with the children that they are going to learn more about the sacraments of Baptism and Confirmation.

DISCOVER

- Ask the children to share how a family welcomes a new baby. Establish that the baby's arrival is a time of joy and blessing.
- Ask the children to describe what is happening in the picture on the page.
- Present "Baptism" by asking the children to find the sentences in the text that tell what happens in Baptism.
- Ask the children to share the sentences they consider important. Fill in any important concepts they overlooked.

Apply

REINFORCE

- Have the children read aloud together the faith word *Baptism* and its meaning. Have them make a word card for this term.
- Share with the children that Baptism is one of the three Sacraments of Christian Initiation.

INTEGRATE

Have the children complete the prayer and pray it quietly.

Baptism and Confirmation

Priest blessing water to be used for Baptism

Faith Focus

What happens at Baptism and Confirmation?

Faith Words

Baptism

Baptism is the sacrament that joins us to Christ and makes us members of the Church. We receive the gift of the Holy Spirit and become adopted sons and daughters of God.

Confirmation

Confirmation is the sacrament in which the gift of the Holy Spirit strengthens us to live our Baptism.

Baptism

Celebrating Baptism, Confirmation, and Eucharist joins us to Christ and makes us members of the Church. These three sacraments are called Sacraments of Christian Initiation.

Baptism is the first sacrament we celebrate. It often takes place during the celebration of Mass. Through Baptism we are joined to Christ and given the gift of the Holy Spirit. We become adopted sons and daughters of God. We are called to live a holy life. We are to love God and our neighbor as Jesus taught.

Dear God,   Responses will vary.
When I was baptized I received the

_____ _____ . I became

a member of the _____ .
Help me always to follow your

Son, _____ . Amen.

106

Finish this prayer. Pray it quietly in your heart.

Liturgy Tip

Learning Through the Senses. In order to understand a concept, children at this age often need to use their five senses. The lesson on Baptism is an opportunity for the children to touch holy water, feel oil on their skin, smell the fragrance of a candle, and hear the words and see the actions used in the celebration of this sacrament. Utilize the senses during prayer time. Use water or fragrant oils in a blessing, or light a candle if possible.

Celebrating Baptism

We celebrate Baptism with words and actions. We are dipped into the water or water is poured over our head three times. The priest or deacon prays, "I baptize you in the name of the Father, and of the Son, and of the Holy Spirit."

Next the priest or deacon anoints, or blesses, the top of our head with blessed oil. We are then dressed in a white garment. We receive a lighted candle.

The words and actions of Baptism show that we share in God's life. We are to live holy lives and be lights in the world as Jesus was.

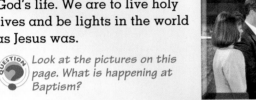 *Look at the pictures on this page. What is happening at Baptism?*

 **Faith-Filled People**

Cornelius

Cornelius was a Roman soldier. One day while he was praying, an angel visited him. The angel told him to go to Saint Peter the Apostle. After learning about Jesus from Peter, Cornelius asked Peter to baptize his whole family (based on Acts of the Apostles 10:1–49).

The newly baptized child is being anointed with blessed oil.

The parents are receiving the lighted candle.

(107)

Background: Faith-Filled People

Cornelius. The story of Cornelius is told in Acts of the Apostles 10:1–43. Cornelius was a Roman centurion: A centurion commanded one hundred soldiers. Cornelius believed in God, prayed regularly, and tried to live a good life. One day as he was praying, Cornelius had a vision. An angel instructed him to send for Peter. Peter went to Cornelius's house and baptized Cornelius's whole family. The baptism of Cornelius, a Gentile, shows that God invites all people to faith and salvation in Christ.

Teach

FOCUS

Remind the children that Baptism is the first sacrament we receive. Tell them they are going to learn more about the words and actions the Church uses in the sacrament of Baptism.

DISCOVER

- Show the children a bowl of water, a candle, a white baptismal garment, and a small bowl of oil. Tell the children that these objects are all used in the celebration of Baptism.
- Ask volunteers to read aloud important words and actions of Baptism in the first paragraph of "Celebrating Baptism."
- Invite volunteers to read the second paragraph. Have the group highlight or underline four signs of Baptism. Water, oil, white garment, lighted candle.
- Share with the children the story of Cornelius in "Faith-Filled People."

Apply

REINFORCE

Ask a volunteer to read aloud the words the priest prays at Baptism.

INTEGRATE

- Have the children look at the two pictures and tell what part of Baptism they show.
- Point out that besides the baby's parents, the godparents are also present. Godparents help us live as Catholics.

.

Teach

FOCUS

Remind the children of the importance of their Baptism. Tell them they are now going to learn about the sacrament of Confirmation.

DISCOVER

- Tell the children that we can only receive Confirmation after we have been baptized. Ask the children to share if they have been to a celebration of Confirmation.
- Explain the first paragraph of "Celebrating Confirmation" to the children in your own words.
- Ask the children to read the second paragraph to discover what happens next in the celebration of Confirmation.

Apply

REINFORCE

- Ask the children to look at the picture and describe what is happening. The bishop is placing his hand on the head of the boy and anointing the boy's forehead with chrism.
- Ask volunteers to come to the front of the room and mime a celebration of Confirmation. Remind them not to use any words. Ask the rest of the class to tell what words would be spoken.

INTEGRATE

Write the words for the puzzle activity on the board and give directions. Invite volunteers to share words that fit.

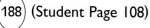
Celebrating Confirmation

We celebrate the sacrament of **Confirmation** after we are baptized. The bishop usually leads the celebration of Confirmation. During the celebration he prays over us, "Send your Holy Spirit upon them to be their Helper and Guide."

Then the bishop places his right hand on top of our head. He signs our forehead with the blessed oil called holy chrism as he prays, "Be sealed with the gift of the Holy Spirit." We say, "Amen." The bishop then shares a sign of peace with us, saying, "Peace be with you." We answer, "And also with you."

In Confirmation the Holy Spirit strengthens us to live our Baptism. The Holy Spirit helps us to remember and share God's love with others.

B i s h **O** p

SP I R I T

H e **L** p e r

108

For each letter in the word oil write a word about Confirmation.

Teaching Tips

Bishops. Many of the children may have never met a bishop and may not know who their bishop is. Borrow a picture of your bishop from the religious education office or the rectory for the children to look at. Tell the children a little about him, and have the children learn their bishop's name.

Our Church Makes a Difference

Fiesta Grande

The children of Saint John Neumann Parish share God's love in a special way. They take part in celebrating Fiesta Grande. Fiesta Grande is a music program performed during Lent.

The parish children dress and decorate individual paper dolls in outfits worn by the people of Central America. These dolls represent the children the people of the parish are helping.

The children also save enough pennies, nickels, dimes, and quarters to sponsor the children. The children write to the children they sponsor and receive messages back. The children also pray for the children they sponsor.

QUESTION *What is one way you and your friends can live your faith in Jesus? How does that share God's love with people?*
Affirm appropriate responses.

Our Catholic Faith

Baptismal Candle
At Baptism we receive a lighted candle. The baptismal candle is lighted from the Easter candle. We are given the lighted baptismal candle to remind us that we are to live our faith.

109

Catholic Social Teaching

Solidarity of the Human Family. The Church teaches that we are all a part of a single human family and that we are responsible for the material and spiritual well-being of one another. This is true regardless of our national, racial, ethnic, and ideological differences. Solidarity is the virtue that promotes the material and spiritual well-being of all people. Solidarity demands that we serve the common good of all and protect the rights of each person.

Tip: Create an "International Bulletin Board." Have each child trace their hands and cut them out. Have them write their names, ethnic backgrounds, and ages on them. Link the hands together across a map of the world to symbolize their solidarity with all people.

HIGHLIGHT

Point out that there are many ways we can share God's love with other people. Point out that the children of Saint John Neumann Parish have a special way of doing this.

DISCOVER

- In your own words tell how the children at Saint John Neumann Parish were signs of God's love.
- Ask the children to tell how these children help other children know God's love. The children give some of their own money to help sponsor a child from Central America who is in need.
- Point out that the paper dolls the children of Saint John Neumann make are signs of their love and care for the orphans of Central America.

INTEGRATE

- Talk with the children about times they have helped someone in need.
- Have the group suggest ways second graders can share God's love with other people.
- Read "Our Catholic Faith" to the children to help them discover how the baptismal candle is a reminder to live our faith.

Connect

HIGHLIGHT

Remind the children that when they live holy lives they really make a difference.

RESPOND

- Point out that the children are already showing God's love to others in many ways.
- Direct their attention to the "Ways to Be Holy" activity. Ask a volunteer to read the directions and tell in their own words what they are to do to complete the activity.
- Have them do the activity on their own and then share their ideas with the group.

CHOOSE

Invite the children to read "My Faith Choice" and write their decisions. Encourage them to put their choices into practice this week.

What Difference Does Faith Make in My Life?

Every time you live your faith in Jesus you show your love for God. The Holy Spirit helps you to live a holy life. You make a difference when you live a holy life.

On the pathway write three things you can do to live a holy life. Responses will vary. Affirm appropriate responses.

Ways to Be Holy

My Faith Choice

This week I will try to live a holy life. I will

Affirm appropriate responses.

110

Teaching Tip

Sing a Welcome Song. Sing these words to the tune of "Mary Had a Little Lamb."

Our Church welcomes us in Baptism, Baptism, Baptism
Our Church welcomes us in Baptism
To be God's family.

The Holy Spirit helps us live good lives, live good lives, live good lives
The Holy Spirit helps us live good lives
To be God's family.

We Pray

Glory to God

A prayer of adoration gives glory to God. Join with your class to give glory to God.

Leader: Let us praise God our Father who has made us his children by our Baptism.

All: **Glory to God, now and forever.**

Leader: Let us bless ourselves with the Sign of the Cross to remind us of our Baptism.

All: *(Dip their right hands in water and bless themselves.)*
Glory to God, now and forever.

We Remember

Find and circle the sacrament words in the puzzle. Use the words that you circle in sentences.

Confirmation		Baptism
oil	water	Holy Spirit

```
H O L Y S P I R I T M C S
W A T E R M D L K B A U H
P N D Q H G X O I L S Y J
B C O N F I R M A T I O N
C Q B A P T I S M P W Z D
```

To Help You Remember

1. Baptism, Confirmation, and Eucharist join us to Christ and make us members of the Church.

2. The sacrament of Baptism brings us into the life of Christ and the Church.

3. The sacrament of Confirmation strengthens us to live our Baptism.

Grade 2 • Chapter 12 (111)

Pray

WE PRAY

- Prepare for the prayer service by writing the responses for the prayer on the board or on poster board. Rehearse the responses.
- Gather the children in the prayer center.
- Invite a child to be the leader.
- Pray this prayer of adoration with the children.

Review

WE REMEMBER

- Ask a volunteer to read each of the "To Help You Remember" statements aloud.
- Introduce the activity and give the children time to complete it.
- Have the children work in partners and use the words in a sentence.

Teaching Tip

Baptismal Fonts and Pools. Many parish churches have baptismal fonts, and others have baptismal pools. Make sure that the children understand that both fonts and pools are used to hold the water used in the celebration of Baptism. Take the children to the church if possible to visit the area where the baptismal pool or font is located. While there, lead the group in a short prayer thanking God for the gift of Baptism.

At Home

ENCOURAGE

Have the children carefully tear out pages 111 and 112 along the perforation. Encourage the children to share the pages with their families and to do the activities together. If they did not complete the review activity on page 111 by the end of the session, emphasize that they can complete it with their families.

VISIT FAITHFIRST.COM

- Share with the children the many activities on the *Faith First* Web site.
- Encourage the children to visit **www.FaithFirst.com.**

---

12 With My Family

This Week . . .

In chapter 12, "We Celebrate Baptism and Confirmation," your child learned about the sacraments of Baptism and Confirmation. Baptism, Confirmation, and Eucharist are called Sacraments of Christian Initiation. They join us to Christ and make us members of the Church. Baptism is the first sacrament we celebrate. The Church baptizes us with water to remind us that original sin and all sins we may have committed are forgiven. We receive the gift of God's life and love, or holiness. At Confirmation the Holy Spirit strengthens us to live our Baptism.

For more on the teachings of the Catholic Church on the sacraments of Baptism and Confirmation, see *Catechism of the Catholic Church* paragraph numbers 1210–1274 and 1285–1314.

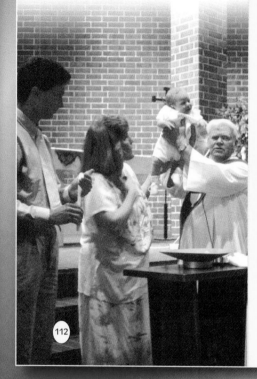

112

Sharing God's Word

Read together the Bible story in Acts of the Apostles 10:1–49 about the baptism of Cornelius. Emphasize that at Baptism we are given the gift of the Holy Spirit and become adopted sons and daughters of God.

Praying

In this chapter your child prayed a blessing prayer with water. Pray together the prayer on page 111.

Making a Difference

Choose one of the following activities to do as a family or design a similar activity of your own.

- After Mass this week visit the place where the sacred oils are kept. Point out that this place is called the ambry.
- Talk about the day of each family member's Baptism. Share the date, location, and who was there. Look at pictures and talk about why Baptism is such an important event for the whole family.
- Godparents help us live as children of God. Send thank-you notes to the godparents of your family members for all they have done to help you grow up in a life of faith.

For more ideas on ways your family can live your faith, visit the "Faith First for Families" page at **www.FaithFirst.com.** You are only a click away from taking a "Tour of the Church" with your child.

Before Moving On . . .

As you finish today's lesson, reflect on the following question before moving on to the next chapter.

Which students could use more attention from me?

✓ Evaluate

Take a few moments to evaluate this week's lesson.
I feel (circle one) about this week's lesson.

   a. very pleased
   b. OK
   c. disappointed

The activity the children enjoyed most was . . .

The concept that was most difficult to teach was . . .

because . . .

Something I would like to do differently is . . .

Our Church Makes a Difference

Saint John Vianney

Saint John Vianney was a special sign of God's forgiveness. John Vianney was a priest. He was honored and respected because of his kindness to people who were sorry for their sins.

There is a story that a special railroad track was built to the village where Father John Vianney lived. The railroad track was built because so many people from all over France wanted to come to John Vianney to celebrate the sacrament of Reconciliation. John Vianney was named a saint in 1925. He is the patron saint of parish priests.

Our Catholic Faith

Act of Contrition

We ask God for forgiveness in many ways. We celebrate the sacrament of Reconciliation. We pray the Act of Contrition. In the Act of Contrition we tell God we are sorry for our sins and ask for forgiveness.

 When have you been kind to someone who asked you to forgive them?
Affirm appropriate responses.

117

Background: Our Catholic Faith

At one time or another we have all been guilty of going through the motions of forgiveness. Our Catholic Faith tells us this is not enough. Real contrition comes from one's heart and is not merely something that is said and not felt. It is true sorrow. The Act of Contrition, or the prayer recited during the celebration of the sacrament of Penance, is a prayer that not only expresses our true sorrow over the sin we have committed and our desire for forgiveness but also includes a true and sincere pledge to avoid sin in the future. All children should know the Act of Contrition found on page 283 by heart before they celebrate the sacrament of Penance.

Connect

HIGHLIGHT

Remind the children that the Church has always taught us about God's love and forgiveness. Then point out that Saint John Vianney brought this message to the people of his day.

DISCOVER

- Remind the children that a saint is a person who tries to make good choices that follow Jesus' example.
- Ask the children to listen for one way in which John Vianney helped the people of France.
- Ask and invite responses to these or similar questions: Who was Saint John Vianney? Why did people come from all over France to speak to him? How did he help people? Accept all appropriate responses.
- Explain that Catholics pray the Act of Contrition to tell God we are sorry for our sins. Invite the children to read silently "Our Catholic Faith" to learn more about the Act of Contrition.

INTEGRATE

- Ask the children to think about how they ask for and give forgiveness. Invite volunteers to share responses with the class.
- Have volunteers tell about a time they have been kind to someone who wanted forgiveness.

Connect

HIGHLIGHT

Point out that the Holy Spirit teaches us how and gives us the grace to forgive others who hurt us, and teaches us how to ask forgiveness when we hurt others.

RESPOND

- Ask the children how the expressions on their faces might tell others how they feel. Ask and discuss: How do I know you are happy? How do I know you are surprised? Accept all appropriate answers.
- Present the introduction and directions to the activity in your own words. Then have the children work alone to complete the activity.
- When the children are finished invite volunteers to share their drawings.

CHOOSE

Have the children read "My Faith Choice" and write their decisions. Encourage everyone to put their choices into practice this week.

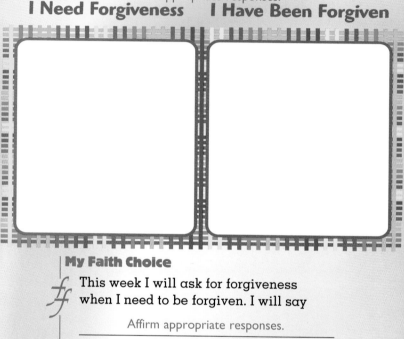

What Difference Does Faith Make in My Life?

The Holy Spirit helps us to ask for forgiveness. He also teaches us to forgive others.

Draw a picture of how you might look when you need to be forgiven. Then draw a picture of how you might look after you have been forgiven.
Affirm appropriate responses.

I Need Forgiveness | **I Have Been Forgiven**

My Faith Choice

This week I will ask for forgiveness when I need to be forgiven. I will say

Affirm appropriate responses.

_____

_____.

118

Teaching Tip

Models of Forgiveness. Role models of forgiveness appear to be in short supply. The media often offer children models of behavior, such as revenge and retaliation, that are contrary to the values taught by Jesus. Invite children to discuss people they know, especially family members or classmates, who are helping them to see how to forgive others and to ask forgiveness. Encourage the children to be good role models of forgiveness for others as well.

We Pray

Lord, Have Mercy!

At Mass we sometimes pray this prayer. We tell God that we trust that he always forgives us.

Leader: Lord, have mercy.
All: **Lord, have mercy.**

Leader: Christ, have mercy.
All: **Christ, have mercy.**

Leader: Lord, have mercy.
All: **Lord, have mercy.**

We Remember

Finish the story. Show that you understand what Jesus taught about forgiveness.

Father	You may use the computer for thirty minutes.
Daughter	Thanks, Dad.
Father	You have been on the computer for one hour.
Daughter	_____Affirm appropriate_____ .
Father	_____responses._____ .
	_____ .

To Help You Remember

1. Jesus told the parable of the Forgiving Father to teach us about forgiveness.

2. When we are truly sorry and ask God for forgiveness, he forgives us.

3. God is so happy when we tell him we are sorry that he rejoices.

Liturgy Tip

Lord, Have Mercy. Though a part of the Rite of Penance at Mass, the Lord, Have Mercy is traditionally a prayer of praise—we first exalt the Lord for his wondrous deeds, and then ask for his mercy. Before beginning the prayer, ask the children to think for what they might praise the Lord and to share their ideas. You might choose to vary the prayer today by asking volunteers to share words of praise and then inviting all to respond, "Lord, have mercy."

Pray

WE PRAY

- Tell the children that today's prayer will recall for them a prayer we say each Sunday at Mass. It is the Lord, Have Mercy prayer that we sometimes pray in the Introductory Rites of the Mass.
- Gather the children in the prayer center.
- Remind them that the word *mercy* means "great kindness."
- Pray the prayer together.

Review

WE REMEMBER

- Write the "To Help You Remember" statements on the board or on poster board, leaving a key word out of each statement.
- Create a word bank above the statements.
- Invite volunteers to come up and fill in the blanks in the statements.
- Ask the children to finish the story in the "We Remember" activity. Invite volunteers to share their endings.

At Home

ENCOURAGE

Have the children carefully tear out pages 119 and 120 along the perforation. Encourage the children to share the pages with their families and to do the activities together. If they did not complete the review activity on page 119 by the end of the session, emphasize that they can complete it with their families.

VISIT FAITHFIRST.COM

- Share with the children the many activities on the *Faith First* Web site.
- Encourage the children to visit **www.FaithFirst.com.**

13 With My Family

This Week . . .

In chapter 13, "The Forgiving Father: A Scripture Story," your child learned that Jesus told parables to help his listeners understand his teaching. The parable is a type of story used by Jesus and other teachers of his times. The teacher or storyteller often compared something their listeners knew well with something they did not know so well. A parable usually ended with a conclusion that surprised those listening to it. This helped people understand the parable's main teaching. Jesus told the parable of the Forgiving Father to help us know and trust in God's forgiveness and merciful love.

For more on the teachings of the Catholic Church on the mercy of God, see *Catechism of the Catholic Church* paragraph numbers 545–546, 587–590, 976–983, 1439, 1465, and 1846–1848.

Sharing God's Word

Read together the parable in Luke 15:11–24 about the forgiving father or read the adaptation of the parable on page 115. Emphasize that the forgiving father was happy that his son returned home.

Praying

In this chapter your child learned to pray a prayer that we sometimes pray in the Introductory Rites of the Mass. Read and pray together the prayer on page 119.

Making a Difference

Choose one of the following activities to do as a family or design a similar activity of your own.

- Make puppets out of paper bags and perform the parable of the Forgiving Father.

- Talk about ways your family asks for forgiveness and forgives one another. Emphasize that there are times in our lives when we need to ask for forgiveness and their are times when we need to forgive others.

- If you have a children's book at home that teaches about forgiveness, read the story together. Discuss what the book teaches about forgiveness.

> For more ideas on ways your family can live your faith, visit the "Faith First for Families" page at **www.FaithFirst.com**. You are only a click away from "Family Prayer."

120

Evaluate

Take a few moments to evaluate this week's lesson.
I feel (circle one) about this week's lesson.

    a. very pleased
    b. OK
    c. disappointed

The activity the children enjoyed most was . . .

The concept that was most difficult to teach was . . .

because . . .

Something I would like to do differently is . . .

Before Moving On . . .

As you finish today's lesson, reflect on the following question before moving on to the next chapter.

What opportunities am I giving the students to express themselves through prayer?

ENRICHING THE LESSON

Making Forgiveness Spinners

Purpose

To reinforce the parable of the Forgiving Father (taught on page 115)

Directions

Draw a six-inch circle on a sheet of paper and divide it into three parts. Draw a large dot in the center of the circle. Make copies of the pattern on colored paper for each child.

- Divide the children into pairs.
- Give each child a copy of the circle, a pencil, and a large paper clip.
- Invite the children to take a pencil and write the following words in the three sections of the circle.
   —"I am very sorry. Please forgive me."
   —"I forgive you."
   —"I will have a party to celebrate."
- Tell the children to work with a partner. Have them place the end of a paper clip over the dot on the circle of one of the pieces of paper and to place the tip of their pencil through the clip and hold it on the dot. Tell the partners to take turns spinning the clip. When it stops spinning, each partner must tell who in the story said the words that the clip is pointing toward.
- Invite the children to take the game home to share with their families.

Materials

copies of circle pattern for each child
large paper clips
pencils

Using Puppets to Learn Forgiveness

Purpose

To reinforce the importance of asking forgiveness and forgiving others (taught on page 116)

Directions

Children can use puppets to help them learn the techniques of showing and asking forgiveness.

- In small groups have the children make simple puppets using small paper plates and Popsicle sticks. Invite them to draw faces on the plates and then glue a Popsicle stick to the back of each one to provide handles for the puppets. Have each child in the group make a puppet—a girl, a boy, an adult, and perhaps a younger child.
- When the groups are ready, have the children give their puppet performances for the whole class.

Materials

glue, paper plates, Popsicle sticks
crayons or markers

Literature Connection

Purpose

To reinforce the parable of the Forgiving Father (taught on page 115)

Directions

Kevin Henkes's story *Lilly's Purple Plastic Purse* (William Morrow & Co., 1996) is a humorous tale that makes a very important point about the need to ask forgiveness.

- Read the story aloud to the children and discuss it with them. Why does the teacher reprimand Lilly? Why is she filled with remorse by his kindness? How is this story like the story of the Forgiving Father? How is it different?

Materials

Lilly's Purple Plastic Purse by Kevin Henkes

Music Connection

- "Somebody's Knockin' at Your Door," (African-American spiritual). *Singing Our Faith (SOF)* #226.
- "Standin' in the Need of Prayer," (African-American spiritual). *SOF* #228.
- "Hold Us in Your Mercy: Penitential Litany," G. Daigle. *SOF* #230.
- "When Jesus the Healer," P. Smith. *SOF* #231.

God's Forgiving Love

Background

Dishonoring God, Others, and Ourselves

When we sin, we deeply offend God's love for us. We dishonor and sever our communion with God. Quite often, one sin leads to another, and eventually we find ourselves, like the prodigal son, far away from our true home, far from our own souls. We can identify a serious sin by its "seriousness."

When sin has finally made us ashamed, we gain an intimate understanding of the magnitude of Christ's gift of reconciliation. When our sorrow and regret humble us, we get a personal insight into Christ's call for conversion. It is a hand reaching through our darkness to rescue us.

The Sacrament of Penance

But where do we go to disclose our wrongs, to obtain a tangible and effective sign of forgiveness, to begin making amends, and to undertake the healing journey back into the welcoming arms of God the Father? Before Jesus returned to his Father, he appeared to his disciples: "[H]e breathed on them and said to them, 'Receive the holy Spirit. Whose sins you forgive are

forgiven them, and whose sins you retain are retained' " (John 20:22–23). Thus, Christ gave to the Church a way to welcome sinners back home.

The sacrament of Penance, or Reconciliation, accomplishes what its name implies. It heals the divisions sin creates between the sinner and God, and between the sinner and others. This sacrament brings God's forgiveness into the life of sinners. It reconciles sinners with God and with the Church.

Sin is before all else an offense against God, a rupture of communion

with him. At the same time it damages communion with the Church. For this reason conversion entails both God's forgiveness and reconciliation with the Church, which are expressed and accomplished liturgically by the sacrament of Penance and Reconciliation.[1]

CATECHISM OF THE CATHOLIC CHURCH 1440

The sacrament of Penance also brings inner healing. It brings the gift of grace into the inner life of the sinner and effects an inner reconciliation as well. It brings the gifts of inner consolation as well as a deep serenity and peace of conscience. Just as the forgiving Father gave the prodigal son a beautiful robe, a ring, and a festive banquet, our forgiving Father gives us what those gifts symbolize—a welcomed return to our true spiritual family.

For Reflection

In what ways do I relate to God's constantly calling me to heal what keeps me from his love?

How has the sacrament of Penance helped me get my life on the right track?

Catechist to Catechist

First Reconciliation

The better prepared the children are for their first celebration of the sacrament of Penance, or Reconciliation, the more positive and comfortable they will be. Give the children in your group time to understand the process and the opportunity to ask questions or share any concerns they may have about receiving this sacrament. This is time well spent and will ensure that the children are well prepared for their first celebration in this sacrament.

Overcoming Obstacles

Even at the age of seven or eight, some children are very shy. Some children may be more nervous than others and may have a more difficult time adjusting to confessing their sins to the priest and sharing with him the things they have done wrong. Help these children and all the children by pointing out that many people feel this way. Assure them that the priest will help them too.

The Church Teaches . . .

The *General Directory for Catechesis* shares with us the intimacy that God the Father desires that we have with him. The *General Directory* states:

> [Jesus] proclaims and reveals that God is not a distant inaccessible Being, "a remote power without a name"[1] but a Father, who is present among his creatures and whose power is his love. This testimony about God as Father, offered in a simple and direct manner, is funda-mental to catechesis. *GDC* 102

By communicating God's gentle love your students will better understand his mercy and forgiveness.

See the Catechism . . .

For more on the teachings of the Catholic Church on the sacrament of Penance, or Reconciliation, see *Catechism of the Catholic Church* 1420–1484.

CATECHIST PRAYER

God, Forgiving Father, I am assured of your love and forgiveness. May I follow the example of your Son and be ready to forgive others quickly and completely. Amen.

Footnote references for these two pages may be found on p. 456.

LESSON PLANNER

Focus
To introduce the children to the Church's special way of celebrating God's forgiveness

Engage

Page 121
Focus
To help the children identify what they already know about forgiveness

Opening Prayer

Discussion
What happens when we make choices we know are against what God wants us to do?

Teach and Apply

Pages 122–124
Focus
To identify that the sacrament of Reconciliation is the Church's special way of celebrating God's forgiveness

Presentation
Read, discuss, and summarize content.
Scripture
• Psalm 51:3
Activities
• Choose a photo and identify the action.
• Learn to sign "I'm sorry."
• Identify the part of the celebration of the sacrament of Reconciliation being celebrated in the picture.

Faith-Filled People
Zacchaeus

Connect

Pages 125–126
Focus
To discover ways the Church is a community of peacemakers

Our Church Makes a Difference
Identify how Saint Dominic Savio is an example of a peacemaker.

Our Catholic Faith
The Gift of Peace

What Difference Does Faith Make?
Activity
Describe ways to share God's gift of peace with words and actions.
Faith Choice
Choose one of the ways from the activity and do it this week.

We Pray

Page 127
Prayer Form
Prayer of praise and petition
Prayer
Choose a leader and then pray together.

We Remember

Review
• Complete the sentences.
• Read the "To Help You Remember" statements aloud.
Preview
Highlight features of "With My Family" page.

Materials

• pens or pencils
• index cards

Enriching the Session

Blackline Masters
Additional Activities booklet:
Chapter 14
Writing about or drawing the confessional
Solving a code
Assessment Tools booklet:
Chapter 14 Test
Enriching the Lesson (CG page 217)
Visiting the Reconciliation Room
Writing Forgiveness Stories
Literature Connection
Music Connection (CG page 217)

www.FaithFirst.com

We update the *Faith First* Web site weekly. Check each week for new content and features. Here are some places to begin:

Catechists and Teachers
• Current Events
• Chapter Downloads
• Catechist Prayer

Faith First **for Families**
• Bible Stories
• Saints
• Make a Difference

Kids' Clubhouse
• *Faith First* Activities
• Chapter Reviews
• Games

Don't Forget! You can make lesson planning a breeze—check out the **Online Lesson Planner.**

God's Forgiving Love

We Pray

Forgive me, O God,
because of your
goodness.

Based on Psalm 51:3

**All-holy Father,
help us to share
your forgiving
love with others.
Amen.**

*What happens
when we make a
bad choice?*

Sometimes we do
something wrong
by accident. At
other times we
may do something
wrong on purpose
that is against what
God wants us to do.

*What happens
when we make
choices we know
are against what
God wants us to do?*

(121)

Teaching Tip

Saying "I'm Sorry." We can thank God each and every day
that we are gifted with a lifetime of new beginnings. Many people
have a tendency to answer "It's all right" when someone apologizes
or asks to be forgiven. Reinforce with the children that saying that
we are sorry helps reconcile us with those we have hurt. When a
person finds the courage and takes the time to apologize, we should
accept the apology graciously and tell them that they are forgiven.

PRAY

- Have the children quiet
  themselves for prayer.
- Begin with the Sign of the
  Cross.
- Proclaim Psalm 51:3. Then lead
  the opening prayer and invite
  the children to echo each
  phrase after you.
- Close the prayer with the Sign
  of the Cross.

DISCOVER

Purpose: To discover what the
children may already know about
forgiveness

- Invite the children to describe
  what they see happening in the
  photograph. Affirm all
  appropriate responses.
- Read aloud the introductory
  paragraph and invite responses
  to the question.

Teach

(Student Page 122)

FOCUS

Ask a volunteer to read aloud the "Faith Focus" question. Share with the children that in this chapter they will learn how the Catholic Church celebrates God's forgiveness.

DISCOVER

- Have the children think about some of the choices they have made today.
- Ask them if they think these were good or bad choices. Explain that many choices we make every day are neither right nor wrong. Other choices do make a difference.
- Have the children silently read "We Make Choices" to learn the meaning of the word *sin*.
- Emphasize that sin hurts our friendship with God, others, and ourselves.

Apply

REINFORCE

- Ask a volunteer to read the meaning of the word *sin* under "Faith Words."
- Have the children make a word card for the word *sin*.
- Remind the children of the difference between accidents and sins.

INTEGRATE

- Have the children discuss the pictures on page 122. Invite them to tell what they think the people in the pictures are saying to each other.
- Have the children complete the activity.

210 (Student Page 122)

God Always Forgives Us

Faith Focus

What happens in the sacrament of Reconciliation?

Faith Words

sin
Sin is freely choosing to do or say something we know God does not want us to do or say.

Reconciliation
Reconciliation is a sacrament that brings God's gifts of mercy and forgiving love into our lives.

We Make Choices

Each day we make many choices. We make good choices. We make bad choices. Some of our bad choices are sins.

We **sin** when we choose to do or say something that we know God does not want us to do or say. We also sin when we choose not to do something we know God wants us to do.

Sin always harms our friendship with God and with other people.

ACTIVITY *Choose one of the photos on this page. On the lines write what you think the child in the photo that you chose is saying.*

Affirm
_____
appropriate
_____
responses.

122

Faith Vocabulary

Prejudice. This would be an excellent time to speak to the children about the sin of prejudice. Point out to the children that prejudice happens when we prejudge a person or a whole group of people without really knowing them. Prejudice often happens when people from different cultures come together. Neither group knows much about the other, but they judge the other group by the color of their skin, or the language they speak, or the religion they practice. Point out to the children how prejudice can affect our lives and the lives of others in serious ways. Then, with the children, brainstorm a list of practical things they could do to avoid prejudice, such as getting to know a child in their neighborhood who has a different cultural background than they do.

We Need Forgiveness

We need to ask for forgiveness when we sin. The Holy Spirit helps us to turn to God and other people and say, "I am sorry. Please forgive me." We also need to make things better when we sin. This shows we are truly sorry for our sins.

Jesus gave us the sacrament of **Reconciliation**. In this sacrament we tell God we are sorry for our sins. We ask for and receive God's forgiveness. We are forgiven the sins we commit after we are baptized. We receive God's help, or grace, to make good choices to live as children of God. Reconciliation is also called the sacrament of Penance. It is also called Confession.

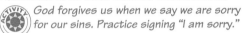 *God forgives us when we say we are sorry for our sins. Practice signing "I am sorry."*

 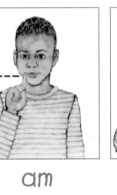 

I   am   sorry.

(123)

✦ **Background: Faith-Filled People**

Zacchaeus. The story of Zacchaeus is only told in the Gospel according to Luke (see Luke 19:1–10). Zacchaeus was the chief tax collector in Jericho on behalf of the Roman authorities. He was extremely unpopular since he acquired wealth by being dishonest. Zacchaeus was probably aware of Jesus' pastoral outreach to all people, even unpopular people like himself. He climbed a sycamore tree to avoid a large crowd. Jesus saw Zacchaeus and invited himself to Zacchaeus' house. Joyful Zacchaeus was a changed man. He gave half of his possessions to the poor and gave back to people from whom he had dishonestly taken money four times the amount he had taken. Zacchaeus's new life reflects the joy of being accepted by Jesus.

Teach

FOCUS

Remind the children that some of our wrong choices are called sins. In the sacrament of Reconciliation we tell God we are truly sorry for our sins.

DISCOVER

- Read the story of Zacchaeus to the children (Luke 19:1–10).
- Summarize "We Need Forgiveness" for the children. Explain that when we sin, we need to ask for forgiveness and try to make things better.
- Ask the children to find and underline two other names for the sacrament of Reconciliation found on page 123. Penance, Confession.
- Ask the children to explain in their own words what takes place during the celebration of Reconciliation.
- Emphasize that we receive God's forgiveness for our sins.

Apply

REINFORCE

Ask a volunteer to read the definition of *Reconciliation* in "Faith Words." Have the children make a word card for this term.

INTEGRATE

Invite the children to study the pictures and then practice signing "I am sorry" with a partner.

Teach

FOCUS

Remind the children of why we celebrate the sacrament of Reconciliation, which is also called the sacrament of Penance and sometimes Confession. Tell them they are going to now learn the way we celebrate this sacrament.

DISCOVER

- Invite the children to read the first paragraph of "We Celebrate Reconciliation" silently to discover two ways we celebrate the sacrament of Reconciliation.
- List on the board the four parts of every celebration of the sacrament of Reconciliation.
- Take the part of the priest yourself and invite several volunteers to pantomime one of the parts of the rite with you.
- Emphasize that confessing our sins to the priest is always done in private even when we celebrate with other members of our parish. The priest will never tell anyone what we confess to him.

Apply

REINFORCE

Write the four parts of the sacrament of Reconciliation on poster board. Mix up the order and invite volunteers to place them in the correct order.

INTEGRATE

Invite the children to tell what part of the sacrament of Reconciliation is happening in the photo and to write their answer under the picture.

Absolution

We Celebrate Reconciliation

We can celebrate Reconciliation by meeting with the priest by ourselves. Or we can gather with other members of our parish and then meet with the priest. There are four things that are part of every celebration of Reconciliation.

1. Confession. We meet with the priest by ourselves and tell him our sins.	**2. Contrition.** We tell God we are truly sorry for our sins. We pray an act of contrition.
3. Penance. We are given a penance. Doing our penance helps repair, or heal, the harm we have caused by our sins.	**4. Absolution.** The priest lays his hands on or over our head. We receive God's forgiveness from our sins through the words and actions of the priest.

ACTIVITY *Look at the picture at the top of this page. Under the picture write the name of the part of Reconciliation that is shown.*

In Reconciliation we share in God's mercy and forgiving love. We receive the gift of peace. We are reconciled with God and with the Church.

(124)

Liturgy Tip

Establishing a Contrition Ritual. Take just a few extra minutes at the end of each session to help the children develop a habit of listening to their consciences. First, have the children think about the things they might have done that were unkind or disobedient. Then have them silently pray an act of sorrow. Next, have the children think about the good choices they made. Then have the children pray aloud together, "Thank you, God, for helping me make good choices."

Our Church Makes a Difference

Saint Dominic Savio

Dominic Savio was a peacemaker. He once said, "I cannot do big things, but I want to do everything, even the small things, for God." Here is a story of one thing Dominic did when he was a teenager.

One day Dominic Savio saw two angry-looking boys holding stones in their hands. Dominic asked, "Why are you holding those stones? You are not going to fight, are you?"

"Before you fight," Dominic told the boys, "think of Jesus. Think of how much people hurt him, and how he forgave them." The boys were ashamed that they were going to fight and dropped the stones.

Dominic was a peacemaker, and the boys became friends again. The Church celebrates the feast day of Saint Dominic Savio on March 9.

QUESTION *What is one way to solve problems without fighting?*
Affirm appropriate responses.

Our Catholic Faith

The Gift of Peace

Peace is a gift of God. At the end of the celebration of Reconciliation, we hear words such as "The Lord has freed you from your sins. Go in peace." Christians are to be peacemakers. We are to share the gift of peace we receive from God with others.

125

Catholic Social Teaching

Call to Family, Community, and Participation. The worldwide Catholic Church is a community of many races, languages, and ethnic groups. As People of God we are concerned about issues, such as prejudice, violence, and injustice. We have an obligation and the responsibility to participate in society and to work harmoniously and peacefully to promote the common good of all people.

Tip. Point out the meaning of prejudice and when it happens. Then give the children the opportunity to brainstorm ways they can reach out to others in their community who are different than they are. Encourage the children to be peacemakers.

HIGHLIGHT

Tell the children that the Church helps us in many ways to be peacemakers and to be signs of God's forgiveness.

DISCOVER

- Ask the children what it means to be a peacemaker. Ask them to name a person they know who lives as a peacemaker.
- Tell the story of Saint Dominic Savio. Ask the children how he helped children learn to be peacemakers. Accept appropriate responses; for example, he told them to think of Jesus first.
- Invite the children to read "Our Catholic Faith" silently to learn more about the gift of peace.
- Ask the children to recall when they share a sign of peace with one another at church. Tell them we are invited to share a sign of peace at Mass.

INTEGRATE

- Invite the children to tell how they might solve the following problems peacefully.
  —You are first in line, and someone cuts in front of you.
  —Your brother took your bicycle without asking, and you want to ride it.
- Have the children name other ways to solve problems peacefully.

Connect

Remind the children that God forgives us our sins in the sacrament of Reconciliation and gives us his gift of peace.

RESPOND

- Invite the children to read the introductory paragraph.
- Ask: When are you a peacemaker? Accept appropriate responses; for example, when I forgive others, I can be a peacemaker.
- Explain that the "Sharing God's Gift of Peace" activity will give them an opportunity to be peacemakers.
- Provide the children with sufficient time to complete the activity.

CHOOSE

- Invite the children to read "My Faith Choice."
- Encourage everyone to keep their faith choices in the week ahead.

What Difference Does Faith Make in My Life?

In the sacrament of Reconciliation, God forgives you and gives you the gift of peace. You need to forgive others too. When you forgive others, you are a peacemaker.

Fill in the empty spaces. Describe how you can be a peacemaker. Affirm appropriate responses.

Sharing God's Gift of Peace

I will ask the Holy Spirit to help me live as a peacemaker.

I will forgive my sister, brother, or friend.

I will show my forgiveness by saying

_____.

I will show my forgiveness by doing

_____.

My Faith Choice

This week I will forgive others. I will do what I have written on the lines above.

126

Teaching Tip

Affirm the Children. Each time you observe the children acting as peacemakers or offering forgiveness, make a point of affirming them. When the children are praised for making good choices, they will be encouraged to make more good choices. It is important to affirm the children for living as Jesus calls them to live.

We Pray

Father, We Are Sorry

Leader: Lord, our God, you always forgive us because of your great love.

All: **Fill our hearts with joy.**

Based on Psalm 51:3, 10

Reader: A reading from the holy Gospel according to John.

All: **Glory to you, O Lord.**

Reader: *Read John 20:19–23.*
The gospel of the Lord.

All: **Praise to you, Lord Jesus Christ.**

Leader: Lord, our God, you always forgive us.

All: **Fill our hearts with peace.**

We Remember

Complete the sentences. Use the words in the word bank.

Absolution	Confession
Contrition	Penance

1. Confession _____
   is the telling of our sins to the priest.

2. Contrition _____
   is true sorrow for our sins.

3. Penance _____
   is making up for our sins.

4. Absolution _____
   is receiving God's forgiveness for our sins.

To Help You Remember

1. We receive God's forgiveness for our sins in the sacrament of Reconciliation.

2. We sin when we choose to do or say something we know God does not want us to do or say.

3. Contrition, confession, penance, and absolution are always part of Reconciliation.

Grade 2 • Chapter 14 127

Liturgy Tip

Mass Responses. Point out to the children that the responses just before and after the Gospel reading in this lesson's prayer are the responses the assembly makes before and after the Gospel is proclaimed at Mass. Tell the children to learn these responses by heart as they prepare for their First Communion. Use these responses whenever a Gospel passage is read as part of your classroom prayer service.

Pray

WE PRAY

- Tell the children that the prayer today is a prayer of petition and praise and will include a reading from the Gospel of John. Then practice the responses.
- Invite a volunteer to read John 20:19–23, the Risen Jesus' appearance to his disciples, giving them the power to forgive sins.
- Gather the children in the prayer center.
- Lead the prayer.

Review

WE REMEMBER

- Scramble the letters of the words *forgiveness*, *Reconciliation*, and *absolution* on the board.
- Ask volunteers to come up and write the words correctly underneath each of the scrambled words.
- Ask other volunteers to find each of the words in the "To Help You Remember" statements and read the statements aloud to the class.
- Give directions for the "We Remember" activity and allow time for the children to complete it.

At Home

ENCOURAGE

Have the children carefully tear out pages 127 and 128 along the perforation. Encourage the children to share the pages with their families and to do the activities together. If they did not complete the review activity on page 127 by the end of the session, emphasize that they can complete it with their families.

VISIT FAITHFIRST.COM

- Share with the children the many activities on the *Faith First* Web site.
- Encourage the children to visit **www.FaithFirst.com.**

---

14 With My Family

This Week . . .

In chapter 14, "God's Forgiving Love," your child learned about sin and forgiveness. Sin is freely choosing to do or say something we know is against God's Law. We also sin when we freely choose not to do or say something that we know God wants us to do or say. Sin harms our relationship with God and others. Jesus gave us the sacrament of Reconciliation. In this sacrament we ask for and receive God's forgiveness for the sins we have committed after Baptism. We are reconciled with God and with the Church. We believe that God forgives our sins through the words and actions of the priest. Just as God forgives us, we must forgive others. It is the Holy Spirit who helps us tell God we are sorry, ask for forgiveness, and repair the harm we have caused by our sins.

For more on the teachings of the Catholic Church on the sacrament of Penance, or Reconciliation, see *Catechism of the Catholic Church* paragraph numbers 1420–1484.

Sharing God's Word

Read together John 20:19–23. Emphasize that in the sacrament of Reconciliation we receive God's forgiveness for our sins and God's gift of peace.

Praying

In this chapter your child celebrated a service of the word of God. Read and celebrate together the service of the word of God on page 127.

Making a Difference

Choose one of the following activities to do as a family or design a similar activity of your own.

- Read together the Bible story about Zacchaeus in Luke 19:1–10. Talk about the importance of repairing the harm that we cause by our sins.

- Using the four essential parts of Reconciliation described on page 124, pantomime the sacrament. Take turns being the priest. Be sure to include all four parts of the sacrament: confession, contrition, penance, and absolution.

- Talk about being peacemakers at home. Promise to help one another live as a family of peacemakers. At dinnertime this week pray to the Holy Spirit to help you live as peacemakers.

For more ideas on ways your family can live your faith, visit the "Faith First for Families" page at **www.FaithFirst.com**. The "Make a Difference" page goes especially well with this chapter.

Evaluate

Take a few moments to evaluate this week's lesson.
I feel (circle one) about this week's lesson.

- a. very pleased
- b. OK
- c. disappointed

The activity the children enjoyed most was . . .

The concept that was most difficult to teach was . . .

because . . .

Something I would like to do differently is . . .

Before Moving On . . .

As you finish today's lesson, reflect on the following question before moving on to the next chapter.

How flexible am I in adjusting time frames if the students are working well on an activity?

ENRICHING THE LESSON

Visiting the Reconciliation Room

Purpose

To reinforce the parts of the sacrament of Reconciliation (taught on page 124)

Directions

Bring the children to your parish church. Have them visit and become familiar with the place where they will meet privately with the priest during the celebration of the sacrament of Reconciliation.

- Take the role of the priest and invite volunteers to take turns being the penitents.
- Pantomime the steps of the sacrament.

Materials

Forgiveness Stories

Purpose

To reinforce the importance of being a peacemaker (taught on pages 125 and 126)

Directions

- In partners have the children write the outlines for a forgiveness story. Have them fill in the characters, the setting (place), and the problem to be solved.
- Have each pair of the children pass their outline to another set of partners and have them fill in the "solution."

Materials

paper and pencils

Continuing the Sacrament Booklets

Purpose

To reinforce the words and actions used in the sacrament of Reconciliation (taught on page 124)

Directions

Have the children continue to work in their sacrament booklets by adding a page for the sacrament of Reconciliation.

- Distribute the booklets to the children.
- Help them recall some key actions of the sacrament of Reconciliation.
- Invite them to write the word *Reconciliation* at the top of the next blank page of their booklets. Direct them to draw a picture of an action of the sacrament and to label their picture. Invite them to share their pictures with one another.
- Collect the booklets and store them for the children.

Materials

sacrament booklets
crayons or markers
pencils

Literature Connection

Purpose

To reinforce the need to ask for forgiveness when we sin (taught on page 123)

Directions

Read the story called "Ol' Meany McCrank," found in *A Child's First Book of Virtues* by Emily Hunter (Harvest House Publishers, 1995). It is a wonderful story of how repeated forgiveness can actually change a person.

Materials

A Child's First Book of Virtues by Emily Hunter

Music Connection

- "Psalm 51: Be Merciful, O Lord," P. Craig. *Singing Our Faith (SOF)* #24.
- "Standin' in the Need of Prayer" (African-American spiritual). *SOF* #228.
- "We Come to Ask Forgiveness," C. Landry. *Rise Up and Sing (RUS)* #90.
- "My God, My God," C. Walker. *RUS* #131.

We Gather for Mass

Background

"Do This in Remembrance of Me"

When we love someone, we want to be with that person. If we know we will be apart from them, we want to leave them something by which to remember us. We want to leave them something that is a sign of our presence with them and our love for them.

As Jesus was about to take his leave from his beloved friends, he gave them a gift. Christ gave the Church the Eucharist as a perpetual remembrance of his love and the unique sign of his presence with the Church. The Eucharist is the sacrament of the real presence of Christ with his Church. Through the words of the priest and the power of the Holy Spirit, the bread and wine become the Body and Blood of Christ. Christ is really and truly present with us. What appears to be bread is the Body of Christ. What appears to be wine is the Blood of Christ. What greater gift of love and presence could the Lord have given us!

Sharers in Christ's Sacrifice of Love

The Holy Sacrifice of the Mass makes present the one sacrifice of Christ on the cross. By his cross

and Resurrection, Christ has set us free from sin and death. Participation in the Eucharist makes us sharers in Christ's sacrifice on the cross, his great act of love for all humanity. When we receive Holy Communion, it is the Body and Blood of Christ we receive. When we participate in the Eucharist and receive Communion, we are joined to Christ, the Lamb of God. Christ not only gave himself for us on the cross; he gives himself to us again and again so that we may be made one with him, the Father, and the Holy Spirit, and live in communion with the Trinity now and forever. The Eucharist is the banquet of life. Jesus said, "[T]he one who feeds on me will have life because of me" (John 6:57). As natural foods nourish our physical life, Holy Communion nourishes our spiritual life.

There is danger that our appreciation of this gift of divine love may grow dull. Our participation in the Eucharist may become routine and be taken for granted. Perhaps after taking part in the

celebration of Mass for so many years, our focus drifts to the quality and length of the homily, or the impact of the music, or other elements of the celebration. We let these get in the way of our appreciating the mystery of love God invites us to share.

It is vital that we continuously ask the Holy Spirit to help us actively, consciously, and fully participate in the celebration of this "sacrament of sacraments" each and every time. We need to prepare our minds and hearts to embrace Christ, present with us. We need to remember who has invited us and celebrates with us—Jesus Christ himself. Befitting such a sublime banquet, we need to prepare ourselves for the honor of greeting the King of kings.

For Reflection

How can I prepare myself to actively, consciously, and fully participate in Mass?

How can I help make my participation in Mass an expression of love between Christ and me?

Catechist to Catechist

We Celebrate the Mass

Each child you teach comes with his or her own unique set of experiences of Mass. Some take part in Mass every Sunday with their families. Others may only attend on special occasions. Some may have been in Sunday school programs while parents and older siblings attended Mass. No matter what the children's previous experience, your role is to help them appreciate their rightful place in the worshiping assembly of the Church.

Prayer Gestures

When introducing the Mass to the children, there are many prayers, postures, responses, and songs to teach, but those are secondary to what must first take place. A  sense of love and sharing, celebration and reverence is most important. Through the efforts of the parish staff and caring parents, you can help the children realize that Jesus is present with us when we listen to his word and celebrate the Eucharist.

The Church Teaches . . .

Sharing experiences of participating in the celebration of Mass is rudimentary to catechesis. *The General Directory for Catechesis* reminds us:

> Every dimension of the faith, like the faith itself as a whole, must be rooted in human experience and not remain a mere adjunct to the human person.
> . . . In the liturgy, all personal life becomes a spiritual oblation. *GDC* 87

Therefore, we gather as the People of God for the celebration of Mass and, putting aside private prayer, participate in the Holy Sacrifice of the Mass.

See the Catechism . . .

For more on the teachings of the Catholic Church on the Eucharist, especially the Introductory Rites and the Liturgy of the Word, see *Catechism of the Catholic Church* 1322–1332 and 1345–1349.

CATECHIST PRAYER

In your wisdom, Lord,
you gifted us with the Church.
May I always remember
that at Mass
we come together
as your people
to give you praise and thanks.
Amen.

LESSON PLANNER

Focus To discover what happens when we celebrate the Liturgy of the Word

Engage

Page 129
Focus

To help the children identify why we gather for Mass

Opening Prayer

Discussion

All over the world Catholics gather to celebrate Mass.

Teach and Apply

Pages 130–132
Focus

To understand that at Mass we always listen to readings from Sacred Scripture

Presentation

Read, discuss, and summarize content.

Scripture

• Psalm 147:1

Activities

• Describe the action in the picture.
• Underline the Mass responses.
• Number the parts of the Liturgy of the Word in order.

Faith-Filled People
The Assembly

Connect

Pages 133–135
Focus

To discover ways we take part in the Liturgy of the Word

Our Church Makes a Difference

Understand that processions help us take part in Mass.

Our Catholic Faith
Sanctuary

What Difference Does Faith Make?
Activity

Draw or write about a Bible story heard at Mass.

Faith Choice

Check the ways you will take part in Mass.

We Pray

Page 135
Prayer Form
Prayer of petition
Prayer
Choose a leader, and pray together "Lord, Hear Our Prayer."

We Remember

Review
• Complete the matching activity.
• Read the "To Help You Remember" statements aloud.
Preview
Highlight features of the "With My Family" page.

Materials

pens and pencils

Enriching the Session

Blackline Masters
Additional Activities booklet:
Chapter 15
Singing a Good News song
Coloring vestments
Assessment Tools booklet:
Chapter 15 Test
Faith First Grade 2 Video
Segments 1 and 4: "Bible Songs"
Enriching the Lesson (CG page 229)
Role-playing the Liturgy of the Word
Sacrament Booklets
Literature Connection
Music Connection (CG page 229)

www.FaithFirst.com

We update the *Faith First* Web site weekly. Check each week for new content and features. Here are some places to begin:

Catechists and Teachers
• Current Events
• Chapter Downloads
• Catechist Prayer

Faith First **for Families**
• Bible Stories
• Saints
• Make a Difference

Kids' Clubhouse
• *Faith First* Activities
• Chapter Reviews
• Games

Don't Forget! You can make lesson planning a breeze—check out the **Online Lesson Planner.**

We Gather for Mass

We Pray

It is good to give praise to God!
Based on Psalm 147:1

God our Father, we worship you. We give you thanks. We praise you for your glory.
Amen.

When do families gather to celebrate?

Families gather to celebrate birthdays, holidays, and other special days. All over the world Catholics gather to celebrate Mass.

What do you see and hear at Mass?

129

PRAY

- Have the children quiet themselves for prayer.
- Pray the Sign of the Cross together.
- Invite a volunteer to read Psalm 147:1. Pray the opening prayer together.
- Conclude the prayer with the Sign of the Cross.

DISCOVER

Purpose: To discover what the children may already know about what happens at Mass

- Invite the children to share ways they celebrate birthdays, holidays, and other special days with their families.
- Invite volunteers to tell what they see in the photograph on page 129. Tell them that all over the world Catholics gather to celebrate the Mass.
- Invite responses to the question at the bottom of the page.

Liturgy Tip

Learning More About Liturgy. Since your second graders are probably preparing for their First Communion this year, you will want to give them the best understanding of the liturgy of the Catholic Church that you can. Be sure to check the resource shelves in your parish religious education office for books that can give you more background and ideas. Two books by Liturgy Training Publications, *Children in the Assembly of the Church* by Eleanor Bernstein and John Brooks-Leonard, editors, and *Preparing Liturgy for Children and Children for Liturgy* by Gabe Huck, are good sources.

FOCUS

Ask a volunteer to read the "Faith Focus" question aloud. Share with the children that in this chapter they will learn some things that happen when Catholics gather for Mass.

DISCOVER

- Explain that the most important celebration of our Church is the Mass.
- Invite a volunteer to read the first paragraph of "The Introductory Rites." Have the children follow along to discover who leads us in the celebration of Mass. A priest or bishop.
- Tell the children that the Mass begins with the Introductory Rites. This is a time when we sing, and the priest greets us and leads us in the opening prayer. We are reminded that God is with us.
- Summarize the second paragraph for the children. Write the priest's greeting and the assembly's response on the board. Invite a child to take the part of the priest, and invite the others to practice the response.

Apply

REINFORCE

Ask the children to read and highlight the word *Mass* and read its definition found in the "Faith Words." Have them create a word card for this term.

INTEGRATE

Ask a volunteer to describe what is happening in the picture.

(222) (Student Page 130)

The Mass

Faith Focus

What happens when we celebrate the Liturgy of the Word?

Faith Words

Mass
The Mass is the most important celebration of the Church. At Mass we worship God. We listen to God's word. We celebrate and share in the Eucharist.

Liturgy of the Word
The Liturgy of the Word is the first main part of the Mass. God speaks to us through the readings from the Bible.

The Introductory Rites

The **Mass** is the most important celebration of the Church. Only a priest or bishop can lead us in the celebration of Mass. He wears special clothes called vestments. At Mass we praise and thank God for all he has done, especially in Jesus. We listen to God's word. We celebrate and share in the Eucharist.

The Mass begins with the Introductory Rites. We stand and sing a hymn as the priest and other ministers enter the church in procession. After we sing the hymn, we pray the Sign of the Cross. The priest greets us, saying, "The Lord be with you." We respond, "And also with you." These words remind us that God is with us. The priest leads us in praying the Collect, or the opening prayer. We respond, "Amen."

ACTIVITY *Describe what is happening in the picture at the top of the page.*
The priest is greeting the assembly.

(130)

Special Needs

Providing Visual Cues. Read the two paragraphs under the heading "The Readings from the Bible" on page 131. On chart paper or on large poster board write the words "The word of the Lord" and "The gospel of the Lord." As you read the passage to the students point to the words. Ask the children to highlight or underline the response words in their books. Read the passage again and pause for the students to read the highlighted words together.

Need: Children with reading difficulties

The Liturgy of the Word

After the Introductory Rites, we celebrate the **Liturgy of the Word.** We listen and respond to God's word.

The Readings from the Bible

At Mass on Sundays and on Saturday evenings we listen to three readings. We sit for the first two readings. The first reading is usually from the Old Testament. After this reading, we sing or pray the responsorial psalm. The second reading is from the New Testament. At the end of both the first and the second readings, the reader says, "The word of the Lord." We respond, "Thanks be to God."

The third reading is from one of the four Gospels. On most days we get ready to listen to the Gospel by standing and singing "Alleluia." The deacon or priest proclaims the Gospel. When he is finished, he says, "The gospel of the Lord." We respond, "Praise to you, Lord Jesus Christ."

ACTIVITY *Underline the responses on pages 130 and 131. Learn them by heart. This will help you to take part in the Mass.*

✗ Faith-Filled People

The Assembly

The assembly is the people who gather to celebrate Mass. All members of the assembly share in the celebration of Mass.

131

✦ Background: Faith-Filled People

The Role of the Assembly. At the beginning of Mass we gather together and form a worshiping community. We call this praying community the assembly. Every member of the assembly has an active role in the Mass. In the Liturgy of the Word the assembly listens and responds to the word of God. In the Liturgy of the Eucharist we join with the priest in preparing our gifts of bread and wine. We join with him in giving thanks to God the Father, and we remember and take part in the death and Resurrection of Jesus. We prepare our minds and hearts to receive the Body and Blood of Christ. We receive the Eucharist and then are dismissed to go forth and bring peace to the world.

Teach

FOCUS

Remind the children that the Mass begins with the Introductory Rites. Then tell them that they are going to learn about the first main part of the Mass, which is called the Liturgy of the Word.

DISCOVER

- Ask the children to read the meaning of *Liturgy of the Word* found in the "Faith Words." Have them make a word card for this term.
- Present "The Liturgy of the Word" in your own words, and have the children listen for how many readings we listen to during the Liturgy of the Word. On Sunday we listen to three readings.
- Tell the children that each time they gather with their families for Mass, they are members of the assembly.
- Ask a volunteer to read "Faith-Filled People" to learn more about the assembly.

Apply

REINFORCE

Write the assembly's responses to the Bible readings at Mass on the board. Invite volunteers to come forward and take the part of the priest. Practice the responses with the children.

INTEGRATE

Ask the children to learn the responses by heart.

Teach

FOCUS

Recall the parts of the Liturgy of the Word that the children have learned. Tell the children they are going to learn about the other parts of the Liturgy of the Word.

DISCOVER

- Ask the children to listen for the meaning of *homily* as a volunteer reads this section.
- Invite another volunteer to read "The Profession of Faith."
- Explain to the children that when we pray the Creed, we are professing our faith in one God, who is Father, Son, and Holy Spirit.
- Ask the children to read "The Prayer of the Faithful" silently to find out who we pray for in this prayer. The Church, our country, and ourselves.

Apply

REINFORCE

Have the children work in pairs to complete the activity on this page.

INTEGRATE

Invite the children to share the part or parts of the Liturgy of the Word that they enjoy the most. Tell them your favorite part.

The Homily

After the Gospel is read, we sit. The priest or deacon helps us to understand the readings. This is called the homily.

The Profession of Faith

After the homily, we stand. Together we pray aloud a profession of faith, or a creed of the Church. We profess our faith in God the Father, God the Son, and God the Holy Spirit.

The Prayer of the Faithful

The last part of the Liturgy of the Word is the Prayer of the Faithful. We ask God to help the Church and our country. We pray for other people and for ourselves.

ACTIVITY *Number the parts of the Liturgy of the Word in the correct order.*

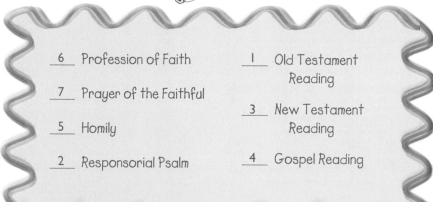

6 Profession of Faith	1 Old Testament Reading
7 Prayer of the Faithful	
5 Homily	3 New Testament Reading
2 Responsorial Psalm	4 Gospel Reading

132

Background: Cultural Diversity

The Lord's Day. Remind the children that Sunday is a special day for Christians. This is the day we call the Lord's Day. It is the day the Lord Jesus was raised from the dead. Catholics keep the Lord's Day holy by taking part in Mass, not doing unnecessary work, and spending time with our families.

Tell the children that Sunday is not the Lord's Day for non-Christians. Explain that the Jewish people celebrate Saturday as their Sabbath and holy day. The Jewish Sabbath begins at sundown on Friday night. They gather as families to praise and thank God for all his gifts and gather at their synagogues to worship God together as a people of faith. Then explain that our Muslim friends celebrate Friday as their holy day.

Our Church Makes a Difference

Processions at Mass

Processions are prayers in action. A procession is people prayerfully walking together. Processions help us to take part in the celebration of the Mass. There are five processions at Mass.

1. The entrance procession at the beginning of Mass

2. The Gospel procession during the Liturgy of the Word

3. The procession bringing up the gifts to the altar at the beginning of the Liturgy of the Eucharist

4. The procession to receive Holy Communion

5. The procession at the end of Mass

Processions help us remember that we are on a journey. We are on the journey to the kingdom of heaven.

 What processions do you take part in during Mass?

Affirm appropriate responses.

Our Catholic Faith

Sanctuary

The sanctuary is the place in the church where you see the altar and the ambo. The word *sanctuary* means "holy place." The ambo is the stand at which the readers, the deacon, and the priest proclaim the word of God.

133

Liturgy Tip

Gospel Preparation. Try to make time during your weekly session to prepare the children for the upcoming Sunday's Gospel reading. Hearing the Gospel reading ahead of time and discussing it with one another will prepare them to be more receptive to the Gospel when they listen to it on Sunday. It will also give them something familiar to look forward to hearing. And, for those children who may not take part in Mass this weekend they will have the chance to hear God's word. You can find resources at **www.FaithFirst.com** to help you in presenting the Gospel reading.

Connect

HIGHLIGHT

Share that we participate in the Mass in many ways.

DISCOVER

- Ask the children if they have ever been part of a procession. Ask them to describe their experiences.
- Summarize the first paragraph on page 133. Point out the difference between walking and processing.
- Tell the children that there are five processions at Mass. Invite five volunteers to read about the five processions.

INTEGRATE

- Ask the children to follow along as you read "Our Catholic Faith." Ask the children to tell what other things they have seen happening in the sanctuary.
- Divide the class into five groups. Have each group prepare to act out what they see in one of the processions at Mass. Encourage them to improvise props for their processions.

Connect

HIGHLIGHT

Remind the children that during Mass we listen and respond to the word of God.

RESPOND

- Have the children work with a partner to complete the activity. Remind the children that they can either draw or write their responses.
- Invite volunteers to share what their Bible story tells them about God's love.

CHOOSE

- Invite the children to read silently "My Faith Choice" and put a check next to their faith choices.
- Encourage everyone to put their faith choices into practice this week.

You take part in the celebration of Mass in many ways. During the Liturgy of the Word you listen and respond to the word of God.

Draw or write about a Bible story you heard at Mass. Write the title of your story on the line. Share what the story tells you about God's love.

Affirm appropriate responses.

My Faith Choice

The next time I take part in Mass, I will

- ❏ say the responses
- ❏ sing the hymns
- ❏ listen carefully to the readings
- ❏ pray the profession of faith
- ❏ _____ Affirm appropriate responses.

134

Teaching Tip

Cultural Diversity. Explain to the children that in some parishes on Sunday, the Scripture readings are proclaimed in more than one language. This is done because there are many parishioners who come to Mass whose first language is not English. They may or may not understand English as well as their second language, so the priest, deacon, or lector reads the Scriptures in the people's first language. That language may be Spanish, Korean, Chinese, one of the Native-American dialects, or another language. Tell the children that this is one way in which the Church helps all people to hear and understand God's word.

We Pray

Lord, Hear Our Prayer

At Mass we sometimes pray "Lord, hear our prayer" during the Prayer of the Faithful. Pray this prayer with your class.

Leader: God our Father, we ask for your help.
Let us pray for the Church,
for our family, and for friends.

All: **Lord, hear our prayer.**

Leader: Let us pray for people who are sick.

All: **Lord, hear our prayer.**

Child: For _____,
we pray to the Lord.

All: **Lord, hear our prayer.**

Leader: God our Father, send the Holy Spirit
upon all who need your help.
We ask this in the name of Jesus.

All: **Amen.**

We Remember

Match each word with its correct description.

Words

__c__ 1. readings

__a__ 2. homily

__b__ 3. creed

__d__ 4. Prayer of the Faithful

Descriptions

a. We listen to the priest or deacon as he helps us to understand God's word.

b. We profess our faith in God the Father, God the Son, and God the Holy Spirit.

c. We listen to God's word.

d. We ask God to help us and other people.

To Help You Remember

1. The Mass is the most important celebration of the Church.

2. At Mass we listen to the word of God.

3. At Mass we respond to the word of God.

Grade 2 • Chapter 15 (135)

☀ Teaching Tip

Videotaping a Sunday Liturgy. Get permission from your DRE, pastor, or parish administrator to have a qualified parishioner videotape one of your parish's Sunday liturgies so that it can be used as an instructional tool. Then, during each session that presents a part of the Mass, play just that part for the children. You may want to teach the lesson first, and then use the videotape as reinforcement. Be sure to point out the important sections and put the tape on pause while you add your own commentary.

WE PRAY

- Tell the children that today's prayer is a prayer of intercession that is similar to the Prayer of the Faithful at Sunday Mass.
- Practice the responses with the children.
- Gather the children in the prayer center.
- Lead the prayer.

Review

WE REMEMBER

- Write the word *Mass* on the board. As the children recall for you what happens at Mass, write key words from their responses around the word *Mass.*
- Invite volunteers to read the "To Help You Remember" statements and ask the children which key words written on the board are also in the statements.
- Give directions for the "We Remember" activity and allow time for the children to complete it.
- Ask volunteers to share their answers.

At Home

ENCOURAGE

Have the children carefully tear out pages 135 and 136 along the perforation. Encourage the children to share the pages with their families and to do the activities together. If they did not complete the review activity on page 135 by the end of the session, emphasize that they can complete it with their families.

VISIT FAITHFIRST.COM

- Share with the children the many activities on the *Faith First* Web site.
- Encourage the children to visit **www.FaithFirst.com.**

15 With My Family

This Week . . .

In chapter 15, "We Gather for Mass," your child learned about the Mass. The Mass is the most important celebration of the Church. We lift up our hearts to God the Father, through Jesus, in the Holy Spirit. We listen and respond to the word of God. We are made sharers in the life, suffering and death, Resurrection, and Ascension of Jesus. The Mass begins with the Introductory Rites during which the worshiping assembly prepares itself for the celebration of the Liturgy of the Word and the Liturgy of the Eucharist. During the Liturgy of the Word, we listen to God's word and make it part of our lives. We profess our faith and pray for the living and the dead.

For more on the teachings of the Catholic Church on the liturgical celebration of the Mass, especially the Introductory Rites and the Liturgy of the Word, see *Catechism of the Catholic Church* paragraph numbers 1322–1332 and 1345–1349.

Sharing God's Word

Read together Acts 2:42–47. Emphasize that from the beginning of the Church, Christians gathered to listen to the teachings and writings of the Apostles and to celebrate the Eucharist.

Praying

In this chapter your child prayed a prayer of the faithful. Read and pray together the prayer on page 135.

Making a Difference

Choose one of the following activities to do as a family or design a similar activity of your own.

- Sunday is called the Lord's Day. It is a day that Catholics take part in the celebration of Mass. We also spend time with members of our family. Talk about how your family keeps Sunday, the Lord's Day, holy.
- The first main part of the Mass is called the Liturgy of the Word. Review the responses for the Liturgy of the Word on page 290. Knowing the responses helps us participate in the Mass.
- Talk about the ways your family joins with the assembly and participates in the Mass.

For more ideas on ways your family can live your faith, visit the "Faith First for Families" page at **www.FaithFirst.com.** Visit "Bible Stories" this week and share the word of God with your child.

136

Before Moving On . . .

As you finish today's lesson, reflect on the following question before moving on to the next chapter.

What am I doing to involve students who seldom volunteer for activities?

✓ Evaluate

Take a few moments to evaluate this week's lesson.
I feel (circle one) about this week's lesson.

   a. very pleased
   b. OK
   c. disappointed

The activity the children enjoyed most was . . .

The concept that was most difficult to teach was . . .

because . . .

Something I would like to do differently is . . .

ENRICHING THE LESSON

Role Playing the Entrance Procession

Purpose

To reinforce the elements of the Introductory Rites of the Mass (taught in chapter 15)

Directions

- Teach the children the refrain to a familiar entrance hymn sung at your parish's Sunday liturgy.
- Invite children to take the parts of members of a Sunday entrance procession.
- Place signs around the children's necks that identify them as the priest, the deacon, extraordinary ministers of Holy Communion, lector, altar servers, and crossbearer. Role-play the entrance procession. Have the rest of the class be the assembly.
- Have everyone sing the entrance hymn as the children process to the prayer table.
- Repeat the activity so that other children can be a part of the procession.

Materials

small pieces of poster board
pieces of yarn or sturdy string
a processional cross and a Bible

Continuing Sacrament Booklets

Purpose

To reinforce the words and actions used in the Liturgy of the Word (taught on pages 131 and 132)

Directions

- Have the children continue to work on their sacrament booklets. Have them label the next page in their booklet *Eucharist: Liturgy of the Word.*
- Invite the children to draw a picture that shows something that happens during the Liturgy of the Word at Mass. Tell them to label their pictures.
- Invite them to share their drawings with one another.

Materials

sacrament booklets
pencils, crayons or markers

Literature Connection

Purpose

To reinforce the teaching about the Liturgy of the Word (taught on pages 131–132)

Directions

The beautifully illustrated children's storybook *Marianthe's Story: Painted Words and Spoken Memories* by Aliki (Greenwillow, 1998) tells the story of a young immigrant girl who struggles to tell the story of her people to her class. Because she does not speak English, she decides to tell her story in pictures, or "painted words."

- You then turn the book over and a second book appears. Marianthe has now learned English and tells her family's history in what are now "spoken memories."
- Ask the children what stories they know about their grandparents or other ancestors. Ask them to tell why they enjoy telling or listening to others tell these stories.

Materials

Marianthe's Story by Aliki

Music Connection

- "Circle Song," B. Farrell. *Rise Up and Sing (RUS)* #177.
- "Jesus, Be with Us," P. Inwood. *RUS* #191.
- "We Come to Your Table," C. Landry. *Singing Our Faith (SOF)* #237.
- "Song of the Body of Christ/Canción del Cuerpo de Cristo" (Hawaiian traditional), arr. D. Haas. *SOF* #240.

The Last Supper
A Scripture Story

Background

The Last Supper

At the Last Supper, Jesus took the bread and wine and changed them into his Body and Blood. In Luke's Gospel we read:

> Then he took the bread, said the blessing, broke it, and gave it to them, saying, "This is my body, which will be given for you; do this in memory of me." And likewise the cup after they had eaten, saying, "This cup is the new covenant in my blood, which will be shed for you."
>
> *LUKE 22:19–20*

Jesus' command to "do this in memory of me" has been acted upon by the Apostles and their successors. It has come to us as the Eucharist, the living sacrament of the Body and Blood of Christ.

Central to the celebration of the Eucharistic liturgy are the everyday items of bread and wine, which Jesus used at the Last Supper. At the Eucharist the bread and wine through the words of the priest and the power of the Holy Spirit become the Body and Blood of Christ.

Keeping the Love of Jesus Alive

The Last Supper discourses pass on to the Church the love Jesus had for the disciples. It is the same love that Jesus continues to have for the Church (see John 13:1).

At the Last Supper Jesus told his disciples that they were to love one another with the same love he had for them. To demonstrate his love, Jesus did an astonishing thing. He took off his outer garments, tied a towel around his waist, and proceeded to wash his disciples' feet. When he had finished, he commanded them,

> "If I, therefore, the master and teacher, have washed your feet, you ought to wash one another's feet. I have given you a model to follow, so that as I have done for you, you should also do." *JOHN 13:14–15*

For those of us who are catechists and ministers in the Church, Christ gives us the gift of his example. We have been chosen to be present to others and to serve them as Christ served.

At the Last Supper Jesus gave his disciples—as he gives us each time we share in the Eucharist— the gift of hope. He promised them that he would go and prepare a place for them in his Father's house (see John 14:3). He also assured them that those who love

one another love him and will be loved by the Father (see John 14:21). Finally, he promised that after he returned to his Father, the Father would send the Holy Spirit in his name. The Holy Spirit would keep his memory and love alive in their hearts—and in their actions.

For Reflection

How does my reflection on the Gospel accounts of the Last Supper keep the memory of Christ alive in my mind and heart?

How am I present to others as Christ is present to me as one who serves me out of love?

Catechist to Catechist

The Gift of the Eucharist

The celebration of special meals is a part of most children's experience. Use these experiences to help children understand the story of the Last Supper. Capitalize on their vivid imaginations and memories of celebrations that are special to them.

A Special Meal

Help the children understand what a special meal the Last Supper was for Jesus and his disciples. Help them see that the gift of his Body and Blood Jesus first gave to the disciples at the Last Supper he also gives to us at every celebration of the Mass. Every week, every day if we wish, we can approach the Lord's table to be fed with Jesus' own Body and Blood. We too hear the same request, "Do this in memory of me." We are now entrusted to retell and do what Jesus did at the Last Supper.

The Church Teaches . . .

The *General Directory for Catechesis* reminds us that the catechist assists parents in leading their children to faith. It states:

> Parents are the primary educators in the faith. . . . The family is defined as a "domestic Church."[1] . . . The family as a *locus* of catechesis has unique privilege: transmitting the Gospel by rooting it in the context of profound human values.[2] . . . It is, indeed, a Christian education more witnessed to than taught, more occasional than systematic, more ongoing and daily than structured into periods. *GDC* 255

Much of family life happens around the kitchen table. You can help a child root his or her faith in the experience of sharing a meal.

See the Catechism . . .

For more on the teachings of the Catholic Church on the Last Supper and the Eucharist, see *Catechism of the Catholic Church* 1333–1344.

CATECHIST PRAYER

I wonder, Lord, if I had been at the Last Supper, whether I would have realized how special the evening was. Help me know the honor of being invited to receive you in the Eucharist. Amen.

Footnote references may be found on p. 456.

LESSON PLANNER

Focus
To discover why the Last Supper is important to Christians

Engage

Page 137
Focus
To help the children relate what they know about the Last Supper

Opening Prayer

Discussion
Talk about family meals.

Teach and Apply

Pages 138–140
Focus
To discover that at the Last Supper Jesus gave us the gift of his Body and Blood, the Eucharist

Presentation
Read, discuss, and summarize content.
Scripture
• Psalm 150:2
• Luke 22:17–20
Activities
• Discover the message.
• Answer the question about the Church and the Last Supper.
• Stained-glass window of the Eucharist.

Connect

Pages 141–142
Focus
Explain how the Church shares her blessings with others

Our Church Makes a Difference
Discover how the Saint Francis Breadline is a way to love and serve others.

Our Catholic Faith
Washing of Feet

What Difference Does Faith Make?
Activity
Write a prayer of thanks.
Faith Choice
Identify a way to share your blessings this week.

We Pray

Page 143
Prayer Form
Prayer of Blessing
Prayer
Pray together "Blessed Be God."

We Remember

Review
• Complete the coded activity.
• Read the "To Help You Remember" statements aloud.

Preview
Highlight features of the "With My Family" page.

Materials

• pens or pencils
• crayons or markers

Enriching the Session

Blackline Masters
Additional Activities booklet:
Chapter 16
Singing a Mass Song
Solving a Last Supper crossword puzzle
Assessment Tools booklet:
Chapter 16 Test

Faith First Grade 2 Video
Segment 7: "The Lord's Supper"

Enriching the Lesson (CG page 241)
A Blessing to Thank God
Drawing the Last Supper
Literature Connection

Music Connection (CG page 241)

www.FaithFirst.com

We update the *Faith First* Web site weekly. Check each week for new content and features. Here are some places to begin:

Catechists and Teachers
• Current Events
• Chapter Downloads
• Catechist Prayer

Faith First for Families
• Bible Stories
• Saints
• Make a Difference

Kids' Clubhouse
• *Faith First* Activities
• Chapter Reviews
• Games

Don't Forget! You can make lesson planning a breeze—check out the **Online Lesson Planner.**

The Last Supper
A Scripture Story

16

We Pray

Praise God. . . .
Give praise for his
mighty deeds.
Psalm 150:1–2

**Let us give
thanks to the
Lord our God.
Amen.**

*What kinds of
stories does your
family share
at family meals?*

Jesus shared many
meals with his
disciples. At one
special meal each
year, they shared
the story of God's
love for his people.

*What do you know
about the last meal
Jesus shared with
his disciples?*

The chalice, bread, and
grapes—symbols for
the Eucharist

(137)

Liturgy Tip

Passover. The Passover is a Jewish feast during which the Jewish people remember and celebrate God's liberating them from slavery in Egypt and guiding them to freedom in the land he promised them. At the Passover meal Jewish people give thanks to God and praise him for all his wondrous deeds. It was at a Passover meal that Jesus instituted the Eucharist. At the Eucharist, the Church gives thanks and praise to God the Father. We join with Christ to give honor and glory in unity with the Holy Spirit to the Father.

PRAY

- Have the children quiet themselves for prayer.
- Pray the Sign of the Cross together.
- Invite a volunteer to read Psalm 150:2. Pray the opening prayer together.
- Close the prayer with the Sign of the Cross.

DISCOVER

Purpose: To discover what the children may already know about the Last Supper

- Invite the children to tell the kinds of stories that they share with their families at special family meals.
- Present the introductory paragraph and invite responses to the question.
- Invite the children to describe what they see in the photograph of the stained-glass window. Give help if needed.

Teach

FOCUS

Ask a volunteer to read the "Faith Focus" question aloud. Share with the children that in this chapter they will learn why the Last Supper is important for Christians.

DISCOVER

- Remind the children that some of the Scripture stories you have shared with them about Jesus involved eating a meal. Share that the Gospel story you will proclaim to them today also involves a meal.
- Summarize the first paragraph of "Jesus Celebrates Passover" to explain the meaning of this Jewish feast.
- Invite the children to read the second paragraph to learn how Passover and the Last Supper are connected. Point out to the children that the pictures on pages 138 and 139 both represent the Last Supper.

Apply

REINFORCE

Ask a volunteer to read aloud the definition of *Last Supper* in "Faith Words." Have the children make a word card for this term.

INTEGRATE

Have the children work in partners to complete the activity. Ask volunteers to share their answers to the puzzle.

Bible Background

Faith Focus

Why is the Last Supper important for Christians?

Faith Words

Last Supper
The Last Supper is the special meal that Jesus ate with his disciples on the night before he died.

Jesus Celebrates Passover

Passover is a holy time of the year for the Jewish people. Jesus belonged to the Jewish people. In the Old Testament the Jewish people are also called the Israelites. During Passover the Jewish people gather for a special meal. They bless and thank God for everything he has done and does for them.

Jesus ate this special meal with his disciples on the night before he died. This meal was the last meal Jesus and his disciples ate together. Christians call this meal the **Last Supper.**

ACTIVITY *Circle the first letter and every other letter. Discover what Jesus and the disciples did at the Last Supper.*

T O H B E R Y C B P L Z E
T S R S O E B D Z A F N I
D W T C H L A S N T K V E
F D J G U O S D.

_____
They blessed
_____
and thanked God   .

138

Teaching Tip

Acting Out the Last Supper. Many second graders remember a story best if they are actively involved with the telling of it. Invite the children to gather around a table or sit in a circle on the floor. Place a pitcher of grape juice (white grape juice will be best), some small paper cups, and a platter of unleavened bread, such as pita bread, in the center of the space. Pass cups of grape juice to each child. Pass around the platter of bread and ask each child to tear off a piece. Emphasize that they are simply acting out the Last Supper and that this is not in any way the celebration of the Eucharist. Take the part of Jesus yourself, and act out the story as told in Luke 22:17–20.

Reading the Word of God

The Last Supper

Jesus and his disciples shared the Last Supper in the city of Jerusalem. Jerusalem is the most important city of the Jewish people. Read what happened at the Last Supper.

During the meal Jesus took bread into his hands and said a blessing prayer. He broke the bread into pieces. Giving the bread to his disciples, Jesus said, "Take this. It is my body. Do this in memory of me."

Jesus took a cup of wine and gave thanks to God. Giving the cup of wine to his disciples, he said, "Drink it." They all drank from the cup. Jesus said, "This is my blood, which is poured out for many." Based on Luke 22:17–20

QUESTION When does the Church gather to do what Jesus asked us to do at the Last Supper? At the Eucharist

139

Background: Liturgy

Participation in the Eucharist. The "Constitution on the Sacred Liturgy (*Sacrosanctum concilium*)" was the first major document issued during the Second Vatican Council (December 4, 1964). It provided direction for revision of the rites of the Mass. Here are some of the major points from this document, which are now very familiar to us:

• The use of the vernacular, or language of the people, was approved so that the people could participate in the Mass more actively.

• The choice of Scripture readings proclaimed at Mass was extended.

• The homily was restored to greater prominence.

• The Prayer of the Faithful was restored.

Teach

FOCUS

Remind the children that Jesus celebrated a special Passover meal with his disciples. Christians call this meal the Last Supper. Tell the children they are going to find out about something very special that Jesus did at the Last Supper.

DISCOVER

• Set the scene for the story of the Last Supper by reading or asking a volunteer to read the first paragraph on page 139.

• Proclaim the Gospel story of the Last Supper based on Luke 22:17–20.

• Invite volunteers to tell the group what Jesus said and did at the Last Supper.

• Emphasize that Jesus told his disciples that bread and wine had become his Body and Blood.

Apply

REINFORCE

Ask the children to underline the words Jesus said at the Last Supper when he gave his disciples his Body and his Blood.

INTEGRATE

• Have the children close their eyes and imagine they are one of the disciples at the Last Supper with Jesus. Ask: Which disciple are you? Where are you sitting? What do you see Jesus doing? What do you hear Jesus saying?

• Ask volunteers to share their responses to the question on the bottom of the page.

Teach

FOCUS

Recall that Jesus gave his disciples his Body and Blood, the Eucharist, at the Last Supper. Share with the children that at the Eucharist, we do what Jesus and his disciples did at the Last Supper.

DISCOVER

- Present "We Gather Around the Altar" in your own words.
- Draw on the board a Venn Diagram of two large overlapping ovals. Ask the children to share how the Last Supper and the Mass are the same and how they are different. Write the differences in the large parts of the ovals and the similarities in the middle.

Apply

REINFORCE

Ask the children to highlight or underline the words in the second paragraph on page 140 that tell how the bread and wine become the Body and Blood of Christ at Mass.

INTEGRATE

Explain the activity. Ask volunteers to share their stained-glass windows and titles.

Understanding the Word of God

We Gather Around the Altar

Jesus gathered around a table with his disciples to celebrate the Last Supper. We gather around the altar to celebrate the Eucharist. Another name for the altar is the Table of the Lord.

At the Eucharist the Church does what Jesus did at the Last Supper. The priest takes bread and wine. Through the words of the priest and the power of the Holy Spirit, the bread and wine become the Body and Blood of Christ. We receive the Body and Blood of Christ in Holy Communion.

ACTIVITY Color the stained-glass window. Color the Xs white and Os yellow. Use other colors for the other spaces. On the line write a title for your window.

Responses will vary.

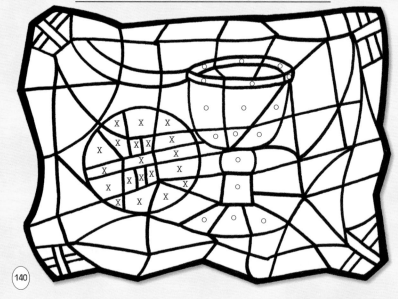

140

✝ Liturgy Tip

Altar Bread. Ask your parish priest or sacristan if you may have some unconsecrated altar bread or hosts to show to the children. Point out that it is the bread that is used for the celebration of Mass. Emphasize for the students that this bread is not the Eucharist we receive at Mass in Holy Communion. Tell the children that the bread used for Mass is called altar bread, Eucharistic bread, or hosts.

Our Church Makes a Difference

The Saint Francis Breadline

At the Last Supper, Jesus told his disciples to love and serve one another as he did. The Franciscans in New York City follow Jesus' command. Franciscans are followers of Saint Francis of Assisi.

People in New York City who need food or clothing come to the Church of Saint Francis of Assisi. The Franciscans are there every morning to greet them.

The Franciscans give each person sandwiches and something to drink. Most importantly, the Franciscans share a smile and words of welcome. They share the love and respect Saint Francis of Assisi himself shared with everyone he met.

Our Catholic Faith

Washing of Feet

Each year on Holy Thursday the Church celebrates the Evening Mass of the Lord's Supper. Jesus gave the Church the Eucharist at the Last Supper. Jesus also washed the feet of the disciples at the Last Supper. At this Mass on Holy Thursday, we celebrate the rite, or ceremony, of the washing of the feet. We remember that we must serve one another as Jesus served us.

QUESTION *What ways can you and your family serve people as Jesus told us to do?* Affirm appropriate responses.

141

Connect

HIGHLIGHT

Tell the children that they are going to discover a special way some members of the Church help others.

DISCOVER

- Tell the children about the Franciscans in New York who every day feed people who are hungry.
- Invite volunteers to read aloud "The Saint Francis Breadline."
- Remind the children that we need to remember to serve one another.

INTEGRATE

- Ask a volunteer to read "Our Catholic Faith" to learn more about the washing of feet on Holy Thursday.
- Remind the children that the followers of Jesus are called to help people in need.
- Discuss ways the children and their families might serve others. If time allows, have the children draw members of their families helping people. Be sure the children include themselves in their pictures.

Background: Our Catholic Faith

Jesus taught us the meaning of true service. When he washed the feet of his disciples, he taught the disciples (and us) by his example. As a catechist, you, together with the parents of the children, are a powerful team that can model Christ's teaching about serving others through your actions. Students learn best to serve others by seeing those whom they admire doing so. Do not underestimate the influence of your actions.

Connect

HIGHLIGHT

We thank God for his blessings by sharing them with others.

RESPOND

• Have the children read the introductory paragraph.

• Emphasize that we give thanks to God for his blessings by sharing our blessings with others.

• Explain the "Thank You, God" activity and give the children time to write their prayers of thanks. You can choose to have the children do this on their own, with a partner, or as a group.

CHOOSE

Invite the children to read "My Faith Choice" and write their faith decisions. Encourage everyone to put their choices into practice this week.

What Difference Does Faith Make in My Life?

At Mass you receive the gift of the Body and Blood of Christ. One way you can thank God for the blessings he gives you is by sharing your blessings with other people.

Write a prayer of thanks to God for all his blessings. Ask the Holy Spirit to help you share your blessings with others.

THANK YOU, GOD

Responses will vary.

My Faith Choice

This week I will share the blessings God has given me. I will

__Affirm appropriate responses.__

_____ .

142

Teaching Tip

Being Nourished. The children are well aware that nutritious food and daily exercise help them remain physically healthy. They are also aware that their brains need to keep thinking and learning new things. Relate this knowledge to develop the children's awareness of their responsibility to nourish their spiritual lives by reading and listening to Scripture, by praying each day, and by participating in the Mass.

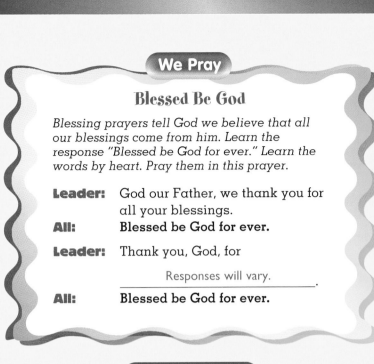

We Pray

Blessed Be God

Blessing prayers tell God we believe that all our blessings come from him. Learn the response "Blessed be God for ever." Learn the words by heart. Pray them in this prayer.

Leader: God our Father, we thank you for all your blessings.

All: **Blessed be God for ever.**

Leader: Thank you, God, for

_____ Responses will vary._____ .

All: **Blessed be God for ever.**

We Remember

Use the code to discover Jesus' words at the Last Supper.

1 = a	2 = e	3 = i	4 = o	5 = y

"T a k e   th i s.   I t   i s
   1   2   3   3   3

m y   b o d y.   Th i s
   5   4   5   3

i s   m y   bl o o d."
   3   5   4   4

To Help You Remember

1. Jesus ate the Last Supper with his disciples on the night before he died.

2. At the Last Supper Jesus gave his followers his Body and Blood.

3. At Mass we gather around the altar and do what Jesus did at the Last Supper.

Background: Doctrine

Jewish Roots. Help the children come to see that our Christian faith has its roots in the faith of the Jewish people, the first people chosen by God to be his people. One example of this connection is the blessing prayer, or *Berakah* in Hebrew, prayed at Mass. Point out to the children that during the Preparation of the Gifts at the beginning of the Liturgy of the Eucharist, the priest prays a prayer of blessing over the bread and a prayer of blessing over the wine, which will become the Body and Blood of Jesus. The assembly responds twice, "Blessed be God for ever."

Pray

WE PRAY

- Tell the children that today's prayer is a blessing prayer that is similar to the one we pray at Mass. Practice the response and invite the children to raise their hands in praise as they say it aloud.
- Gather the children in the prayer center.
- Lead the prayer.

Review

WE REMEMBER

- Write the terms *Last Supper*, *Body* and *Blood*, and *Mass* on the board. Ask volunteers to tell what each term means.
- Invite volunteers to read aloud each "To Help You Remember" statement one at a time.
- Introduce the review activity and explain the directions.
- Allow the children time to finish the activity. Then ask a volunteer to read the solution.

At Home

ENCOURAGE

Have the children carefully tear out pages 143 and 144 along the perforation. Encourage the children to share the pages with their families and to do the activities together. If they did not complete the review activity on page 143 by the end of the session, emphasize that they can complete it with their families.

VISIT FAITHFIRST.COM

- Share with the children the many activities on the *Faith First* Web site.
- Encourage the children to visit **www.FaithFirst.com.**

---

16 With My Family

This Week . . .

In chapter 16, "The Last Supper: A Scripture Story," your child learned about the Last Supper and the connection between the Last Supper and the Eucharist. At the Last Supper Jesus took the bread and gave it to his disciples, saying, "This is my body." He took the cup of wine and gave it to his disciples, saying, "This is my blood." Then he said, "Do this in memory of me." At the celebration of the Eucharist, the Church does what Jesus asked. We celebrate what happened at the Last Supper. Through the power of the Holy Spirit and the words of the priest, the bread and wine become the Body and Blood of Christ. Jesus is really and truly present under the appearances of bread and wine.

For more on the teachings of the Catholic Church on the Last Supper and the Eucharist, see *Catechism of the Catholic Church* paragraph numbers 1333–1344.

Sharing God's Word

Read together the Bible story in Luke 22:14–20 about the Last Supper or read the adaptation of the story on page 139. Emphasize that at the Last Supper Jesus instituted, or gave, the Church the Eucharist.

Praying

In this chapter your child prayed a blessing prayer, using a response from the Mass. Read and pray together the blessing prayer on page 143.

Making a Difference

Choose one of the following activities to do as a family or design a similar activity of your own.

- After your family takes part in Mass this week, take time to visit your parish tabernacle. The tabernacle is where the consecrated bread, or Blessed Sacrament, is kept.

- This week at Mass remind your child that what Jesus did at the Last Supper is part of the Eucharistic Prayer. After Mass talk with your child about the Last Supper and the Mass.

- The Eucharist strengthens us to love and serve others as Jesus commanded his followers to do. Choose one thing your family can do this week to live as followers of Jesus.

For more ideas on ways your family can live your faith, visit the "Faith First for Families" page at **www.FaithFirst.com.** Click on "Questions Kids Ask." Help your child grow in faith.

144

Before Moving On . . .

As you finish today's lesson, reflect on the following question before moving on to the next chapter.

How well do I communicate to the children that I enjoy being their catechist?

✓ Evaluate

Take a few moments to evaluate this week's lesson.
I feel (circle one) about this week's lesson.

- a. very pleased
- b. OK
- c. disappointed

The activity the children enjoyed most was . . .

The concept that was most difficult to teach was . . .

because . . .

Something I would like to do differently is . . .

ENRICHING THE LESSON

A Blessing to Thank God

Purpose

To reinforce the importance of thanking God for everything he has done (taught on page 138)

Directions

- Discuss with the children the importance of thanking God before their meals.
- Practice the grace before meals found on page 285.
- Using an easy recipe for bread, have the children work with you to prepare the ingredients and place them in plastic bags.
- Send the ingredients for making bread home with the children. Include both a card with baking instructions and a card with the grace before meals.
- Remind the children to pray the grace before meals before they serve and eat the bread.

Materials

ingredients for bread
disposable baking pans
cards with the grace before meals

Drawing the Last Supper

Purpose

To reinforce the Scripture story of the Last Supper (taught on page 139)

Directions

- Borrow from your local library or from your family and friends images of the Last Supper. Display the images and talk about them with the children.
- Invite the children to draw their own images of the Last Supper.
- Display the children's drawings in a place where parishioners can enjoy them.

Materials

construction paper
markers or crayons

Literature Connection

Purpose

To reinforce the concept of Passover (taught on page 138)

Directions

There are many wonderful books for children that retell the story of Passover. This great Jewish story of faith is a story the children will enjoy reading.

- Here are a few titles that you might use: *The Story of Passover* by Norma Simon (HarperCollins, 1998); *Four Special Questions, A Passover Story* by Jonny Zucker (Barron's Educational Series, Inc., 2003); and *Why on This Night?* by Louise August (Simon & Schuster Children's Press, 2000).
- After reading one of these stories, reinforce with the children the similarities and differences between the Passover meal and the Mass.

Materials

one of the above books

Music Connection

- "Jesus, Be with Us," P. Inwood. *Rise Up and Sing (RUS)* #191.
- "Memorial Acclamation C," M. Haugen. *Singing Our Faith (SOF)* #75.
- "We Come to Your Table," C. Landry. *SOF* #237.
- "Take and Eat," C. Landry. *SOF* #238.

Chapter 17

We Give Thanks to God

Background

The Breaking of Bread

The Mass has several other names that help us come to know the meaning of the mystery of the Eucharist. One such name is the "Breaking of Bread." Just as Christ broke and distributed bread at the Passover meal of the Last Supper, the Mass repeats these actions. Jesus told his disciples that by doing this they will recognize him in times to come. Thus, the celebrating of the Eucharist in the first Christian assemblies was known as the Breaking of Bread.

It was above all on "the first day of the week," Sunday, the day of Jesus' resurrection, that the Christians met "to break bread."[1] From that time on down to our own day the celebration of the Eucharist has been continued so that today we encounter it everywhere in the Church with the same fundamental structure. It remains the center of the Church's life.

CATECHISM OF THE CATHOLIC CHURCH 1343

The Mass Today

The Acts of the Apostles tells that the early Church in Jerusalem devoted itself to the "teaching of the apostles and to the communal life, to the breaking of the bread and to the prayers" (Acts of the Apostles 2:42). Every day the followers of Christ, with "exultation and sincerity of heart," would break bread together in their homes (Acts of the Apostles 2:46).

The rites of the Mass as they are celebrated today bear a close resemblance to the breaking of bread, or the celebration of the Eucharist, in the early Church. Around the year 155, Saint Justin the Martyr wrote a description of the Eucharistic celebration. Here is a summary of what he had to say:

- "On the day we call the day of the sun, all who dwell in the city or country gather in the same place."

- They would read from the "memories of the apostles and the writings of the prophets." (Liturgy of the Word)
- The presider challenges the faithful "to imitate these beautiful things." (Homily)
- Then they all stand and "offer prayers for ourselves . . . and for all others." (Intercessions)
- "When the prayers are concluded, we exchange a kiss." (Sign of Peace)
- Then bread and a mixture of water and wine are brought to the presider. (Presentation of the Gifts)
- The presider offers praise and glory to God: Father, Son, and Holy Spirit. "He gives thanks that we have been judged worthy of these gifts." (Eucharistic Prayer)
- The "eucharistic bread" is then given to those present and sent to those absent. (Communion)

For Reflection

What does the name "breaking of bread" evoke in me about my participation in the Eucharist?

How does my participation in the Eucharist strengthen my participation in the communal life of the Church?

Catechist to Catechist

What We Give

Children love to receive and give gifts. However, because they are children, there is often much more excitement over receiving gifts than over giving gifts. Many times children and adults alike will say they get nothing out of going to Mass. We need to teach the children that they need to give at Mass. They need to offer the gift of themselves along with the gifts of bread and wine—their attention, their voices, their desire to go out and make a difference by living as Jesus did.

Participating in Mass

While it is important to teach children reverence and respect, sometimes we place more emphasis on how well children behave during Mass than on how well they participate. It is important for the children, who have come to join with the parish community, to celebrate, to be nourished, and to praise and thank God the Father with their whole beings.

The Church Teaches . . .

The *General Directory for Catechesis* clearly states that the Eucharist is the "sacrament of sacraments."

[T]he Holy Eucharist occupies a unique place to which all of the other sacraments are ordained. The Eucharist is to be presented as the "sacrament of sacraments"[1] (*GDC* 115).

In your teaching about the Eucharist always emphasize that the Eucharist is the "source and summit of Christian life"[2] (*CCC* 1324).

See the Catechism . . .

For more on the teachings of the Catholic Church on the Eucharist, see *Catechism of the Catholic Church* 1345–1405.

CATECHIST PRAYER

Jesus, Bread of Life,
may I always approach
your table conscious of
the gift I am to receive.
Help me to lead your children
to know your love
as they approach the day
of their First Communion.
Amen.

Footnote references may be found on p. 456.

LESSON PLANNER

Engage

Page 145
Focus
To help the children identify the special gift we thank God for at Mass

Opening Prayer

Discussion
What do you say when you receive a gift?

Materials

pens or pencils

Teach and Apply

Pages 146–148
Focus
To recognize that the Eucharistic Prayer is the Church's great prayer of thanksgiving

Presentation
Read, discuss, and summarize content.
Scripture
• Psalm 92:2
Activities
• Pray "Blessed Be God Forever."
• Color the letters "Amen.'
• Choose ways to live as followers of Jesus.
Faith-Filled People
Saint Pope Pius X

Enriching the Session

Blackline Masters
Additional Activities booklet:
Chapter 17
Creating a thank-you billboard
Writing an e-mail about being grateful
Assessment Tools booklet:
Chapter 17 Test
Faith First **Grade 2 Video**
Segment 7: "The Lord's Supper"
Enriching the Lesson (CG page 253)
Writing Letters to Jesus
Completing Sacrament Booklets
Reinforcing Faith Words
Music Connection (CG page 253)

Connect

Pages 149–150
Focus
To identify ways the Church loves and serves the Lord as we are told to do at Mass

Our Church Makes a Difference
Understand the Concluding Rites of the Mass.
Our Catholic Faith
The Holy Sacrifice of the Mass
What Difference Does Faith Make?
Activity
Name reasons Catholics celebrate Mass.
Faith Choice
Identify a way to show thanks to God this week.

www.FaithFirst.com

We update the *Faith First* Web site weekly. Check each week for new content and features. Here are some places to begin:

Catechists and Teachers
• Current Events
• Chapter Downloads
• Catechist Prayer
Faith First **for Families**
• Bible Stories
• Saints
• Make a Difference
Kids' Clubhouse
• *Faith First* Activities
• Chapter Reviews
• Games

Don't Forget! You can make lesson planning a breeze—check out the **Online Lesson Planner.**

We Pray

Page 151
Prayer Form
Prayer of petition
Prayer
Pray "The Lamb of God" together.

We Remember

Review
• Complete the sentence activity.
• Read the "To Help You Remember" statements aloud.
Preview
Highlight features of the "With My Family" page.

We Give Thanks to God

17

We Pray

It is good to give thanks to the LORD.
Psalm 92:2

Father, always and everywhere we give you thanks through Jesus Christ, your Son.
Amen.

What is a gift you have received?

When we receive a gift, we say, "Thank you." At Mass we thank God for Jesus and for everything he did for us.

What are you thankful to God for?

145

Background: The Importance of Gratitude

Children often have a sense that they deserve all they have or that they are entitled to things. Emphasize that expressing thanks and gratitude is always important. People like to hear "Thank you" when they have done something kind for someone or given someone a gift. Help the children understand that we do not deserve anything from God. We have done nothing on our own to deserve all the blessings God has given us.

Engage

PRAY

- Have the children quiet themselves for prayer.
- Begin the prayer experience with the Sign of the Cross.
- Have a volunteer read Psalm 92:2.
- Lead the opening prayer and invite the children to echo each phrase after you.
- Close the prayer with the Sign of the Cross.

DISCOVER

Purpose: To discover what the children may already know about the importance of showing gratitude

- Ask the children to tell you about times that they use the words *Thank you*. Ask volunteers to describe a gift they have received.
- Present the introductory paragraph in your own words and invite responses to the question.
- Invite the children to look at the photograph and describe what is happening. The priest is holding the Body and Blood of Christ and giving honor and glory to God the Father at the conclusion of the Eucharist prayer.

Teach

FOCUS

Ask a volunteer to read the "Faith Focus" question aloud. Tell the children that in this chapter they will learn about the Liturgy of the Eucharist, the second main part of the Mass.

DISCOVER

- Remind the children that the Eucharist is Jesus' gift of his Body and Blood to us.
- Tell them that the word *Eucharist* means "to give thanks."
- Ask if any of the children have ever brought the gifts of bread and wine to the altar during Mass. Have volunteers describe their experience. If no one responds, briefly share what happens.
- Ask the children to read to discover what the priest does and says when he accepts the gifts of bread and wine from us.

Apply

REINFORCE

- Ask the children to highlight the responses "Blessed be God for ever" and "Amen" on the page.
- Read together the meanings of the faith words *Eucharist* and *Liturgy of the Eucharist*. Ask the children to create flash cards from the terms.

INTEGRATE

Invite the children to complete the activity.

Give Thanks and Praise to God

Faith Focus

What happens when we celebrate the Liturgy of the Eucharist?

Faith Words

Eucharist
The Eucharist is the sacrament of the Body and Blood of Jesus Christ.

Liturgy of the Eucharist
The Liturgy of the Eucharist is the second main part of the Mass. The Church does what Jesus did at the Last Supper.

The Liturgy of the Eucharist

The **Liturgy of the Eucharist** is the second main part of the Mass. The word *eucharist* means "to give thanks."

The Preparation of the Gifts

The Liturgy of the Eucharist begins with the preparation of the gifts. Members of the assembly bring our gifts of bread and wine to the altar. The priest tells God all our blessings come from him. We respond, "Blessed be God for ever." The priest then leads us in the Prayer over the Offerings. We respond, "Amen."

ACTIVITY *Think of the blessings God has given you and your family. Pray with your class, "Blessed be God for ever."*

146

Liturgy Tip

Bread and Wine. At Mass we use unleavened bread made from wheat and wine made from grapes as Jesus did at the Last Supper. Unleavened bread is made without yeast. At Mass the bread and wine become the Body and Blood of Jesus through the words of the priest and the power of the Holy Spirit.

The Eucharistic Prayer

The Eucharistic Prayer is the Church's great prayer of thanksgiving. During this prayer the Church does what Jesus did at the Last Supper.

> The priest holds the bread in his hands and says,
> "Take this, all of you, and eat it: this is my body which will be given up for you."
>
> Then the priest holds up the chalice of wine and says,
> "Take this, all of you, and drink from it: this is the cup of my blood, the blood of the new and everlasting covenant. It will be shed for you and for all so that sins may be forgiven. Do this in memory of me."

The bread and wine become Jesus' Body and Blood through the power of the Holy Spirit and the words of the priest. What looks like bread and wine is no longer bread and wine. It is really Jesus. At the end of the Eucharistic Prayer the assembly stands and sings "Amen."

Faith-Filled People

Pope Pius X

Saint Pius X was a pope. He is called "Pius the Tenth" because he was the tenth pope to use the name Pius. Saint Pius X made a rule that Catholics as young as seven years old could receive Holy Communion. He also told Catholics that it was important that they receive Holy Communion often. The Church celebrates the feast day of Saint Pius X on August 21.

ACTIVITY Amen means "It is true." Color the letters in the word Amen. Think of what happens at Mass and pray "Amen."

147

Background: Faith-Filled People

Saint Pius X. Saint Pius X was elected pope on August 4, 1903. The motto for his papacy was "To restore all things in Christ." The new pope was determined to make his papacy truly pastoral. In addition to lowering the age for receiving First Communion to the age of discretion, approximately seven years of age, he reorganized the Roman Curia, updated Canon Law and seminary curricula, and encouraged the laity to advance the kingdom of God. He fully realized that the Eucharist unites us more closely with Christ and one another.

Teach

FOCUS

Remind the children that the Liturgy of the Eucharist is the second main part of the Mass. Then point out that they are going to learn about a special prayer that is part of the Liturgy of the Eucharist.

DISCOVER

- Help the children recall what Jesus said and did at the Last Supper. Then explain that at Mass the priest does what Jesus did at the Last Supper.
- Invite volunteers to read aloud "The Eucharistic Prayer."
- Emphasize that when we receive Holy Communion, what looks like bread and wine is really the Body and Blood of Christ.
- Read "Faith-Filled People" aloud to help the children learn what rule Saint Pius X made about receiving Holy Communion.

Apply

REINFORCE

Emphasize that through the power of the Holy Spirit and the words of the priest, the bread and wine become Jesus' Body and Blood at Mass.

INTEGRATE

- Have the children underline the words the priest says. Together read the words aloud.
- Read the activity aloud to the children. Invite them to color the letters spelling *Amen*. After they have finished coloring the letters recall with the children what happens at Mass and together pray "Amen."

Teach

FOCUS
Remind the children that the Eucharistic Prayer is the Church's great prayer of thanksgiving. We are now going to learn what happens after we finish praying the Eucharistic Prayer.

DISCOVER
- Write the word *communion* on the board. Explain that being in communion with someone means being very close to them.
- Read the text on this page aloud to the children.
- Ask the children to highlight our response to the words "The Body of Christ" and "The Blood of Christ."

Apply

REINFORCE
Review the meaning of the faith word *Eucharist* together.

INTEGRATE
- Look at the picture on page 148. Use the information in the "We Celebrate the Mass" section in the back of this guide to review with the children how to receive Holy Communion.
- Allow the children time to complete the activity. Ask a volunteer to share what they have written.

Communion

We walk in procession to receive the consecrated bread at the altar. The Eucharist is offered to us with the words "The body of Christ." We bow our heads to honor Jesus present in the sacrament and respond, "Amen." We receive and eat the consecrated bread.

If we receive from the cup, the cup of consecrated wine is offered to us. We hear the words "The blood of Christ." We bow our heads and respond, "Amen." We take the cup and drink from it.

We receive strength to live as followers of Jesus. We become closer to Jesus, Mary, the saints, and all the members of the Church. We receive Jesus' promise, or pledge, that we too will live forever in heaven.

ACTIVITY On each note card write one way you live as a follower of Jesus.
Responses will vary.
Affirm appropriate responses.

148

Liturgy Tip

Source of the Christian Life. Taking part in Sunday liturgy carries through the entire week—our whole lives lead to and from the celebration of Eucharist. The Eucharist nourishes us to live our faith. The Eucharist is the source and summit of the Christian life. That is why active participation in the liturgy is so vital to the Christian life. Lead by example and be present at Sunday Mass. Let the children know what Mass you go to and encourage them to come and bring their families.

Our Church Makes a Difference

Love and Serve the Lord

The celebration of Mass ends with the Concluding Rites. We receive God's blessing. The deacon or priest sends us forth using these or similar words, "Go in peace to love and serve the Lord." We respond, "Thanks be to God."

We show our thanks to God when we try our best to live as Jesus taught. We try to love one another. We do things that are difficult to do because of our love for God and for others. When we do this, we love God and people as Jesus did.

Our Catholic Faith

The Holy Sacrifice

Jesus' sacrifice on the cross is the greatest act of love for God the Father and for all people. The Mass is also called the Holy Sacrifice. At Mass we share in the sacrifice of Jesus. We join with Jesus and show our love for God. We receive God's grace to love one another as Jesus commanded us to do.

QUESTION *These children have chosen ways to live as Jesus taught. What is one way you can live as Jesus taught?*

149

Liturgy Tip

To Love and Serve the Lord. Remind the children of the actions that precede and follow the Dismissal. The priest first prays that we will take the graces we have received at the Eucharist and carry them into our everyday lives. He then invokes God's blessing upon us and dismisses us to continue the work of the Eucharist. The words remind us that it is only in a spirit of peace that we can do the fruitful work of loving and serving the Lord and one another. Our response is a prayer of thanksgiving for all the gifts we have received and the opportunity we now have to share them with others. We pray "Thanks be to God" and join in singing a final hymn as the priest, deacon, lectors, and servers process from the Church.

Connect

HIGHLIGHT

Share that the Mass ends with the Concluding Rites.

DISCOVER

- Begin reading aloud "Love and Serve the Lord." When you get to the words "Go in peace . . ." read them prayerfully and ask the group to read the response.
- Invite the children to finish reading the rest of the page silently.
- Have the children listen for why we call the Mass a Holy Sacrifice as you read "Our Catholic Faith."

INTEGRATE

Introduce the activity. Have the children share ways they can live as Jesus taught.

Connect

Remind the children that in the Eucharist we receive the grace to live as followers of Jesus.

RESPOND

- Explain the activity directions to the children clearly.
- Have the children complete the activity on their own or with a partner.

CHOOSE

- Invite the children to read "My Faith Choice" and to write their decisions.
- Encourage them to put their choices into practice this week.

What Difference Does Faith Make in My Life?

When you share in the Eucharist, you receive the grace to live as a follower of Jesus.

On each door write one reason Catholics celebrate Mass.

Celebrating Mass

Responses will vary.

My Faith Choice

I will show my thanks to God this week for the gift of the Eucharist. I will

Affirm appropriate responses.

_____

150

Teaching Tip

Making Altar Bread and Wine. Tell the children that many orders of religious sisters support themselves by making altar bread (hosts). The hosts are bought by parishes and other Catholic groups for use as sacred bread at Mass. Contact your diocesan office to locate a monastery in your area that is involved in this special ministry. Contact the monastery and ask the sisters if they could loan you photographs of the sisters involved in each step of the host-making process.

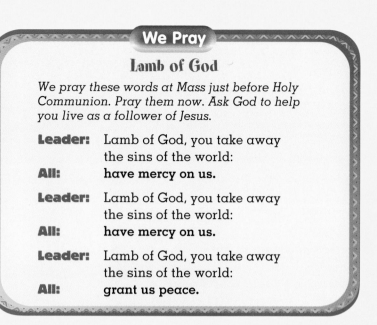

We Pray

Lamb of God

We pray these words at Mass just before Holy Communion. Pray them now. Ask God to help you live as a follower of Jesus.

Leader: Lamb of God, you take away the sins of the world:

All: **have mercy on us.**

Leader: Lamb of God, you take away the sins of the world:

All: **have mercy on us.**

Leader: Lamb of God, you take away the sins of the world:

All: **grant us peace.**

We Remember

Draw a line from each word in the left column to the sentence it completes in the right column.

Words	Sentences
sacrament	The _____ is the Church's great prayer of thanksgiving.
Eucharistic Prayer	At the Eucharist we do what Jesus did at the _____.
Last Supper	The Eucharist is the _____ of the Body and Blood of Christ.

To Help You Remember

1. At the celebration of the Eucharist the bread and wine become the Body and Blood of Jesus.
2. We receive the Body and Blood of Jesus in Holy Communion.
3. Receiving Holy Communion makes us closer to Jesus and to one another.

Grade 2 • Chapter 17 151

Liturgy Tip

Praying the "Lamb of God." The children will be praying this ancient prayer at liturgy for the rest of their lives. Help them to appreciate its significance. In this invocation, repeated three times, the priest and assembly petition Jesus Christ, the Lamb of God, to grant us mercy and peace. Before the Second Vatican Council this prayer was recited or sung in Latin. Teach the children to pray this invocation using gestures, for example, they might cross their arms over their chests and bow their heads as they say, "Have mercy on us." You could then close your prayer service by having the children exchange a sign of peace with one another as would happen at Mass.

Pray

WE PRAY

- Gather the children in the prayer center. Tell them that our prayer today is a prayer we say just before Holy Communion.
- Rehearse the three responses and point out that the third response is different from the first two.
- Tell the children to bow their heads as they pray each response.
- Lead the prayer.

Review

WE REMEMBER

- Write a word bank with the words *Eucharist, Jesus,* and *Holy Communion* on the board. Read the "To Help You Remember" statements aloud, omitting "Eucharist" in the first statement, "Holy Communion" in the second, and "Jesus" in the third statement.
- Ask volunteers to use the word bank to fill in the missing words.
- Ask a volunteer to read each of the "To Help You Remember" statements aloud to check the responses.
- Introduce the activity and give the children time to complete it.

At Home

ENCOURAGE

Have the children carefully tear out pages 151 and 152 along the perforation. Encourage the children to share the pages with their families and to do the activities together. If they did not complete the review activity on page 151 by the end of the session, emphasize that they can complete it with their families.

VISIT FAITHFIRST.COM

- Share with the children the many activities on the *Faith First* Web site.
- Encourage the children to visit **www.FaithFirst.com.**

Before Moving On . . .

As you finish today's lesson, reflect on the following question before moving on to the next chapter.

What more could I do to incorporate music into our sessions?

---

17 With My Family

This Week . . .

In chapter 17, "We Give Thanks to God," your child learned about the Liturgy of the Eucharist and the Concluding Rites of the Mass. The Eucharistic Prayer, the Church's great prayer of thanksgiving to God, is at the center of the Liturgy of the Eucharist. During the Eucharistic Prayer the Church remembers and does what Jesus did at the Last Supper. Through the power of the Holy Spirit and the words of the priest, the bread and wine become the Body and Blood of Jesus. The consecrated bread is really Jesus. The consecrated wine is really Jesus.

For more on the teachings of the Catholic Church on the Eucharist, see *Catechism of the Catholic Church* paragraph numbers 1345–1405.

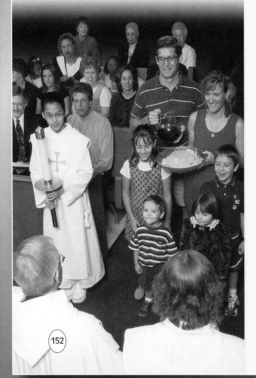

Sharing God's Word

Read together 1 Corinthians 11:23–26. Emphasize that at Mass the bread and wine become the Body and Blood of Jesus.

Praying

In this chapter your child prayed one of the prayers of the Mass. Read and pray together the prayer on page 151.

Making a Difference

Choose one of the following activities to do as a family or design a similar activity of your own.

- Sign up as a family to bring up the gifts at Mass.
- The Liturgy of the Eucharist is the second main part of the Mass. Review the Liturgy of the Eucharist on pages 291–294 and help your child learn the appropriate responses by heart. Knowing the responses helps us participate more fully and actively in the Mass.
- In the Concluding Rites, the priest sends us forth, using these or similar words, "Go in peace to love and serve the Lord." Talk about how your family can love and serve the Lord this week.

For more ideas on ways your family can live your faith, visit the "Faith First for Families" page at **www.FaithFirst.com**. Click on "Contemporary Issues" to find an interesting article on religion in today's world.

152

Evaluate

Take a few moments to evaluate this week's lesson.
I feel (circle one) about this week's lesson.

    a. very pleased
    b. OK
    c. disappointed

The activity the children enjoyed most was . . .

The concept that was most difficult to teach was . . .

because . . .

Something I would like to do differently is . . .

ENRICHING THE LESSON

Completing Sacrament Booklets

Purpose

To reinforce the teaching about the Liturgy of the Eucharist (taught in chapter 17)

Directions

Today the children will complete the sacrament booklets they have been making throughout Unit 2.

- Invite the children to turn to the next page in their booklets and write the words *Eucharist: Liturgy of the Eucharist* at the top of the page.
- Help the children recall some of the actions of this part of the Mass. Have them draw a picture of one of these actions beneath the page title. Invite them to share their drawings with one another.
- Praise the children for all their work on the sacrament booklets. Encourage the children to take their booklets home and share them with their families.

Materials

note paper, pens or pencils

Reinforcing Faith Words

Purpose

To reinforce the new vocabulary (taught in chapters 11 to 17)

Directions

- Tell the children to take out the word cards they have been making during this unit. In partners have the children play a guessing game.
- Model the activity for them by choosing a vocabulary word and giving a clue about it. Continue offering clues until someone in the class guesses the word.
- Ask the children to take turns quizzing each other on the words in the same way. Have them continue until they have covered all the faith words in the unit.

Materials

the children's word cards

Literature Connection

Purpose

To reinforce the theme of thanksgiving in the Eucharist (taught on pages 146–147)

Directions

The picture book *Thank You, Grandpa* by Lynn Plourde (Dutton, 2003) explores the theme of thanksgiving for the fleeting gifts of life. In this touching story, a young girl and her grandpa take walks together. In their encounters with nature the old man shows the little girl how to say "thank you and good-bye" to the gifts of nature that come and go. Finally, as her grandfather dies, the girl, now older, is able to look back with gratitude on the many gifts he gave to her.

- Read the story aloud to the children. Share the illustrations with them and help them notice the differences in the two characters as they grow older.
- Ask the children to share the things for which they are most grateful in their lives.
- Remind them that the Eucharistic Prayer at Mass is the Church's great prayer of thanksgiving for the gift of Jesus.

Materials

Thank You, Grandpa by Lynn Plourde

Music Connection

- "We Come to Share God's Special Gift," C. Walker. *Rise Up and Sing* #193.
- "Lamb of God," R. Proulx. *Singing Our Faith (SOF)* #95.
- "Friends, All Gather 'Round," J. Doucet/C. Landry. *SOF* #233.
- "We Come to Your Table," C. Landry. *SOF* #237.

Unit 2 Review

The unit review provides the opportunity to assess the children's understanding of the concepts presented in the unit and to affirm them in their growing knowledge and love of God.

Here are a few suggestions for using these pages:

- Share that the next two pages are an opportunity to stop and review what they have learned.
- Provide time for the children to ask questions.
- Have the children complete the review alone or with a partner.

PART A: The Best Word

This section reviews the main concepts of the unit.

- Read the directions for section A. Illustrate what you expect the children to do by completing the first question together. By working together on the first question, you are teaching the children a strategy for answering these types of questions.
- When the children have finished this section, invite volunteers to share their answers. Review any questions that the children seem to have difficulty answering.

FAMILY CONNECTION

Encourage the children to share the unit review pages with their families. This provides an excellent opportunity to involve the families in the faith formation of their children.

Review Unit 2   Name _____

A. The Best Word

Complete the sentences. Color the circle next to the best choice for each sentence.

1. The seven ___ are signs of God's love for us.

   ○ Bibles   ● sacraments   ○ prayers

2. Water and oil are used in the sacrament of ___.

   ● Baptism   ○ Reconciliation   ○ Matrimony

3. Jesus told the parable of the Forgiving ___ to teach us about God's forgiveness.

   ○ Son   ● Father   ○ Brother

4. In the sacrament of ___ we receive God's forgiveness for our sins.

   ○ Matrimony   ● Reconciliation   ○ Confirmation

5. The ___ is the most important celebration of the Church.

   ● Mass   ○ rosary   ○ Nativity

153

Teaching Tip

Assessment as Affirmation. Assessment is a time of affirmation. Take the time to affirm the children in all that they have learned. Be sure to point out their many efforts at living the faith they have been learning about. Do not use this time to overemphasize the ways they have fallen short. If you do discover areas they have not learned well, take what you learn through this review and reteach the concepts at appropriate times. Remember that *Faith First* is a spiral curriculum through which the children will be reintroduced to key concepts year after year. Children will have opportunities in succeeding years to relearn or extend their knowledge of these concepts.

B. Sacraments

Draw a line to connect the clues to the correct sacrament.

Sacrament	Clue
1. Baptism	a. strengthened by the Holy Spirit
2. Confirmation	b. forgiveness of sins committed after Baptism
3. Eucharist	c. first sacrament we receive
4. Reconciliation	d. Body and Blood of Christ

C. What I Have Learned

1. *Name two things you learned in this unit. Tell a partner.*

_____
Affirm appropriate responses.
_____

2. *Look at the faith words listed on page 96. Circle the ones that you know now.*

D. From a Scripture Story

Draw two pictures about the parable of the Forgiving Father. Tell the beginning and the end of the parable. Give a title to each picture.

Affirm appropriate responses.

154 Grade 2 • Unit 2 Review

PART B:
Sacraments

This section further reinforces the children's understanding of the sacraments.

- Read the directions to the children and together do the first item. Have the children continue working in partners to finish the section.
- Invite volunteers to share their answers.

PART C:
What I Have Learned

This section provides the children with the opportunity to write or talk about what they have learned.

1. Have the children share with the group two things they remember from the unit chapters.
2. Invite the children to return to the unit opener pages and affirm how they have grown in building a faith vocabulary.

PART D:
From a Scripture Story

This section is a review of the parable of the Forgiving Father. Have the children work with a partner to retell the story and complete the activity. Have each pair share their responses.

Teaching Tip

Another Reminder. As you complete this unit take the time to reinforce the importance of the faith choices. Have the children share their success stories, and discuss with the children any challenges they may have had. Encourage them not to abandon their faith choices if they are not successful in keeping them the first time.

Unit 3 Opener

The unit opener pages use a variety of questioning techniques to assess the children's prior knowledge about the key faith concepts presented in the unit. Processing these pages should not take more than ten or fifteen minutes.

USING ILLUSTRATIONS

Pictures help stimulate the religious imaginations of the children. The pictures on page 155 illustrate some of the important concepts in the unit.

- Invite the children to look at the pictures and invite volunteers to describe what each picture says to them.
- Invite the children to share a response to the question.

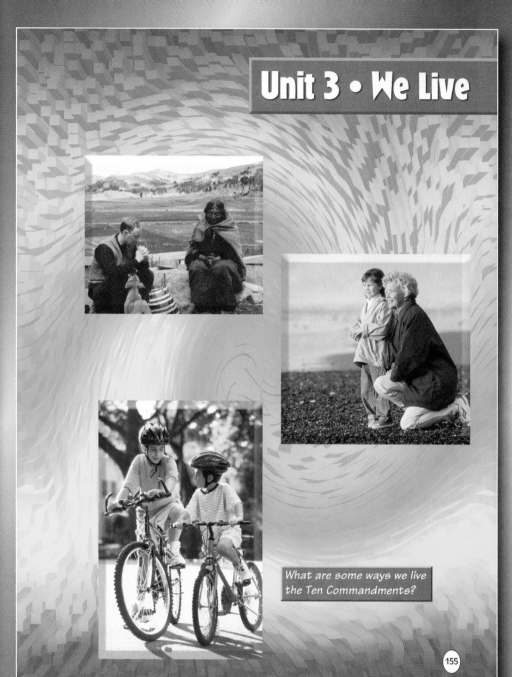

Unit 3 • We Live

What are some ways we live the Ten Commandments?

155

Teaching Tip

Visual Learners. *Faith First* acknowledges that contemporary youth live in a visual world. The *Faith First* catechetical process builds on this characteristic of the twenty-first century learner. Throughout the *Faith First* texts, the minds of the young learners are first engaged by visuals that draw them into the mysteries of faith. The written text then opens up in more detail the teachings of the Catholic Church on the faith concepts presented in the lesson.

Getting Ready

What I Have Learned

What is something you already know about these faith words?

The Ten Commandments

Responses will vary.

_____

Your conscience

Responses will vary.

_____

Words to Know

Put an X next to the faith words you know. Put a ? next to words you need to know more about.

Faith Words

_____ grace

_____ Great Commandment

_____ conscience

_____ heaven

_____ sanctifying grace

A Question I Have

What question would you like to ask about the Great Commandment?

Responses will vary.

_____

_____

A Scripture Story

Jesus teaching the Great Commandment

What is the Great Commandment?

Responses will vary.

(156)

Faith Vocabulary

Religious Literacy. One of the goals of children's religious education is to help them become more articulate about their Catholic faith. The "Faith Words" feature in each chapter is one way in which the children are building religious literacy. Through the acquisition of a faith vocabulary the children develop the language to express Catholic belief. At the outset of each unit, the "Words to Know" feature forecasts the new words that the upcoming chapters will address. In each chapter they will work with these words and create word cards for them. In the Unit Reviews, they will have the opportunity to review the words once again. The glossary on pages 298–301 of the student book contains all the faith words taught in the grade 2 text.

GETTING READY

The "Getting Ready" pages help the children share prior knowledge and assist you in planning your lessons to meet the children's needs.

What I Have Learned

Ask the children to write one thing they know about the Ten Commandments and conscience.

Words to Know

This section is a quick assessment of the children's familiarity with some of the faith vocabulary they will be learning. Read each term to the group. Have them put an X next to terms they already know, and a ? next to the terms they need to learn more about. During the review for this unit ask them to return to this page and once again share their understanding of the faith words.

A Question I Have

Invite the children to write one question they have about the Great Commandment. Ask volunteers to share their questions aloud. You may wish to write their questions on a chart. Refer back to the chart from time to time and ask volunteers to respond when they can answer the questions.

A Scripture Story

Unit 3 will review the Scripture story about the Great Commandment. Have the children look at the picture and answer the question to help you assess their prior knowledge of this story.

We Are God's Children

Adopted Sons and Daughters of God

When we are baptized into Christ, we become adopted sons and daughters of God the Father. This adoption transforms us. We receive the gift of the Holy Spirit and the grace to live our new life in Christ. In union with Jesus and empowered by the Holy Spirit, we can love one another as Jesus commanded, live heartfelt lives of charity, and experience a peace unlike anything found in this world.

While we receive the grace to live our new life in Christ, we also need to accept that grace and respond to it. We have to freely choose to follow Christ. This is not a one-time decision. Choosing to follow Christ is a decision that must be made day in and day out, many times each day.

We can utter lovely words about God and charity and our concern for the poor, but as Eliza Doolittle says to Henry Higgins in

My Fair Lady, "Show me!" Saint James the Apostle taught the same. Unless our words are translated into practical, concrete actions, they have a hollow ring to them. The Letter to James admonishes,

> What good is it, my brothers [and sisters], if someone says he has faith but does not have works? . . . [F]aith of itself, if it does not have works, is dead.
>
> JAMES 2:14–17

Grace Upon Grace

Our life in Christ must, of necessity, flow outward from us. The sacraments strengthen us for living Jesus' new commandment of love. The Holy Spirit lavishes grace upon us so that Christ's life will increase in us. What we do right here, right now, with whatever is in front of us, is the arena of grace. We are to live, as Christ taught, in the present moment (see John 13:34–35).

In what ways can we implement the daily decisions to live our new life in Christ? Saint Augustine of Hippo puts the answer in a nutshell, "Love and do what you like." When love of God becomes so operative in our lives that all our thoughts and actions are rooted in his will, then we let that love be our guide. Not an easy task, but practice makes for perseverance.

For Reflection

How convinced am I that when it comes to living the gift of faith in Christ, practice makes for perseverance?

In what situations do I find it most difficult for me to live the new commandment of Jesus, "Love one another as I love you"?

Catechist to Catechist

Responsibility

Each day seven- and eight-year-olds are learning more and more about responsibility. They have a growing sense of the obligation to be responsible for themselves and for the choices they make. While this is certainly true at home and in school, it is also true in the Church. It is your responsibility to help the children learn that they need to become more aware that belonging to God's family also carries its own set of obligations and responsibilities.

Children of God

As these second graders learn more about how they are expected to live as children of God and followers of Jesus Christ,  there is an underlying truth that needs always to be reinforced in their young minds and hearts. The children need to know and trust that God loves them completely, that he will always be there for them. An important place where they can learn this truth is in your catechetical space. Your encouragement and affirmations can be visible signs of God's love for them.

The Church Teaches . . .

Children learn best through example. While "the Church recognizes diversity, the essential equality of all, and the need for charity and mutual respect among all groups in a pluralistic Church and society" (*NCD* 193), the children will need your guidance and wisdom as they experience ethnic or religious diversity or children with special needs in their day-to-day encounters. Guide the children to make the love of Christ for all people the standard by which they treat all people.

See the Catechism . . .

For more on the teachings of the Catholic Church on the dignity of the human person, grace, and holiness, see *Catechism of the Catholic Church* 1699–1756 and 1996–2016.

CATECHIST PRAYER

*Lord God our loving Father,
I am still learning and growing
and striving to be the person
you created me to be. Give me
the strength and the courage to
follow the example of Jesus,
your Son, and with the help
of the Holy Spirit to live my
life as his companion. Amen.*

LESSON PLANNER

To discover what the children of God do for God, their Father

Engage

Page 157
Focus
To help the children appreciate that they are children of God

Opening Prayer

Discussion
Knowing that people love us makes us feel good inside.

Teach and Apply

Pages 158–160
Focus
To recognize that Jesus taught that we are to love and respect all people

Presentation
Read, discuss, and summarize content.
Scripture
• Psalm 18:2
• John 14:6
Activities
• What would you say to Jesus?
• Follow the path.
• Identify people who help you make good choices.
Faith-Filled People
Saint Teresa of Avila

Connect

Pages 161–162
Focus
To demonstrate how the Church lives as Jesus taught

Our Church Makes a Difference
Understand Saint Thérèse's Little Way.
Our Catholic Faith
Fruits of the Holy Spirit

What Difference Does Faith Make?
Activity
Identify acts of kindness that show you are a child of God.
Faith Choice
Surprise someone with an act of kindness.

We Pray

Page 163
Prayer Form
Prayer of petition
Prayer
Pray "May God Bless Us" together.

We Remember

Review
• Find the hidden words.
• Read the "To Help You Remember" statements aloud.
Preview
Highlight features of the "With My Family" page.

Materials

• index cards
• pens or pencils

Enriching the Session

Blackline Masters
Additional Activities booklet:
  Chapter 18
    Following footprints
    Connecting the dots
Assessment Tools booklet:
  Chapter 18 Test
Faith First **Grade 2 Video**
  Segment 2: "The Clown of God"
  Segment 6: "Blessing of the Children"
Enriching the Lesson (CG page 269)
  Creating a Picture Story About Choices
  Pantomiming Acts of Kindness
  Literature Connection
Music Connection (CG page 269)

www.FaithFirst.com

We update the *Faith First* Web site weekly. Check each week for new content and features. Here are some places to begin:

Catechists and Teachers
• Current Events
• Chapter Downloads
• Catechist Prayer
Faith First **for Families**
• Bible Stories
• Make a Difference
Kids' Clubhouse
• *Faith First* Activities
• Chapter Reviews
• Games
• Saints

Don't Forget! You can make lesson planning a breeze—check out the **Online Lesson Planner.**

We Are God's Children

18

We Pray

I love you, LORD.
Psalm 18:2

Blessed be Jesus, whom you sent to be the friend of children.
Amen.

Who loves you?

Knowing people love us makes us feel good inside. God loves us more than anyone. We are children of God.

What do you think it means to be a child of God?

157

Background: Doctrine

We Are All Children of God. It is important that children come to value themselves and all people as children of God. God created every person in his image and likeness. God lives among us and within us. That is the foundation of the dignity of every person. Jesus taught that when we reach out and help our neighbor, we are reaching out and helping him. Help the children brainstorm ways they can reach out to others.

PRAY

- Have the children quiet themselves for prayer.
- Pray the Sign of the Cross together.
- Proclaim Psalm 18:2. Lead the opening prayer, inviting the children to echo each phrase after you.
- Close the prayer with the Sign of the Cross.

DISCOVER

Purpose: To discover what the children may already know about living the way God wants us to live

- Ask the children, "Who loves you?"
- Present the opening paragraph in your own words. Then invite responses to the "What do you think it means to be a child of God?" question.
- Invite the children to look at the photograph. Ask volunteers to describe how these children are living as children of God.

Teach

FOCUS

Ask a volunteer to read the "Faith Focus" question aloud. Share with the children that in this chapter they will learn what children of God need to do to live as he wants us to live.

DISCOVER

- Have the children read aloud the faith word *honor* and its meaning. Talk with them about some of the people in their own lives whom they honor and respect.
- Read aloud the first paragraph of "Jesus and the Children." Have the children follow along and listen for how God honors us.
- Ask the children to read the second paragraph silently to find out how Jesus taught us to honor God.

Apply

REINFORCE

Have the children make a word card for *honor*.

INTEGRATE

Invite the children to look carefully at the picture of Jesus and the little children. Ask volunteers what they would say to Jesus if they were there.

We Are Children of God

Faith Focus

What do we do to live as children of God?

Faith Words

honor
To honor someone is to treat them with kindness, respect, and love.

grace
Grace is the gift of God sharing his life with us. It is also God helping us to make good choices to live as children of God.

 QUESTION *Imagine you are one of the children in the picture. What would you say to Jesus?*

Jesus and the Children

The Bible teaches that God gives every person a great **honor.** He creates every person in his image and likeness. God shares his life with us. He creates us to be children of God.

Jesus taught us to honor God, ourselves, and other people. He taught us to treat people with kindness, respect, and love. He taught us to honor all people as children of God.

Detail from *Christ with the Children* by American artist Shannon Stirnweis

158

Teaching Tip

Accepting Others. Most children are very accepting of others. We can use this opportunity to point out that differences are to be enjoyed and celebrated. It is important to reinforce that God made all people in his image and likeness, and he loves all people equally. As children of God, we are called to love and respect all others. Organize a class affirmation party. Write the name of each child on a card and place it in a basket. Ask each child to draw a name and then write on the card a gift or talent they see in that child. Place all the cards back in the basket. Once again, ask each child to draw a card, say the name on the card aloud, and then read the words of the affirmation to the class.

Jesus Is Our Teacher

The disciples of Jesus honored him in many ways. They honored and respected him as a teacher. In Jesus' time to call someone "Teacher" was a sign of great honor and respect.

Jesus' disciples carefully listened to him. They learned from him. He told them this about himself. He said,

"I am the way, the truth, and the life. I will lead you to God."

Based on John 14:6

Jesus is our teacher. We listen to him. We try our best to live as he taught.

ACTIVITY *Follow each path to Jesus. Ask Jesus to teach you to live as a child of God.*

LIFE
WAY
TRUTH

159

Background: Faith-Filled People

Saint Teresa of Avila: Doctor of the Church. Saint Teresa of Avila's life (1515–1582) was marked by great independence and energy. She saw her life as a never-ending spiritual journey to grow in faith and closeness to God. Though ill for long periods of time, she was an optimist who lived life to the fullest. Saint Teresa was the first woman to be honored as a Doctor of the Church, one officially acknowledged by the Church as an accomplished teacher because of his or her tremendous insight and wisdom into the faith. Saint Teresa of Avila is the patron saint of Spain.

Teach

FOCUS

Remind the children that Jesus teaches us to honor all people as children of God. Tell them they are going to learn more about Jesus the Teacher.

DISCOVER

- Ask the children to describe what teachers do. Then ask: How do you learn from teachers? Watching, listening.
- Ask the children to listen as you read aloud "Jesus Is Our Teacher."
- Have the children find and highlight what Jesus told his disciples about himself.
- Emphasize that Jesus teaches us how to live.
- Read aloud "Faith-Filled People." Tell the children about Saint Teresa of Avila, a great teacher of the Church.

Apply

REINFORCE

Invite the children to memorize the words "I am the way and the truth and the life" (John 14:6).

INTEGRATE

- Remind the children that they are followers of Jesus.
- Have the children look at the puzzle. Explain that each path leads to Jesus. Tell the children to follow each path to Jesus.

Teach

FOCUS

Remind the children that Jesus taught us how to live as children of God. Point out that children of God make good choices.

DISCOVER

- Invite a volunteer to read aloud the first paragraph of "Making Choices." Ask the class to listen to find out what making good choices shows others.
- Ask the children to read the second paragraph silently. Ask them to underline the sentence that tells what grace means. Ask who gives us grace to make good choices to live as children of God. The Holy Spirit.

Apply

REINFORCE

- Invite a volunteer to read aloud the definition of *grace* in "Faith Words." Tell the children to make a word card for *grace*.

INTEGRATE

- Remind the children that many people help us learn to make good choices to live as children of God.
- Have the children do the activity.
- Invite volunteers to share whose name they wrote and what that person has taught them.

Making Choices

Jesus taught us how to make good choices to live as children of God. When we make good choices, we show that we are proud and honored to call Jesus "Teacher." We show we are trying our best to live as children of God. We love God and other people as Jesus did.

We ask God for the **grace,** or help, to make good choices to live as children of God. The Holy Spirit helps us to make good choices. When we make good choices, we grow as children of God.

ACTIVITY Put a ✔ in the boxes next to the people who help you learn to make good choices to live as a child of God.

Affirm appropriate responses.

- ☐ parent
- ☐ grandparent
- ☐ priest
- ☐ friend
- ☐ teacher
- ☐ coach

☐ _____
(name of someone else)

(160)

Background: Doctrine

A World of Grace. The *Catechism of the Catholic Church* teaches us that grace is a free gift from God that could never be earned. Through grace we are able to respond to God's call to be his children and to live forever with him. We can talk about God's grace in several ways. Sanctifying grace is what is called a habitual grace, because it disposes us to live in harmony with God and for others. God also intervenes in the course of our lives through what are called actual graces. At times the Holy Spirit offers us these graces to empower us to make good choices (see *Catechism of the Catholic Church* 1996–2000).

Our Church Makes a Difference

Saint Thérèse of Lisieux

Saint Thérèse of Lisieux was proud to be a child of God. Thérèse tried her best to do little things well.

Thérèse wrote a story about her life. She wrote about the little things we can do each day out of love. We can say "Thank you," help at home, and care for our things. When we do little things out of love as Saint Thérèse did, we honor and respect God. We honor and respect other people and ourselves. We do what Jesus taught us to do.

Saint Thérèse of Lisieux is also called Saint Thérèse of the Child Jesus. She is also known as The Little Flower. Her feast day is October 1.

QUESTION *What are some of the little things people do to honor and respect God, themselves, and other people?* Affirm appropriate choices.

Our Catholic Faith

Fruits of the Holy Spirit

The Bible names some signs that show we are trying our best to live as children of God. Three of these signs are joy, generosity, and kindness. We call these signs fruits of the Holy Spirit.

161

Teaching Tip

Blessed Mother Teresa of Calcutta. Blessed Mother Teresa of Calcutta and her missionary sisters model for us the living of the Gospel mandate to respect the dignity of every human person. As with Saint Thérèse of Lisieux their way was the little way, respecting the dignity of the poor and the hungry. Give the children some background on the life of Blessed Mother Teresa, which is readily available from many sources. Invite the children to follow the example of Blessed Mother Teresa and the Sisters of the Missionaries of Charity by engaging the children in a project that will serve people in need. Consider having the children and their families donate new pairs of socks of all sizes that can be shared with families living in your local homeless shelter.

Connect

HIGHLIGHT

Remind the children that the Church gives us many holy people whose examples help us make good choices. Point out that Saint Thérèse of Lisieux is one of these people.

DISCOVER

• Encourage the children to tell what they might know about Saint Thérèse of Lisieux.
• Read aloud the story of Saint Thérèse.
• Invite the children to explain in their own words why they think Saint Thérèse was named a saint by the Church.
• Read aloud "Our Catholic Faith." Explain that when we live as Saint Thérèse lived, others see in us signs of holiness. We call these signs of holiness the fruits of the Holy Spirit.

INTEGRATE

• Talk about some of the "little" good deeds that people do each day. Share how each shows honor and respect for God and for people.
• Ask the children to suggest a list of "little" good deeds they can do at home or at school this week to show that they are trying to live as children of God.

Connect

HIGHLIGHT

Help the children recall that the Holy Spirit gives us the grace to make good choices each day. Point out that by making choices to live as Jesus taught, we are living as children of God.

RESPOND

- Brainstorm with the children some of the choices they can make to show others that they are children of God. List the choices in two separate columns on the board labeled "Say" and "Do."
- Invite the children to write their own choices in their books. Tell them they may use some of the examples listed on the board.

CHOOSE

- Invite the children to read "My Faith Choice" and write their decisions.
- Encourage everyone to put their choices into practice this week.

What Difference Does Faith Make in My Life?

Each day the Holy Spirit helps you to live as a child of God. The Holy Spirit helps you to make choices that show you are proud to be a child of God.

Write some words of kindness you say. Then write acts of kindness you do that show you are a child of God.

Living as a Child of God

Say

Affirm appropriate choices.

_____

_____

Do

Affirm appropriate choices.

_____

_____

My Faith Choice

This week I will surprise someone with this act of kindness. I will

Affirm appropriate choices.

_____ .

162

Teaching Tip

Good Manners. While you are discussing acts of kindness, remind the children that good manners are ways of being kind. Encourage the children to remember the value of using such words as "please" and "thank you." Ask the children if they have noticed that teachers and parents listen more carefully when the children speak politely. Extend this teaching by further reminding the children that good manners can also be shown in church when they take part in Mass. By acting respectfully while at Mass, the children are showing honor and respect to God who is present among them.

We Pray

May God Bless Us

At the conclusion of Mass the priest asks God to bless the people. Pray this prayer to ask God to bless your class.

Leader: Father, we ask your blessing on us.

All: **Father, we are your children.**

Leader: Guide us to choose what is good and to do your will.

All: **Father, we are your children.**

Leader: *As each child comes forward, place a hand on the child's head, saying:* May God bless us and keep us.

All: **Amen.**

We Remember

Find and circle the words hidden in the puzzle. Use the words to share with a partner how you can live as a child of God.

RESPECT   GOOD   LOVE

FOLLOW   CHOICES   HONOR   FAITH

```
(R E S P E C T) L H O Q L T H R A
O (F O L L O W) P N Z T (F A I T H)
(C H O I C E S) T R W (L O V E) P T
Y (H O N O R) L I (G O O D) R W Z A
```

To Help You Remember

1. All people are to be honored and respected because God has created everyone to be a child of God.

2. Jesus taught that we are to live as children of God.

3. The Holy Spirit helps us to make choices to live as children of God.

Grade 2 • Chapter 18   163

✝ Liturgy Tip

Blessings. Asking for God's blessing can be very powerful. This form of prayer strengthens us in times of illness or stress. It unites God's family and sends us forth to do God's work of treating others with respect and dignity. Include prayers asking for God's blessing as a regular part of each lesson.

WE PRAY

- Gather the children in the prayer center.
- Practice the responses.
- Tell the children that they are going to pray a blessing prayer together.
- Lead the prayer.

WE REMEMBER

- Write the words *respected*, *Jesus*, and *choices* on the board. Tell the children that each of these words was an important word in today's lesson.
- Read aloud the "To Help You Remember" statements, leaving out the words *respected*, *Jesus*, and *choices*. Ask volunteers to guess the missing words.
- Introduce the activity and allow the class sufficient time to complete it. If time allows, ask volunteers to use the words they circled in sentences.

At Home

ENCOURAGE

Have the children carefully tear out pages 163 and 164 along the perforation. Encourage the children to share the pages with their families and to do the activities together. If they did not complete the review activity on page 163 by the end of the session, emphasize that they can complete it with their families.

VISIT FAITHFIRST.COM

- Share with the children the many activities on the *Faith First* Web site.
- Encourage the children to visit **www.FaithFirst.com.**

---

18 With My Family

This Week . . .

In chapter 18, "We Are God's Children," your child learned to honor and respect all people. Every person deserves our respect. Every person has the dignity of being a child of God, who is created in the image and likeness of God. Jesus is our Teacher. He showed us how to live as children of God. He said, "I am the way, the truth, and the life. I will lead you to God" (based on John 14:6). We honor and respect Jesus as our Teacher when we try our best to live as he taught. All our words and actions are to show respect for God, other people, and ourselves.

For more on the teachings of the Catholic Church on the dignity of the human person, grace, and holiness, see *Catechism of the Catholic Church* paragraph numbers 1699–1756 and 1996–2016.

Sharing God's Word

Read together the Bible story in Mark 10:13–16 about Jesus and the children. Emphasize that Jesus taught us to respect all people as children of God.

Praying

In this chapter your child prayed a prayer asking God's blessing on all the members of the class. Pray together the prayer on page 163.

Making a Difference

Choose one of the following activities to do as a family or design a similar activity of your own.

- Talk about making good choices. Help your child learn how we know that we are making or have made good choices. Discuss how the Church helps us make good choices.

- Saint Thérèse of Lisieux focused on doing the little things in life out of love. Share how your family can live as Saint Thérèse did and do the little things that are part of daily life out of love.

- Share ideas on how acts and words of kindness show we are children of God. Choose and do something this week to live as children of God.

For more ideas on ways your family can live your faith, visit the "Faith First for Families" page at **www.FaithFirst.com.** Click on "Saints" and learn about other faith-filled people of the Church.

✓ Evaluate

Take a few moments to evaluate this week's lesson.
I feel (circle one) about this week's lesson.

    a. very pleased

    b. OK

    c. disappointed

The activity the children enjoyed most was . . .

The concept that was most difficult to teach was . . .

because . . .

Something I would like to do differently is . . .

Before Moving On . . .

As you finish today's lesson, reflect on the following question before moving on to the next chapter.

How much effort do I make to reinforce and summarize before moving on to a new concept?

ENRICHING THE LESSON

Creating a Picture Story About Choices

Purpose

To reinforce that when we make choices to live as Jesus taught, we are trying our best to live as children of God (taught on page 160)

Directions

- Draw three boxes on the board, labeling them "Problem," "Choice," and "Consequences."
- Invite the children to create a picture story by drawing three boxes on their paper. Have them include dialogue bubbles that illustrate what the people in each picture are saying.
- Tell the children the first box should depict a problem. The second box should tell the choice being made to solve the problem. The third box relates the consequences of the choice. Have the children title their story "Proud to Be a Child of God."
- Display the children's work.

Materials

construction paper, crayons or markers

Pantomiming Acts of Kindness

Purpose

To reinforce that to honor someone is to treat them with kindness, respect, and love (taught on page 158)

Directions

- In small groups have the children discuss some of the ways that they show kindness and respect to others.
- Have them select one of the ways that they named and pantomime it.
- Invite the children to present their pantomimes, and have the other children title each pantomime after it is presented.

Materials

Literature Connection

Purpose

To reinforce the importance of making good choices (taught on page 160)

Directions

You might wish to obtain a copy of *For the Children: Words of Love and Inspiration from His Holiness Pope John Paul II* (Scholastic, 2000) and read a selection to the children from time to time. In this beautifully produced book, the pope challenges the children of the world to be full participants in their Christian faith and to make the best possible choices. The book is lavishly illustrated with photographs of the pope with children, many of whom are dressed in their national costumes.

- Read a selection to the children and show them the accompanying pictures.
- Invite the children to brainstorm various ways to respond to the pope's challenge. What faith choice could they make?

Materials

For the Children: Words of Love and Inspiration from His Holiness Pope John Paul II

Music Connection

- "We Are the Church," C. Walker. *Rise Up and Sing* #234.
- "Psalm 100: We Are God's People," D. Haas. *Singing Our Faith (SOF)* #38.
- "Walking By Faith," D. Haas. *SOF* #179.
- "At Evening," D. Haas. *SOF* #280.

The Great Commandment
A Scripture Story

Background

The Great Commandment

The Great Commandment stands at the center of living the gift of faith. It was at the center of the Law of the Old Covenant. It is at the center of living the New Covenant, life in Christ.

"Teacher, which commandment in the law is the greatest?" [Jesus] said to him, "You shall love the Lord, your God, with all your heart, with all your soul, and with all your mind. This is the greatest and the first commandment. The second is like it: You shall love your neighbor as yourself. The whole law and the prophets depend on these two commandments."

MATTHEW 22:36–40

Practically speaking, how do we keep the two parts of this commandment at the center of living our new life in Christ? We can gain an insight into the answer to this question by exploring how we don't keep it.

Caught up in the demands of their busy schedules, many people go about their daily chores with little reference to God. Their hearts, souls, and

minds are focused on other more immediate concerns, such as paying bills, raising children, and a seemingly endless round of daily errands.

The Art of Christian Living

Should we simply drop these responsibilities and sit in watchful attendance with God? Of course not! The art of Christian living involves integrating our love of God into the activities of the day. It involves placing God at the center of our lives, or allowing God to take center stage.

This involves working on developing good habits, especially the good habit of setting a deliberate, daily place for God at

the tables of our lives. For example, we can regularly include morning prayer and evening prayer in our daily schedule; we can take part in the celebration of Mass not only on Sunday but also on weekdays; we can pray a short prayer upon entering our car or when we make a phone call. In other words, we decide upon and put into action a few appropriate and practical resolutions to allow God some elbow room in our everyday existence. Eventually, all of these actions will become good habits, or virtues.

To live the Great Commandment of love requires attentiveness. It requires a period of concentration which, over time, evolves into a natural rhythm and oneness with God. Over time, expressing our love for God and for others will become as natural as breathing and will become a spontaneous part of living our life in Christ.

For Reflection

How can I integrate attentiveness to God in my daily routine?

What are some of the things I can do to develop a natural rhythm for living the Great Commandment?

Catechist to Catechist

As We Love Ourselves

By age seven or eight, most children can talk about what it means to love God and to love their neighbor. As you help them develop their understanding of the Great Commandment, spend some time helping them better appreciate the concept of love of self. This is a part of the Great Commandment that often goes untreated—God calls us to love and respect ourselves.

The Importance of a Positive Self-Image

Some children and many adults as well have a difficult time really loving themselves. At this young age self-image and feelings of self-worth are continuing to develop. How you treat each child in your care will have a definite influence on how lovable and capable they believe themselves to be.

The Church Teaches . . .

Sharing the Light of Faith: National Catechetical Directory for Catholics of the United States (NCD) reminds us:
"Love implies an absolute demand for justice, namely a recognition of the dignity and rights of one's neighbor."[1] Justice is therefore the foundation of charity: i.e., if I love my neighbor, it is absolutely required that I respect his or her rights and meet his or her needs. It is impossible to give of oneself in love without first sharing with others what is due them in justice. This can be expressed very succinctly by saying that justice is love's absolute minimum. *NCD* 165
The Great Commandment asks us to love as Jesus did, without boundaries.

See the Catechism . . .

For more on the teachings of the Catholic Church on the Law of God and the Great Commandment, see *Catechism of the Catholic Church* 2052–2055, 2083, and 2196.

CATECHIST PRAYER

Lord, I've known the Great Commandment since I was a child. Help me be aware of my actions and reactions as I strive to live by the law of love. Amen.

Footnote references may be found on p. 456.

LESSON PLANNER

Focus **To discover what the Great Commandment commands us to do**

Engage

Page 165
Focus

To help the children express what it means to live as a child of God

Opening Prayer

Discussion

What are some ways we live as children of God?

Teach and Apply

Pages 166–168
Focus

To recognize that the Great Commandment sums up all of God's laws

Presentation

Read, discuss, and summarize content.

Scripture
- Psalm 1:2
- Matthew 22:37–40

Activities
- Draw yourself worshiping God in church.
- Read the Scripture verses.
- Describe the action in the pictures.

Connect

Pages 169–170
Focus

To describe how the Church lives the Great Commandment

Our Church Makes a Difference

Understand how Christian missionaries live the Great Commandment.

Our Catholic Faith
Mission Cross

What Difference Does Faith Make?
Activity

Tell a kindergarten class about the Great Commandment.

Faith Choice

Identify a way to live the Great Commandment this week.

We Pray

Page 171
Prayer Form
Prayer of blessing and adoration
Prayer
Pray "An Act of Love" together.

We Remember

Review
- Complete the writing activity.
- Read the "To Help You Remember" statements aloud.

Preview
Highlight features of the "With My Family" page.

Materials

- pens or pencils
- crayons or markers

Enriching the Session

Blackline Masters
Additional Activities booklet:
Chapter 19
Making a Commandment chain
Creating a Web page
Assessment Tools booklet:
Chapter 19 Test

Faith First **Grade 2 Video**
Segment 3: "Story of St. Clare"

Enriching the Lesson (CG page 281)
Art Activity
Making Prayer Stones
Literature Connection

Music Connection (CG page 281)

www.FaithFirst.com

We update the *Faith First* Web site weekly. Check each week for new content and features. Here are some places to begin:

Catechists and Teachers
- Current Events
- Chapter Downloads
- Catechist Prayer

Faith First **for Families**
- Bible Stories
- Make a Difference

Kids' Clubhouse
- *Faith First* Activities
- Chapter Reviews
- Games Arcade
- Saints

Don't Forget! You can make lesson planning a breeze—check out the **Online Lesson Planner.**

The Great Commandment
A Scripture Story

19

We Pray

LORD God, your law brings us joy and happiness.
Based on Psalm 1:2

Lord our God, we love you with all our heart. Amen.

What new thing have you learned this week?

Watching, listening, and asking questions are all ways of learning. Jesus helps us to learn how to live as children of God.

What are some ways you live as a child of God?

165

Teaching Tip

The Life and Times of Jesus. The children are learning about the life and times of Jesus. Seven- and eight-year-olds still relate most of what they learn through the window of their own experiences. As you introduce this week's Scripture story, invite the children to share with you how they picture where Jesus lived, how he was taught, or what people wore. This sharing will make you aware of any prior knowledge and mistaken impressions they may have about the life and times of Jesus.

Engage

PRAY

- Have the children quiet themselves for prayer.
- Begin with the Sign of the Cross.
- Proclaim Psalm 1:2. Then lead the opening prayer and invite the children to echo each phrase after you.
- Conclude the prayer with the Sign of the Cross.

DISCOVER

Purpose: To discover what the children may already know about ways to live as children of God

- Ask the children what new things they have learned this week. Then invite several volunteers to share the ways they know that help them learn something new. Tell them to think of new games and skills as well as things they learn at school.
- Tell the class that they are going to learn something the Bible teaches about being children of God.
- Direct the children's attention to the photograph on page 165. Invite volunteers to explain how the older child is living as a child of God.

Teach

FOCUS

Ask a volunteer to read the "Faith Focus" question aloud. Share with the children that in this chapter they will learn how the Great Commandment guides us to live as children of God.

DISCOVER

- In your own words talk with the children about "The Temple in Jerusalem."
- Establish that at the time of Jesus, Jewish people went to the Temple to pray, to worship God, and to learn more about God and his laws.

Apply

REINFORCE

- Ask the children why the Jewish people went to the Temple. To listen and learn about God's Law.
- Together read in "Faith Words" the meaning of *Temple in Jerusalem*. Have the children make a word card for this term.

INTEGRATE

Talk with the children about some of the places where they learn about God and his laws, such as at home and at church. Help them compare the similarities between the people of Jesus' time learning about God and his laws and their own learning about God and his laws.

Bible Background

Faith Focus

What does the Great Commandment help us to do?

Faith Words

Temple in Jerusalem
A temple is a building built to honor God. The Jewish people in Jesus' time worshiped God in the Temple in Jerusalem.

Great Commandment
The Great Commandment is to love God above all else and to love others as we love ourselves.

The Temple in Jerusalem

In Jesus' time the Jewish people came to the **Temple in Jerusalem** to worship God. A temple is a building built to honor God. The Temple in Jerusalem was the largest building in the city. It was a beautiful white building with a golden roof.

The people met in the Temple courtyard with the teachers of God's Law. They gathered there to listen to and to learn about God's Law.

ACTIVITY *Christians gather in churches to worship God and to learn about God. Draw yourself worshiping God in your parish church.*

Affirm appropriate responses.

Drawing of Temple in Jerusalem

166

Faith Vocabulary

Temple in Jerusalem. The Hebrew word for *temple* means "great house." The Temple of Jerusalem was built by King Solomon who fulfilled the plans of King David, his father. David's choice for the site was based on the belief that the rock on which it was to be built was the center of the world. Obtain from your religious education office or your local library picture books that show the Temple at the time of Jesus. Information and pictures are also available on the Internet.

Reading the Word of God

Jesus Teaches in the Temple

One day Jesus was in the Temple. A teacher of God's Law asked Jesus which commandment of God is the greatest. Jesus gave him this answer.

"You shall love the Lord your God with all your heart, and with all your soul, and with all your mind. This is the first and greatest commandment. The second commandment is like the first one. You shall love your neighbor as yourself. There is no other commandment greater than these two." *Based on Matthew 22:37–40*

Jesus named two commandments. Together both commandments make up one **Great Commandment.**

ACTIVITY Read the Scripture verses again. Name the two commandments that make up the Great Commandment.

167

✦ Background: Scripture

The Scholar of the Law. Matthew 22:37–40 is a response to a question put to Jesus as part of a longer series of questioning by a scholar of the Law. Having been asked which commandment was the greatest, Jesus responded by quoting Deuteronomy 6:5 and Leviticus 19:18. This was an answer, of course, that a scholar of the Law already knew. Jesus' summary statement, "The whole law and the prophets depend on these two commandments" (Matthew 22:40), turned the question back to the scholar of the Law and invited him to reflect on his own living of the Law.

Teach

FOCUS

Remind the children that the Jewish people went to the Temple in Jerusalem both to worship God and to listen and learn about his Law.

DISCOVER

- Tell the children that one day when Jesus was in the Temple a teacher of the Law asked Jesus which commandment of God's was the greatest.
- Ask the children to listen carefully as you read Jesus' response.
- Proclaim the Scripture based on Matthew 22:37–40.
- Ask the children what Jesus told the people.
- Explain that when we keep the Great Commandment, we keep the Ten Commandments as well.

Apply

REINFORCE

- Have the children make a word card for *Great Commandment.*
- Ask the children to complete the activity and allow volunteers time to share their responses.

INTEGRATE

- Tell the children that they are keeping the Great Commandment every time they show their love for God and for others.
- Divide the class into two groups. Have each group prepare to role-play how they can live the Great Commandment.

(Student Page 167) 275

Teach

FOCUS

Remind the children that Jesus taught that there is no greater commandment than the Great Commandment.

DISCOVER

- Tell the children that Jesus taught the people that the Great Commandment was the greatest law of God.
- Present "The Great Commandment" in your own words, clearly distinguishing the two parts of the commandment.
- Ask volunteers to explain what we mean when we say that God is the center of our lives. Everything we do and say must show that God is the center of our lives and we love him above all else. Accept all other appropriate responses.
- Then ask: How do we live the second part of the Great Commandment? By treating others as we like to be treated. Accept all other appropriate responses.

Apply

REINFORCE

Have the children work with a partner and come up with a list of ways that they can be kind to others.

INTEGRATE

- Invite volunteers to share their list with the whole group.
- Explain the activity. After giving the children time to complete this exercise, ask for volunteers to share their work.

Understanding the Word of God

The Great Commandment

The first part of the Great Commandment teaches that God is the center of our life. It teaches us to love God above all else.

- We show our love for God when we honor and respect God in all we do and say.
- We show our love for God when we pray.

The second part of the Great Commandment teaches us to treat others as we like to be treated. We are to respect and honor all people.

- We respect and honor all people when we help them care for their things.
- We respect and honor people when we treat them fairly.

ACTIVITY Tell how the people in the pictures are showing love for God and for one another. Draw how you can live the Great Commandment. Affirm appropriate responses.

Responses will vary.

168

Teaching Tip

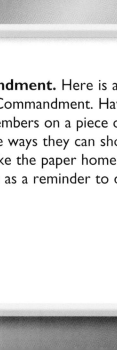

Living the Great Commandment. Here is a simple way to help the children live the Great Commandment. Have the children write the names of two family members on a piece of paper. Beside each name have them write three ways they can show kindness to this person. Have the children take the paper home and put it in a place where they will see it often as a reminder to do what they have written.

Our Church Makes a Difference

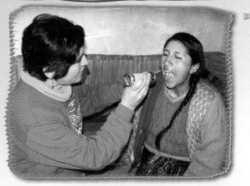

Missionaries

Christians live the Great Commandment in many different ways. Missionaries travel to teach others about Jesus. Missionaries are often priests, religious sisters, religious brothers, or laypeople who are married or single. They can be teachers, doctors, nurses, farmers, and scientists.

Christian missionaries live the Great Commandment. They help people come to know and believe in Jesus and God's love for them. They help people to live as Jesus taught and to treat one another with respect.

 How are the missionaries in these pictures living the Great Commandment?

Affirm appropriate responses.

(169)

✝ Background: Doctrine

The Missionary Nature of the Church. The Second Vatican Council in the *Decree on the Church's Missionary Activity* teaches: "The Church on earth is by its very nature missionary since, according to the plan of the Father, it has its origin in the mission of the Son and the Holy Spirit." In the sacrament of Baptism we are joined to Christ, receive the gift of the Holy Spirit, and become members of the Church. In essence, as the Church is missionary, so all the baptized are "missionaries." We all according to our vocation, or state in life, are to preach the Gospel in word and deed.

Connect

HIGHLIGHT

Point out that Christian missionaries are members of the Church who live the Great Commandment in a special way.

DISCOVER

- Explain that Christian missionaries show their love for God and others by teaching and caring for people in their own country and in other countries.
- Ask the children to follow along as you read "Missionaries." Ask them to listen for the work every missionary has. Communicate to the children that missionaries do many kinds of jobs, but every missionary has the work of telling others about Jesus.
- Present "Our Catholic Faith" so that the children might learn about the cross that missionaries are given.
- Invite volunteers to suggest why some Christians wear a cross around their necks.

INTEGRATE

- Direct the children's attention to the pictures on this page. Have the children tell how the missionaries are living the Great Commandment.
- If there are children in the group who know a missionary, invite them to tell how that missionary serves the Church.

Connect

HIGHLIGHT

Remind the children that when they pray and do acts of kindness they are already living the Great Commandment. Explain that the Holy Spirit gives them the grace to live the Great Commandment.

RESPOND

- Have the children look at the activity on this page as you read the directions.
- Invite the children to complete the activity and then share their ideas with a partner.

CHOOSE

- Present "My Faith Choice" and have the children write their choices.
- Encourage everyone to put their choices into practice this week.

What Difference Does Faith Make in My Life?

The Holy Spirit helps you to live the Great Commandment.

Pretend you are teaching a kindergarten class about the Great Commandment. Write or draw what you are telling the class.

Sharing with Others

Affirm appropriate responses.

My Faith Choice

This week I will live the Great Commandment. I will

Affirm appropriate responses.

170

Teaching Tip

Lay Mission Helpers. Try to locate with the help of your diocesan office someone who has served the Church as a lay missionary. Invite him or her to come to the next session and speak with the children about the work of missionaries. Encourage the speaker to bring photographs or video images of the people whom he or she served. Allow the children to ask appropriate questions after the guest's presentation.

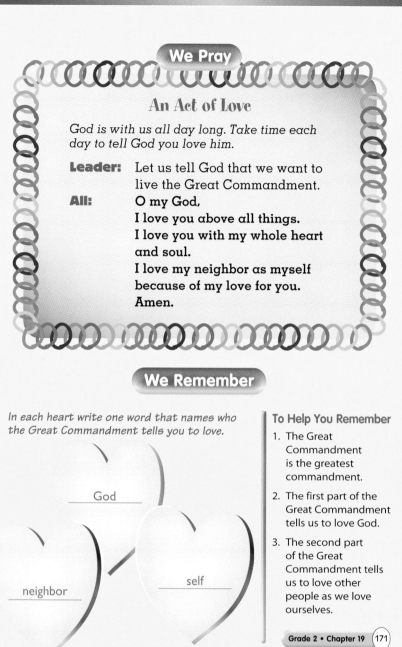

We Pray

An Act of Love

God is with us all day long. Take time each day to tell God you love him.

Leader: Let us tell God that we want to live the Great Commandment.

All: O my God,
I love you above all things.
I love you with my whole heart and soul.
I love my neighbor as myself because of my love for you.
Amen.

We Remember

In each heart write one word that names who the Great Commandment tells you to love.

God

neighbor   self

To Help You Remember

1. The Great Commandment is the greatest commandment.

2. The first part of the Great Commandment tells us to love God.

3. The second part of the Great Commandment tells us to love other people as we love ourselves.

Grade 2 • Chapter 19 (171)

Liturgy Tip

Prayer Postures and Gestures. There are many ways to pray. We can pray verbally or in silence, alone or with the community. We pray with our whole bodies. Standing, sitting, kneeling, making the sign of the cross are just a few examples. Other prayer postures and prayer gestures include bowing in reverence, crossing arms over one's heart to express love, shaking hands with a partner to express love of neighbor, and so on. Include the use of prayer gestures in praying "An Act of Love" and other prayers during your sessions with the children.

Pray

WE PRAY

- Gather the children in the prayer center with their books. Tell them that the closing prayer today is an act of love. In the prayer we tell God that we want to keep the Great Commandment. Encourage the children to memorize the prayer and pray it every day.
- Read through the prayer aloud once as the children follow along in their books.
- Begin the prayer with the Sign of the Cross.
- Lead the children in prayer.
- Close your prayer by having all offer each other a sign of peace.

Review

WE REMEMBER

- Write the "To Help You Remember" statements on the board or on poster board in the form of a single paragraph. Leave spaces for the words *greatest*, *God*, and *ourselves*.
- Read the sentences aloud together, pausing for the children to fill in the missing words. At the conclusion, write the correct words in the sentences.
- Introduce the review activity and allow time for the children to complete it. Have them share their work with a partner.

At Home

Have the children carefully tear out pages 171 and 172 along the perforation. Encourage the children to share the pages with their families and to do the activities together. If they did not complete the review activity on page 171 by the end of the session, emphasize that they can complete it with their families.

VISIT FAITHFIRST.COM

- Share with the children the many activities on the *Faith First* Web site.
- Encourage the children to visit **www.FaithFirst.com.**

---

19 With My Family

This Week . . .

In chapter 19, "The Great Commandment: A Scripture Story," your child learned that the heart of God's Law is the Great Commandment. A teacher of God's Law asked, "What is the greatest of all the commandments?" Jesus responded that the driving spirit of all God's laws is summarized in two commandments, namely, love God and love others as yourself. The first part of the Great Commandment comes from Deuteronomy 6:5; the second part is from Leviticus 19:18. Jesus taught that both of these commandments together make up the Great Commandment.

For more on the teachings of the Catholic Church on the Law of God and the Great Commandment, see *Catechism of the Catholic Church* paragraph numbers 2052–2055, 2083, and 2196.

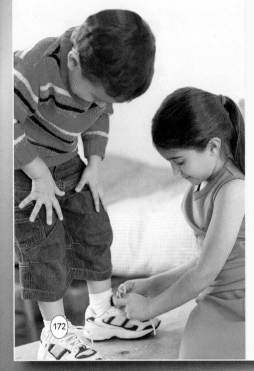

Sharing God's Word

Read together the Bible story in Matthew 22:34–40 about the Great Commandment or read the adaptation of the story on page 167. Emphasize that the Great Commandment has two inseparable parts: love God and love your neighbor as yourself.

Praying

In this chapter your child prayed an act of love. Read and pray together the act of love on page 171.

Making a Difference

Choose one of the following activities to do as a family or design a similar activity of your own.

- Talk about how your family lives the Great Commandment. Choose one thing you will do this week to live the Great Commandment.

- Create a large heart out of poster paper. Write the Great Commandment within the heart. Display the heart where it will serve as a reminder to the whole family to live the Great Commandment.

- The Great Commandment tells us to treat others as we would like to be treated. Talk about some of the practical ways your family can live this part of the Great Commandment at home.

For more ideas on ways your family can live your faith, visit the "Faith First for Families" page at **www.FaithFirst.com.** This week share some of the ideas on the "Gospel Reflections" page with one another.

Before Moving On . . .

As you finish today's lesson, reflect on the following question before moving on to the next chapter.

What activity options am I providing so that all of the children get a chance to express themselves in the way that is best for them?

✓ Evaluate

Take a few moments to evaluate this week's lesson.
I feel (circle one) about this week's lesson.

    a. very pleased
    b. OK
    c. disappointed

The activity the children enjoyed most was . . .

The concept that was most difficult to teach was . . .

because . . .

Something I would like to do differently is . . .

ENRICHING THE LESSON

Art Activity

Purpose
To reinforce the meaning of the Great Commandment (taught on page 167)

Directions
- Print the words of the Great Commandment on a sheet of paper.
- Then draw a wide decorative border around it and duplicate it on white paper so that each child has a copy.
- Invite the children to decorate the border, using colors of their choice. Make construction paper frames for the children to use to frame their artwork.
- Suggest that they hang it at home to remind them to live as children of God.

Materials
copies of the words of the Great Commandment with a decorative border
construction paper
scissors
glue sticks

Making Prayer Stones

Purpose
To reinforce that we show our love for God when we pray (taught on page 168)

Directions
A great help to remind the children to pray is the use of prayer stones.
- Have the children make their own prayer stones by providing them with stones no bigger than three inches long.
- Give each child a ribbon to tie a swatch of material around the stone.
- Tell the children to keep the prayer stones on their pillows during the day as a reminder to pray their night prayers. At night, the children could place the prayer stones in their shoes as a reminder to pray their morning prayers.

Materials
stones
swatches of material and ribbons

Literature Connection

Purpose
To reinforce the teaching about the Great Commandment (taught on pages 167–168)

Directions
The Paper Dragon, a classic Chinese folk tale, is retold here by Marguerite W. Davol and exquisitely illustrated by Robert Clarke Sabuda (Simon and Schuster, 1997). Mi Fei is a humble, contented painter in a quiet village. But when the dragon Sui Jen awakens one day, it falls to Mi Fei to find a way to return the dragon to his slumber. He chooses a way of love.
- Read the story dramatically to the children, making sure to share the dramatic tissue-paper illustrations and fold-out spreads.
- Discuss the tactic that Mi Fei uses, and help the children compare his solution to the message of the Great Commandment.

Materials
The Paper Dragon by Marguerite W. Davol

Music Connection
- "What Can I Give to God?" P. Freeburg/ D. Walker. *Rise Up and Sing* #275.
- "This Is My Commandment," traditional. *Singing Our Faith (SOF)* #207.
- "Love One Another," R. Glover. *SOF* #213.
- "I Want to Walk as a Child of the Light," K. Thomerson. *SOF* #255.

20

The Ten Commandments

Background

"I'm Talking to You"

The Ten Commandments as found in Exodus 20 contain a curious diversion from the way God usually addresses the people of the Old Testament. In the Old Testament, he generally addresses the people of Israel collectively, as a community. This is not what happens in the rendering of the Ten Commandments.

God, using the first person singular, says, "I am the Lord" (see Exodus 20:2), as in "Listen up, what I'm about to say is very important." Then he says, "you," not the plural, collective "you," but "you" as an individual. God, in other words, is addressing each person individually as he speaks to the whole community. In other words, we need to listen up. These Commandments are not "just for others"; they are for me. It is as though he is saying, "Take this personally; I'm talking to you."

In the Revelation of the Ten Commandments, God was not revealing something new. He was not revealing a mystery beyond the comprehension of humans. He was putting in human words what he had already written on every human heart. God was making us aware of what his people, both the community of

Israel and each member of it, already should have known and come to understand.

The Fulfillment of the Law

The Ten Commandments do not only belong to the Old Law. Jesus, the Incarnate Son of God, revealed the importance of the Command-ments. He taught:

> "Do not think that I have come to abolish the law or the prophets. I have come not to abolish but to fulfill. . . . But whoever obeys and teaches these command-ments will be called greatest in the kingdom of heaven."
> MATTHEW 5:17, 19

The story of the rich young man gives us an insight into how Jesus fulfilled the Law. The young man approached Jesus and asked him, "[W]hat good must I do to gain eternal life?" (Matthew 19:16). Jesus replied, "If you wish to enter into life, keep the commandments" (19:17). The young man then said, "All of these I have observed. What do I still lack?" (19:20). Jesus confounds the young fellow—and us—with his response, "If you wish to be perfect, go, sell what you have and give to [the] poor, and you will have treasure in heaven. Then come, follow me" (19:21).

Jesus asks his disciples to live the Law of God as it is written on the human heart. Always make love for God and others your motivation in all you say and do. Fulfill Jesus' New Commandment: "love one another as I love you" (John 15:12).

For Reflection

When am I most aware of God speaking to me? How attentive and responsive am I?

In what ways do I strive to fulfill the Law of God as Jesus taught?

Catechist to Catechist

The Value of Rules

Sometimes both children and adults see rules as something negative—statements that restrict their freedom. But the contrary is really true. By following the Ten Commandments we are actually freeing ourselves to live our lives to the fullest. We need to help the children appreciate that good and authentic rules and laws protect our rights and privileges. They teach us how to handle freedom and responsibility. They help us grow in love and respect for God, for others, and for ourselves.

Classroom Rules

Be sure the children understand that the rules you have for your time together are meant to give each person the opportunity to be respected and be

respectful. Point out that parents too act out of love when they make rules for their children.

This is a good time to review any classroom rules you have established at the beginning of your time together. Ask the children which rules may still need some attention. Ask the children to discuss the positive effects these rules have had on your class.

The Church Teaches . . .

One of the first catechetical documents after Vatican II pointed out the need for catechists to do more than teach facts. Merely "teaching about" religion is not enough. Instead, such programs must strive to teach doctrine fully, foster community, and prepare their students for Christian service.

To Teach as Jesus Did 87

This is why we not only teach about God's rules but also help children practice applying them to daily life.

See the Catechism . . .

For more on the teachings of the Catholic Church on the Ten Commandments, see *Catechism of the Catholic Church* (2083–2550).

CATECHIST PRAYER

Lord,
in looking closely
at the Commandments,
I see how I sometimes
casually go about my days
without giving them a
thought. Help me
strive each day to live
the spirit of your laws.
Let me grow in age and
wisdom and grace.
Amen.

LESSON PLANNER

Focus To discover how the Ten commandments help people live a holy life

Engage

Page 173
Focus
To help the children identify the Ten Commandments as rules God gave us to free us

Opening Prayer

Discussion
What are some of your family's rules?

Teach and Apply

Pages 174–176
Focus
To introduce the Ten Commandments as laws given by God for living a holy life

Presentation
Read, discuss, and summarize content.
Scripture
• Psalm 25:5
Activities
• Write ways to keep the first three Commandments.
• Describe the action in the pictures.
• Write what the pictures tell about living as a child of God.

Connect

Pages 177–178
Focus
To describe ways the Commandments make a difference for the Church and for all people

Our Church Makes a Difference
Understand how parish members today follow the example of Saint Vincent de Paul.

Our Catholic Faith
Almsgiving

What Difference Does Faith Make?
Activity
Describe how to live the Commandments.
Faith Choice
Choose which Commandment you will most try to keep this week.

We Pray

Page 179
Prayer Form
Signing a prayer
Prayer
Sign the "Prayer to the Holy Spirit" together.

We Remember

Review
• Complete the sentences.
• Read the "To Help You Remember" statements aloud.
Preview
Highlight features of the "With My Family" page.

Materials

• pens or pencils
• crayons or markers
• poster board or chart paper

Enriching the Session

Blackline Masters
Additional Activities booklet:
    Chapter 20
        Tracing and coloring
        Making pocket-size
        Commandments
Assessment Tools booklet:
    Chapter 20 Test
Enriching the Lesson (CG page 293)
Collecting Food for Those in Need
Respect for Parents and
    Grandparents
Literature Connection
Music Connection (CG page 293)

www.FaithFirst.com

We update the *Faith First* Web site weekly. Check each week for new content and features. Here are some places to begin:

Catechists and Teachers
• Current Events
• Chapter Downloads
• Catechist Prayer

Faith First for Families
• Bible Stories
• Make a Difference

Kids' Clubhouse
• *Faith First* Activities
• Chapter Reviews
• Games Arcade
• Saints

Don't Forget! You can make lesson planning a breeze—check out the **Online Lesson Planner.**

The Ten Commandments

20

We Pray

LORD God, teach me your ways.

Based on Psalm 25:5

God our Father, help us to live your laws.

Amen.

Name a rule in your home that everyone has to follow.

Family rules help us to love one another. The Ten Commandments are rules God gave us. They help all people to live as children of God.

Name the Commandments you know.

173

Engage

PRAY

- Have the children quiet themselves for prayer.
- Begin the prayer with the Sign of the Cross.
- Proclaim Psalm 25:5. Lead the opening prayer, and invite the children to echo each phrase after you.
- Close the prayer with the Sign of the Cross.

DISCOVER

Purpose: To discover what the children may already know about the Ten Commandments

- Ask volunteers to name several family rules and have them tell who helps them learn these rules. Tell the children that God has rules too. Invite a volunteer to read aloud the sentences that tell about God's rules.
- Ask volunteers to name the Commandments they know.
- If any child names the Great Commandment, remind them of the distinction between the Ten Commandments and the Great Commandment.
- Have the children study the image of the Ten Commandments on the page. Ask them to tell why they think the Ten Commandments are not divided into two equal groups in the stained-glass window. Tell them they will find the answer in this chapter.

Teach

FOCUS

Ask a volunteer to read the "Faith Focus" question aloud. Tell the children that the Ten Commandments guide us to live a holy life. They are now going to learn about the first three Commandments.

DISCOVER

- Invite the children to imagine playing a soccer game without any rules. Ask: What would happen? Accept all reasonable answers.
- Emphasize that players need rules. Tell the children that God gave us the Ten Commandments to help us know how to love him, all people, and ourselves.
- Ask different volunteers to read aloud about the first three Commandments.
- Invite volunteers to describe each of the first three Commandments. Jot their answers on a numbered chart. (You will be adding more to this chart later.)

Apply

REINFORCE

Ask volunteers to read aloud the faith words and their meanings. Have the children make word cards for these terms.

INTEGRATE

- Discuss how the people in the picture are keeping one of the Commandments.
- Invite volunteers to name more ways to keep one of the first three Commandments.

Living the Commandments

Faith Focus

How do the Ten Commandments help people to live holy lives?

Faith Words

commandments
Commandments are rules that help us to live holy lives.

Ten Commandments
The Ten Commandments are the laws that God gave Moses that teach us to live as God's people.

Love God

Commandments are rules. The **commandments** God gives us help us to live holy lives. God gave us the **Ten Commandments.** The first three Commandments teach us to love and respect God.

The First Commandment teaches us that there is only one God. We worship God alone. We love God above all else.

The Second Commandment teaches us that God's name is holy. We speak God's name with reverence. We always speak it with respect and honor.

The Third Commandment teaches us to keep one day each week as God's day. Sunday is that day for Christians. It is the Lord's Day. Each Sunday Catholics gather together and celebrate the Eucharist. We make time to show that God is our Father and we are his children.

ACTIVITY Write one way you can keep one of the first three Commandments.

Affirm appropriate responses.

174

Teaching Tip

Respecting Other Religions. The children live in a multiculturally diverse world. They will notice that Christians gather to worship God on Sunday. Jewish people observe the Sabbath on Saturday, and Muslims come together in prayer assemblies on Friday. All three of the major religions of the world set aside a day each week for their community to give honor to God. God deserves our honor and respect. Help the children grow in their respect for all people who strive to sincerely love God with their whole heart. Discuss ways they can show respect for those of all faiths.

Love Others

The Fourth Commandment teaches us to honor and obey our parents. It also tells us to honor and obey grandparents, teachers, and other people who parents ask to help guide their children.

The Fifth Commandment teaches us to take care of our own lives and the lives of other people. We take care of our health. We do not harm ourselves or other people.

The Sixth Commandment and the Ninth Commandment teach us to respect our own bodies and the bodies of other people. We are not to let people touch us in the wrong way.

ACTIVITY *Look at the pictures on this page. Describe how the people are showing love for other people.*

(175)

Background: Faith-Filled People

Saint John Bosco. Saint John Bosco (1815–1888) was ordained a priest in 1841. He worked with homeless boys, teaching them job skills. His theory of education stressed the whole person. He believed that Christ's love and our faith in that love should be a part of every aspect of life—our work, our study, and our play. In 1884 John Bosco founded the Society of Saint Francis de Sales, whose members are called Salesians. He was canonized in 1934. In paying tribute to him Pope Pius XI praised John Bosco for doing so many positive things in his teaching ministry with young people, especially in changing the ordinary into the extraordinary. He is the patron saint of young apprentices.

Teach

FOCUS

Remind the children that the first three Commandments help us love God. Point out that the last seven Commandments teach us to love and respect others and ourselves.

DISCOVER

- Ask: Why do all people deserve to be treated with care and respect? All people are children of God.
- Ask volunteers to read about the next three Commandments. Ask about their meanings, and jot appropriate answers on the chart you have prepared.
- Read aloud "Faith-Filled People" about Saint John Bosco.

Apply

REINFORCE

Ask the children to give examples of how they can show care and respect for themselves and others at home, at school, and in their neighborhoods.

INTEGRATE

Have the children work with a partner to describe how the people in the illustrations are showing love for others.

FOCUS

Remind the children that the Fourth, Fifth, and Sixth Commandments have to do with ways to love others. Tell the children they are going to learn about the Seventh, Eighth, and Tenth Commandments.

DISCOVER

- Tell the children that loving others also means respecting their property.
- Ask volunteers to read aloud each paragraph of "Three More Commandments." As others read, ask the rest of the class to notice ways to keep each of the Commandments.
- After each paragraph, stop to discuss ways to keep each Commandment. Jot key answers about each Commandment on the chart.

Apply

REINFORCE

Emphasize that the virtues, or habits, of being fair and generous toward others will help us live these three Commandments.

INTEGRATE

Discuss the illustrations on this page. Then have the children describe how each picture tells us about living as a child of God.

We are to respect what belongs to others. Affirm all appropriate responses.

Three More Commandments

The Seventh Commandment teaches us to respect the property of other people. We do not steal or cheat. When we want to use something that belongs to someone else, we ask permission. We use what we borrow correctly and return it in good condition.

The Eighth Commandment teaches us to be honest and truthful. We do not lie.

The Tenth Commandment teaches us to use food and water and all creation fairly. The good things we have and the things we can do are all gifts from God. We share our gifts. We are not jealous of other people.

When we live the Ten Commandments, we are living as children of God. We are living holy lives.

On the lines describe what each picture tells us about living as a child of God.

We are to care for our health and safety. Affirm all appropriate responses.

176

Teaching Tip

Discussion Starters. To help the children recognize situations in which they will be called upon to live out the Ten Commandments, present these discussion starters and lead the children in a class discussion.

- A child in your class has cancer. He wears a baseball cap to school because the cancer treatments have made his hair fall out. Everyone feels sorry for him but no one talks to him because they don't know what to say. Is there anything you can say or do for him?
- Some children in your neighborhood don't want to play with a new girl who has just moved into the neighborhood because she doesn't know the rules to the game they are playing. What can you do?
- You know one of your friends took candy from the store and is giving it to his friends. What can you do?

Our Church Makes a Difference

Saint Vincent de Paul

People who live the Commandments help to build a kind and fair world. They treat people as children of God. They share God's love with people as Jesus did.

Saint Vincent de Paul took care of the sick. He gave clothes and food to the poor. He helped people to find jobs and to build homes.

Today people in many parishes follow the example of Saint Vincent de Paul. They are members of the Saint Vincent de Paul Society.

 What do the people of your parish do to show they are building a kind and fair world? Affirm appropriate responses.

Our Catholic Faith

Almsgiving

Almsgiving is a word that means "sharing something to help the poor." Jesus told us that when we help the poor and the hungry, we are helping him. From the very beginning of the Church, Christians have always done what Jesus asked. The first Christians did this very well. Their neighbors used to say, "See how much they love one another."

(177)

Catholic Social Teaching

Dignity of Work and the Rights of the Worker. Work has dignity because of the dignity of the worker, who is created in the image and likeness of God. Through our work we express and fulfill our humanity, share in God's work of creation, and contribute to the world through our work. We all have the obligation and the right to make use of our talents and to use them to work for the common good. Governments should guarantee to their workers a just wage, provide access to meaningful jobs, and promote fairness in the workplace.

Tip: Create a job chart for the month and assign children to rotating tasks each week.

Connect

HIGHLIGHT

Help the children recall that the Church lives the Ten Commandments in many ways. Point out that one way the Church lives out the Commandments is by following the example of Saint Vincent de Paul.

DISCOVER

- Ask the children if they have ever heard of the Saint Vincent de Paul Society.
- Explain that this group within the Church cares for people in need in the spirit of Saint Vincent de Paul. Tell about the saint in your own words.
- Ask children to read the page silently to themselves. Invite volunteers to give examples of Saint Vincent's work. He cared for the sick, gave food and clothing to the poor, helped people find jobs and build homes.
- Read "Our Catholic Faith" about almsgiving to the children.

INTEGRATE

Direct the children's attention to the picture. Ask the children to think about what people of their parish do to show they are building a kind and fair world. Have them share their thoughts with a partner.

Connect

HIGHLIGHT

Remind the children that when they live the Ten Commandments they are helping to build a world where God is respected and people are fair and loving toward one another.

RESPOND

- Have the children suggest ways to live the Commandments.
- Then have the children read the sentences in the activity frame.
- Choose a volunteer to read the directions, and invite the children to complete the activity alone or with partners.

CHOOSE

Present "My Faith Choice." Have the children write their choices and encourage them to put their choices into practice this week.

What Difference Does Faith Make in My Life?

When you live the Ten Commandments, you are living as a child of God. You are living a holy life. You are building a kind and fair world.

The sentences in the frames name seven ways to live the Ten Commandments. Choose one. Write or draw how you can do what it says.

Living the Commandments

Respect your parents.

Take care of yourself.

Go to church.   Be kind.

Be generous.

Treat others fairly.

Listen to your grandma and grandpa.

My Faith Choice

I will keep the _____ Commandment this week. I will

Affirm appropriate responses.

_____

_____ .

178

Teaching Tip

The Giraffe Project. The Ten Commandments help us live holy lives. Doing the right thing often requires "sticking our neck out." Use this opportunity to tell the children about the Giraffe Project. The Giraffe Project, a nonprofit organization, was founded in 1982 (www.giraffe.org/prjectinfo.html). Its purpose is to publicize stories of ordinary people, especially children, who have "stuck their necks out" to do the right thing. The genius of the Giraffe Project is that it tells us about real heroes. Share some of the stories with the class and send home the Web site information so that the children's families can share in this project.

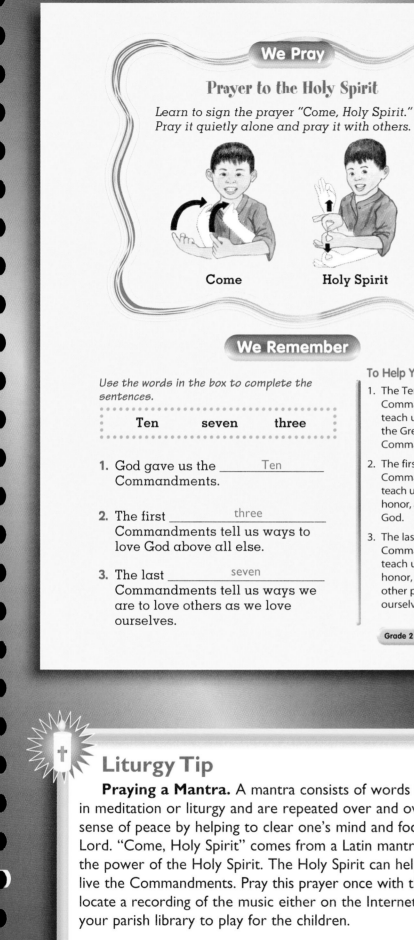

We Pray

Prayer to the Holy Spirit

Learn to sign the prayer "Come, Holy Spirit."
Pray it quietly alone and pray it with others.

Come   Holy Spirit

We Remember

Use the words in the box to complete the sentences.

> **Ten**   **seven**   **three**

1. God gave us the _____Ten_____ Commandments.

2. The first _____three_____ Commandments tell us ways to love God above all else.

3. The last _____seven_____ Commandments tell us ways we are to love others as we love ourselves.

To Help You Remember

1. The Ten Commandments teach us to live the Great Commandment.

2. The first three Commandments teach us to love, honor, and respect God.

3. The last seven Commandments teach us to love, honor, and respect other people and ourselves.

Grade 2 • Chapter 20 (179)

Liturgy Tip

Praying a Mantra. A mantra consists of words that are used in meditation or liturgy and are repeated over and over to bring a sense of peace by helping to clear one's mind and focus on the Lord. "Come, Holy Spirit" comes from a Latin mantra that invokes the power of the Holy Spirit. The Holy Spirit can help each of us live the Commandments. Pray this prayer once with the children or locate a recording of the music either on the Internet or from your parish library to play for the children.

WE PRAY

- Gather the children in the prayer center.
- Remind them that the Holy Spirit is always with us to give us the grace to live the Ten Commandments.
- Tell them we are going to learn a signing prayer to the Holy Spirit.
- Teach the signs, then quiet the children in prayer. If possible, play quiet background music.
- Lead the prayer, and repeat it three times.

Review

WE REMEMBER

- Turn the "To Help You Remember" statements into questions. Invite volunteers to answer them. Then have the children read the statements aloud together.
- Explain the directions to the activity. Allow time for the children to complete it. Invite them to check their answers with a partner.

At Home

ENCOURAGE

Have the children carefully tear out pages 179 and 180 along the perforation. Encourage the children to share the pages with their families and to do the activities together. If they did not complete the review activity on page 179 by the end of the session, emphasize that they can complete it with their families.

VISIT FAITHFIRST.COM

- Share with the children the many activities on the *Faith First* Web site.
- Encourage the children to visit **www.FaithFirst.com**.

Before Moving On . . .

As you finish today's lesson, reflect on the following question before moving on to the next chapter.

What have I done to let the children know that they are helping me to grow in faith as I work with them?

---

20 With My Family

This Week . . .

In chapter 20, "The Ten Commandments," your child learned that the Commandments guide us in living the Great Commandment. The first three Commandments name ways that we are to love, honor, and respect God. The last seven Commandments name ways we are to love, honor, and respect other people, ourselves, and all of God's creation. When we live the Ten Commandments, we live as children of God. We live holy lives. We prepare for the coming of the kingdom of God.

For more on the teachings of the Catholic Church on the Ten Commandments, see *Catechism of the Catholic Church* "First Commandment" (2083–2132), "Second Commandment" (2142–2159), "Third Commandment" (2168–2188), "Fourth Commandment" (2196–2246), "Fifth Commandment" (2258–2317), "Sixth Commandment" (2331–2391), "Seventh Commandment" (2401–2449), "Eighth Commandment" (2464–2503), "Ninth Commandment" (2514–2527), and "Tenth Commandment" (2534–2550).

Sharing God's Word

Read together Exodus 20:1–3, 7–17. Talk about how the Ten Commandments help us to live holy lives. Emphasize that the Ten Commandments are God's laws. They help us to live the Great Commandment.

Praying

In this chapter your child signed a prayer to the Holy Spirit. Read and pray together the prayer on page 179.

Making a Difference

Choose one of the following activities to do as a family or design a similar activity of your own.

- Write and illustrate your own storybook about how your family shows respect for God and other people.

- We can show our love for God by setting aside time each day to pray. Make prayer rocks to carry in your pockets. Use them as reminders to set aside time to pray often throughout the day. When you put your hand into your pocket, you will be reminded to pray. You will also be reminded that God is always with you.

- Talk about what your parish does to live the Ten Commandments. You might use a copy of your parish bulletin or visit your parish web site as a guide for your discussion.

For more ideas on ways your family can live your faith, visit the "Faith First for Families" page at **www.FaithFirst.com**. The "Make a Difference" page goes especially well with this chapter.

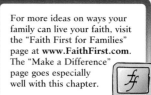

Evaluate

Take a few moments to evaluate this week's lesson.
I feel (circle one) about this week's lesson.

  a. very pleased
  b. OK
  c. disappointed

The activity the children enjoyed most was . . .

The concept that was most difficult to teach was . . .

because . . .

Something I would like to do differently is . . .

ENRICHING THE LESSON

Collecting Food for Those in Need

Purpose
To reinforce how we live the Ten Commandments by sharing our gifts (taught on page 176)

Directions
Children enjoy giving and showing their love for others.
- Suggest that the children participate in a monthly food drive.
- Together create a calendar of different food items for each month. A sample calendar of items follows:
  September   canned fruit
  October   canned soup
  November   hot and cold cereals
- Remind the children to bring in their food items the week before they are due.
- Arrange with your local food bank to receive these donations monthly.

Materials
poster board for calendar

Respect for Parents and Grandparents

Purpose
To reinforce the Fourth Commandment (taught on page 175)

Directions
- Brainstorm with the children words and actions that show respect for their parents and grandparents.
- Invite the children to create a collage of words and pictures cut from magazines that indicate respect for elders.
- Have the children glue the words and pictures on large pieces of construction paper that you have labeled "We Honor Our Elders."

Materials
magazines, scissors, glue sticks
construction paper with prepared title

Literature Connection

Purpose
To reinforce the concept of rules and how they help us (taught on pages 173–174)

Directions
Children for several generations have enjoyed the hilarious *Mrs. Piggle Wiggle* books by Betty Bard McDonald. The first volume, *Mrs. Piggle Wiggle* (HarperCollins paperback, 1976), introduces children to the wonderful grandmotherly lady in the upside-down house who smells like cookies and makes it fun to learn to behave.
- You might read the episode to the children about Hubert who never puts anything away or Patsy who hates to take a bath.
- Discuss the rules Mrs. Piggle Wiggle imposes and, most importantly, discuss the happy outcome of each of her strategies.
- Remind the children that God's rules, the Ten Commandments, bring us happiness and freedom.

Materials
Mrs. Piggle Wiggle by Betty Bard McDonald

Music Connection
- "Bread of Friendship," O. Alstott. *Rise Up and Sing (RUS)* #230.
- "What Can I Give to God?" P. Freeburg/ D. Walker. *RUS* #275.
- "This Is My Commandment," traditional. *Singing Our Faith (SOF)* #207.
- "Love One Another," R. Glover. *SOF* #213.

Proverbs
A Scripture Story

Background

Maxims for Living a Holy Life

The Book of Proverbs is a collection of instructive, or didactic, poetry. It is an example of an early catechism on living a holy life, aimed at the young and the inexperienced among the Israelites. Its title, "Proverbs," is derived from the Hebrew word *Mishle*, which is the first word of the book.

The usefulness and popularity of these proverbs, however, were not limited to the young. These pithy statements were well known and used as guides to wise decision making by those who wished to advance in piety. They frequently seasoned the conversations of God's people in much the same way as maxims color our language today.

The subject matter of the sayings in Proverbs runs the gamut from secular good sense to lofty inspiration. They can teach us a great deal about God and our relationship with him. For example:

God's power: Many are the plans in a man's heart, / but it is the decision of the Lord that endures.

PROVERBS 19:21

God's providential care: Say not, "I will repay evil!" / Trust in the Lord and he will help you.

PROVERBS 20:22

God's justice: The Lord is far from the wicked, / but the prayer of the just he hears. *PROVERBS 15:29*

It is difficult to say how this wondrous anthology of wisdom came about. Some proverbs were independent collections attributed to authors like King Solomon. Some believe that a religious scholar, probably in the early part of the fifth century before Christ, gathered these disparate collections into the inspired Book of Proverbs.

Proverbs in the New Testament

It is evident that the Jewish people of New Testament time were familiar with Proverbs, and Jesus used them to teach. In speaking to the Pharisees and guards sent to arrest him, Jesus refers to Proverbs 1:28. He says,

"I will be with you only a little while longer, and then I will go to the one who sent me. You will look for me and not find [me], and where I am you cannot come."

JOHN 7:33–34

The maxims of Proverbs are an anthology of holy maxims given to us by God, who is Wisdom. They help us appreciate wisdom and discipline and train us in wise conduct, in what is right, just, and honest.

For Reflection

What are some holy maxims that guide my daily decision making to live as a disciple of Christ?

How does the gift of wisdom, one of the seven Gifts of the Holy Spirit, guide and influence my decisions each day?

Catechist to Catechist

Words of Wisdom

The people of the Old Testament used "wise sayings" collected in the Book of Proverbs to help them live holy lives. These sayings or proverbs can help us think about God and live as his children.

Second graders are familiar with what can be considered "wise sayings." They hear them at home and in school, on the radio and TV. They often have to do with safety, such as "Cross at the green, not in-between" and "Buckle up for safety." Families often have their own "wise sayings" that are passed down from one generation to the next.

Words of Influence

Ask the children to share any sayings their parents or grandparents use frequently. Remind them that words like these, when heard often, will stay with them for a long, long time.

Remember that what you say to the children, even the most simple advice, can influence them and help them live holier lives. You can and do make a difference by sharing your own loving words of wisdom with the children.

The Church Teaches . . .

Children have many ways of learning, and there is little you cannot use to invite them to discipleship.

The Church . . . discerns contemporary methods in the light of the pedagogy of God and uses with liberty "everything that is true, everything that is noble, everything that is good and pure, everything that we love and honor and everything that can be thought virtuous or worthy of praise." (Phil. 4:8). In short, she assumes those methods which are not contrary to the Gospel and places them at its service.   *GDC* 148

Family sayings, proverbs, or poems can help the children remember the elements of good decision making.

See the Catechism . . .

For more on the teachings of the Catholic Church on the Gifts of the Holy Spirit and the importance of praying the Scriptures, see *Catechism of the Catholic Church* 1830–1832, 2568–2589, and 2653–2654.

CATECHIST PRAYER

Father, help me grow in love as I share our faith story with the children. Help me use proverbs so that I too may live as a child of God. Amen.

LESSON PLANNER

To explore the Book of Proverbs and its meaning for our lives as Christians

Engage

Page 181
Focus
To help the children share some wise sayings they know

Opening Prayer

Discussion
Some wise sayings help us make good choices.

Teach and Apply

Pages 182–184
Focus
To explain how proverbs help us make wise choices

Presentation
Read, discuss, and summarize content.

Scripture
• Psalm 25:5
• Proverbs 3:5, 16:3

Activities
• Illustrate a wise saying.
• Explain the meaning of two proverbs.
• Complete the proverb.

Connect

Pages 185–186
Focus
To Identify people in the Church, past and present, who help us make good choices to live as followers of Jesus

Our Church Makes a Difference
Learn what Saint Ignatius of Loyola said to help us remember that God is always with us.

Our Catholic Faith
The Bishop's Motto

What Difference Does Faith Make?
Activity
Describe how the Holy Spirit helps you use wise sayings.

Faith Choice
Identify someone to help you this week.

We Pray

Page 187
Prayer Form
Prayer of petition and praise
Prayer
Pray "We Pray to the Lord" together.

We Remember

Review
• Complete the "agree or disagree" activity.
• Review the "To Help You Remember" statements.

Preview
Highlight features of the "With My Family" page.

Materials

• pens or pencils
• crayons or markers

Enriching the Session

Blackline Masters
Additional Activities booklet:
    Chapter 21
    A door to God's help
    Make a book of Proverbs
Assessment Tools booklet:
    Chapter 21 Test

Enriching the Lesson (CG page 305)
Making a Hanging Art Proverb
Writing Letters of Thanks
Literature Connection

Music Connection (CG page 305)

www.FaithFirst.com

We update the *Faith First* Web site weekly. Check each week for new content and features. Here are some places to begin:

Catechists and Teachers
• Current Events
• Chapter Downloads
• Catechist Prayer

Faith First **for Families**
• Bible Stories
• Make a Difference

Kids' Clubhouse
• *Faith First* Activities
• Chapter Reviews
• Games
• Saints

Don't Forget! You can make lesson planning a breeze—check out the **Online Lesson Planner.**

Proverbs
A Scripture Story

We Pray

The precepts of
the LORD are right.
Psalm 19:9

**Lord God, teach
me to live your
Commandments.
Amen.**

*What sayings do
you know that help
you to remember to
do something?*

The saying "Buckle
Up" helps us to
make a safe choice.
The Bible has many
sayings that help
us to make wise
choices.

*What sayings
from the Bible do
you know?*

181

PRAY

- Have the children quiet themselves for prayer.
- Explain that the word *precepts* means "laws."
- Pray the Sign of the Cross together.
- Proclaim Psalm 19:9.
- Pray the opening prayer together and close with the Sign of the Cross.

DISCOVER

Purpose: To discover what the children already know about proverbs

- Have the children look carefully at the picture. Invite them to share what the woman might be looking at with the little girl.
- Ask the opening question and have them recall any wise sayings that grandparents or others in their family have shared with them. Give some examples from your own family.
- Read aloud the introductory paragraph and invite responses to the question.

Background: Scripture

Proverbs and Good Decisions. A proverb is a short saying that helps us make good choices. More than anything else proverbs in the Bible tell us ways to live as children of God. For instance, all people know the value of living the Golden Rule. You have a special opportunity as the children's catechist to help them make the Golden Rule a part of their daily lives.

Teach

FOCUS

Ask a volunteer to read the "Faith Focus" question aloud. Share with the children that in this chapter they will explore the Book of Proverbs, which is found in the Old Testament.

DISCOVER

- Write on the board a popular saying such as "The early bird gets the worm." Be sure to explain the saying if needed.
- Point out that simple, wise sayings can help us make wise choices.
- Ask the children to read the meaning of the faith words.
- Read aloud "Sayings in the Bible."
- Ask the children how some people in Old Testament times learned to make good choices. Learning proverbs by heart.

Apply

REINFORCE

Ask the children to share with a partner a wise choice that they have made.

INTEGRATE

- Encourage the children to share other wise sayings they know. Then have them do the activity.
- Ask volunteers to share their drawings or sayings.

Bible Background

Faith Focus

What are proverbs?

Faith Words

proverbs
Proverbs are short sayings that help us to make wise choices.

wise choice
A wise choice is a choice that helps us to live as children of God.

Sayings in the Bible

The Bible has many wise sayings. These sayings are called **proverbs**. They help God's people to make **wise choices** to live as children of God.

Many of God's people in Old Testament times could not read or write. Listening very carefully and learning proverbs by heart helped them to make wise choices.

ACTIVITY *Think of wise sayings you know. For example, "Buckle Up" or "Stop, Drop, and Roll." Write or draw a picture of another saying you know that helps you to make wise choices.*

Stop, Drop, and Roll

Buckle Up!

Responses will vary.

(182)

Teaching Tip

Connecting with Home. Involve the families in this lesson by sending a note home with the children asking each family to write on a sheet of paper one or more wise sayings that help them make good choices. Collect the families' sayings and create a bulletin board with them. Be sure that every child is represented.

Reading the Word of God

The Book of Proverbs

The writers of the Bible collected many proverbs. You can read them in the Book of Proverbs in the Old Testament. Each proverb helps us to love God, other people, and ourselves.

Read these two proverbs. Think about how each can help you to live as a child of God.

Trust God with all your heart.
Do not think you always have
the answers.
Based on Proverbs 3:5

Ask God's help before
you do something.
It is the secret to doing
the right thing.
Based on Proverbs 16:3

QUESTION ? How does each of these two proverbs help you to live as a child of God?

183

Teaching Tip

Different Learning Styles. Many of the children enjoy drawing to show they understand the concepts taught. However, try to remember that other children love to use music to learn. Perhaps putting some of the proverbs into music or acting them out will make the proverbs more personal and vivid.

FOCUS

Remind the children that the proverbs in the Bible help us make good choices to live as children of God.

DISCOVER

• Ask the children in which part of the Bible they would find the Book of Proverbs.

• Ask them to listen for the answer as you read the first paragraph of "The Book of Proverbs."

Apply

REINFORCE

Show the children where the Book of Proverbs is in the Bible, and read one or two appropriate proverbs to them. Discuss the meanings of the proverbs you selected with the children.

INTEGRATE

Invite the children to tell how each proverb helps them live as a child of God.

Teach

FOCUS
Remind the children that God's people in Old Testament times learned proverbs by heart.

DISCOVER
- Point out that it is important to learn some things by heart. There are many things we would not do if we had to look up information every time we wanted to do them.
- Read aloud or invite volunteers to read aloud "Living as Children of God" to discover the meaning of the two proverbs on the previous page.

Apply

REINFORCE
Emphasize that the Bible has many proverbs that help us live as God's children.

INTEGRATE
- Direct the children to complete the proverb in the activity at the bottom of the page.
- Invite volunteers to share ways their proverbs can help us live as children of God.

Understanding the Word of God

Living as Children of God

The first proverb on page 183 begins "Trust God with all your heart." Learn it by heart. Following its advice will help you to keep God first in your life. It will help you to love God above all else.

The second proverb teaches us to pray before we make our choices. Praying helps us to make wise choices.

Write a second part for this proverb. Share ways that your proverb can help you to live as a child of God.

Writing a Proverb

Speak kindly,
     and you will make peace.
Speak unkindly,
     and you will

Responses will vary.

184

Teaching Tip

Importance of Brainstorming. Before beginning a writing activity, take time to brainstorm ideas with the children and write their ideas on the board. This gives the children ideas and vocabulary to use to tackle writing activities with more self-confidence and excitement.

Our Church Makes a Difference

Christian Sayings

The Church has always had people to help us to live as followers of Christ. Many of these people said things that are like proverbs.

Saint Ignatius of Loyola once said, "See God in all things." What a wonderful way to help us to remember that God is always with us. What a wonderful way to remember to love God above all else with our whole heart.

Our Catholic Faith

The Bishop's Motto

A motto is another kind of short saying. Bishops use a motto to describe their work as a bishop. Pope John Paul II showed his love for Mary by choosing the motto "I Am Completely Yours, Mary."

QUESTION? *Who are some of the people who give you good advice? What good advice do they give you? How does that advice help you to love God with your whole heart?* Responses will vary.

See God in All Things

185

HIGHLIGHT

The proverbs and other sayings in the Bible help us live as children of God. Point out that holy members of the Church have also given us wise sayings that are similar to the proverbs.

DISCOVER

- Present "Christian Sayings" and ask the children to listen to a wise saying of Saint Ignatius of Loyola as you read the page.
- Ask: What does this saying help us remember?
- Present "Our Catholic Faith."
- Point out to the children that the bishops' mottos, the sayings of the saints, and the Book of Proverbs are all wise sayings that help us live as children of God.

INTEGRATE

- Talk with the children about who gives them good advice.
- Invite volunteers to share what good advice someone has given them and how it helps them love God with their whole heart.

Teaching Tip

A Well-Formed Conscience. Everyone has the responsibility to make the effort to assure that their conscience is well formed. Catechists have the ministry to support parents in bringing up their children in the practice of the faith. One way catechists meet this responsibility is by helping the children entrusted to them to develop the habit of training their conscience. Teach the children that we do many things to train our conscience. We pray and listen to and learn from Bible stories. We pay attention to our parents, godparents, and other adults who have the responsibility to help us grow in faith. We learn and follow the teachings of the Church. It is important to guide the children, even at this young age, to develop these important habits of conscience formation.

Connect

HIGHLIGHT

The Holy Spirit gives us the grace to use wise sayings to make good choices to live as followers of Jesus Christ.

RESPOND

- Explain the activity and invite the children to complete it.
- Let volunteers share how they have followed the good advice of a parent, teacher, coach, and so on.

CHOOSE

- Invite the children to read "My Faith Choice" and write their decisions.
- Encourage them to put their choices into practice this week.

What Difference Does Faith Make in My Life?

What sayings do you know that help you to make wise choices? The Holy Spirit will help you to use these sayings to live as a follower of Jesus Christ.

Think about some of the good advice your parents or teachers have given you to live as a child of God. Write or draw the actions that show you are following that advice.

Wise Choices

Responses will vary.

My Faith Choice

This week when I need help making a choice to live as a child of God, I will ask someone for help. I will ask

Affirm appropriate responses.

186

Teaching Tip

Positive Reinforcement. Remember that words of positive reinforcement can help us build our faith. Children need to know that we respect them as faith-filled learners. Use words such as "nice job," "good work," "interesting question," and "great idea" to show that you value their participation and efforts. You will soon hear the children use these expressions themselves to affirm one another.

We Pray

We Pray to the Lord

At Baptism we receive the grace to live the Commandments as Jesus taught. Pray this prayer. Tell God you will try your best to live as a follower of Jesus.

Leader: Remember the Lord's teachings. Keep his laws with all your heart.

All: **Lord, teach us your laws.**

Leader: Trust in the Lord with all your heart. The Lord will lead you on a straight path.

All: **We will trust the Lord always.**

Based on Psalm 119:33–34

We Remember

Circle Yes if you agree with a sentence. Circle No if you do not agree with a sentence.

1. Proverbs help us to make wise choices. Yes No

2. Most of the proverbs in the Bible are found in the New Testament. Yes No

3. Learning proverbs by heart can help us to live as children of God. Yes No

To Help You Remember

1. Proverbs are wise sayings.

2. Proverbs are found in the Book of Proverbs in the Old Testament.

3. The proverbs in the Bible help us to make choices to live as children of God.

Grade 2 • Chapter 21 187

Liturgy Tip

Praying the Scriptures. Sacred Scripture is the living word of God. Through Scripture God speaks to us, inviting us to live in communion and intimacy with him. Include Scripture in your prayer with the children. Teach them to memorize short Scripture verses, such as verses from the Psalms, Proverbs, and the Gospels, and to pray those verses quietly in their hearts. God's own word then becomes their prayer, leading them to deeper and deeper intimacy with him.

Pray

WE PRAY

- In advance, write the two prayer responses on newsprint.
- Gather the children in the prayer center.
- Tell them that our prayer today will include two proverbs.
- Practice the responses. Point out that each one is different.
- Tell the children to raise their hands in a prayer gesture as they make each response.
- Lead the prayer.

Review

WE REMEMBER

- Write the word *Proverbs* on the board. Put three bullets underneath it.
- Ask the children to tell you three things they know about proverbs and write their answers on the board next to the bullets.
- Read aloud the three "To Help You Remember" statements.
- Compare the children's bulleted points with the "To Help You Remember" statements.
- Introduce the activity. Ask the children to stand if they agree and to put their heads down on the table or desk if they do not agree. Then give them time to circle the Yes or No.

At Home

Have the children carefully tear out pages 187 and 188 along the perforation. Encourage the children to share the pages with their families and to do the activities together. If they did not complete the review activity on page 187 by the end of the session, emphasize that they can complete it with their families.

VISIT FAITHFIRST.COM

- Share with the children the many activities on the *Faith First* Web site.
- Encourage the children to visit **www.FaithFirst.com.**

With My Family

This Week . . .

In chapter 21, "Proverbs: A Scripture Story," your child learned about proverbs, in particular the proverbs found in Sacred Scripture. Proverbs in the Bible are short sayings that help us make wise decisions. Wisdom is one of the seven gifts of the Holy Spirit. This gift helps us know the purpose and plan of God and see the world as God sees it. Wisdom and the other gifts of the Holy Spirit help us live our relationship with God and with other people. They guide us to use and respect all of creation according to God's loving plan for creation.

For more on the teachings of the Catholic Church on the gifts of the Holy Spirit and the importance of praying the Scriptures, see *Catechism of the Catholic Church* paragraph numbers 1830–1832, 2568–2589, and 2653–2654.

Sharing God's Word

Read together Proverbs 3:5 and Proverbs 16:3 or read the adaptation of these verses on page 183. Emphasize that the proverbs in the Bible can help us make choices to live as children of God.

Praying

In this chapter your child prayed a prayer based on verses from Psalm 119. Read and pray together the prayer on page 187.

Making a Difference

Choose one of the following activities to do as a family or design a similar activity of your own.

- Choose one of the proverbs in this chapter. Tell how the proverb can help your family live as children of God.

- Talk about Gospel sayings your family may use; for example, "God bless you" or "God reward you."

- Share with one another the names of people who give you advice that helps you make wise family decisions. Share what wise advice these people have given you.

> For more ideas on ways your family can live your faith, visit the "Faith First for Families" page at **www.FaithFirst.com.** Visit the "Game" site. Ask your child to show you her or his favorite game. Play it together.

Before Moving On . . .

As you finish today's lesson, reflect on the following questions before moving on to the next chapter.

Do I make a faith choice each week just as I encourage the children to do? If so, have I ever shared a way I acted on my choice?

Evaluate

Take a few moments to evaluate this week's lesson.
I feel (circle one) about this week's lesson.

    a. very pleased

    b. OK

    c. disappointed

The activity the children enjoyed most was . . .

The concept that was most difficult to teach was . . .

because . . .

Something I would like to do differently is . . .

We Make Choices

We Pray

LORD God, doing your will makes me happy.
Based on Psalm 40:9

We thank you, God our Father. You made us to love you and one another.

Amen.

What wise choices did you make today?

We make many wise choices each day. Jesus teaches us how to make wise choices.

What can help you to make wise choices?

189

PRAY

- Have the children quiet themselves for prayer.
- Pray the Sign of the Cross together.
- Proclaim Psalm 40:9. Then lead the opening prayer, and invite the children to echo each phrase after you.
- Close the prayer with the Sign of the Cross.

DISCOVER

Purpose: To discover what connections the children make between their own good decisions and the teachings of Jesus

- Present the introductory paragraph in your own words.
- Invite responses to the two questions.
- Ask volunteers to share why they think the picture was chosen for the chapter opener.

Teaching Tip

Accidents, Mistakes, and Sins. Some children this age become very confused about accidents and mistakes, especially if they have serious consequences. We need to make it very clear to them that hurtful accidents and mistakes, which are out of their control, are NOT a result of choices they made. Accidents and mistakes are not sins. No one makes a mistake on purpose. Sins are always bad choices we make on purpose, knowing that what we say or do is against God's will and hurts our relationship with God, others, or ourselves.

Teach

FOCUS

Ask a child to read the "Faith Focus" question aloud. Tell the children that in this chapter they will learn to recognize their ability to use their conscience to make good choices. Point out that our choices to do what God wants us to do bring us the happiness he created us to have.

DISCOVER

- Ask the children what makes them happy.
- Present "Wise Choices Bring Happiness" in your own words.
- Ask: How did Jesus show that he loved God the Father more than anyone or anything else? Jesus always chose to do what his Father asked him to do.
- Emphasize that God wants us to be truly happy with him now and forever in heaven.

Apply

REINFORCE

Remind the children that God the Father sent Jesus to show us how to make good choices.

INTEGRATE

- Have the class look at the illustrations of the girls at the bottom of the page.
- Discuss the possible choices for each situation.
- Ask the children what they would do if they were in one of these situations. Possible answers: Tell someone about the broken window. Clean up the room.

We Follow Jesus

Faith Focus

Why is it important to follow God's will when we make choices?

Faith Words

consequences
Consequences are the good or bad things that happen when we make choices.

conscience
Conscience is a gift from God that helps us to make wise choices.

Wise Choices Bring Happiness

God sent Jesus to show us how to make wise choices. Jesus always did what his Father asked him to do. We will be truly happy when we make choices as Jesus taught us.

God wants us to be happy now and forever in heaven. Heaven is being happy with God and with all the saints forever.

ACTIVITY *Look and think about what is happening in these pictures. Tell what choice you would make next. Share why your choices are good choices.*

Responses will vary.

Choices

190

Background: Doctrine

Rewards and Punishment. It is not always an easy thing to admit fault and take responsibility for the harm that results from our choices. It is, of course, easier and more pleasant to take credit for the good that results from our choices. Children this age tend to assess the "goodness" or "badness" of their acts from the punishment or the reward that results from their choices. While moral growth demands that parents and catechists guide the children to progress beyond this stage of moral development, punishment and reward can be properly and appropriately used as tools to help the children stop and assess their choices—both words and deeds. When punishment is used, its goal should be to lead the child to knowingly and freely make better choices.

Choosing Right and Wrong

God lets us make choices for ourselves. We can choose to do or not to do God's will. In the Bible we read,

> When God created us, he gave us free choice. It is our choice to do God's will.
>
> Based on Sirach 15:14–15

Things happen when we make choices. These are called **consequences.** We are responsible for the consequences of our actions. This means that we accept what happens because of our choices.

Sometimes we make a choice that we know God does not want us to make. We need to fix the harm our bad choices have done.

✗ Faith-Filled People

Philip Neri

Saint Philip Neri sold all his possessions and gave away his money. He visited banks, shops, and places where people gathered. Every place he visited, he tried to convince people to serve God in all they did. The Church celebrates the feast day of Saint Philip Neri on May 26.

ACTIVITY Read this story. Write or draw one consequence of Sarah's choice.

Sarah's Choice
Sarah's little sister Katie is sick. Sarah asks her parents, "May I read Katie a story?"

Responses will vary.

191

Background: Faith-Filled People

Saint Philip Neri. Saint Philip Neri (1515–1595) had a lively sense of humor. His own words explained that "the importance of getting through each day is not to fear what might happen tomorrow." Philip had that rare ability to help people probe their hearts while at the same time he could add a joke. He is honored as the "Second Apostle of Rome." The feast of Saint Philip Neri is celebrated on May 26.

Teach

FOCUS

Remind the children that happiness is a consequence of making choices to do God's will.

DISCOVER

- Read "Choosing Right and Wrong." Invite a volunteer to read the Scripture verse. Be sure the children understand the meaning of free choice.
- Explain that we have to accept responsibility for our choices and for what happens because of our choices.
- Have the children read aloud the meaning of the faith word *consequences.*
- Tell the children about the good choice Saint Philip Neri made.

Apply

REINFORCE

- Ask the children how they know when they have not made a good choice. They feel sorry about their choice. They experience bad consequences.
- Ask the children to share an action that they do every day— tie their shoes, ride their bike, do their chores. Go over the consequences of these actions or inactions. They could trip and fall if the shoe isn't tied, and so on.
- Have the children create a word card for *consequences.*

INTEGRATE

- Introduce the activity. Have the children suggest possible consequences.
- Invite them to complete the activity on their own.

Teach

FOCUS

Remind the children that all of our moral choices have consequences. Point out that God gives us the gift of our conscience to help us make choices to live as his children.

DISCOVER

- Ask the children how they know if something is what God wants them to do or not do.
- Read aloud "The Gift of Our Conscience." Ask the children to listen for the meaning of conscience.
- Ask the children what happens if we refuse to listen to our conscience. *We may make choices that are against what God wants us to do or not do.*
- Ask the children to reread the second paragraph silently. Have them underline four ways we form our conscience.
- Ask a volunteer to name one way we form our conscience.

Apply

REINFORCE

Have the children turn back to page 190 in their text and read aloud the faith word *conscience* and its meaning and then create a word card.

INTEGRATE

- Read the directions for the activity on this page.
- Guide the children through the examination of conscience by reading each statement aloud and allowing the children to silently record their responses in their books. Do not ask the children to share their answers.

The Gift of Our Conscience

God gives us a gift that helps us to make wise choices. This gift is our **conscience.** Our conscience tells us whether a choice we are about to make or a choice we have made is a wise choice.

We need to form our conscience. We need to learn what God wants us to do. We pray to the Holy Spirit. We read and listen to the Bible. We learn what the Church teaches. We ask our parents and other grown-ups to help us.

ACTIVITY *Read each statement and think about your day. Circle the happy and sad faces to help you to review the choices you made.*

Thinking about Our Choices

Responses will vary.

1. I prayed to God to ask for help. ☺ ☹

2. I showed my love to family members. ☺ ☹

3. I showed my love to my friends. ☺ ☹

4. I showed my love to other people. ☺ ☹

192

Liturgy Tip

Examination of Conscience. Examining one's conscience is a skill children can develop. For the next few sessions, include this simple examination of conscience in the closing prayer.

- How well do I show my love for God? Do I pray? Do I listen to his word at Mass? Do I use the name of God reverently?

- How am I showing love for others and for myself? Do I show respect for my parents? Do I care for my health and follow safety rules? Do I treat others kindly?

Invite the children to silently ask God's forgiveness for any wrong choices they might have made.

Our Church Makes a Difference

Morning and Night Prayers

We can pray in the morning and at night. In the morning we ask God to help us to make wise choices.

We pray at night to help us to think about the day. We examine our conscience. We talk to God about the choices we have made. God helps us to make better and better choices.

We pray at the beginning and end of each day. This helps us to make choices to live as Jesus taught us to live. It helps us to thank and praise God all day long.

 QUESTION *When do you pray each day? How does praying each day help people to make wise choices?*

Our Catholic Faith

Examination of Conscience

We examine our conscience to know if the choices we made were wise choices. This helps us to live holy lives. We always examine our conscience to prepare for the celebration of the sacrament of Reconciliation.

193

Teaching Tip

Teaching Short Prayers. Help the children pray often throughout the day for help in making good choices by teaching them short prayers such as the following.

1. "God our Father, help me to do my best." (every time they pick up their pencils)

2. "Jesus, the Son of God, help me to be fair." (every time they go out to play)

3. "Holy Spirit, help me to be a good friend today." (every time they join their friends)

Connect

HIGHLIGHT

Share that praying in the morning and at night each day helps us make choices to live as children of God.

DISCOVER

- Some of the children may already be in the habit of saying morning and/or night prayers every day. This is a good time to encourage all the children to form this habit.
- Point out that we can begin each day by thanking God for the new day and the gift of life. We can ask God to help us make choices to live as his children.
- Help the children connect the idea of praying at night with examining their conscience.

INTEGRATE

- Invite the children to follow along as a volunteer reads "Our Catholic Faith."
- Ask the children to highlight the sentence that tells why we examine our conscience.
- Working in partners have the children come up with one way praying helps people make wise choices.

Connect

HIGHLIGHT

Our conscience helps us know right from wrong.

RESPOND

• Ask the children if they know anyone who wears a bracelet with the letters WWJD on it.

• Explain that the letters stand for the words "What Would Jesus Do," and many Christians wear these bracelets. The words remind them to follow their conscience and make good choices.

• Read aloud the introductory paragraph.

• Have the children look at the activity pictures. Explain the directions. Ask volunteers to share their work.

CHOOSE

Invite the children to read "My Faith Choice" and write their decisions. Encourage them to put their choices into practice this week.

Your conscience helps you to know right from wrong. It helps you to make choices to live as Jesus taught.

Circle the pictures that show children making a good choice to live as Jesus taught. Write an X on the pictures that show a bad choice.

Making Choices

My Faith Choice

ff I can choose to make choices to live as Jesus taught. This week I will

_____

Affirm appropriate choices.

_____.

(194)

Teaching Tip

Extend the Activity. Get the children into the habit of asking what Jesus' teachings might lead them to do in important situations. Have them role-play the following or similar scenarios. After each role-play, ask, "What would Jesus want me to do?"

1. The child in the next desk at school has a new hand-held computer game that you like. You think about sneaking it out of her backpack when no one is looking.

2. Your friends are talking about a boy at school who is not popular. They are saying very mean things about him that you know are not true.

We Pray

Prayer of Saint Francis

Saint Francis of Assisi prayed about making wise choices. He prayed that God would help him to be a peacemaker. Peace happens when we live as God wants us to live.

All: Lord, make us instruments of your peace.

Group 1: Where there is hatred,
Group 2: let us bring love.

Group 1: Where there is injury,
Group 2: let us bring forgiveness.

All: Lord, make us instruments of your peace.

We Remember

Unscramble the letters to make a word you learned in this chapter. Make up a sentence using the word. Share your sentence with others.

S C I C O N E N C E

C O N S C I E N C E

_____

_____

_____

To Help You Remember

1. We are happy when we make choices that follow God's will.

2. Wise choices show we are following our conscience.

3. All of our choices have consequences.

Grade 2 • Chapter 22 (195)

Pray

WE PRAY

- Gather the children in the prayer center with their books.
- Tell them that Saint Francis worked hard to bring peace into the world. Tell them that today's prayer is one he wrote.
- Divide the children into group 1 and group 2 and point out their parts.
- Pray the Prayer of Saint Francis together.

Review

WE REMEMBER

- Ask volunteers to share at least one thing they learned in this chapter.
- Compare their statements to the "To Help You Remember" statements.
- Tell the children that good choices show we are following our conscience.
- Ask the children to name two things that happen when we make good choices. We are happy; good things happen.
- Have the children complete the activity and share their answers.

Teaching Tip

Establishing Rules and Consequences. Most second graders are at a very elementary level of moral thinking. It is normal for them at this age to be more motivated by the possibilities of reward or punishment than by a lofty ideal. That is why we make rules and establish consequences for breaking them. Experiencing the consequences of their choices will help the children grow in their understanding of the reason for the rules and in growing in their love for God and others.

(Student Page 195) (315)

At Home

ENCOURAGE

Have the children carefully tear out pages 195 and 196 along the perforation. Encourage the children to share the pages with their families and to do the activities together. If they did not complete the review activity on page 195 by the end of the session, emphasize that they can complete it with their families.

VISIT FAITHFIRST.COM

• Share with the children the many activities on the *Faith First* Web site.
• Encourage the children to visit **www.FaithFirst.com.**

---

22 With My Family

This Week . . .

In chapter 22, "We Make Choices," your child learned that we are responsible for the choices we make. God has given us the gift of a conscience to help us discern right from wrong. Every person has the responsibility to form a good conscience. Parents and others who have children under their care have the responsibility to help their children develop a well-formed and correct conscience. This will help the children live according to God's will and find happiness both here on earth and forever in heaven.

For more on the teachings of the Catholic Church on true happiness, responsibility, and conscience, see *Catechism of the Catholic Church* paragraph numbers 1716–1724, 1730–1738, and 1776–1794.

Sharing God's Word

Read together Sirach 15:14–15 or read the adaptation of these verses on page 191. Emphasize that God created us with a free will and the ability to make our own choices.

Praying

In this chapter your child prayed part of the peace prayer of Saint Francis of Assisi. Read and pray together the prayer on page 195.

Making a Difference

Choose one of the following activities to do as a family or design a similar activity of your own.

• Watch a TV show together. Point out when characters on the show make wise choices and when they make bad choices. If someone makes a bad choice, make suggestions for a wise choice.

• Talk about how your family can help and support one another to make wise decisions and choices.

• Celebrate wise choices. At dinnertime this week share with one another the wise choices family members made during the day and talk about their consequences. Share how the good consequences of your choices help to build a world of peace and fairness.

For more ideas on ways your family can live your faith, visit the "Faith First for Families" page at **www.FaithFirst.com**. Click on "Saints." Talk about the consequences of the wise choices the saint made.

196

Before Moving On . . .

As you finish today's lesson, reflect on the following question before moving on to the next chapter.

What can I do to help the children who are more mathematically or scientifically inclined to bring their gifts to our religion activities?

✓ Evaluate

Take a few moments to evaluate this week's lesson.
I feel (circle one) about this week's lesson.

    a. very pleased
    b. OK
    c. disappointed

The activity the children enjoyed most was . . .

The concept that was most difficult to teach was . . .

because . . .

Something I would like to do differently is . . .

We Share in God's Life

We Pray

I trust God, who always cares for me.

Based on Psalm 57:3

Lord God, we bless you and thank you. You have called us to share in your life. Amen.

What is a favorite gift you have received?

A gift is a sign of love. God gives us the gift of sharing in his life.

What does it mean to share in the gift of God's life?

(197)

Teaching Tip

Living as God's Children. When we love someone, we enjoy their company. Many of the children in your group, like the children in the picture, are friends who enjoy each other's company. God is always present with us, sharing his life and love with us and inviting us to live as his children. Help the children see that we live as God's children when we overcome disagreements peacefully, respect each other's differences and opinions, and make up when we hurt one another.

Engage

PRAY

- Have the children quiet themselves for prayer.
- Pray the Sign of the Cross together.
- Invite a volunteer to read Psalm 57:3. Then lead the opening prayer, and invite the children to echo each phrase after you.
- Close the prayer with the Sign of the Cross.

DISCOVER

Purpose: To discover how well the children understand that life is a gift from God

- Ask the children to name a favorite gift they have received. Then ask them to name a gift they have received that is not a thing. A grandparent comes to visit; a parent takes them on a special outing; someone reads them a story at bedtime.
- Tell the children that God gives us many gifts. Then have them read the opening paragraph.
- Ask the last question and invite responses. Accept appropriate responses; for example, we are children of God.

Teach

FOCUS

Ask a volunteer to read the "Faith Focus" question aloud. Tell the children that in this chapter they will learn what it means to share in God's life and love.

DISCOVER

- Invite the children to read the meaning of the faith words *sanctifying grace*.
- Read aloud "God Shares His Life with Us" and ask the children to listen to find out when we first receive the gift of sanctifying grace.
- Ask: What does God's gift of grace do for us? Makes us sharers in God's life and love; helps us live as his children.

Apply

REINFORCE

Have the children create a word card for *sanctifying grace*. Remind the children to keep it in a place where it can be a reference for them.

INTEGRATE

Explain the activity and have the children complete it on their own. Ask the children what good thing the gift of God's grace could help them do. Accept all appropriate answers.

God Shares His Life with Us

Faith Focus

What does the gift of grace help us to do?

Faith Words

sanctifying grace
Sanctifying grace is the gift of God sharing his life with us.

God Shares His Life with Us

God has given us the gift of **sanctifying grace.** The word *sanctifying* means "something that makes us holy." We first receive this gift at Baptism.

The gift of sanctifying grace makes us children of God. God shares his life with us. As God's children, filled with grace, we are holy. The Bible tells us,

Through your faith in Jesus, you are all children of God.
Based on Galatians 3:26

God also helps us to live as his children. The Holy Spirit always gives us the grace to make wise choices. This helps us to live as children of God.

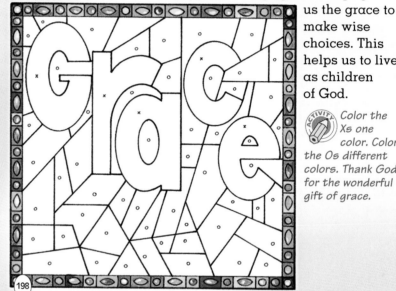

Activity Color the Xs one color. Color the Os different colors. Thank God for the wonderful gift of grace.

198

Background: Doctrine

Grace. The word *grace* means "gift." God's grace is both the gift of his sharing his life and love with us (sanctifying grace) and his grace, or help, to live as his friends (actual graces). The more we come to know God, the more we want to spend time with him in prayer and the more we want to show how proud we are to be his friends. Spending time with God in prayer is also a graced moment. We come to him in prayer because he first invites us.

Choosing to Live a Holy Life

It is not always easy to choose to live a holy life. Sometimes we choose to sin. All sins hurt our relationship with God and other people. Some sins are very serious. These sins are mortal sins. When we commit a mortal sin, we lose the gift of sanctifying grace.

We need to confess mortal sins in the sacrament of Reconciliation. When we are sorry for our sins and confess them in Reconciliation, God forgives our sins. We receive the gift of sanctifying grace again.

Other sins are not as serious as mortal sins. These sins are venial sins. It is good to confess these sins too. In Reconciliation we receive God's grace to live a holy life.

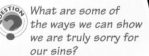 **What are some of the ways we can show we are truly sorry for our sins?**

Affirm appropriate responses.

Receiving absolution in sacrament of Reconciliation

199

Faith-Filled People

Monica

Saint Monica's son Augustine often made unwise choices. Monica prayed that her son would make better choices. He did and lived a holy life. Today her son is honored as Saint Augustine. The Church celebrates the feast day of Saint Monica on August 27.

Background: Faith-Filled People

Saint Monica. Saint Monica (331–387) is the patron saint of mothers. Her examples of kindness, love, patience, and persistence apply to all Christians. As a young man, her son, Augustine, lived a wild life, and Monica's life was devoted to faithfully praying for Augustine's conversion to Christianity. Augustine accepted God's gift of grace and became a Christian. He became one of the greatest teachers of the Church and is honored as a Doctor of the Church.

Teach

FOCUS

Remind the children that while we do try to make good choices to live as children of God, we sometimes freely choose to do what we know is against his will. When we do, we sin.

DISCOVER

- Present "Choosing to Live a Holy Life" in your own words, focusing on the difference between mortal sin and venial sin.
- Ask the children to describe the two kinds of sin in their own words.
- Remind the children that we can ask forgiveness for our sins in the sacrament of Reconciliation. Emphasize that we need to confess all mortal sins in the sacrament of Reconciliation.
- Have the children read the second paragraph silently to find out how the sacrament of Reconciliation helps us. God forgives us; we receive the grace to live a holy life.
- Read "Faith-Filled People" to the children. Point out that Saint Monica prayed for many years that her son would make better choices.

Apply

REINFORCE

Emphasize that God's gift of grace helps us make choices to live as children of God.

INTEGRATE

Introduce the question at the bottom of the page and invite responses.

Teach

FOCUS

Remind the children that we must confess mortal sins in the sacrament of Reconciliation. Point out that God is always ready to forgive our sins when we are truly sorry.

DISCOVER

- Invite volunteers to read aloud "Jesus Teaches About Forgiveness."
- Ask the children what Jesus teaches us about forgiveness. "Forgive and you will be forgiven" (Luke 6:37).

Apply

REINFORCE

- Ask the children what Jesus meant when he said, "Forgive and you will be forgiven."
- Write the children's responses on the board.

INTEGRATE

- Ask the children to name some people who forgive them when they ask for forgiveness. Then ask them to think about someone they have forgiven.
- Have the children complete the activity. Remind them that the Holy Spirit helps us be forgiving and live the Great Commandment.

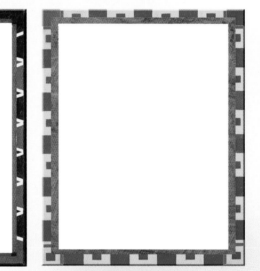

Jesus Teaches About Forgiveness

Jesus reminded us over and over again that God is always ready to forgive our sins. Jesus also taught us another important thing about forgiveness. We need to forgive other people. He said,

"Forgive and you will be forgiven." *Luke 6:37*

The Holy Spirit always gives us the help to forgive others. Forgiving others is not always easy. When we forgive others, we are living the Great Commandment.

ACTIVITY *In one frame draw yourself forgiving someone. In the other frame draw someone forgiving you.*

Affirm appropriate responses.

200

Background: Doctrine

Making up. Making up is a behavior children learn early and sometimes quickly. They learn that making up when they are hurtful to their family and friends is a vital part of life and developing healthy relationships. They also learn the negative consequences of not making up with those whom they harm and of not accepting the efforts to make up of those who harm them. The Church teaches that when we sin, we need to make up. We need to make reparation for our sins. Help the children grow in their ability to apologize to the people whom their words and actions harm. This is a first step in learning to make up.

Our Church Makes a Difference

Saint Catherine of Siena

Catherine of Siena lived at a time when the people in the Church were having disagreements. Some of these disagreements led to fighting.

Catherine helped people in the Church to see the harm their fighting was causing. She brought people together. They began to forgive one another and to solve their problems without fighting.

The Church celebrates the feast day of Saint Catherine of Siena on April 29. We ask the Holy Spirit to help us to forgive those who hurt us. We ask the Holy Spirit to help us to live as peacemakers.

 QUESTION *What are some of the ways you see people showing forgiveness to others?*

Responses will vary.

Our Catholic Faith

Religious Medals

Catholics sometimes wear a cross or a religious medal of Mary or of a saint. This helps us to remember to live as children of God. It also helps us to remember to pray to Mary and the other saints to help us live as Jesus taught.

201

💡 Teaching Tip

Being Peacemakers. Encourage the children to follow Saint Catherine's example by being peacemakers. They will find many opportunities both at home and at school to use their peacemaking skills. Beforehand, make a one-week calendar and give each child a copy. They can write or draw what they do to be peacemakers each day. Remind them that they may not do something every day, and that's okay, but encourage them to look for opportunities each day to be peacemakers. Have the children return their calendars to the next session and share them with the other children.

Connect

HIGHLIGHT

Help the children understand that God constantly gives us the grace to live as his children. Point out that Saint Catherine made good choices to help others.

DISCOVER

- Tell the children the story of Saint Catherine of Siena in your own words.
- Point out that Catherine was a peacemaker. She helped the pope and other members of the Church settle disagreements and work together in peace.
- Present "Our Catholic Faith."
- Help the children understand that wearing religious medals of Mary and the saints reminds us to live as Jesus taught us to live.

INTEGRATE

- Divide the class into groups of three. Ask the children to role-play the way they see people resolving problems and showing forgiveness to others.
- Have each group present their role-play for the class.

Connect

HIGHLIGHT

Help the children recall that the Holy Spirit helps us live as children of God. Point out that one way we live as children of God is to live as peacemakers.

RESPOND

- Read the introductory paragraph with the children.
- Talk about ways we can be peacemakers.
- Help the children with the activity or have them complete it at home with their families.

CHOOSE

- Invite the children to read "My Faith Choice" and write their decisions.
- Encourage them to put their choices into practice this week.

What Difference Does Faith Make in My Life?

God shares the gift of his life with us. The Holy Spirit helps us to live as children of God. One way you can live as a child of God is to be a peacemaker.

Work with your teacher or parent. Create a message for the Internet that tells how people your age can live as peacemakers.

Teaching Peace

My Faith Choice

This week I will show I am a peacemaker. I will

Affirm appropriate choices.

_____

_____ .

202

Teaching Tip

Acting Out a Story of Forgiveness. The story of Zacchaeus provides a good example of the power of God's grace and his willingness to forgive. Zacchaeus was a tax collector despised by the people. Yet when Jesus showed God's love to him, Zacchaeus was transformed and became Jesus' follower. Read the complete story in Luke 19:1–10 to the children. If time allows, invite some children to act out the story for the group as you read it a second time.

We Pray

Hail Mary

Learn the Hail Mary by heart. Pray it every day to show your love for Mary. Ask Mary to help you to live a holy life.

Group 1: Hail Mary, full of grace, the Lord is with you!

Group 2: Blessed are you among women, and blessed is the fruit of your womb, Jesus.

All: **Holy Mary, Mother of God, pray for us sinners, now and at the hour of our death. Amen.**

We Remember

Write words on the path that show ways we can live holy lives.

To Help You Remember

1. Grace is a gift from God.

2. Sanctifying grace is the gift of God's life that he shares with us.

3. Other graces help us to live holy lives.

Grade 2 • Chapter 23 (203)

Liturgy Tip

Praying the Hail Mary. The Hail Mary is a traditional Catholic prayer and a beautiful way to honor the Mother of God. Go over the parts of the Hail Mary with the children before beginning the concluding prayer. Help the children understand the language of the prayer so they might be able to better appreciate it as one of the prayers Catholics pray frequently.

Pray

WE PRAY

- Remind the children that Mary, the mother of Jesus, was always filled with God's grace.
- Tell the children that you are going to pray the Hail Mary with them today as the closing prayer.
- Divide the children into two groups. Have each group find the part of the Hail Mary that they are going to pray aloud.
- Gather the children in the prayer center.
- With hands folded, have the children pray the Hail Mary together.

Review

WE REMEMBER

- Write each "To Help You Remember" statement on a sentence strip.
- Cut each strip into two parts, dividing the term from its meaning.
- Mix the sentences up and tape them to a flat surface with double-stick tape.
- Invite volunteers to come up and match the terms with their meanings.
- Have the children complete the activity.

At Home

ENCOURAGE

Have the children carefully tear out pages 203 and 204 along the perforation. Encourage the children to share the pages with their families and to do the activities together. If they did not complete the review activity on page 203 by the end of the session, emphasize that they can complete it with their families.

VISIT FAITHFIRST.COM

- Share with the children the many activities on the *Faith First* Web site.
- Encourage the children to visit **www.FaithFirst.com.**

This Week . . .

In chapter 23, "We Share in God's Life," your child learned that God shares divine life with us. We receive the gift of sanctifying grace. By sharing his life with us, God calls us to live a holy life. Sin turns us away from God's love and deters us from living holy lives. When we sin, we need to be sorry and ask God for forgiveness. Asking for forgiveness and forgiving others are part of living a holy life.

For more on the teachings of the Catholic Church on grace and the call to holiness, see *Catechism of the Catholic Church* paragraph numbers 1846–1869 and 1996–2016.

Sharing God's Word

Read together Matthew 6:14–15. Emphasize that God gives us the gift of his help, or grace, to live as children of God. God helps us forgive others as he forgives us.

Praying

In this chapter your child prayed the Hail Mary. Read and pray together the Hail Mary on page 203.

Making a Difference

Choose one of the following activities to do as a family or design a similar activity of your own.

- Name people who have showed you ways to be forgiving. Discuss that when we do not make wise choices and sin, we need to be sorry and ask God for forgiveness. As God forgives us, we need to forgive others too.
- Become more familiar with the Hail Mary. Use the Hail Mary for your family prayer this week.
- Create forgiveness place mats. Use the place mats at family meals as reminders to forgive others as you want to be forgiven by God and others.

For more ideas on ways your family can live your faith, visit the "Faith First for Families" page at **www.FaithFirst.com**. As a family share some of the ideas on the "Gospel Reflections" page this week.

204

Before Moving On . . .

As you finish today's lesson, reflect on the following question before moving on to the next chapter.

How am I using the gifts of the artists in my class?

Evaluate

Take a few moments to evaluate this week's lesson.
I feel (circle one) about this week's lesson.

    a. very pleased

    b. OK

    c. disappointed

The activity the children enjoyed most was . . .

The concept that was most difficult to teach was . . .

because . . .

Something I would like to do differently is . . .

Our Church Makes a Difference

Blessed Kateri Tekakwitha

Kateri Tekakwitha was a Native American. She was a member of the Turtle Clan of the Iroquois.

Kateri loved to go into the woods and be alone with God. Her favorite place to pray was in the tall trees amid the quiet sounds. "There," she said, "God speaks to my heart."

The Church honors Kateri Tekakwitha as "Blessed." The Church names a person "Blessed" before it names a person a saint.

QUESTION *Who do you know who both prays and does kind things for other people? What does that person do?*

Responses will vary.

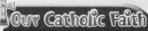

Our Catholic Faith

Family Prayer

We first learn to pray in our families. Families often pray at mealtimes. Another favorite time for families to pray is at the end of the day before bedtime.

213

Background: Catholic Tradition

Blessed Kateri Tekakwitha. Blessed Kateri was the daughter of a Christian Algonquin mother and a non-Christian Mohawk chief. She was born in 1656 near the Mohawk River in what is now upstate New York. When she was four years old, Kateri contracted smallpox. She survived, but her eyesight was impaired and the illness left her badly scarred. Kateri was baptized in 1676. She eventually settled at a mission near Montreal and devoted her life to teaching prayers to children and helping the sick and elderly until she died in 1680 at age twenty-four. Kateri was beatified, or named "Blessed," by Pope John Paul II in 1980. Her feast day is July 14.

Connect

HIGHLIGHT

- Invite a volunteer to read aloud "Our Catholic Faith" to remind the children that we first learn to pray in our families.
- Share that one way our Church helps us learn to pray is by sharing with us examples of saints and other holy people.

DISCOVER

- Tell the children that you are going to tell them the story of a Native American girl who is an example of prayer.
- Ask the children to look at the stained-glass window on page 213 and explain that this holy person is Blessed Kateri Tekakwitha. The Church honors Kateri with the title "Blessed" because she led a holy and prayerful life and may one day be named a saint.
- Tell the story of Blessed Kateri Tekakwitha.
- Ask: What can you learn from Blessed Kateri Tekakwitha?
  Going to a quiet place can be a good place to pray. Affirm all appropriate responses.

INTEGRATE

Ask the question at the bottom of the page and invite volunteers to respond.

Connect

Point out that the Holy Spirit invites and teaches us to pray.

RESPOND

- Ask the children to read along with you as you explain the directions to the "Talking with God" activity.
- Have the children complete the activity.

CHOOSE

- Invite the children to read "My Faith Choice" and write their decisions.
- Encourage everyone to put their choices into practice this week.

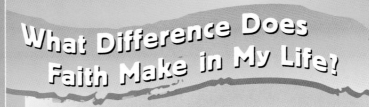

What Difference Does Faith Make in My Life?

The Holy Spirit asks you to make prayer an important part of your life. The Holy Spirit invites you to pray often during the day.

Talking with God

On the clock, circle three times during the day when you might pray. On the lines below write the times you circled and prayers you can say.

8:00	Thank you, God, for a new day!
_:__	Responses will vary.
_:__	
_:__	

My Faith Choice

This week I will try my best to pray several times each day. I will

_____

_____.

(214)

Background: Liturgy

Liturgy of the Hours. Here is some information about the Liturgy of the Hours that you can share with the children. After Jesus ascended to his Father, his disciples met to pray together. As the years passed, the Church began to pray many Psalms several times a day. This practice developed and became known eventually as the Liturgy of the Hours. But working people did not have time to pray for long hours. So monks, priests, and nuns prayed the Liturgy of the Hours. They prayed eight times a day. Recently, the Church revised the Liturgy of the Hours and has encouraged all the members of the Church to pray it, at least in part, every day.

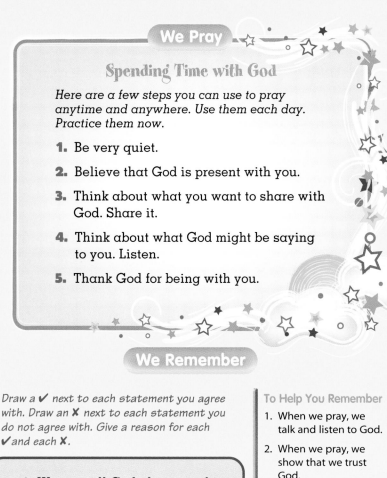

We Pray

Spending Time with God

Here are a few steps you can use to pray anytime and anywhere. Use them each day. Practice them now.

1. Be very quiet.

2. Believe that God is present with you.

3. Think about what you want to share with God. Share it.

4. Think about what God might be saying to you. Listen.

5. Thank God for being with you.

We Remember

Draw a ✔ next to each statement you agree with. Draw an ✘ next to each statement you do not agree with. Give a reason for each ✔ and each ✘.

___ 1. We can tell God about anything.

___ 2. We must wait our turn before God is ready to listen.

___ 3. We can pray anytime.

___ 4. God always listens to our prayers.

Affirm appropriate responses.

To Help You Remember

1. When we pray, we talk and listen to God.

2. When we pray, we show that we trust God.

3. When we pray, we make God part of our day.

Grade 2 • Chapter 24 (215)

Liturgy Tip

Prayer Formula. Help the children learn to pray using a prayer formula. Copy this prayer formula onto a sheet of paper and make a copy for each child. Have the children paste it on an index card and put it in their religion book.

• Greet God.
• Tell God you love him.
• Tell God why you love him.
• Thank God for some of the special gifts he has given you.
• Ask God for other blessings or favors for other people and for yourself.
• Tell God you are sorry for the times you have done wrong.
• Promise to stay close to him by praying often.
• Say "Amen."

Pray

WE PRAY

• Gather the children in the prayer center and have them sit in a circle on chairs or on the floor.

• Tell them to close their eyes and imagine that they are alone in the quiet woods as Blessed Kateri often was when she prayed. You might play a CD or tape recording of quiet nature sounds as background.

• Lead the meditation, using the steps on the children's page.

• Pause for a moment after each step to allow the children to enter into the experience.

• Pause at the end of the last step for a moment before inviting the children to open their eyes.

Review

WE REMEMBER

• While the children are still seated in the prayer center, summarize today's teaching on prayer by sharing the "To Help You Remember" statements. Read each statement, leaving out a word. Ask volunteers to respond with the missing word.

• Invite the children to return to their seats. Introduce the agree/disagree activity and give the children time to complete it.

At Home

ENCOURAGE

Have the children carefully tear out pages 215 and 216 along the perforation. Encourage the children to share the pages with their families and to do the activities together. If they did not complete the review activity on page 215 by the end of the session, emphasize that they can complete it with their families.

VISIT FAITHFIRST.COM

- Share with the children the many activities on the *Faith First* Web site.
- Encourage the children to visit **www.FaithFirst.com.**

24 With My Family

This Week . . .

In chapter 24, "We Talk with God," your child learned the importance of prayer in the life of a follower of Jesus. Jesus taught us the importance of prayer by his example. Our Christian family is the first place we learn to pray. We can pray anywhere and anytime. God is always present, listening and responding to our prayer.

For more on the teachings of the Catholic Church on the prayer of Jesus and the many expressions of Christian prayer, see *Catechism of the Catholic Church* paragraph numbers 2559–2616 and 2697–2719.

Sharing God's Word

Read together 1 Thessalonians 5:17. Emphasize that we are to pray often during the day.

Praying

In this chapter your child learned some steps that can be used for prayer anywhere and anytime. Read these steps on page 215 together. Take the time this week to follow the steps to pray alone and as a family.

Making a Difference

Choose one of the following activities to do as a family or design a similar activity of your own.

- We can pray anywhere and anytime. Ask each family member to share where and when they pray.

- We learn to pray first in our families. Talk about your family prayer times. Discuss how and when you pray as a family. Decide on times you will pray as a family this week.

- Write a family prayer thanking God for each family member. Pray this prayer at dinnertime this week.

For more ideas on ways your family can live your faith, visit the "Faith First for Families" page at **www.FaithFirst.com.** Click on "Family Prayer" to find a special prayer to pray this week.

216

Before Moving On . . .

As you finish today's lesson, reflect on the following question before moving on to the next chapter.

What can I do to ensure that the children leave the session feeling more positive about themselves as faith-filled people?

Evaluate

Take a few moments to evaluate this week's lesson.
I feel (circle one) about this week's lesson.

    a. very pleased

    b. OK

    c. disappointed

The activity the children enjoyed most was . . .

The concept that was most difficult to teach was . . .

because . . .

Something I would like to do differently is . . .

Jesus Teaches Us to Pray

A Scripture Story

25

We Pray

Come, let us sing to God.

Based on Psalm 95:1

Lord Jesus, teach us to pray. Amen.

Who first taught you to pray?

We first learn to pray at home. People in our Church also teach us to pray. Jesus taught his disciples to pray.

What did Jesus teach about prayer?

Jesus teaching the people about the kingdom of God

(217)

PRAY

- Have the children quiet themselves for prayer.
- Pray the Sign of the Cross together.
- Invite a volunteer to read Psalm 95:1 aloud.
- Pray the opening prayer together.
- Close the prayer with the Sign of the Cross.

DISCOVER

Purpose: To discover what the children may already know about how Jesus taught us to pray

- Ask the children who first taught them to pray.
- Ask the children to look at the picture and imagine that they are talking with Jesus like the boy in the picture. What might Jesus be saying to you about how to pray?
- Read the opening paragraph to the children. Then ask and discuss the question, "What did Jesus teach about prayer?"

✝ Liturgy Tip

The Prayer of All Christians. Invite a few parishioners to the session who are fluent in other languages, such as Spanish, Korean, Japanese, and German. Tell these visitors that you want to provide the children with an experience of hearing the Our Father prayed in languages other than English. By listening to the Our Father prayed in a variety of languages, the children will get a more personal experience of the Church being universal, made up of people of all nations and cultures.

Teach

FOCUS

Ask a volunteer to read the "Faith Focus" question aloud. Share with the children that they will learn that Jesus taught us to pray.

DISCOVER

- Invite the children to name some of the places where they like to pray.
- Present the first paragraph of "Jesus Prayed" by describing Galilee to the children.
- Have the children follow along as volunteers read the last two paragraphs to discover the ways Jesus prayed and why he prayed to his Father.

Apply

REINFORCE

- Draw a simple outdoor scene on the board suggesting the landscape of Galilee. Include the outlines of hills, a lake, trees, and some stick figures to represent people. Draw a path through the landscape.
- Ask the children to name some of the places where Jesus prayed. As they answer, place the letter J at appropriate places on the landscape.

INTEGRATE

- Invite the children to circle the places in the puzzle activity that tell where they can pray.
- Ask for volunteers to write on the board the words they circled.

Bible Background

Faith Focus

Why do we pray to God the Father?

Faith Words

Lord's Prayer
The Lord's Prayer is another name for the Our Father.

Jesus Prayed

Jesus lived in Galilee. Galilee is a large area of land with mountains, lakes, and fields.

Jesus prayed in many places in Galilee. He prayed alone in quiet places. He prayed in the mountains and in the fields. He prayed with other people.

When he prayed, Jesus asked his Father what he wanted him to do. He told his Father that he would do whatever the Father asked him. Jesus knew and trusted that his Father was always listening.

ACTIVITY Find and circle four places you can pray. On the line write your favorite place to pray. Share with a partner why it is your favorite place to pray.

God Is Always with Us

```
D  B  L (H  O  M  E) T  P  K
L  Q  R (P  A  R  K) G  T  B
(P  L  A  Y  G  R  O  U  N  D)
N (C  H  U  R  C  H) Q  V  W
_____
```

218

Teaching Tip

A Closer Look. Some children are visual learners, but most children benefit from learning by using as many senses as possible. Seeing pictures of the Holy Land and of what people wore in Jesus' time will help all the children come to better understand the Scripture stories. You might use the Visual Bible® segments on the *Faith First* Grade 3 video, or one of the commercial videos or DVDs of the life of Jesus. The use of visuals will spark the children's interest and help them enter into the Gospel stories as they read and listen to them.

Reading the Word of God

Jesus Teaches the Disciples to Pray

One day Jesus went up a mountain to pray. His disciples went with him. They wanted Jesus to teach them to pray. This is what Jesus taught them.

"This is how you are to pray.
Our Father in heaven,
 hallowed be your name,
 your kingdom come,
 your will be done,
  on earth as in heaven.
Give us today our daily bread;
and forgive us our debts,
as we forgive our debtors;
and lead us not into temptation,
 but deliver us from evil."

Based on Matthew 6:9–13

Jesus taught the disciples to pray to God the Father. He taught them to love and trust his Father as he did.

QUESTION *When do you pray the Our Father?*

Affirm appropriate responses.

219

Liturgy Tip

Proclaiming the Word of God. When you proclaim the Gospel in the classroom, using the proper liturgical form will help the children learn by heart the responses they use at Mass. The proper form is as follows:

A reading from the holy gospel according to _____.

Response: Glory to you, O Lord. *(Proclaim the Gospel.)*

The gospel of the Lord. *(Raise the Bible as you say this.)*

Response: Praise to you, Lord Jesus Christ.

Teach

FOCUS
Remind the children that Jesus prayed often to his Father. Point out that Jesus taught us to pray to his Father too.

DISCOVER
- Read the first paragraph to set the scene explaining that the disciples of Jesus wanted to pray as he prayed.
- Then have a volunteer read the Gospel passage.
- Ask volunteers to name the prayer that Jesus taught his disciples.

Apply

REINFORCE
Ask the children to tell you which words of the Our Father do these three things:
 —Praise God.
 —Ask for all to do God's will.
 —Ask for help in doing what is good.

INTEGRATE
- Have the children share when they pray the Our Father with others. At Mass; at home; in school. Affirm appropriate responses.
- Remind the children to pray the Our Father every day.

Teach

FOCUS

Point out that the Our Father, or Lord's Prayer, is the prayer of all Christians.

DISCOVER

- Ask the children to think about how and when they pray. Then ask: How do you pray as Jesus prayed?
- Invite the children to consider where and when the Catholic Church prays the Lord's Prayer together. At Mass. Affirm all appropriate responses.
- Read "The Lord's Prayer" aloud and have the children raise their right hands when they hear why we also call the Our Father the Lord's Prayer.
- Emphasize that when we pray the Lord's Prayer, we tell God the Father we love and trust him.
- Emphasize that the Lord's Prayer is the prayer of all Christians.

Apply

REINFORCE

Ask a volunteer to read aloud the definition of *Lord's Prayer* in "Faith Words" on page 218. Have the children make a word card for this term.

INTEGRATE

Invite the children to do the drawing activity. When all have finished, ask the children to imagine that they are with children from all over the world. Have everyone pray the Our Father silently.

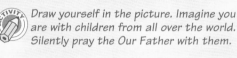

Understanding the Word of God

The Lord's Prayer

We also call the Our Father the **Lord's Prayer.** We call it the Lord's Prayer because it is the prayer that Jesus our Lord taught the disciples. The Our Father is the prayer of the whole Church. Catholics all over the world pray the Our Father every day.

 *Draw yourself in the picture. Imagine you are with children from all over the world. Silently pray the Our Father with them.*

(220)

💡 Teaching Tip

Singing the Our Father. A great way to teach or pray the Our Father with the children is by singing it. Ask one of your parish music ministers to visit with the children and teach them a simple version of the Our Father. Be sure to use the sung version, then, as part of the closing prayer for this session and the next.

ENRICHING THE LESSON

Making a Thank-You Carnation

Purpose

To reinforce appreciation for the people who have helped us learn to pray (taught on page 219)

Directions

- Provide the children with square sheets of tissue paper to make paper carnations.
- Have the children fold the paper in accordion folds.
- Then direct them to fold the completed strip in half crosswise and twist the paper on the fold. They can either tape the fold or secure it with one end of a pipe cleaner. The rest of the pipe cleaner will become a stem.
- Finally have them fan the folds apart to create a flower shape.
- Tell the children to give their completed paper carnations to someone who has helped them learn how to pray.

Materials

tissue paper
pipe cleaners or tape

Memorizing Prayers

Purpose

To reinforce learning the Our Father (taught on pages 219 and 283)

Directions

- Make a puzzle with eight to ten pieces outlined within a triangle. Write the words of the Our Father within the outlines of the puzzle pieces.
- Give each child a copy of the puzzle.
- Have the children cut out their puzzle pieces, shuffle them, and put the prayer back together again.

Materials

copy of puzzle outline
pens or pencils

Literature Connection

Purpose

To reinforce the importance of the Our Father (taught in chapter 25)

Directions

The beautifully illustrated book *When Daddy Prays* by Nikki Grimes and Tim Ladwig (Eerdmans, 2002) recounts the prayers of a strong, faith-filled African-American father as seen and heard by his young child. His prayers in the ordinary struggles of everyday life—a late school bus, a sick child, or even Rollerblades left in a hallway—reveal his dependence on God and teach children that prayer should be an integral part of daily life.

- Read all or part of this book to the children as an introduction to classroom spontaneous prayer.
- Talk with the children about who has taught them to pray and when they now pray. Ask them to name other times they can think of when they might call on God in prayer.

Materials

When Daddy Prays by Nikki Grimes and Tim Ladwig

Music Connection

- "Canticle of the Sun," M. Haugen. *Gather Comprehensive* #7.
- "Like a Child Rests," C. Walker. *Rise Up and Sing* #212.
- "Psalm 23: The Lord Is My Shepherd," R. Sensmeier. *Singing Our Faith (SOF)* #11.
- "The Lord, the Lord, the Lord Is My Shepherd" (African-American spiritual). *SOF* #166.

The Our Father

The Prayer of All Christians

The Our Father is the prayer of all Christians. It is the one prayer Christians have all prayed, alone and with others, innumerable times. It springs from our memory and onto our lips so quickly that our hearts and minds may be easily bypassed. Its recitation may become so rote and mechanical that its awesome importance and endless depth may elude us.

Jesus could have chosen any number of words with which to teach us to pray. But he chose words of the Our Father that flowed from his heart and from his love for the Father—and for us. He invites and encourages us to speak to the Father in such familiar terms as "Abba." He invites our participation and cooperation in his Father's unfolding kingdom. He evokes our trust in and surrender to God's providential will. It is almost as if Jesus is saying to us, "Let go, all will be well." He accentuates our prayerful concern for our daily necessities, placing forgiveness prominently among those needs. Finally, he joins his prayers with ours to be delivered from anything that would erode our relationship with God the Father.

A Summary of the Gospel

Saint Augustine of Hippo described the Our Father as the summary of the whole Gospel. He wrote:

> Run through all the words of the holy prayers (in Scripture), and I do not think that you will find anything in them that is not contained and included in the Lord's Prayer. *EPISTLE 130*

The Lord's Prayer presents us with sufficient material for a lifetime of meditation. But its first two words, "Our Father," are particularly rich with significance. Jesus did not say to pray "My Father." We are to pray "Our Father."

When we pray "Our Father," we join with Jesus and the whole Church, the Body of Christ. We acknowledge God the Father to be the Father of the entire human community. By telling us to address God as "Our Father," Jesus moved us away from selfishness and toward charity to all; he moved us from division to unity.

Jesus' revelation of God as "Our Father" transforms our

relationship with God from that of mere creatures to that of adopted sons and daughters. When we pray "Our Father" we express our desire to become like him, to emulate his loving kindness, and be concerned for those who share our birthright. By acknowledging God as Father, we claim a dignity that no one can take from us.

For Reflection

What do I believe are some of the implications of being adopted children of God the Father?

What does Jesus' invitation to us to address his Father as "Abba, Father" say to me?

Catechist to Catechist

The Family of God

Imagine it! You can go into any Christian church anywhere in the world and hear the Our Father being prayed. When Christians all over the world address God, "Our Father," it gives a special meaning to the phrase "family of God."

Stay Focused

We really should focus attentively on the meaning of the words of the Our Father every time we pray them. We need to slow down and  let the meaning of this prayer give meaning to our lives. When we do, it changes our day. We respond with love and forgiveness. We understand the meaning of caring for others. We take responsibility for our choices. We see the world as God's gift to us, a sign of his love for us. We see and value others as children of God, created in his image and likeness.

The Church Teaches . . .

Jesus is our model and guide in the ways of prayer. In the *General Directory for Catechesis* we read:

> To learn to pray with Jesus is to pray with the same sentiments with which he turned to the Father: adoration, praise, thanksgiving, filial confidence, supplication and awe for his glory. All of these sentiments are reflected in the *Our Father*, the prayer which Jesus taught his disciples and which is the model of all Christian prayer. The *"handing on of the Our Father"*[1] is a summary of the entire Gospel[2] and is therefore a true act of catechesis.   *GDC* 85

See the Catechism . . .

For more on the teachings of the Catholic Church on the Our Father, see *Catechism of the Catholic Church* 2777–2856.

CATECHIST PRAYER

Be patient with me, Lord. I know and believe that you accept me with love and understanding. Lord, I know you will continue to fill me with your grace to help me grow in faith, hope, and love. Amen.

Footnote references may be found on p. 456.

LESSON PLANNER

To understand the meaning of the parts of the Our Father

Engage

Page 225
Focus
To help the children recall what they know about the Our Father

Opening Prayer

Discussion
Jesus gave the Church the Our Father to teach us to live as God's children.

Teach and Apply

Pages 226–228
Focus
To introduce the children to the meaning of the parts of the Our Father

Presentation
Read, discuss, and summarize content.
Scripture
• Psalm 136:1
Activities
• Identify words and actions that show love for God the Father.
• Complete the Our Father matching activity.
Faith-Filled People
Saint Benedict

Connect

Pages 229–230
Focus
To understand that praying the Our Father helps us to live as the family of God

Our Church Makes a Difference
Understand that we are all members of God's family.
Our Catholic Faith
Vocation

What Difference Does Faith Make?
Activity
Complete the "Living as Jesus Taught" activity.

Faith Choice
Choose a way to live the Our Father this week.

We Pray

Page 231
Prayer Form
Prayer of thanks
Prayer
Pray "Go Forth" together.

We Remember

Review
• Solve the crossword puzzle.
• Read the "To Help You Remember" statements aloud.
Preview
Highlight features of the "With My Family" page.

Materials

pens or pencils

Enriching the Session

Blackline Masters
Additional Activities booklet:
Chapter 26
Circling words in a puzzle
Illustrating the kingdom of God
Assessment Tools booklet:
Chapter 26 Test
Unit 4 Test
Faith First **Grade 2 Video**
Segment 4: "Bible Songs"
Enriching the Lesson (CG page 369)
Preparing the Way for the Kingdom of God
A Year of Faith Stories
Literature Connection
Music Connection (CG page 369)

www.FaithFirst.com

We update the *Faith First* Web site weekly. Check each week for new content and features. Here are some places to begin:

Catechists and Teachers
• Current Events
• Chapter Downloads
• Catechist Prayer

Faith First **for Families**
• Bible Stories
• Make a Difference

Kids' Clubhouse
• *Faith First* Activities
• Chapter Reviews
• Games
• Saints

Don't Forget! You can make lesson planning a breeze—check out the **Online Lesson Planner.**

The Our Father

We Pray

God's love for us lasts forever.
Based on Psalm 136:1

God our Father, we praise you with the whole Church, all the world over.

Amen.

What are new things you have learned this year?

This year we have learned what it means to be a child of God. Jesus taught his disciples the Our Father.

What is one thing you know about the Our Father?

(225)

PRAY

- Have the children quiet themselves for prayer.
- Pray the Sign of the Cross together.
- Invite a volunteer to read Psalm 136:1. Then pray the opening prayer together.
- Close the prayer with the Sign of the Cross.

DISCOVER

Purpose: To discover what the children may already know about praying the Our Father

- Ask the opening question. Encourage the children to share their answers.
- Have one of the children read the introductory paragraph aloud.
- Invite volunteers to respond to the question.
- Direct the children's attention to the picture and invite volunteers to suggest where the people are and what they are doing. Praying the Our Father at Mass.

✦ Background: Doctrine

Being Holy. Children as young as seven or eight may think that the word *holy* is only used for God, Mary, and the saints. The children need to appreciate that they too are holy. *Holy* is a word we use to describe all those who live as children of God the Father. Through Baptism every Christian is made a sharer in the holiness of God. We receive the gift of the Holy Spirit who helps us live holy lives.

Teach

FOCUS

Ask a volunteer to read the "Faith Focus" question aloud. Tell the children that today they will learn more about the meaning of the Our Father.

DISCOVER

- Ask the children why we pray the Our Father.
- Summarize the children's responses by telling them that praying the Our Father shows God the Father we trust him and we want to live as his children.
- Divide the class into two groups. Invite group one to read aloud "Our Father, Who Art in Heaven" and group two to read the meaning.
- Ask what God the Father does to show that he is our loving Father. List their responses on the board. He shares his life and love with us now and forever.
- Switch the groups for the next sections so that each group gets a chance to read a meaning.

Apply

REINFORCE

Ask a volunteer to read the definition of *kingdom of God* in "Faith Words." Have the children make a word card for this term.

INTEGRATE

Invite the children to complete the activity by naming the things they do and say to show their love for God the Father.

362 (Student Page 226)

We Pray the Our Father

Faith Focus

Why do we pray the Our Father?

Faith Words

kingdom of God
The kingdom of God is also called the kingdom of heaven.

The Our Father

The Our Father helps us to pray and understand how to live as God's children.

Our Father, Who Art in Heaven: God is the Father of all people. God creates us in his image and likeness. God shares his life and love with us now and forever.

Hallowed Be Thy Name: The word *hallowed* means "very holy." We love God above all else. We adore and worship God. We honor and respect the name of God in all we say and do.

Thy Kingdom Come: Jesus announced the coming of the **kingdom of God.** The kingdom of God is also called the kingdom of heaven. When we love God above all else, we live as Jesus taught. We prepare for the coming of the kingdom of God.

QUESTION *What are the things you do and say that show your love for God the Father?* Affirm appropriate responses.

226

Faith Vocabulary

The Kingdom of God. The kingdom of God is another term for the kingdom of heaven. Children this age have many questions about heaven. Help them grow in their understanding of heaven as a life of happiness with God forever. It is the very reward Jesus promises to those who love him. Children at this age are concrete thinkers. It is very natural for them to imagine heaven as a physical place similar to some happy place on Earth that is part of their experience. The children's understanding of heaven as a state of eternal happiness with God will evolve as they grow in their understanding of the Catholic faith.

Thy Will Be Done on Earth as It Is in Heaven: The Holy Spirit helps us to continue the work of Jesus. We share God's love with our family, friends, and everyone we meet.

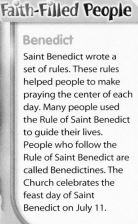

Faith-Filled People

Benedict

Saint Benedict wrote a set of rules. These rules helped people to make praying the center of each day. Many people used the Rule of Saint Benedict to guide their lives. People who follow the Rule of Saint Benedict are called Benedictines. The Church celebrates the feast day of Saint Benedict on July 11.

Give Us This Day Our Daily Bread: We always trust God. God knows what we need. We ask God to help us to live as his children. We pray for all people to receive God's blessings.

ACTIVITY *Draw lines to connect each part of the Our Father to its meaning.*

Our Father	God's name is said with love.
In heaven	God's love for us is now and forever.
Hallowed be thy name	God is the Father of all.
Thy kingdom come	The kingdom of God is called heaven.
Thy will be done	God gives us what we need.
Give us this day our daily bread	We continue the work of Jesus.

227

Background: Faith-Filled People

Saint Benedict of Nursia. Saint Benedict (480–543) is the patron saint of monks. Benedict saw community as a way of life that brings out the best in each individual. The Rule of Saint Benedict teaches patience with ourselves, with others, and with God. Modern spiritual writers have adapted the Rule of Saint Benedict to be a spiritual guide for laypeople as well as those who live the monastic life. The feast of Saint Benedict is celebrated on July 11.

Teach

FOCUS
Explain that the Our Father guides us to pray for things we need to live as children of God.

DISCOVER
- Share with the children a story about waiting. Tell the children that we often have to wait for something to happen or someone to come to visit us.
- Have the children read the line "Thy Will Be Done on Earth as It Is in Heaven." Ask a volunteer to share who helps us continue to do the work of Jesus. The Holy Spirit.
- Have all the children read the section "Give Us This Day Our Daily Bread" silently.
- Ask the children to read "Faith-Filled People" silently to find out how Saint Benedict helped people make praying the center of each day.

Apply

REINFORCE
Tell the children that everyone can make prayer the center of their day by praying in the morning when they get up, at night before they go to bed, and at meals. Some of the children may ask God to help them many times during the day. All this is prayer.

INTEGRATE
Have the children complete the activity on their own. Check their answers as they work. Have volunteers share their answers.

Teach

FOCUS

Remind the children that the Our Father guides us to pray for things we need to live as children of God.

DISCOVER

- Have the children read the words of the Our Father for each section on page 228. Paraphrasing the text, describe for them what each of these lines of the Our Father means.
- Ask the children if they know why we end our prayer by saying, "Amen."
- Explain that when we say "Amen," we are telling God that we believe he will hear our prayers and give us what we need to live as his children.

Apply

REINFORCE

Remind the children that the Holy Spirit will help us to make wise choices and to say no to all that is evil.

INTEGRATE

Invite the children to complete the activity. Ask volunteers to share their responses.

And Forgive Us Our Trespasses as We Forgive Those Who Trespass Against Us: Jesus taught us to be forgiving persons. Asking for forgiveness and forgiving others help us to live as children of God and followers of Jesus.

And Lead Us Not into Temptation, But Deliver Us from Evil: We ask God to help us to say no to temptation. Temptation is everything that can lead us away from God's love and from living as children of God. The Holy Spirit helps us to make wise choices. The Holy Spirit helps us to say no to temptation and all that is evil.

Amen: We end our prayer by saying, "Amen." Amen means, "Yes, it is true. We believe!"

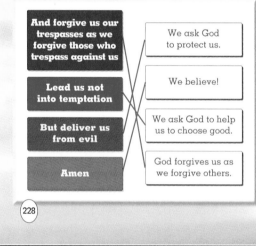

ACTIVITY Draw lines to connect each part of the Our Father to its meaning.

228

✦ Background: Doctrine

Avoiding Temptation. Telling the truth can be challenging at times for children this age. They want to avoid punishment, but they also really want to do what is right. Tell the children that one of the important signs of a follower of Jesus is a willingness to take responsibility for their choices—good and bad. Tell them to ask God for help if ever they are tempted to lie about their bad choices.

Our Church Makes a Difference

The Family of God

God calls everyone who is baptized to live as a follower of Jesus. God calls many men and women to live a married life. God also calls some people to live a single life.

God calls some men to serve the whole Church as bishops, priests, and deacons. He calls other men to live in a religious community as priests, deacons, or brothers. He calls some women to live in a religious community as sisters.

Whatever way God calls us to live, we are all members of God's family. We work together to continue the work of Jesus. We prepare for the kingdom of God.

Our Catholic Faith

Vocation

The word *vocation* means "what we are called to do." Every Christian has the vocation to live as a follower of Jesus. God calls us to do this in different ways in the Church.

QUESTION What do you want to do when you grow up? How will it help you to live as a follower of Jesus?

229

Liturgy Tip

Prayer for Vocations. Each year on the Fourth Sunday of Easter, "Good Shepherd" Sunday, the Church celebrates a World Day of Prayer for Vocations. On this day we are reminded that Jesus the Good Shepherd calls us to participate in his work of building the kingdom of God as priests, deacons, religious brothers and sisters, married, or single persons. On this day we pray for the grace to respond to our vocational call. You might extend the activity on this page by inviting second graders to role-play scenarios in which they imagine themselves serving in one of the vocational lifestyles. Conclude the activity by praying the prayer for vocations on page 285.

Connect

HIGHLIGHT

Remind the children that God is the Father of all people. Point out that each of us has special gifts and talents that he has given us to serve him and others.

DISCOVER

- Read "Our Catholic Faith."
- Talk with the children about the kinds of work and ministries they see their family members engaged in.
- Present "The Family of God," describing the various ways, or vocations, the baptized are called to live as followers of Christ.
- Ask the children what God is calling them to do right now. Accept appropriate responses, such as, to be good children, good brothers and sisters, good friends, and so on.

INTEGRATE

- Invite the children to look at the pictures and answer the question.
- Ask the children to suggest ways they can live as followers of Christ in their families and at school.

Connect

HIGHLIGHT

Remind the children that the Holy Spirit teaches us to pray and helps us to pray.

RESPOND

- Discuss with the children ways they can do the things we pray for in the Our Father.
- Give the children sufficient time to complete the activity. You may wish to have them copy this activity onto art paper to make a small poster to hang in their rooms over the summer.

CHOOSE

- Invite the children to read "My Faith Choice" and write their decisions.
- Encourage everyone to put their choices into practice throughout the summer.

What Difference Does Faith Make in My Life?

The Holy Spirit is helping you to live the Our Father now. He is helping you to live as a member of the family of God's people.

Put a ✔ next to one way that you will try to live the words of the Our Father this summer. Make a plan to put your choice into action.

Living as Jesus Taught

Affirm responses.

✔ I will pray.

✔ I will make wise choices.

✔ I will forgive those who hurt me.

✔ I will say I am sorry when I hurt someone else.

✔ I will listen to the Holy Spirit who helps me to make wise choices.

My Faith Choice

I will live the Our Father. This week I will do one of the things I checked. I will continue to do the things I checked all summer.

(230)

Teaching Tip

Share a Story. Explain to the children that God the Father has given all of his children special gifts and talents to use to prepare for his kingdom to come in fullness. Every person has a vocation, regardless of where they live, which culture they belong to, or which language they speak. Share with the children a story, such as *My Name Is Yoon* by Helen Recorvits (Farrar, Straus, Giroux, Inc., 2003), to help them grow to appreciate that they are blessed.

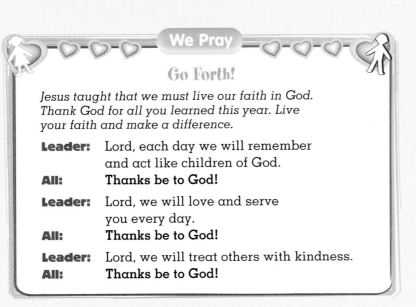

We Pray

Go Forth!

Jesus taught that we must live our faith in God. Thank God for all you learned this year. Live your faith and make a difference.

Leader: Lord, each day we will remember and act like children of God.

All: Thanks be to God!

Leader: Lord, we will love and serve you every day.

All: Thanks be to God!

Leader: Lord, we will treat others with kindness.

All: Thanks be to God!

We Remember

Use the clues to solve the puzzle.

DOWN

1. ____ means "very holy."
2. When you ____, you lift up your heart to God.

ACROSS

3. God is our ____.
4. ____ is something that leads us away from God.
5. Living as God wants us to live helps us to prepare for the ____ of God.

CLUES

Temptation   pray
kingdom   Father
Hallowed

Crossword answers:
3. Father (across)
4. Temptation (across)
5. kingdom (across)
1. Hallowed (down)
2. pray (down)

To Help You Remember

1. We pray the Our Father to show our love and adoration of God.

2. The Our Father helps us to live as children of God.

3. The Our Father helps us to prepare for the kingdom of God.

Liturgy Tip

Closing Prayer. The closing prayer is one of praise and thanksgiving. Show the children how to raise their hands high in a gesture of praise and thanks as they say each response. Consider using bells or other rhythm instruments to play during the responses. You might also like to play background music to aid in the prayer celebration.

Pray

WE PRAY

- Tell the children that the closing prayer for the year should be a prayer of thanksgiving. Just as we do at the end of Mass, we are going forth to love and serve the Lord and one another until we meet again.
- Practice the prayer response.
- Gather the children in the prayer center and lead the prayer.
- Conclude the prayer by going to each child and tracing a cross on his or her forehead, saying, "God bless you, _____, and keep you safe until we meet again."

Review

WE REMEMBER

- Ask the children to share some things they have learned this week about the meaning of the Our Father. Read the "To Help You Remember" statements aloud to the children for emphasis.
- Invite the children to use the clues to solve the crossword puzzle.

At Home

ENCOURAGE

Have the children carefully tear out pages 231 and 232 along the perforation. Encourage the children to share the pages with their families and to do the activities together. If they did not complete the review activity on page 231 by the end of the session, emphasize that they can complete it with their families.

VISIT FAITHFIRST.COM

- Share with the children the many activities on the *Faith First* Web site.
- Encourage the children to visit **www.FaithFirst.com.**

---

26 With My Family

This Week . . .

In chapter 26, "The Our Father," your child learned the meaning of the parts, or petitions, of the Our Father. The Our Father is not only a prayer. It is also a school of prayer. Praying the Our Father teaches us how we are to pray. When we pray the Our Father, we understand what it means to live as children of God and to prepare for the coming of the kingdom of God.

For more on the teachings of the Catholic Church on the parts of the Our Father, see *Catechism of the Catholic Church* paragraph numbers 2777–2856.

232

Sharing God's Word

Read together Matthew 6:9–13. Emphasize that the Our Father is not only a prayer. It is a "summary of the whole Gospel." Praying the Our Father teaches us how to pray and how to live as children of God.

Praying

In this chapter your child prayed a prayer of thanksgiving. Read and pray together the prayer on page 231.

Making a Difference

Choose one of the following activities to do as a family or design a similar activity of your own.

- Make an Our Father booklet. As you read each part of the Our Father, write the words of that part in your booklet. Write or draw how you can live each part of the Our Father.

- Talk about some of the ways your family lives the Our Father. Pray to the Holy Spirit. Ask the Holy Spirit to help your family live the Our Father.

- Ask each family member to name one thing they learned about the Our Father from this chapter. Afterward, pray the Our Father together.

For more ideas on ways your family can live your faith, visit the "Faith First for Families" page at **www.FaithFirst.com.** "Gospel Reflections" will continue to change each week over the summer. Don't forget to check it out.

Looking Back . . .

As you finish today's lesson, reflect on the following question.

What is something I learned from the children that has enriched my own faith life?

Evaluate

Take a few moments to evaluate this week's lesson.
I feel (circle one) about this week's lesson.

    a. very pleased
    b. OK
    c. disappointed

The activity the children enjoyed most was . . .

The concept that was most difficult to teach was . . .

because . . .

Something I would like to do differently is . . .

ENRICHING THE LESSON

Preparing the Way for the Kingdom of God

Purpose

To reinforce the meaning of the petition "Your kingdom come," which is prayed in the Our Father (taught on page 226)

Directions

- Have the children quietly pray "Your kingdom come" several times.
- Brainstorm with the children ways that they live as Jesus taught. List their responses.
- Ask how each of the things on the list prepares the way for the coming of the kingdom of God.
- Encourage the children to continue doing the things on the list. Ask each child to identify one thing that they are not doing and to ask their families to help them do it.

Materials

pencils, note paper

A Year of Faith Stories

Purpose

To reinforce the many stories from the Bible and the faith-filled people taught this year (taught in the chapters in the book)

Directions

- In partners have the children look through their books and name their favorite Bible stories and faith-filled people. List the names on the board.
- Using clues, such as "What story am I?" or "Who am I?", ask the children to stand as soon as they know the story or person. Invite volunteers to name the story or person.
- After doing several examples, allow the children to present their own clues.
- Affirm how much the children have grown in their understanding of Scripture.

Materials

Literature Connection

Purpose

To reinforce that in the Our Father we ask God to give all people what they need (taught on page 227)

Directions

This closing chapter on the Our Father is an ideal time to retell the classic children's story *Stone Soup*. In the retelling by Marcia Brown of the classic French tale (Simon and Schuster Children's Paperbacks, 1986), three hungry soldiers enter a village. Through their cleverness they are able to entice the villagers to contribute bit by bit to their "stone" soup— first a carrot, then a bit of beef—until a rich and satisfying soup is prepared and enjoyed by all. Children love the story and will not mind hearing it again.

- Read the story aloud to the children with expression and humor.
- Ask the children to describe their ideas of what the main point of the story is. Point out that when we all share, all are assured of enough to eat.
- Remind the children that all God's children are entitled to their "daily bread." This is what we pray for in the Our Father.

Materials

Stone Soup by Marcia Brown

Music Connection

- "Lord's Prayer," D. Hass. *Gather Comprehensive (GC)* 37.
- "The Lord's Prayer," M. Joncas. *GC* #16.
- "Thank You, God," J. Vogt. *Rise Up and Sing* #198.
- "If You Believe and I Believe" (Zimbabwean traditional), arr. J. Bell. *Singing Our Faith* #258.

Unit 4 Review

The unit review provides the opportunity to assess the children's understanding of the concepts presented in the unit and to affirm them in their growing knowledge and love of God. Here are a few suggestions for using these pages.

- Share that the next two pages are an opportunity to stop and review what the children have learned.
- Provide time for the children to ask questions.
- Have the children complete the review alone or with a partner.

PART A:
The Best Word or Phrase

This section reviews the main concepts of the unit.

- Read the directions for section A. Illustrate what you expect the children to do by completing the first question together. By working together on the first question you are teaching the children a strategy for answering these types of questions.
- When the children have finished this section, invite volunteers to share their answers. Review any questions that the children seem to have had difficulty answering.

FAMILY CONNECTION

Encourage the children to share the unit review pages with their families. This provides an excellent opportunity to involve the families in the faith formation of their children.

Review Unit 4   Name _____

A. The Best Word or Phrase

Complete the sentences. Color the circle next to the best choice for each sentence.

1. ___ is raising our hearts and minds to God.
   ○ Standing   ● Praying   ○ Kneeling

2. Jesus taught his disciples the ___.
   ○ Hail Mary   ○ Glory Prayer   ● Our Father

3. The kingdom of ___ is all people living as God wants them to live.
   ○ saints   ● God   ○ earth

4. We can pray ___.
   ● anytime   ○ on Sundays   ○ at bedtime

5. We can pray ___.
   ● anywhere   ○ at home   ○ in church

233

Teaching Tip

Affirm Everyone. Use this final unit review to deepen the children's sense of accomplishment this year. Share how much they have learned and what a difference they have made for your life. Take time to remind the children that Jesus spent many years in Nazareth with Mary and Joseph and the people of his synagogue and village learning the teachings, prayers, and practices of the Jewish religion. Encourage the children to pray each day during the summer that they might come to know and love Jesus more and more.

B. Making Sentences

Color the box to mark the sentences that are true.

- ■ Jesus taught us to pray to God the Father.
- ■ God speaks to us quietly in our minds and hearts.
- ■ We can always thank God for his blessings.
- ☐ We can only pray in Church.

C. What I Have Learned

1. *Name two things you learned in this unit. Tell a partner.*

_____Affirm appropriate responses._____

_____

2. *Look at the words listed on page 208. Circle the ones that you know now.*

D. From a Scripture Story

Draw lines to connect the parts of the Our Father to their meanings.

Parts

1. Our Father
2. Hallowed be thy name
3. Give us this day our daily bread
4. Forgive us our trespasses as we forgive those who trespass against us
5. Deliver us from evil

Meanings

a. God gives us what we need.
b. God forgives us as we forgive others.
c. God is the Father of all.
d. We ask God to protect us.
e. God's name is said with love.

Teaching Tip

Family Faith Sharing. Send a note home with the children that encourages their families to use the "Catholic Prayers and Practices" section of the child's book with their children over the summer. For example, families might use the:

- "Glossary" to share faith about some of the key faith concepts the children learned this year.
- "We Celebrate the Mass" section to talk about the Mass, using the pictures of the Mass.
- "Rosary" section to help the children continue to honor Mary and remember the important events in the life of Jesus and Mary.

PART B: Making Sentences

This section reinforces the unit vocabulary.

- Read the directions to the children and together do the first item in the true-or-false activity. Have the children continue working in partners to finish the section.
- Invite volunteers to share their answers.

PART C: What I Have Learned

This section provides the children with the opportunity to write or talk about what they have learned.

- Have the children share with the group two things that they learned from the chapters in this unit.
- Invite the children to return to the "Getting Ready" page in this unit and observe for themselves how they have grown in building a faith vocabulary.

PART D: From a Scripture Story

This section is a review of the Scripture story on the Our Father. Have the children complete the activity and share their responses.

We Celebrate

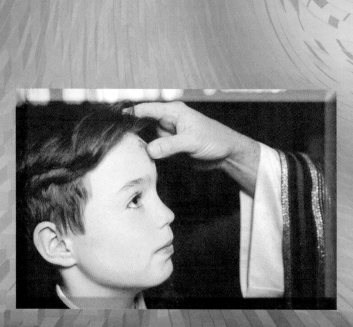

How does the Church celebrate its faith all year long?

235

The Liturgical Year

The Church's year of prayer and worship is called the liturgical year. These are the seasons of the Church's year.

Advent

We prepare for Christmas. The color for Advent is purple.

Christmas

We praise and thank God for sending us Jesus, the Savior of the world. The color for Christmas is white.

Lent

We make sacrifices to help us to remember our love for God and others. We prepare for Easter. The color for Lent is purple.

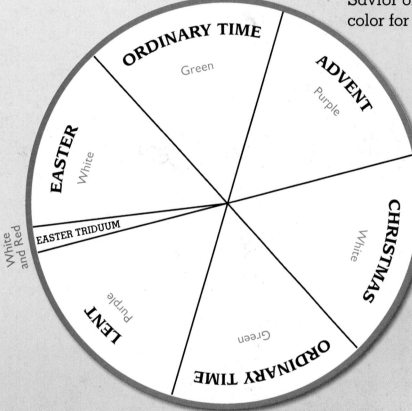

ORDINARY TIME — Green
ADVENT — Purple
CHRISTMAS — White
ORDINARY TIME — Green
LENT — Purple
EASTER TRIDUUM — White and Red
EASTER — White

Easter Triduum

Triduum is the three days during Holy Week when we remember Jesus' death and Resurrection. We welcome new members into the Church.

Easter

For fifty days we celebrate and remember and share in Jesus' Resurrection. The color for Easter is white.

Ordinary Time

The rest of the Church's year is called Ordinary Time. We learn to live as followers of Jesus. The color for Ordinary Time is green.

ACTIVITY *Color each of the seasons of the Church on the chart. What is your favorite season? Tell one thing you can do to celebrate it.*

Affirm appropriate responses.

The Liturgical Year/Ordinary Time

Background

Seasons and Feasts

We all know that we need consistency in our lives. But we also need a break from consistency; we need surprises and festive days. Absolute consistency introduces monotony and makes us a dull people. Endless festivity dissipates the spirit and wears us down. Experience teaches us the value of balancing the daily and the festive, or the ordinary and the extraordinary.

The Church is uniquely positioned to gather us for celebration. It does this through liturgy. Filled with anticipation during Advent, we prepare to celebrate the festive season of Christmas. The traditional Lenten practices of fasting, praying, and almsgiving prepare us to enter into Triduum and the Easter season.

Easter is central to the liturgical year. Because Jesus was raised from the dead on Sunday, the Church gathers to celebrate each week on that day. Every Sunday is a memorial of the Paschal Mystery and a commemoration of Easter.

Festive seasons, such as the Easter season, stand in contrast

to the long, steady season of Ordinary Time. Generally, of the thirty-four Sundays in Ordinary Time, about ten occur on the Sundays between the seasons of Christmas and Lent. The remainder of the Sundays in Ordinary Time are celebrated after the Solemnity of the Body and Blood of Christ (two weeks after Pentecost) and culminate in the feast of Christ the King. This late autumn feast brings the liturgical year to a close.

The Rhythm of the Liturgical Year

The seasons of the liturgical year help us keep balanced as nature's seasons pass. Through the seasons of autumn, winter, spring, and summer, significant changes occur. As time passes from season to season, the Church provides a steady rhythm.

Sunday after Sunday, we are reminded and called to live out the reality of the abiding presence of the Risen Lord among us. Sunday after Sunday from the extremes of deep winter to high summer, we remember with gratitude that all time and all ages belong to Christ, who is yesterday and today, the beginning and the end.

The liturgical year is our way to remember with gladness and joy that every day is the day the Lord has made. We remember that we are called to rejoice in this.

For Reflection

How does the liturgical year provide a wonderful balance of ordinary and festive time for my life of faith?

Which of the liturgical seasons is my favorite? Why?

Catechist to Catechist

Ordinary Time

The word *ordinary,* which is used to designate this time of the liturgical year, is a misnomer that might lead us to undervalue the importance of Ordinary Time. The word *ordinary* is not used to describe the value of Ordinary Time. It is used to indicate that these Sundays are identified by numbers or ordinals; for example, Second Sunday in Ordinary Time, Third Sunday in Ordinary Time, and so on. During this time of the liturgical year we develop the daily, or ordinary, habit of integrating God's word into our daily lives—turning ordinary lives into extraordinary lives of faith.

Signs of the Liturgical Year

Display signs of the liturgical year in your learning space. Surround the children with reminders that will help set the tone of both the seasons and

feasts of the liturgical year. For example, consider using a table runner the color of each liturgical season in the prayer area. Place a Bible opened to the Sunday Gospel reading on the prayer table.

The Church Teaches . . .

During Ordinary Time and the other seasons of the liturgical year, the feast days of many of the canonized saints are remembered in the celebration of the liturgy. The *Catechism of the Catholic Church* points out:

> When the Church keeps the memorials of martyrs and other saints during the annual cycle, she proclaims the Paschal mystery in those "who have suffered and have been glorified with Christ."[1] *CCC* 1173

You may wish to celebrate the feast days of some of the saints during your sessions, particularly those who may be the patron saints of the children.

See the Catechism . . .

For more on the teachings of the Catholic Church on the liturgical year, see *Catechism of the Catholic Church* 1168–1171 and 1172–1173.

CATECHIST PRAYER

God, Father and Creator, you always watch over your people. Through the prayer of Jesus, your Son, may your blessings be poured out on us and keep us safe in your care. Amen.

[BASED ON THE OPENING PRAYERS FOR FIFTH SUNDAY IN ORDINARY TIME]

Footnote references may be found on p. 456.

Teach

FOCUS

Ask a volunteer to read the "Faith Focus" question aloud. Share with the children that the Church has seasons as the calendar year does. Point out that the seasons of the Church's year help us celebrate our faith throughout the year.

DISCOVER

- Introduce "The Celebrations of Our Church" by presenting the first paragraph aloud to the children and have them name the things that they like to celebrate.
- Have volunteers read aloud the next two paragraphs.
- Summarize by telling the children that during Ordinary Time we listen to stories from the Gospel that tell us about Jesus' teachings and work on earth.
- Invite the children to look at the picture, and tell them it depicts the Gospel story of Jesus feeding over five thousand people with fish and loaves of bread. Tell them it is one of the stories we listen to at Mass during Ordinary Time.
- Ask volunteers to tell what Jesus might be saying and doing for the people. Affirm appropriate responses.
- Remind the children that the color for Ordinary Time is green. Then ask a volunteer to read aloud "What You See."

Ordinary Time

Faith Focus

How does the Church celebrate our faith all year long?

The Word of the Lord

These are the Gospel readings for the Third Sunday in Ordinary Time. Ask your family to read this year's Gospel reading with you. Talk about the reading with your family.

Year A
Matthew 4:12–23 or Matthew 4:12–17

Year B
Mark 1:14–20

Year C
Luke 1:1–4, 4:14–21

What You See

When we see the color green, we think of plants and other living things. The color green reminds us of the life we are living as Christians.

The Celebrations of Our Church

Birthday parties are fun. So are Christmas parties and parties with our teammates. We seem to have something to celebrate all throughout the year.

Our Church celebrates our faith all year long too. We celebrate during the seasons of Advent and Christmas, Lent and Easter, and Ordinary Time.

Each week at Mass we listen to a different story from the Gospel. We hear Jesus teaching his disciples. Closing our eyes, we can imagine we are with Jesus. We think about what Jesus is saying and doing. We decide how we can live as a follower of Jesus.

237

Teaching Tip

Liturgical Calendar. Make a special effort to mark the important feast days of the Church's year on a calendar. These should include the Immaculate Conception (December 8), Christmas (December 25), Solemnity of Mary (January 1), Ascension (forty days after Easter), Assumption (August 15), and All Saints (November 1). Also enter children's birthdays on the calendar. Pray for those children in the session that is held during the week of their birthdays. On your last day of the year, pray for the children who will celebrate their birthdays during the summer vacation.

Living Our Faith

Think about your favorite stories about Jesus. Draw one of those stories in this box. Share how this story helps you to live as a follower of Jesus.

Responses will vary.

Affirm appropriate responses.

238

Teaching Tip

Including All Learners. Talk to the children about multicultural celebrations during the year. Invite the children to share the special ways their families celebrate the seasons of the Church's year, holy days, feasts of Mary, and other feasts of the Church with their families. Encourage the children to tell about the special things they do with their families and the special foods they might prepare and eat.

Apply

REINFORCE

Ask a volunteer to describe how the Church celebrates our faith all year long. Accept all appropriate responses, such as, The Church celebrates the seasons of Advent, Christmas, Lent, Easter, and Ordinary Time.

INTEGRATE

- Invite the children to look at the picture on page 237 and tell them it depicts the Gospel story of Jesus feeding more than five thousand people with fish and loaves of bread. Tell them it is one of the stories we listen to at Mass during Ordinary Time. Ask volunteers to tell what Jesus might be saying and doing for the people. Affirm appropriate responses.
- Invite the children to share other stories they remember about Jesus teaching the disciples. List the stories on the board.
- Then introduce the "Living Our Faith" activity and have the children complete it.

PRAY

Gather the children in the prayer area. Ask them to close their eyes and imagine they are with Jesus. Then read aloud Matthew 14:13–21, the account of the multiplication of the loaves and fishes. Conclude by leading the children in praying the Our Father together.

The Season of Advent

Hope-filled Expectation

Advent begins the liturgical year. The expectation of the coming of the Lord literally colors the season. Advent's violet, or purple, color is reminiscent of the sky just before dawn. After a long night, we naturally look to the east and long for the dawn. We are able to do this because we are sure the sun will rise. Our certitude is based on past experience.

In Advent we prepare for the coming of the Incarnate Son of God among us. Our confidence about his coming is based on faith. Through faith we can be even more sure of his coming than we are of the rising of the sun in the east.

Faith-filled Anticipation

During Advent the Church urges us toward quiet meditation as we make the necessary practical preparations to welcome the Savior at Christmas. We prepare for his coming by recalling the Incarnation. We live with the mystery and grace of his presence with us now. And, lastly, we look to his coming in majesty at the end of time as the Lord of all time and all space.

God Fulfills Our Hope

The opening Gospel readings of the Advent season in each of the three cycles proclaim the Day of the Lord. The Gospel readings awaken us to our present Christian life and our promised future.

The Sunday Gospel readings then move ever closer to the birth of Jesus. John the Baptist announces his coming. Finally, Elizabeth, Mary, and Joseph prepare themselves—and us—as the time of the celebration of Jesus' birth draws near.

Throughout the four Sundays of Advent, the Old Testament prophets, who longed for Emmanuel, also accompany us. As we pray for the Savior's arrival among us, we prepare our homes and hearts for the gift of his presence.

For Reflection

How does celebrating Advent help me live in the mystery of God's presence?

What are my hopes for this Advent season? How can I prepare to welcome the fulfillment of those hopes?

Catechist to Catechist

The Three Comings of Christ

Advent is a time of joyful preparation. There is a fascination created by our preparation for Christmas that captures the imaginations and hearts of all Christians. This fascination can narrow our celebration of Advent to the point that we mistakenly only focus on Christ's birth and his coming to us in the past.

We constantly need to prepare our hearts to welcome Christ who comes to us each and every moment of our lives. We need to prepare ourselves throughout our entire life, each and every day, to be ready to welcome him when he comes again in glory at the end of time.

Waiting in Silence

Advent favors quiet anticipation. An extra effort is needed to offset the pre-Christmas holiday bustle of this season.  Whatever you do this season, do it patiently, quietly, and with the awareness of the coming of Jesus Christ right here, right now. Be sure to add moments of quiet and silent prayer to your classroom prayer, to balance the hectic nature of the secular Christmas season.

The Church Teaches . . .

The *Catechism of the Catholic Church* teaches:

> When the Church celebrates the *liturgy of Advent* each year, she makes present this ancient expectancy of the Messiah, for by sharing in the long preparation for the Savior's first coming, the faithful renew their ardent desire for his second coming.[1]
>
> *CCC* 524

Preparing for Christ in prayer and liturgy each week during Advent heightens expectation among the children and helps them focus on the true meaning of the season.

See the Catechism . . .

For more on the teachings of the Catholic Church on Advent, John the Baptist, and Jesus the Messiah, see *Catechism of the Catholic Church* 522–524, 748, and 2466.

CATECHIST PRAYER

*Father in heaven,
increase our longing
for your Son, Christ our Savior.
Give us strength to grow in
love. Open our minds
and hearts to welcome the
light of his truth.
Amen.*

[BASED ON THE OPENING PRAYERS FOR
THE MASS ON SECOND SUNDAY OF ADVENT]

Footnote references may be found on p. 456.

Teach

FOCUS

Ask a volunteer to read the "Faith Focus" question aloud. Share with the children that Advent has four Sundays.

DISCOVER

- Invite volunteers to tell how they wait and prepare for days that are special to them.
- Invite the children to read silently "Getting Ready" on page 239 to find out how Advent helps us to prepare to welcome Jesus into our lives.
- Ask the class to look at the picture and describe what they see. The children are lighting a candle on the Advent wreath.
- Share "What You See" with the class to help them learn about the Advent wreath.

Faith Focus

How does celebrating Advent help us to welcome God into our lives?

The Word of the Lord

These are the Gospel readings for the First Sunday of Advent. Ask your family to read this year's Gospel reading with you. Talk about the reading with them.

Year A
Matthew 24:37–44

Year B
Mark 13:33–37

Year C
Luke 21:25–28, 34–36

What You See

The Advent wreath is made of evergreens. There are three purple candles and one pink candle. The candles stand for the four weeks of Advent.

Getting Ready

Every year you get excited about your birthday coming. Your family gets ready to celebrate. During Advent we get ready to celebrate the birth of Jesus. We also celebrate that Jesus is always with us. We celebrate that he will come in glory at the end of the world.

Advent has four Sundays. On these Sundays we gather in our parish church. Together we get our hearts ready to welcome Jesus.

During Advent we remember that Jesus asks us to do good things. We pray. We try to be extra kind. We help people who need our help.

239

Teaching Tip

Making an Advent Chain. Tell the children that they are going to make an Advent chain at home, representing the 24 days that we prepare for Christmas Day. Give each child an envelope that contains 24 six-inch strips made from purple construction paper, which are individually numbered 1 through 24. Tell the children to make and connect the links one at a time each day during Advent. Suggest that they write on each link either a short prayer or one way they can prepare for Christmas. Also give the children star stickers to put on the numbered links for December 6 (Saint Nicholas), December 8 (Immaculate Conception), and December 12 (Our Lady of Guadalupe).

We Welcome Jesus

ACTIVITY *Think about ways you can get ready to welcome Jesus. Write something you can do each day this week.*

Responses will vary.
Affirm appropriate responses.

Sunday　　Use the Advent wreath at dinnertime.

Monday　　Tell someone about Jesus.

Tuesday　　Thank God the Father for sending Jesus.

Wednesday　Make a Christmas card for my family.

Thursday　　Ask my family to read the Christmas story to me from the Bible.

Friday　　　Pray to Jesus in the morning and at bedtime.

Saturday　　Help at home to get ready for Christmas.

240

Apply

REINFORCE

Ask the children how the Church prepares to welcome Jesus at Christmas. We gather in our parish church and together get our hearts ready to welcome Jesus. We light the candles on the Advent wreath. Accept other appropriate responses.

INTEGRATE

- Have the children brainstorm what they might do to get ready to welcome Jesus.
- Explain the "We Welcome Jesus" activity to the children.
- Give the class time to complete the activity. If they do not complete the activity during the session, encourage them to complete it at home with their families.
- Encourage them to put what they wrote into action each day this week.

PRAY

Gather the children in the prayer area around an Advent wreath which you have set up in advance. Read this year's Gospel reading for the first week of Advent. Have the children respond "Come, Lord Jesus! Come!"

✝ Liturgy Tip

Songs of the Season. Each time you meet with the children during Advent, teach them a few lines of a Christmas carol, such as "Silent Night" or "Joy to the World." This will prepare the children to sing along with the assembly as these songs are sung at Mass on Christmas Day and throughout the Christmas season. Appropriate music for all the liturgical seasons can be found on **www.FaithFirst.com.**

Teach

FOCUS

Ask a volunteer to read the "Faith Focus" question aloud. Remind the children that the color for Advent is purple. Then have the children read "What You See" on page 241.

DISCOVER

- Recall with the children that God promised to send his people a very special leader.
- Invite volunteers to read aloud "Waiting for the Lord" and listen for the name of the leader God promised to send.
- Ask them to raise their right hand when they hear the name of the One whom God sent to fulfill his promise.
- Summarize by telling the children how important it is that we prepare for the coming of the Lord Jesus into our lives.

The Second Week of Advent

Faith Focus

Who are we waiting for during Advent?

The Word of the Lord

These are the Gospel readings for the Second Sunday of Advent. Ask your family to read this year's Gospel reading with you. Talk about the reading with them.

Year A
Matthew 3:1–12

Year B
Mark 1:1–8

Year C
Luke 3:1–6

What You See

The Church uses the color purple during Advent. In Jesus' time purple was a color used by kings. We remember Jesus is the newborn King God promised to send his people.

Waiting for the Lord

We like to be with people we trust. We like people who keep their promises. The Bible says that God made a promise. God promised to send his people a very special leader.

The people believed God. They waited for God's promise to come true. They waited like guards who keep watch at night. When the sun comes up, how glad the guards are to see darkness creep away!

Jesus is the One who God promised to send. We welcome Jesus the Lord just as the guards welcome the rising sun.

241

Teaching Tip

Bookmarks for Advent. Write the words "Come, Lord Jesus" on the board. Distribute purple sheets of construction paper with the outline of two bookmarks on them. Ask the children to copy the words within the outlines of the bookmarks on the strips of construction paper. Have available scissors, seals, and stickers that the children can share to decorate their Advent bookmarks. If time allows, have the children make one bookmark for themselves and one to give to someone else.

An Advent Prayer

Color the letters and decorate this Advent prayer.
Learn the prayer by heart. Pray it each day of Advent.

242

REINFORCE

Ask the children to look at the photo of the rising sun on page 241 and invite a volunteer to share how it helps them prepare for Christmas. We welcome Jesus as we welcome the rising sun each and every day. Accept other appropriate responses.

INTEGRATE

- Share with the children the words of the Advent hymn "O Come, O Come, Emmanuel." Explain to the children that the name *Emmanuel* means "God with us." Then tell them that the Bible uses the name *Emmanuel* for Jesus.
- Teach the children the first line of this song. This will help them to join in singing this hymn with the assembly at Mass.
- Have a volunteer read the directions for the Advent prayer activity. Then invite the children to color the letters of the prayer.

PRAY

- Have the children bring the prayer they have colored and gather in the prayer area around the Advent wreath.
- Invite the children to quiet themselves. Then read aloud the following prayer.
  God our Father,
  hear our prayer
  as we watch and wait.
  Bless us as we prepare to welcome your Son, Jesus. Amen.
- Conclude by having the children pray aloud, "Come, Lord Jesus, Come."

Teaching Tip

Individual Differences. As the holidays approach, it is important to allow the children more movement, more activity and creativity. Remember that some children do their very best work with their hands; others are better at drawing or writing. Allow children to use their individual talents to create and design a special gift box. Each time you observe a child doing something that helps the class prepare for Jesus, have them write their name on a card and put it in the box. Such acts of individual affirmation will encourage the children to prepare their minds and hearts to welcome Christ at Christmas and every day.

Teach

FOCUS

Ask a volunteer to read the "Faith Focus" question aloud. Share that during Advent we celebrate our faith and joy that God is always near us.

DISCOVER

- Have the children look at the photo on page 243 and ask them to describe the feelings of the girl in the photo. Accept all appropriate responses, including joy.
- Help them connect their feelings of joy with the Advent season as we prepare for Christmas.
- Then ask the children to follow along as you read aloud "Hope in God." Comment that Advent is also a time to praise God.
- Write the word *hope* on the board. Explain that hope is a gift from God that helps us desire him above all things.

The Third Week of Advent

Faith Focus

How do we show our hope in God during Advent?

The Word of the Lord

These are the Gospel readings for the Third Sunday of Advent. Ask your family to read this year's Gospel reading with you. Talk about the reading with them.

Year A
Matthew 11:2–11

Year B
John 1:6–8, 19–28

Year C
Luke 3:10–18

Hope in God

Sometimes we need people we trust to help us. The Bible tells us that God is our helper. We can always trust God.

During Advent we praise God too. We remember the story of God's promises to us. We believe that God is always near. We are filled with hope that God will come again in glory at the end of the world. We will celebrate that faith and hope with great joy during Advent.

(243)

Background: Scripture

The Hail Mary. Tell the children the story of the Annunciation (Luke 1:26–38) and the Visitation (Luke 1:39–56) in your own words, or read the stories from a children's version of the Bible. Ask them to listen for the joy that filled the hearts of Mary and Elizabeth. Then point out that the first part of the Hail Mary is based on these two stories. Perhaps many of the children already know the Hail Mary by heart. This is a good time to teach the prayer to those who do not know it.

People of Joy

In each green leaf write one way someone has brought you joy. In each yellow leaf write one way you can bring joy to someone. Make a plan and put your choice into action this Advent.

244

Teaching Tip

Finger Puppet Plays. Have each child work with a partner to make simple paper finger puppets of Mary, the angel Gabriel, and Elizabeth. Then invite them to create a puppet show, "The Story of Mary's Joy," based on the Gospel stories of the Annunciation and the Visitation.

REINFORCE

Ask the children why Advent is a season of joy and hope. Then have them look for the answer on page 243 and underline or highlight it. We believe that God is always near. We are filled with hope that Jesus will come again in glory at the end of time.

INTEGRATE

Read the directions for the "People of Joy" activity. Have the children complete the activity. Then distribute a generous supply of leaf shapes that you have cut out of green and yellow construction paper. Have the children transfer what they wrote on the leaves in their books to the construction-paper leaves. Paste the leaves on a large sheet of poster board and work with the children to create an Advent Tree of Joy.

PRAY

Invite the children to the prayer area, and have them quiet themselves. Share with them the joy that filled Mary's heart at the Annunciation. Lead the children in praying the first part of the Hail Mary.

Teach

FOCUS

Ask a volunteer to read the "Faith Focus" question aloud. Tell the children that today they will learn why Mary and Joseph went to Bethlehem.

DISCOVER

- Write the word *Bethlehem* on the board. Then ask volunteers to tell you what they know about Bethlehem. Accept all appropriate responses, such as, Jesus was born there.
- Read aloud "Little Bethlehem" to the children or have volunteers read the text to the class.
- Reread the "Faith Focus" question to the children and invite volunteers to answer it in their own words.

The Fourth Week of Advent

Faith Focus

Why was Jesus born in Bethlehem?

The Word of the Lord

These are the Gospel readings for the Fourth Sunday of Advent. Ask your family to read this year's Gospel reading with you. Talk about the reading with them.

Year A
Matthew 1:18–24

Year B
Luke 1:26–33

Year C
Luke 1:39–45

Little Bethlehem

People live in small towns all over the world. Very often people who have become famous were born in these small towns. Long ago a man named David lived in the small town of Bethlehem. He became king of God's people.

Years later another leader wanted to know how many people lived in his land. So everyone had to go to their family's hometown to be counted. Joseph and Mary went to Bethlehem because Joseph belonged to David's family.

The prophet Micah said that the Savior who God promised to send his people would come from Bethlehem. Just as Micah said, Jesus was born in Bethlehem.

245

Teaching Tip

Create a Christmas Card. Have the children make Christmas cards for family members and friends. Do not assume every child lives in a two-parent home with siblings. Be sensitive to the fact that children come from different family structures; for example, some children may have grandparents as caregivers; others may live with just one parent. Encourage the children to give the cards to their family members and friends.

The Legend of the Christmas Donkey

Read this story as a group. Think about the story. Decide ways you can be kind to others.

All: Mary and Joseph had to go to Bethlehem. They walked a long way.

Reader 1: Mary was going to have a baby. She was very tired. Joseph saw a donkey eating grass nearby. He lifted Mary up onto the donkey's back.

All: The donkey was a peaceful animal. He felt honored to help Mary. He proudly carried Mary uphill and downhill.

Reader 2: When they got to the stable, Mary slipped off the donkey's back. She thanked him for his service.

All: From that day to this day, some donkeys bear the trace of a cross on their back. People say this is a sign that God rewards the smallest acts of kindness.

This week I will try to do one small act of kindness each day. One thing I will do is

Affirm appropriate responses.

_____

_____.

(246)

Teaching Tip

Sharing Christmas Stories. Seven- and eight-year-olds love to hear and watch Christmas stories. Ask the children to share their favorite Christmas story and tell you why they like it. Remind them that the real story of the birth of Christ is the greatest Christmas story of all. It is the reason for all the other stories about Christmas.

Apply

REINFORCE

Invite the children to look at the photo on page 245. Explain to them that it is a photo of a shepherd with his flock near the town of Bethlehem today. Ask the children what promise that God made came true in Bethlehem. Accept all appropriate responses, such as, The prophet Micah said that the Savior whom God promised to send his people would come from Bethlehem.

INTEGRATE

- Have the children practice reading aloud "The Legend of the Christmas Donkey." Select two readers and have the class present the activity as a choral reading.
- Write the word *kind* on the board and ask why *kind* is a good word to describe the donkey. Accept appropriate responses, such as, The donkey let Joseph put Mary on his back and let Mary ride him to Bethlehem.
- Then have the children do the activity at the bottom of the page.

PRAY

Gather the children around the Advent wreath in the prayer area. Lead them in singing "O Come, O Come, Emmanuel." Conclude by praying this or a similar prayer:
    God our Father,
    you are always kind to us.
    Help us to prepare
    for the coming of your Son, Jesus,
    by being kind to others.
    Amen.

The Season of Christmas

The Light of the World

The celebration of the Incarnation is suffused with light. In the third century, missionaries to Britain encountered festivals of light celebrated in the dark December night. The Church supplanted these light rituals with the celebration of the "Christ Mass" and the feast honoring the birth of Jesus, the true "sun of justice" (Malachi 3:20) and "light of the world" (John 8:12).

The Church in the East preferred to celebrate Epiphany as the major feast commemorating the coming of the Savior into the world. This celebration focused on the manifestation of Emmanuel to the whole world, represented by the Magi. Today the liturgical Season of Christmas enfolds these two feasts and more.

The Season of Christmas

Though the Christmas season begins with the Mass of the Vigil of Christmas, most Catholics begin the season by celebrating one of the three Masses of Christmas: the Mass at Midnight, the Mass at Dawn, or the Mass During the Day. The Gospel for the Mass at Midnight is the account of the birth of Jesus in the stable. The Gospel for the Mass at Dawn tells the story of the shepherds. The Gospel for the Mass During the Day begins with the towering account: "In the beginning was the Word . . ." (John 1:1).

The Christmas season continues with the celebration of the feast of the Holy Family on the Sunday after Christmas (or on December 30); the Solemnity of Mary, Mother of God (January 1); Epiphany (the Sunday between January 2 and 8); and the Baptism of the Lord on the Sunday following Epiphany. The celebrations of the Christmas season cover the entire spectrum, from the intimacy of the Bethlehem story on Christmas night to the proclamation to the whole world at the liturgical celebration of the Baptism of Jesus that Jesus is the beloved Son on whom the Father's favor rests.

A Season of Light and Abundance

The season of Christmas is very dear to the hearts of Christians. In the birth of the child Jesus, who is named Savior and Emmanuel, Christ and Lord, we are made new. The whole earth rejoices. Delightful traditions are evident along our streets and in our homes. Gifts abound. Evergreens are strung with lights and ornaments. Delicious baked goods are given and received. Special meals are shared.

This season of light and blessing reminds us of our vocation to be light, to bear gifts, to share our blessings both during this season and throughout the year.

In what ways does my celebration of the birth of Jesus, who is named Savior and Emmanuel, renew my life of faith?

How can I best celebrate the Christmas gift, the grace of God's presence?

The Savior of the World

Pretend you are with the Magi. Follow the maze to Jesus. What gift would you bring to Jesus? What would you say to Jesus when you give your gift to him?

250

Teaching Tip

Guests in Our Homes. Remind the children that the Magi, the three kings in the Gospel story, represent people from all over the world who came to honor Jesus. Emphasize that this Gospel story teaches that Jesus is the Savior of all people. Emphasize that this points out God's love for all people. Connect this story to the children's everyday life. For example, discuss the importance of welcoming relatives and friends into our homes. Help the children discover and learn words or actions of hospitality that they can use to welcome guests into their homes.

REINFORCE

Ask the children to describe how the Magi honored Jesus. Accept all appropriate responses, such as, They bowed and gave him gifts.

INTEGRATE

- Introduce "The Savior of the World" activity. Have the children complete the maze and then ask a volunteer to respond to the first question. Accept all appropriate responses.
- Distribute a colored index card to each child. Have the children write on one side of card the name *Jesus* and on the other side of the card one way they will honor Jesus. Tell them that they will use their cards in the prayer service.

PRAY

- Place a decorated gift box on the prayer table that you have prepared in advance.
- Invite the children to the prayer area. Read aloud the second question in the maze activity and have the children quietly think of their response.
- Invite the children to come forward one at a time and place their cards in the box. While the children are placing their cards in the box, you might play a recording of "The Little Drummer Boy."
- After all the children have returned to their places, invite them to quietly leave the prayer area.

The Season of Lent

Life in Christ

The Lenten season prepares us for the celebration of the Triduum and the Easter season during which we initiate new members into the Church, the Body of Christ. Throughout Lent the Church constantly reminds us that through the Passion, death, and Resurrection of Christ, joy came to the whole world. By dying Jesus taught us how to live.

Lent begins on Ash Wednesday. On this day we are reminded of our vulnerability and need for redemption. We are invited to enter into the company of the faithful who willingly and wholeheartedly take on the Lenten discipline of deepening their life in Christ through prayer, fasting, and almsgiving.

We ask the Holy Spirit's guidance and help to enter fully into the death and new life of the Lord. As the Church, the new People of God, we support one another and work together to welcome new members into the Church at the Easter Vigil through the celebration of the three Sacraments of Christian Initiation—Baptism, Confirmation, and Eucharist.

God's Word to Us

The goal of our Lenten journey is to celebrate and deepen our new life in Christ. The Gospel readings for the first two Sundays of Lent speak of the Temptation of Christ and his Transfiguration. We journey with Jesus into the desert and confront both our weakness and our strength. Moved by the Holy Spirit we confront sin and evil in our lives, renewing our commitment to reject sin and the glamour of evil and to live as children of the Father.

We journey up the slopes of the Mount of the Transfiguration and listen, as Saints Peter, James, and John did, to the words of the Father, "This is my beloved Son, with whom I am well pleased; listen to him" (Matthew 17:5). We are privileged to do so in order that we may be transformed into faithful and faith-filled disciples of his Son. The Gospel readings assigned for the remaining Sundays of Lent shine with images of living water, of restored sight and life. We cannot miss the allusion to the Easter sacraments.

Finally, the Mass of Palm Sunday of the Lord's Passion introduces us to the holiest week of the liturgical year. We remember and celebrate Jesus' entrance into the city of Jerusalem, his celebration of Passover for the last time with his disciples, and his journey up the hill of Calvary to the place of his death. As we enter into this week of Jesus' Passion and death, we look forward to his Resurrection.

For Reflection

What will be my Lenten discipline this year

As I journey through Lent and remember that through the cross of Christ joy came to the whole world, how am I strengthened?

Catechist to Catechist

Garden of Faith

Lent is a season of new life, a season of hope, a season of spiritual growth and renewal. Imagine yourself as a spiritual gardener using the threefold Lenten discipline of prayer, almsgiving, and fasting to care for your garden of faith, your spiritual life. Fasting, almsgiving, and prayer all help us live the Great Commandment. Prayer focuses on our life with God and deepens our intimacy with him. Almsgiving is a concrete, practical way to express our love for our neighbor. Fasting strengthens the virtue of detachment in us, guiding us to see that God and the things of God alone are the treasures our hearts should seek above all else.

Working at the Lenten Disciplines

All three Lenten practices are spiritual skills that need to be used appropriately throughout one's lifetime. This Lent offer the children opportunities to develop  the habit of prayer. Encourage their participation in the celebration of the sacrament of Penance and the praying of the Stations of the Cross. Encourage their giving up "little things" and doing "little extras" to show their love for God and others.

The Church Teaches . . .

In the *Ceremonial of Bishops* (251) we read:

> The faithful are to be encouraged to participate in an ever more intense and fruitful way in the Lenten liturgy and in penitential celebrations. They are to be clearly reminded that both according to the law and tradition they should approach the sacrament of penance during this season so that with purified heart they may participate in the paschal mysteries.

During Lent your parish probably will celebrate the communal rite of the sacrament of Penance. This always includes the confession of sins by individuals to the priest. Take the time to review the examination of conscience and rites for the celebration of Penance with the class.

CATECHIST PRAYER

God of compassion, you invite us to turn to prayer, fasting, and almsgiving. Let your compassion fill us with hope and lead us to the beauty of Easter joy.

[BASED ON THE ALTERNATIVE OPENING PRAYER FOR THE MASS FOR THE THIRD SUNDAY OF LENT]

Teach

FOCUS

Ask a volunteer to read the "Faith Focus" question aloud. Point out that the children will begin to find out the answer to the question in this lesson.

DISCOVER

- Read aloud "Keeping Lent." Pause after each paragraph to make sure the children are adequately grasping what is being taught.
- Summarize by connecting the first and last paragraphs on the page. This will help the children establish the relationship between Lent and Easter.

The First Week of Lent

Faith Focus

How does celebrating Lent help us to get ready for Easter?

The Word of the Lord

These are Gospel readings for the First Sunday of Lent. Ask your family to read this year's Gospel reading with you. Talk about the reading with them.

Year A
Matthew 4:1–11

Year B
Mark 1:12–15

Year C
Luke 4:1–13

What You See

During Lent the Church uses the color purple or violet. The colors purple and violet remind us of sorrow and penance.

Keeping Lent

Sometimes a special day seems far away. But we can do many things to get ready for that day.

Lent is forty days long. It begins on Ash Wednesday. We turn to God and pray each day. We make sacrifices, or give up some things. This helps us to show our love for God and others.

Lent is the special time of the year the Church prepares new members for Baptism. It is the time members of the Church prepare to renew the promises we made at Baptism.

We do all these things during Lent to help us to prepare for Easter. Easter is a special day for all Christians. It is the day of Jesus' Resurrection.

251

Teaching Tip

Signs of Lent. Take the time to decorate your prayer space with colors and symbols that represent the Lenten season. For example, cover the prayer table with a purple runner, and place a crucifix and a bowl of holy water on the table. The children will notice that the prayer space has been freshly decorated. This can be a good lead-in to share with them the meaning of the Lenten season.

Prepare for Easter

Pick a partner. Take turns answering each question.
Decide how to keep Lent and prepare for Easter.
On the lines write your answers to each question.

LENT

When does Lent begin?

_____Ash Wednesday_____

How long is Lent?

_____Forty Days_____

What does the word *sacrifice* mean?

_____Give up some things_____

What can you give up during Lent?

_____Responses will vary._____

How can you help others during Lent?

_____Responses will vary._____

What prayer could you say during Lent?

_____Responses will vary._____

EASTER

252

Teaching Tip

Lenten Prayer Service. Precut slips of purple paper and print the words *I will* on each slip of paper. Share with the children that Lent is a time to prepare for Easter by thinking about our Baptism and naming ways we can better live as children of God. Distribute the strips to the children. Ask the children to write or draw one way they can prepare for Easter during Lent. Suggest that they use the items that are listed on the board. Have the children place their paper strips in the basket on the prayer table as part of the closing prayer. After all the children have placed their slips in the basket, pray together, "We will grow in God's love."

Apply

REINFORCE

Ask the children to describe how Lent helps us get ready for Easter. Have them look for the answer on page 251 and underline or highlight it. We turn to God and pray each day. We make sacrifices, or give up some things. Then have them look at the picture on page 251 and connect it to their response.

INTEGRATE

- Introduce the "Prepare for Easter" activity and have the children work in groups to complete it.
- Have each group share their responses with the whole class.
- Encourage the children to do what they have answered to the fourth, fifth, and sixth questions.

PRAY

- Invite the children to gather in the prayer area. Point out that the table is decorated with a purple runner, and then read aloud "What You See" on page 251 to help the children learn why the Church uses purple during Lent.
- Have the children quiet themselves. Then lead them in prayer. Tell them to repeat the words of the prayer after you.
  Lord God,
  as we begin the Lenten season,
  help us to prepare for Easter.
  Remind us to pray each day
  and help us to make a sacrifice
  that will show our love for
  you and others.
  Amen.

Teach

FOCUS

Ask a volunteer to read the "Faith Focus" question aloud. Comment that during Lent we can make an extra effort to grow stronger and stronger in our friendship with Jesus.

DISCOVER

- Invite the children to look at the picture. Explain that it is a picture of grapes growing on a vine. Then read aloud the first paragraph of "The Vine and the Branches."

- Have the children listen for how the picture can help us understand how to celebrate Lent. Then read aloud the second and third paragraphs of the text.

- Ask volunteers to respond to the question, How does the picture of the vine and the branches help us celebrate Lent? Accept all appropriate responses, such as, Jesus is the vine and we are the branches. During Lent we grow strong like the grape branches.

The Second Week of Lent

Faith Focus

How can people know we are followers of Jesus?

The Word of the Lord

These are the Gospel readings for the Second Sunday of Lent. Ask your family to read this year's Gospel reading with you. Talk about the reading with them.

Year A
Matthew 17:1–9

Year B
Mark 9:2–10

Year C
Luke 9:28–36

The Vine and the Branches

Jesus once compared himself and his followers to a grape vine and its branches. Where Jesus lived grapevines grew on hillsides. The vine and the branches make juicy, sweet grapes.

Jesus said he is like the vine. We are his branches. We share his life. Together with Jesus we share God's love with others. During Lent we grow strong like the grape branches. We do good deeds. People know that we are followers of Jesus.

At Baptism we become one with Jesus. We promise to believe and do what he taught us.

(253)

Teaching Tip

Make Lenten Prayer Books. Help the children develop the habit of prayer. Work with them to make prayer books that the class can use during Lent. Write these headings on the board: "Help," "Thank You," "Please," "Pray Alone," and "Pray Together." Each of these headings can become the title of a page of the prayer book. Brainstorm the words for a prayer for each page and write the prayer on the board. Have the children work in small groups. Have one group create a cover and the other groups the pages. Gather the finished pages into a book and place it in the prayer center for all to use.

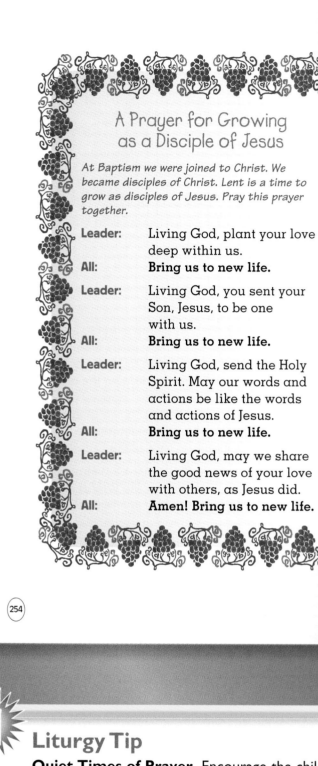

A Prayer for Growing as a Disciple of Jesus

At Baptism we were joined to Christ. We became disciples of Christ. Lent is a time to grow as disciples of Jesus. Pray this prayer together.

Leader: Living God, plant your love deep within us.

All: **Bring us to new life.**

Leader: Living God, you sent your Son, Jesus, to be one with us.

All: **Bring us to new life.**

Leader: Living God, send the Holy Spirit. May our words and actions be like the words and actions of Jesus.

All: **Bring us to new life.**

Leader: Living God, may we share the good news of your love with others, as Jesus did.

All: **Amen! Bring us to new life.**

254

Liturgy Tip

Quiet Times of Prayer. Encourage the children to take time to develop the habit of personal prayer. For example, tell them to set aside a quiet moment each day to praise and thank God. Incorporate such moments of quiet personal prayer throughout your sessions with the children. Since deepening one's prayer life is one of the three Lenten disciplines, this is a good time of the year to focus on this aspect of the children's development as people of prayer.

Apply

REINFORCE

- Read and discuss John 15:1–5, the Gospel story that compares Jesus to the vine and all Christians to branches.
- Invite volunteers to explain why Jesus and his followers are like the vine and the branches. Accept all appropriate responses, such as, We share Jesus' life. He is the vine and we are the branches. We do good deeds as Jesus taught us.

INTEGRATE

- Have the children work in pairs to name some of the good deeds Jesus asked us to do. Have volunteers share their ideas with the whole class.
- Summarize by stating that when we do the things Jesus taught us, people see that we are his followers. Explain that just as our friendship with a good friend can grow much stronger, one way we continue to grow closer to Jesus is by living as he taught us to do.
- Introduce "A Prayer for Growing as a Disciple of Jesus." Explain that during today's prayer time you will say the "Leader" parts and the children will respond with the "All" parts.

PRAY

- Ask the children to bring their books with them and quietly come to the prayer area.
- Lead the class in praying "A Prayer for Growing as a Disciple of Jesus."

Teach

FOCUS

Have the children look at the picture of the stained-glass window. Tell them that it depicts Jesus carrying his cross to the place where he died. Then ask a volunteer to read the "Faith Focus" question aloud.

DISCOVER

- Point to the heading "The Stations of the Cross." Tell the children that Catholics in many parishes come together during Lent to pray the Stations of the Cross.
- Read aloud or paraphrase the text under "The Stations of the Cross."
- Discuss with the children why Catholics might gather in their parishes during Lent to pray the Stations of the Cross.

The Third Week of Lent

Faith Focus

How can we remember Jesus' journey to the place where he died?

The Word of the Lord

These are the Gospel readings for the Third Sunday of Lent. Ask your family to read this year's Gospel reading with you. Talk about the reading with them.

Year A
John 4:5–42 or
John 4:5–15, 19–26, 39, 40–44

Year B
John 2:13–25

Year C
Luke 13:1–9

The Stations of the Cross

Who do you know who has died? What do you remember about that person? What do you do that helps you to remember that person? As we prepare for Easter we remember that Jesus died for us.

Long ago people went to Jerusalem to remember that Jesus died. They walked the same roads as he did to the place where he died on the cross. Along the way they stopped and prayed. Each place they stopped is called a station. The whole journey is called the Stations, or Way, of the Cross.

During Lent some Christians still go to Jerusalem to pray the Way of the Cross. Many others pray the Stations of the Cross in their parish churches. Today most churches have fourteen Stations of the Cross. Some have a fifteenth station. This station shows that Jesus, who died, is risen.

(255)

Liturgy Tip

Ethnic Diversity in Prayer. Some cultures use motion and gestures as an expression of prayer more than other cultures do. But all children enjoy movement, singing, and clapping. Include motion and gestures in your prayers with the children. This is an important point to remember as you work toward recognizing the diversity of ethnic backgrounds within your group.

The Cross of Christ

The cross is a sign of Jesus' love for us. Use the code to discover a prayer about the cross. Learn the prayer by heart and pray it each day during Lent.

1 = A   2 = E   3 = I   4 = O   5 = U

J <u>e</u> sus,
   2

thr <u>o</u> <u>u</u> gh th <u>e</u>   cr <u>o</u> ss
    4 5   2   4

y <u>o</u> <u>u</u>   br <u>o</u> <u>u</u> ght j <u>o</u> y
  4 5   4 5   4

t <u>o</u>   th <u>e</u>   w <u>o</u> rld.
  4   2   4

Th <u>a</u> nk y <u>o</u> <u>u</u> .
   1   4 5

Am <u>e</u> n.
   2

256

Background: Liturgy

Laetare Sunday. Next Sunday, the Fourth Sunday of Lent, is Laetare Sunday. The word *Laetare* means "Rejoice!" In many parishes the priest will wear rose-colored vestments to emphasize that while Lent is a time of penance, the Lenten journey is toward Easter and the celebration of and rejoicing in the new life we have received in Baptism. If possible, cover the table in your prayer area with a pink or rose-colored runner. For more information on Laetare Sunday visit the *Catholic Encyclopedia* Web site.

REINFORCE

Ask a volunteer to read aloud the "Faith Focus" question on page 255. Then ask for volunteers to describe how praying the Stations of the Cross help us remember Jesus' journey to the place where he died.

INTEGRATE

- Introduce and explain the directions for "The Cross of Christ" activity. Discuss the opening sentence with the children. Then ask them to complete the activity.
- Invite a volunteer to share the decoded message with the whole class.
- Distribute markers, crayons, and fourteen cross shapes made from sturdy paper that you have prepared in advance. Have the children decorate the crosses. Explain that the crosses will be used in the closing prayer celebration.

PRAY

- Help the children post their crosses at the children's eye level on the walls of the classroom so that you have fourteen stopping places along the four walls.
- Invite the children to walk from cross to cross. As they reach each station, read aloud the name of the station, and have the children briefly stop and silently pray an act of love to Jesus.
- After they pray silently at the fourteen crosses, invite all to repeat this prayer after you:
  Jesus, through the cross you brought joy to the world. Thank you. Amen.

Teach

FOCUS

Ask a volunteer to read the "Faith Focus" question aloud. Tell the children that in this lesson they will learn about one more way we celebrate Lent.

DISCOVER

- Write the word *sharing* on the board. Explain that during Lent we make a special effort to share our blessings with people in need.
- Read aloud "Making Room for God." Tell the children to listen for the reasons that sharing our blessings with others is an important part of the way we celebrate Lent.

The Fourth Week of Lent

Faith Focus

During Lent how can we make more room in our hearts for God?

The Word of the Lord

These are the Gospel readings for the Fourth Sunday of Lent. Ask your family to read this year's Gospel reading with you. Talk about the reading with them.

Year A
John 9:1–41 or
John 9:1, 6–9, 13–17,
34–38

Year B
John 3:14–21

Year C
Luke 15:1–3,
11–32

Making Room for God

No matter how much we have, we can always share what we have with someone else.

Once a young man asked Jesus how to live as God wanted him to live. Knowing the young man owned many good things, Jesus told him to share his things with others. This would help the man to make more room in his heart for God.

During Lent the Church helps us to make room in our hearts for God too. We can do this by sharing our time, our talents, and our treasure with others.

We can use our time to visit someone who is sick. We can use our talents to help others. We can share the things we treasure with those who have too little.

257

Teaching Tip

Affirm the Children's Lenten Efforts. Tell the children that this Sunday, the Fourth Sunday of Lent, is also called "Laetare Sunday." Explain that the word *Laetare* means "Rejoice." All the efforts we make to cooperate with God's grace and live as his children bring joy to our hearts. Affirm the children for all they have done so far this Lent—and this year—to live as children of God. Point out to them that the priest and deacon might wear rose-colored vestments as a sign of rejoicing because Easter is near.

Sharing with Others

Jesus told us to share the blessings God gives us with others. In the boxes draw or write ways you can share your time, talents, and treasures with people. This week try your best to do what you have drawn or written in each gift box.

Responses will vary. Affirm appropriate responses.

258

REINFORCE

Ask the children to tell why sharing our blessings makes room in our hearts for God and brings us joy. Accept all appropriate responses, such as, We are doing what Jesus taught us to do. We are living as children of God.

INTEGRATE

- Ask the children to look at the picture on page 257 and ask volunteers to tell how the people are sharing their time, talents, and treasures with one another.
- Brainstorm with the children examples of time, talent, and treasure that they can share with others.
- Introduce and explain the directions to the "Sharing with Others" activity. Invite the children to complete the activity. Encourage everyone to try their best to do what they have drawn or written in the boxes.

PRAY

- Tell the children that for the closing prayer they are going to complete the statement, "Jesus, help me make room in my heart for you by _____."
- Invite the children to quietly come to the prayer center and lead them in prayer.

Teaching Tip

Sunday Readings. Be sure to visit the "Lectionary" page of the *Catechist and Teachers* section of the *Faith First Legacy* Web site at **www.FaithFirst.com.** There you will find the Sunday lectionary readings, background to the readings, and a process for sharing the readings with the children. Be sure to send a note home with the children, encouraging families to visit **www.FaithFirst.com,** click on the "Faith First for Families" page, then on "Gospel Reflections," and share some of the ideas on the Sunday Gospel reading.

Teach

FOCUS

Ask a volunteer to read the "Faith Focus" question aloud. Have the children look at the illustrated art on page 259 and share with them that Lent is also a time of forgiveness.

DISCOVER

- Invite the children to suggest words and ways that show forgiveness. List their suggestions on the board.
- Read the first two paragraphs of "A Forgiving Heart" to the children and have them listen for how Jesus wants us to forgive those who hurt us.
- Invite volunteers to read aloud the remaining paragraphs of the text on page 259 as the rest of the group follows along to find out how we grow as people of forgiveness.
- Talk with the children about why asking for forgiveness and forgiving others is important in the life of a Christian. God forgives us over and over. We try to forgive others over and over too.

The Fifth Week of Lent

Faith Focus

How can we grow as people who forgive others as God forgives us?

The Word of the Lord

These are the Gospel readings for the Fifth Sunday of Lent. Ask your family to read this year's Gospel reading with you. Talk about the reading with them.

Year A
John 11:1–45 or
John 11:3–7, 17,
 20–27,
 33–45

Year B
John 12:20–33

Year C
John 8:1–11

A Forgiving Heart

When people hurt us, we sometimes want to hurt them back. Jesus asks us to forgive those who hurt us.

In the Our Father we pray "forgive us our trespasses as we forgive those who trespass against us." Praying these words shows that we want to forgive others. We want to have a forgiving heart.

During Lent we remember that God forgives us over and over. We try to forgive others over and over too.

We also celebrate God's forgiveness in the sacrament of Reconciliation during Lent. We come together with people in our parish and ask God for forgiveness of our sins. We ask God to help us to forgive others.

Forgive Us Our Trespasses

Liturgy Tip

The Prayers of Petition and Intercession. The prayer of petition and the prayer of intercession are two of the five traditional forms of Christian prayer. Reinforce the children's use of these prayers. Here is a suggestion: Create a prayer box. Place a stack of paper and pencils nearby. Invite the children to print on a slip of paper the name of a person or a drawing of the person they would like to pray for. During the session take a moment and invite the children to quietly pray for all the people whose names have been placed in the prayer box.

Growing in Forgiveness

Lent is a time of forgiveness. The Our Father teaches that God forgives us and that we are to forgive others. Listen and pray together.

God's Word

Leader: Let us listen to a reading from Matthew's Gospel.

Reader: Peter asked Jesus, "Lord, if my brother sins against me, how often must I forgive him? As many as seven times?"

Children: **Jesus answered, "I say to you, not seven times, but seventy-seven times."**

Matthew 18:21–22

Reflection and Prayer

Leader: Let us think of those people we forgive . . . Let us now pray the Our Father and ask God to forgive us as we forgive others.

All: **Our Father . . .**

Blessing

Leader: May God who calls you to grow as forgiving children bless you.

All: **Amen.**

Leader: May God who forgives over and over smile on you.

All: **Amen.**

Leader: May God who loves gather you in his tender care.

All: **Amen.**

260

REINFORCE

Ask the children to describe some of the ways we can grow during Lent as a people who forgive others as God forgives us. Accept all appropriate responses, such as, We forgive others. We celebrate the sacrament of Reconciliation.

INTEGRATE

- If the children in your class are going to receive the sacrament of Reconciliation, review both the individual rite of Reconciliation and the communal rite of Reconciliation with the class. You might also send a note home to the families stating the dates and times this sacrament will be celebrated in the parish.

- Introduce the "Growing in Forgiveness" prayer on page 260. Rehearse the "All" lines so they flow smoothly.

PRAY

Invite the children to bring their books and gather in the prayer center. Invite all to participate in the prayer service "Growing in Forgiveness."

Teaching Tip

Think, Pair, and Share. Lent is a time of praying, sharing, and forgiving. All these disciplines help us grow in union with God and with one another. Use the cooperative learning strategy of think, pair, and share in your lessons. Guide the children to cooperate with one another and work together, sharing their time and talents with one another as they learn and pray.

Holy Week

The Easter Triduum

The Easter Triduum is the center of the Church's year. The celebration of the Triduum begins with the celebration of the Evening Mass of the Lord's Supper on Holy Thursday and concludes with Evening Prayer, or Vespers, on Easter Sunday. "Christ redeemed us all and gave perfect glory to God principally through his paschal mystery: dying he destroyed our death and rising he restored our life. Therefore the Easter triduum of the passion and resurrection of Christ is the culmination of the entire liturgical year."

"General Norms for the Liturgical Year and the Calendar," Roman Missal 18

Holy Thursday

The first day of the Triduum begins with the Evening Mass of the Lord's Supper. (The term *day* is somewhat misleading if one thinks of days as independent twenty-four-hour periods of time. The Triduum in reality is a three-day-long celebration and participation in this great mystery of our faith—the Paschal Mystery.) Celebrating this liturgy for Holy Thursday marks our entrance into the solemn observance of the Triduum. We join Christ at the Passover meal. We watch and listen in amazement. We learn

what it means to serve as Jesus did. We receive the gift of his Body and Blood, the Eucharist.

Good Friday

On the second day of the Triduum, Good Friday, we gather for the celebration of the Lord's Passion. Celebrating this liturgy occurs ideally at about three o'clock in the afternoon, the traditional hour of Jesus' death. However, this time is often altered to reflect pastoral needs.

Holy Saturday

In the evening of the third day of the Triduum, Holy Saturday, we celebrate the Easter Vigil. "The Easter Vigil, during the holy night

when Christ rose from the dead, ranks as the 'mother of all vigils.' Keeping watch, the Church awaits Christ's resurrection and celebrates it in the sacraments. Accordingly, the entire celebration of this vigil should take place at night, that is, it should either begin after nightfall or end before the dawn of Sunday."

"General Norms for the Liturgical Year and the Calendar," Roman Missal 21

The Easter Vigil summons us to enter into the Service of Light, with the singing of the Easter Proclamation, the Liturgy of the Word, the Liturgy of Baptism, and the Liturgy of the Eucharist. We initiate and welcome new members into the Church, the Body of Christ, and renew our Baptism. Together we rejoice:

Jesus Christ, our King,
is risen!
Sound the trumpet
of salvation!

Easter Proclamation

How does my taking part in the celebration of the Easter Triduum strengthen my identity as a follower of Jesus Christ?

What can I do to observe these days as the holiest time of the Church's year?

Catechist to Catechist

The Easter Triduum

The heart of Holy Week is the Easter Triduum, which is the "culmination of the entire liturgical year" (*General Norms of the Liturgical Year and Calendar* 18). This three-day celebration, which is calculated according to liturgical time, begins with the celebration of the Evening Mass of the Lord's Supper on Holy Thursday. It continues with the Celebration of the Lord's Passion on Good Friday, and concludes with the Easter celebrations of the Easter Vigil, Easter Sunday Mass, and Evening Prayer on Easter Sunday evening.

Celebrate the Rites

Use some of the concrete rites and symbols of the Holy Week celebrations as a means to help the children discover the meaning of these central  mysteries of the faith of the Church. Decorate the prayer space with palm branches, a goblet or wine glass, a loaf of unleavened bread, a bare cross draped with a red cloth, a clear bowl of water, and candles. Share the Scripture stories and prayers that are part of the liturgical celebrations. Have the children memorize such simple prayers as "Where there is love, there is God" and "Christ has died, Christ is risen, Christ will come again" and encourage them to pray them often.

The Church Teaches . . .

On Preparing and Celebrating the Paschal Feasts, the 1988 circular letter concerning the preparation and celebration of the Easter feast, written by the Congregation for Divine Worship and the Sacraments, reminds us:

> The greatest mysteries of redemption are celebrated yearly by the church beginning with the evening Mass of the Lord's Supper on Holy Thursday and ending with Vespers of Easter Sunday. This time is called "the triduum of the crucified, buried and risen."[1] (38)

Ideally, the children would have an opportunity for catechesis on the Easter Triduum immediately before its celebration. If this is not possible, encourage the families to use the Triduum lessons at home.

CATECHIST PRAYER

God, Father of compassion, send your blessing down upon us who celebrate the death of your Son in the hope of his Resurrection. Amen.

[BASED ON "PRAYER OVER THE PEOPLE" FROM THE LITURGY OF GOOD FRIDAY, ROMAN MISSAL.]

Footnote references may be found on p. 456.

Teach

FOCUS

Ask a volunteer to read the "Faith Focus" question aloud. Share with the children that Palm Sunday of the Lord's Passion is the beginning of Holy Week.

DISCOVER

- Tell the children the week of the year during which the Church remembers and celebrates the events of Jesus' entrance into the city of Jerusalem and his Passion, death, and Resurrection is called Holy Week.
- Select a child to read aloud the first paragraph of "Holy Week Begins."
- Ask a volunteer to describe why the Church calls the day it celebrates this event in the life of Jesus Palm Sunday of the Lord's Passion. Accept all appropriate responses, such as, The people waved palm branches to greet Jesus.
- Then have the children read the rest of page 261 to discover how the Church remembers and celebrates this event.
- Use "What You See" to raise the children's awareness of an important way they can take part in celebrating the liturgy for Palm Sunday of the Lord's Passion.

Palm Sunday of the Lord's Passion

Faith Focus

How do we begin our celebration of Holy Week?

The Word of the Lord

These are the Gospel readings for Palm Sunday of the Lord's Passion. Ask your family to read this year's Gospel reading with you. Talk about the reading with them.

Year A
Matthew 26:14–27, 66 or
Matthew 27:11–54

Year B
Mark 14:1–15:47 or
Mark 15:1–39

Year C
Luke 22:14–23:56 or
Luke 23:1–49

What You See

We carry palm branches in procession. We hold them as we listen to the Gospel reading.

Holy Week Begins

When friends come to visit, we welcome them. Once when Jesus came to visit Jerusalem, many people came out to welcome him. They spread cloaks and branches on the road to honor him. The Church remembers and celebrates that special time on Palm Sunday of the Lord's Passion. It is the first day of Holy Week. Holy Week is the week before Easter.

At Mass on Palm Sunday we honor Jesus. We hold palm branches and say, "Hosanna to the Son of David. Blessed is he who comes in the name of the Lord!" We welcome Jesus as the people welcomed him to Jerusalem.

261

Background: Liturgy

The Liturgy for Palm Sunday of the Lord's Passion. Briefly explain the main details of the liturgy for Palm Sunday of the Lord's Passion to the children. Point out that the liturgy begins with the blessing of palms, which often takes place outside the church, and the procession of palms into the church for the celebration of the Mass. Explain that the Gospel for the Mass is the reading of one of the Gospel accounts of the Passion and death of Jesus.

Prayers for the Whole World

On Good Friday the Church prays a special Prayer of the Faithful. Pray this prayer of the faithful together.

Leader:	Let us pray for the Church.
Child 1:	May God guide us and gather us in peace.
All:	**Amen.**
Leader:	Let us pray for the pope.
Child 2:	May God help the pope to lead us as God's holy people.
All:	**Amen.**
Leader:	Let us pray for those who will soon be baptized.
Child 3:	May God help them to follow Jesus.
All:	**Amen.**
Leader:	Let us pray for our government leaders.
Child 4:	May God bless them and help them keep us safe and free.
All:	**Amen.**
Leader:	Let us pray for those in need.
Child 5:	May God make their faith and hope in him strong.
All:	**Amen.**

266

Background: Catholic Tradition

Good Friday Silence. There is a long-standing Christian practice of making the three hours of 12:00 noon to 3:00 P.M. on Good Friday quiet or silent time. Remind the children's families of the importance of spending some quiet time in prayer on Good Friday. The family might gather to read the Passion and death of Jesus in one of the four Gospels. Point out that they might visit the "Gospel Reflections" page of the "*Faith First* for Families" section of **www.FaithFirst.com** for some ideas on ways to share their faith in the meaning of Jesus' Passion and death for their family.

Apply

REINFORCE

Ask the children to describe how taking part in the celebration of Good Friday helps us grow as followers of Christ. Affirm all appropriate responses, such as, We listen to the story of Jesus' suffering and death. We show our love for Jesus by venerating the cross. We pray for others. We receive Holy Communion.

INTEGRATE

- Work with the children and draw up a list of people for whom they wish to pray. Explain that they can include groups of people, such as priests, people who are sick, and so on.
- Tell the children that at the liturgy on Good Friday the Church prays a special Prayer of the Faithful.
- Introduce and explain the directions for "Prayers for the Whole World." Select five volunteers for the "Child" parts. Explain that everyone will answer "Amen" to each petition. Allow time for the five volunteers to practice their parts.

PRAY

Have the children bring their books and gather in the prayer center. Lead them in prayer. Begin and end with the Sign of the Cross. After the last "Amen," repeat the Sign of the Cross.

Teach

FOCUS

Ask a volunteer to read the "Faith Focus" question. Point out that Easter, the greatest feast of the Church, is the third and final day of the Triduum.

DISCOVER

- Have the children look at the picture of the butterfly. Ask why they think the butterfly and other living things we see in the springtime remind us of Easter. Accept all appropriate responses.

- Read aloud the first paragraph of "The Best Day of All" and allow volunteers to respond to the questions in the paragraph.

- Ask the children to read silently the rest of the page to find out why Easter is the best day of all for Christians. Invite volunteers to share what they have learned.

Faith Focus

Why is Easter the most important season of the Church's year?

The Word of the Lord

These are the Gospel readings for Easter Sunday. Ask your family to read the Gospel reading for this year with you. Talk about it with them.

Year A
John 20:1–9 or
Matthew 28:1–10 or
Luke 24:13–35

Year B
John 20:1–9 or
Mark 16:1–7 or
Luke 24:13–35

Year C
John 20:1–9 or
Luke 24:1–12 or
Luke 24:13–35

The Best Day of All

What is the best day of your life? Why do you say it is the best day you remember? For Christians Easter is the best day of all days. On this day God raised Jesus from death.

During Easter we remember that we are one with Jesus Christ, who is risen. For Christians every Sunday is a little Easter. Sunday is the Lord's Day. It is the day on which Jesus was raised from death to new life.

Easter and every Sunday are days of joy and celebration. On these days we remember that through Baptism we share in the new life of the Risen Jesus. We share in his new life now and forever.

267

Teaching Tip

Decorating with Signs of Life. Easter is a season of new life in Christ. Easter celebrates both the Resurrection of Jesus and our Baptism into new life in Christ. Decorate your prayer area with a variety of signs of life. Cover the prayer table with a flowing white cloth, put a bowl of holy water on the table to remind the children of their Baptism, and place green plants and candles in the prayer area. Have the children create Easter banners and display them throughout your learning space.

Celebrating Our New Life

The earth is filled with signs that remind us of the gift of new life in Christ we receive in Baptism. Find and color the signs of new life in this drawing. With your family look for these and other signs of new life. Talk about what the signs you discover tell about Easter.

268

REINFORCE

Ask the children to explain why Easter is the most important time of the Church's year. Easter is the day on which Jesus was raised from the dead. Affirm all appropriate responses.

INTEGRATE

- Recognize the diversity within your group and invite the children to share the ways their families celebrate Easter.
- Introduce and explain the "Celebrating Our New Life" activity to the children.
- Give the children time to find and color the signs of the new life of Easter in the activity.
- Invite volunteers to talk about what the signs of new life in the picture tell about Easter.
- Encourage the children to stop and think of the Resurrection of Jesus and give thanks and praise to God the Father when they see signs of new life, such as flowers, a rising sun, and so on.

PRAY

- Gather the children in the prayer area. Have them quiet themselves, close their eyes, and imagine they are with the disciples who went to the tomb three days after Jesus was buried.
- Proclaim Matthew 28:1–10 to the children and pause after the Gospel reading.
- Tell the children to open their eyes and echo the prayer "This is the day the Lord has made; let us rejoice and be glad" after you.

Teaching Tip

Understanding Cultural Traditions. A wide variety of ethnic and family customs are used to celebrate Easter. If your parish includes specific cultural traditions in the celebration of Easter, such as the blessing of Easter foods, talk about that celebration so that all the children in your group can understand its significance. You might also send a note home asking families who celebrate Easter using specific cultural traditions to visit with the class during the Easter season and share those traditions with the class. The Easter season is fifty days long, so there is plenty of time for the children to share and to learn from one another.

The Season of Easter

The Great Sunday

The fifty days from Easter Sunday to Pentecost are celebrated as one feast day, sometimes called the great Sunday (see "General Norms for the Liturgical Year and the Calendar," *Roman Missal* 22). The Easter season, which includes the feasts of the Ascension and Pentecost, is a time of praise, assurance, and mission. With our insistent "Alleluias" we lift up praise to God the Father for the new life that comes to us in the Resurrection of Jesus Christ, our Lord and Savior. We cannot but marvel before this great mystery of our redemption. The only fitting or, indeed, possible response is one of praise and thanksgiving.

The Scripture readings and the prayers of the Easter season reassure the hope of all believers. The story of the Risen Jesus encountering the two disciples on the road to Emmaus (see Luke 24:13–35) confirms the continuing presence of the Lord in his Church. In word and sacrament, through the proclamation of the Scriptures (see Luke 24:32) and the celebration of the Eucharist (see Luke 24:35), Jesus, the Risen One, abides with his community of faithful believers. The Easter readings and prayers that present Jesus as the Good Shepherd assure us of his continuing presence, love, and care for us, the sheep he claims as his own.

Proclaim the Resurrection

The Easter season renews the whole People of God and each individual believer in their sense of mission. The Risen Lord promised us that the Father would send the Holy Spirit. That promise was fulfilled on Pentecost, and the Holy Spirit continues to empower and encourage believers to proclaim the Gospel and to invite all people to repentance and Baptism. Those who are sealed with the Easter sacraments of Baptism, Confirmation, and Eucharist continue the mission of Jesus until he returns again in glory.

During the Easter season, the liturgy rekindles the sense of holy responsibility to both celebrate and extend to others the saving mysteries of Christ's death and Resurrection.

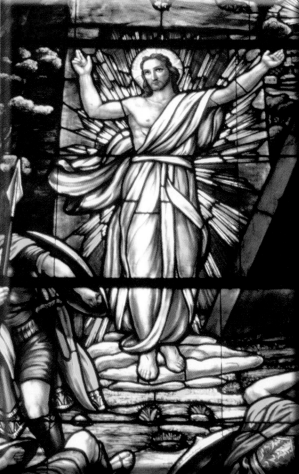

How does singing "Alleluia" for fifty days move me to share the good news of the Resurrection with others?

What are some practical, age-appropriate ways that young people can share in the mission of the Church?

Welcoming People
as Jesus Would

With a partner create a story about welcoming people
as Jesus would welcome them. Write or draw your
story in this space. Act out your story for the class.

Welcome

Aloha! E Komo Mai

Bienvenida

Responses will vary.

Affirm appropriate responses.

Soo-dhawayn

276

Teaching Tip

Love One Another. Remind the children of Jesus' command that we are to love one another as he loved us. Then share with the class the many ways your parish follows Jesus' command. For example, talk about how the priest preaches the Gospel, the people visit the sick, the parish cares for those who need clothing and food, and so on. Point out that what the parish does is similar to what the early Church did.

Apply

REINFORCE

Ask the children to name some of the ways the early Church welcomed its new members. They shared meals and prayed together. They rejoiced together and gave thanks. They helped people who needed food, clothing, and shelter.

INTEGRATE

- Ask the children to look at the photograph on page 275. Have volunteers describe what they see. Accept all appropriate responses, such as, People are serving food to others as Jesus taught them to do.
- Then ask how the people in the picture are doing what the early Church did.
- Invite the children to read and complete the "Welcoming People as Jesus Would" activity. Encourage volunteers to share their story with the class. You might have them read it or act it out.

PRAY

- Gather the children in the prayer area and pray together. Invite the children to close their eyes and imagine that they are members of the early Church helping people as Jesus taught.
- Have them open their eyes and pray this prayer adapted from Hebrews 13:1, echoing the lines after you.
  "Always love one another. Welcome one another."

Teach

The Sixth Week of Easter

FOCUS

Present the opening paragraph of "Share the Good News." Ask a volunteer to read the "Faith Focus" question.

DISCOVER

- Invite the children to silently read the second and third paragraphs of "Share the Good News" to find the answer to the "Faith Focus" question.

- Ask the children to look at the picture and identify who they think these people are and how they might be doing what Jesus asked them to do before he returned to his Father.

The Sixth Week of Easter

Faith Focus

How did the early Christians tell others about Jesus?

The Word of the Lord

These are the Gospel readings for the Sixth Sunday of Easter. Ask your family to read the Gospel reading for this year with you. Talk about the reading with them.

Year A
John 14:15–21

Year B
John 15:9–17

Year C
John 14:23–29

Share the Good News

When the time came for the Risen Jesus to return to his Father, Jesus took his followers to a hillside. We call the return of the Risen Jesus to his Father the Ascension. Jesus told his disciples to tell others about him and to invite them to become his followers.

The Holy Spirit helped the followers of Jesus to share with others what Jesus said and did. Philip the Apostle went to Samaria to tell the people all about Jesus. Samaria was a place Jesus had visited.

When the other Apostles heard what Philip was doing, they sent Peter and John there too. Many people came to believe in Jesus and asked to be baptized.

277

Teaching Tip

Writing Thank-you Notes. This is an excellent time to teach the children the names of ordained ministers of the Church. Share with the children the name of the pope, the bishop of the diocese and his auxiliaries, and the priests and deacons who serve the parish. Encourage the children to pray for these leaders. If there is time, have the children write a class thank-you or individual thank-you notes to the local bishop. Be sure to mail the thank-you note or notes for the children.

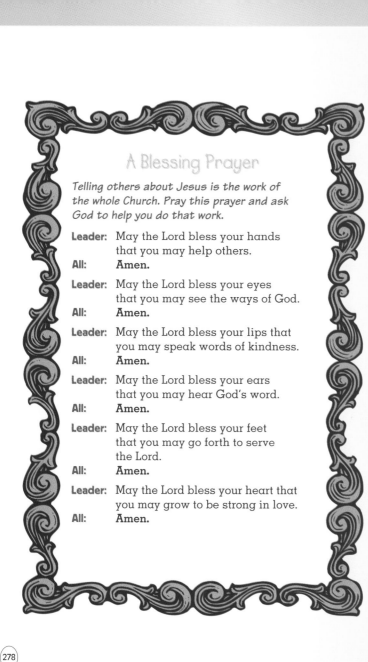

A Blessing Prayer

Telling others about Jesus is the work of the whole Church. Pray this prayer and ask God to help you do that work.

Leader: May the Lord bless your hands that you may help others.

All: Amen.

Leader: May the Lord bless your eyes that you may see the ways of God.

All: Amen.

Leader: May the Lord bless your lips that you may speak words of kindness.

All: Amen.

Leader: May the Lord bless your ears that you may hear God's word.

All: Amen.

Leader: May the Lord bless your feet that you may go forth to serve the Lord.

All: Amen.

Leader: May the Lord bless your heart that you may grow to be strong in love.

All: Amen.

278

Teaching Tip

Learning Preferences. Some children learn better when they both see and hear things. A rebus combines the use of sounds and sights in learning. Work with the children to create their own rebus that shares the Gospel story of Jesus telling the disciples to share the Good News.

Apply

REINFORCE

- Invite volunteers to tell what the Risen Jesus asked his followers to do. Accept all appropriate responses, such as, Jesus told his disciples to tell people about him and invite them to be his followers.

INTEGRATE

- Identify the Church's celebration of the Risen Jesus' return to his Father in heaven as the Ascension. Circle the feast of the Ascension on a calendar for the children to see. Remind the children that the feast of the Ascension is a holy day of obligation.
- Invite the children to think of ways that they can use their skills and talents to share the Good News about Jesus with people. Give everyone who wishes the opportunity to tell what they might do.

PRAY

- Rehearse the prayer service "A Blessing Prayer." Have the children make up gestures to accompany each blessing, such as hands up and out, hand over heart, and so on.
- Invite the children to come to the prayer center and quiet themselves. Choose volunteers to take the part of the leader and pray together "A Blessing Prayer" using the gestures the children have suggested.

Teach

FOCUS

Share with the children that this week's Gospel story is about Jesus praying for his followers. Then select a volunteer to read the "Faith Focus" question aloud.

DISCOVER

- Have the children name some of the ways they see the Church praying together. Accept all appropriate responses.
- Ask the children to read "A Praying Church" and find and underline or highlight two important times that the Church gathers to pray.
- Have the children raise their right hand when they are finished. Call on volunteers to read aloud what they have underlined or highlighted.

The Seventh Week of Easter

Faith Focus

When does the Church gather to pray?

The Word of the Lord

These are the Gospel readings for the Seventh Sunday of Easter. Ask your family to read the Gospel reading for this year with you. Talk about the reading with them.

Year A
John 17:1–11

Year B
John 17:11–19

Year C
John 17:20–26

A Praying Church

This week we listen to a story that tells about Jesus praying for his followers. What Gospel stories do you know that tell about Jesus praying?

The followers of Jesus are people of prayer. Every Saturday evening and every Sunday the Church gathers all over the world to celebrate the Eucharist. The Church also gathers several times every day of the year to pray. We call this daily prayer of the Church the Liturgy of the Hours.

Morning prayer gets us ready to make our day holy. Evening prayer closes our day. We remember and thank God for all his blessings.

Throughout each day of the year all over the world the Church gathers to pray. We bless and thank God for what he has done for us. We ask God to care for his people, the Church, and for all people.

Teaching Tip

Sharing Gospel Stories. Every time we hear a good story retold, we seem to learn something new. It is amazing how often we hear something we did not hear the last time we listened to the story. The Easter story has been told and retold for centuries. It is "the story" that we need to hear over and over again. It is "the story" that we need to share over and over again. The Holy Spirit will open our hearts and minds to hear something new each and every time.

My Daily Prayers

Use the prayers on this page to make Morning Prayer and Evening Prayer prayer cards. Take the time to pray every morning and every evening.

Morning Prayer

May the Lord open my lips.
May my mouth proclaim praise.
Now the sun fills the sky.
I lift my heart to God on high.
May God bless all I do and say,
and keep me free from sin today.
Amen.

Evening Prayer

Thank you, Lord, for this bright day.
Now, stay near. For this we pray.
Let your strong love surround us,
as darkness wraps all around us.
We leave to you, O God unsleeping,
this quiet world for your safekeeping.
Amen.

280

Teaching Tip

Use of Images. The biblical writers used many images to help us understand the meaning of God's word. Images are powerful tools to help us learn the mysteries of the faith. This may be a good lesson to use the image of a butterfly coming out of its cocoon to help the children get a glimpse into the meaning of the Resurrection. You might use a primary-grade-level science book and pictures from the library to show to the children. These visuals will help the children understand this important belief of our faith.

Apply

REINFORCE

Ask the children to explain why we call the Church a praying Church. Accept all appropriate responses, such as, Throughout each day all over the world the Church gathers to pray.

INTEGRATE

- Ask the children when they can take time to pray. List their responses on the board and relate the times during the day the children pray to the times during the day the Church prays.
- Invite the children to silently read "Morning Prayer" and "Evening Prayer" and suggest that they pray them as part of their daily prayer.

PRAY

- Invite the children to come to the prayer area. Tell the children that in today's prayer you will pray the beginning of each line of the prayer and they will complete it silently with their own thoughts. At the end of the prayer everyone will respond "Amen."
- Lead the children in the prayer.
  We thank you for . . .
  We praise you for . . .
  We ask you for . . .
  We are sorry for . . .
  Amen.

Teach

FOCUS

Remind the children that at Baptism they received the gift of the Holy Spirit. Then ask a volunteer to read the "Faith Focus" question aloud.

DISCOVER

- Read the first paragraph under "The Holy Spirit" and have the children answer the questions. Accept all appropriate responses.
- Invite a volunteer to read the next paragraph.
- Then have the children silently read the rest of the page. Tell them to highlight or underline the name of the day on which the Holy Spirit came to Saint Peter the Apostle and the other disciples.
- Write the word *Pentecost* on the board and invite several volunteers to tell why Pentecost is such an important day for the Church. Accept all appropriate answers, such as, Saint Peter the Apostle began the work Jesus told the disciples to do.

Pentecost

Faith Focus

Who helps us to live as followers of Jesus?

The Word of the Lord

These are the Scripture readings for Pentecost. Ask your family to read one of the readings with you. Talk about the reading with them.

First Reading
Acts 2:1–11

Second Reading
1 Corinthians 12:3–7, 12–13

Gospel
John 20:19–23

The Holy Spirit

What do you do when you have to do something that is very difficult to do? How do you feel when someone helps you?

Jesus knew that his disciples would need help to do the work he gave them to do. So he promised that the Holy Spirit would come and help them.

On the day of Pentecost, the Holy Spirit came to Peter the Apostle and the other disciples as Jesus promised. Peter was filled with courage. He told a crowd from many different countries that God had raised Jesus to new life. Everyone was amazed by what Peter was saying. Over 3,000 people became followers of Jesus that day.

The Holy Spirit is our helper and teacher too. The Holy Spirit helps us to tell others about Jesus and teaches us to live as followers of Jesus.

281

Liturgy Tip

Prayer to the Holy Spirit. The traditional prayer of the Church to the Holy Spirit, which comes from the liturgy of Pentecost, begins with the words "Come, Holy Spirit, fill the hearts of your faithful." Write the words on the board for the children to copy, or write the words in advance on pieces of paper to give to the children. Help the children learn the words to the prayer by heart and encourage them to pray this simple prayer each day.

Come, Holy Spirit

The Holy Spirit helps us to live as followers of Jesus. Unscramble the scrambled words in each sentence of this prayer. Write the missing letters of the words on the lines under each sentence. Pray the prayer to the Holy Spirit together.

All: Come, Holy Spirit, be our guest, in our work, be our (ster).

r e s t

Group 1: When we are hurt, (lhea) us.

h e a l

Group 2: When we are weak, make us (torsng).

s t r o n g

Group 1: When we fail, (whas) our sins away.

w a s h

Group 2: Bring us (jyo) that never ends.

j o y

All: Amen.

282

Teaching Tip

Affirm the Giftedness of the Children. At Baptism we all receive the gift of the Holy Spirit and the responsibility to share our faith in Jesus Christ with others. Affirm the children in all their efforts that they have made to share their faith during the sessions this year. In advance you might make construction-paper flames with the words "Thank you, (name of child), for sharing with us your faith in Jesus this year" and give one to each child. Many will value it as a keepsake, reminding them of the time you have spent together this year.

Apply

REINFORCE

Ask the children to share how the Holy Spirit helps Christians today. The Holy Spirit helps us to tell others about Jesus and teaches us to live as followers of Jesus.

INTEGRATE

- Ask the children to name the people who tell them about Jesus. Accept all appropriate responses.
- Then ask the children to name some of the ways the Holy Spirit can help them live as followers of Christ. List their responses on the board. Encourage everyone to choose one or two of the things on the list and do them this week with their families.

PRAY

- Have the children prepare for the prayer by working in pairs to unscramble the words in the "Come, Holy Spirit" prayer and write the words in their books.
- Gather the children in the prayer area. Have them form two groups and slowly pray the prayer.

Saints for All Seasons

Here is a reference chart of all the canonized saints taught in the second grade book as well as other saints, arranged according to their feast days. Since you might not teach the chapter in which the saint is taught during the month when the saint's feast day is celebrated, this chart will allow you to honor these saints as their feasts occur in the Proper of the Saints throughout the school year. Saints who are not in the Proper of the Saints are also listed by their traditional celebration days. You may also wish to prepare a chart of the saints for whom the children in the class are named and honor these saints as well.

January

1 Mary the Mother of God

31 Saint John Bosco

February

11 Our Lady of Lourdes

March

9 Saint Dominic Savio
17 Saint Patrick
19 Solemnity of Saint Joseph

April

25 Saint Mark, Evangelist

29 Saint Catherine of Siena

May

3 Saints Philip and James, Apostles

26 Saint Philip Neri

June

24 Birth of Saint John the Baptist
29 Saints Peter and Paul, Apostles

July

11 Saint Benedict

15 Saint Bonaventure

21 Saint Matthew, Apostle and Evangelist

22 Saint Mary Magdalene

26 Saints Anne and Joachim, parents of Mary

August

4 Saint John Vianney

21 Saint Pius X

27 Saint Monica

28 Saint Augustine

September

27 Saint Vincent de Paul

October

1 Saint Thérèse of Lisieux

4 Saint Francis of Assisi

15 Saint Teresa of Avila

18 Saint Luke, Evangelist

November

1 All Saints

2 All Souls

December

12 Our Lady of Guadalupe
27 Saint John, Apostle and Evangelist

Catholic Prayers and Practices

Sign of the Cross

In the name of the Father,
and of the Son,
and of the Holy Spirit. Amen.

Glory Prayer

Glory to the Father,
and to the Son,
and to the Holy Spirit:
as it was in the beginning, is now,
and will be for ever. Amen.

Lord's Prayer

Our Father, who art in heaven,
hallowed be thy name;
thy kingdom come;
thy will be done on earth
as it is in heaven.
Give us this day our daily bread;
and forgive us our trespasses
as we forgive those who trespass
against us;
and lead us not into temptation,
but deliver us from evil.
Amen.

Hail Mary

Hail Mary, full of grace,
the Lord is with you!
Blessed are you among women,
and blessed is the fruit
of your womb, Jesus.
Holy Mary, Mother of God,
pray for us sinners,
now and at the hour of our death.
Amen.

Act of Contrition

My God,
I am sorry for my sins
with all my heart.
In choosing to do wrong
and failing to do good,
I have sinned against you
whom I should love above all things.
I firmly intend, with your help,
to do penance,
to sin no more,
and to avoid whatever leads me to sin.
Our Savior Jesus Christ
suffered and died for us.
In his name, my God, have mercy.

283

ACT OF CONTRITION

Teaching children to develop the habit of expressing true sorrow is vital to their social and spiritual development. The traditional Act of Contrition is provided so you and the parents can foster this sense of sorrow and desire to make amends for deliberate wrongdoing. Use simple Psalm verses that express sorrow to lay the foundation for the children's use of this act of contrition.

APOSTLES' CREED

The word *creed* comes from two Latin words that mean "I give my heart to" that have been joined together to form one word that means "I believe." In the creed we express our belief in, or give our hearts to, God. The Apostles' Creed is one of the earliest creeds of the Church. It is called the Apostles' Creed because the teachings in this creed date back to the main beliefs that the Church has professed since the days of the Apostles. Read the words of the Apostles' Creed one line at a time, and have the children echo, or repeat, the words after you.

NICENE CREED

The Nicene Creed, or, more correctly, the Nicene-Constantinople Creed, is the creed regularly professed at Mass on Sundays. For this reason it is important to guide your second graders to become familiar with its words so that they can join in professing the creed at Mass. You might slowly integrate the use of this creed into your lessons. For example:

- point out its Trinitarian structure when you present chapter 2, "We Believe in the Holy Trinity";
- read the words of the first part as a summary to your presenting chapter 3, "God Is Our Father"; and so on.

Apostles' Creed

I believe in God,
　the Father almighty,
　creator of heaven and earth.

I believe in Jesus Christ,
　his only Son, our Lord.
　He was conceived by the power
　　of the Holy Spirit
　and born of the Virgin Mary.
　He suffered under Pontius Pilate,
　　was crucified, died, and was
　　buried.
　He descended to the dead.
　On the third day he rose again.
　He ascended into heaven,
　and is seated at the right hand
　　of the Father.
　He will come again to judge
　　the living and the dead.

I believe in the Holy Spirit,
　the holy catholic Church,
　the communion of saints,
　the forgiveness of sins,
　the resurrection of the body,
　and the life everlasting. Amen.

Nicene Creed

We believe in one God,
　the Father, the Almighty,
　maker of heaven and earth,
　of all that is, seen and unseen.

We believe in one Lord, Jesus Christ,
　the only Son of God,
　eternally begotten of the Father,
　God from God, Light from Light,
　true God from true God,
　begotten, not made, one in Being
　　with the Father.

Through him all things were
　made.
For us men and for our salvation
　he came down from heaven:
by the power of the Holy Spirit
　he was born of the Virgin Mary,
　and became man.

For our sake he was crucified under
　Pontius Pilate;
　he suffered, died, and was buried.
　On the third day he rose again
　　in fulfillment of the Scriptures;
　he ascended into heaven
　　and is seated at the right hand
　　of the Father.
He will come again in glory to judge
　the living and the dead,
　and his kingdom will have no end.

We believe in the Holy Spirit, the
　Lord, the giver of life,
　who proceeds from the Father
　　and the Son.
　With the Father and the Son he is
　　worshiped and glorified.
　He has spoken through the
　　Prophets.
We believe in one holy catholic
　and apostolic Church.
We acknowledge one baptism for
　the forgiveness of sins.
We look for the resurrection of the
dead, and the life of the world
　to come. Amen.

(284)

Prayer to the Holy Spirit

Come, Holy Spirit, fill the hearts
of your faithful.
And kindle in them the
fire of your love.
Send forth your Spirit and
they shall be created.
And you will renew the
face of the earth.

A Vocation Prayer

God, I know you will call me
for special work in my life.
Help me to follow Jesus each day
and be ready to answer your call.

Morning Prayer

Dear God,
as I begin this day,
keep me in your love and care.
Help me to live as your child today.
Bless me, my family, and my friends
in all we do.
Keep us all close to you. Amen.

Evening Prayer

Dear God,
I thank you for today.
Keep me safe throughout the night.
Thank you for all the good I did today.
I am sorry for what I have chosen
to do wrong.
Bless my family and friends. Amen.

Grace Before Meals

Bless us, O Lord,
and these your gifts
which we are about to receive
from your goodness,
through Christ our Lord.
Amen.

Grace After Meals

We give you thanks for all your gifts,
almighty God,
living and reigning now and for ever.
Amen.

(285)

RHYTHM OF PRAYER

Praying is to the spiritual life as breathing is to our physical life. Saint Paul the Apostle captures the truth of this adage when he admonishes us to pray always. Guide the children to pray always by helping them develop the habit of prayer, or a rhythm to their prayer life. Make the children aware of and teach them to incorporate prayer into their daily life.

DEVOTION TO MARY

The Blessed Virgin Mary has a favored and unique place in God's loving plan of salvation for the world. The twenty mysteries of the Rosary summarize Mary's role in God's plan as intrinsically related to the mysteries of the life of Christ.

Connect the Rosary with your sessions. For example, when a chapter talks about a mystery from the life of Mary and Jesus—the Annunciation, the Nativity, the Crucifixion, the Resurrection, the Ascension, the descent of the Holy Spirit on Pentecost, and so on—make the connection with the Rosary. Introduce the children to the praying of the Rosary.

Use the information on page 286 to demonstrate to the children how the Rosary is prayed. Point out the centrality of praying the Hail Mary as part of the Rosary. Draw the children's attention to the Hail, Holy Queen prayer, which has been placed on this page so they can begin to become familiar with it.

Rosary

Catholics pray the Rosary to honor Mary and remember the important events in the life of Jesus and Mary. There are twenty mysteries of the Rosary. Follow the steps from 1 to 5.

5. Pray the Hail, Holy Queen prayer. Make the Sign of the Cross.

3. Think of the first mystery. Pray an Our Father, 10 Hail Marys, and the Glory Prayer.

2. Pray an Our Father, 3 Hail Marys, and the Glory Prayer.

4. Repeat step 3 for each of the next 4 mysteries.

1. Make the Sign of the Cross and pray the Apostles' Creed.

Joyful Mysteries
1. The Annunciation
2. The Visitation
3. The Nativity
4. The Presentation
5. The Finding of Jesus in the Temple

Mysteries of Light
1. The Baptism of Jesus in the Jordan River
2. The Miracle at the Wedding at Cana
3. The Proclamation of the Kingdom of God
4. The Transfiguration of Jesus
5. The Institution of the Eucharist

Sorrowful Mysteries
1. The Agony in the Garden
2. The Scourging at the Pillar
3. The Crowning with Thorns
4. The Carrying of the Cross
5. The Crucifixion

Glorious Mysteries
1. The Resurrection
2. The Ascension
3. The Coming of the Holy Spirit
4. The Assumption of Mary
5. The Coronation of Mary

Hail, Holy Queen

Hail, holy Queen, mother of mercy,
hail, our life, our sweetness,
   and our hope.
To you we cry, the children of Eve;
to you we send up our sighs,
mourning and weeping
   in this land of exile.
Turn, then, most gracious advocate,
your eyes of mercy toward us;
lead us home at last
and show us the blessed fruit
   of your womb, Jesus:
O clement, O loving, O sweet
   Virgin Mary.

286

The Great Commandment

"You shall love the Lord, your God, with all your heart, with all your soul, and with all your mind. . . . You shall love your neighbor as yourself."

Matthew 22:37, 39

Jesus' Commandment

"This is my commandment: love one another as I love you."

John 15:12

The Ten Commandments

1. I am the LORD your God: you shall not have strange Gods before me.
2. You shall not take the name of the LORD your God in vain.
3. Remember to keep holy the LORD's Day.
4. Honor your father and your mother.
5. You shall not kill.
6. You shall not commit adultery.
7. You shall not steal.
8. You shall not bear false witness against your neighbor.
9. You shall not covet your neighbor's wife.
10. You shall not covet your neighbor's goods.

Based on Exodus 20:2–3, 7–17

287

LIVING OUR LIFE IN CHRIST

This page offers a brief summary of God's Law of Love. It makes a visual and concrete connection to children living the Ten Commandments as a way of living the Great Commandment. Use this page to:

- introduce the children to Unit 3, "We Live," to provide the big picture of what it means to live as a child of God.
- reinforce the teaching of chapters 18 through 23 and prepare the children for the unit review.

THE SEVEN SACRAMENTS

This page presents an overview of the seven sacraments of the Church. Visual learners will benefit greatly from its incorporation into your lessons. Use this page as:

- an overview during the lesson when you introduce the children to the seven sacraments.
- a reinforcement tool during each session that deals with the sacraments individually and at the end of the second unit as part of a review.

The Seven Sacraments

Jesus gave the Church the seven sacraments. The seven sacraments are signs of God's love for us. When we celebrate the sacraments, Jesus is really present with us. We share in the life of the Holy Trinity.

Baptism
We are joined to Christ. We become members of the Body of Christ, the Church.

Confirmation
The Holy Spirit strengthens us to live as children of God.

Eucharist
We receive the Body and Blood of Jesus.

Reconciliation
We receive God's gift of forgiveness and peace.

Anointing of the Sick
We receive God's healing strength when we are sick or dying, or weak because of old age.

Holy Orders
A baptized man is ordained to serve the Church as a bishop, priest, or deacon.

Matrimony
A baptized man and a baptized woman make a lifelong promise to love and respect each other as husband and wife. They promise to accept the gift of children from God.

288

We Celebrate the Mass

The Introductory Rites

We remember that we are the community
of the Church. We prepare to listen to the word of God
and to celebrate the Eucharist.

The Entrance

We stand as the priest, deacon,
and other ministers enter the
assembly. We sing a gathering song.
The priest and deacon kiss the altar.
The priest then goes to the chair
where he presides over the
celebration.

**Greeting of the Altar and
of the People Gathered**

The priest leads us in praying the
Sign of the Cross. The priest greets
us, and we say,
"And also with you."

The Act of Penitence

We admit our wrongdoings.
We bless God for his mercy.

The Gloria

We praise God for all the good
he has done for us.

The Collect

The priest leads us in praying the
Collect, or the opening prayer.
We respond, **"Amen."**

289

WE CELEBRATE THE MASS
Use "We Celebrate the Mass"
on pages 289–295 of the
children's book to help the
children participate fully and
actively in the celebration of the
Mass. This section of the
children's book includes photos
that will help the children identify
with the rites of the Mass and
prayers and responses that are
used during the Mass. Integrate
these pages into your
presentation of chapters 15
and 17.

Here are some suggestions of ways that you can incorporate these pages into your teaching.

- Have the children examine the photographs of the Mass.
- Relate what is happening in the photographs with the prayers and explanations.
- Point out that although there may be some differences in the way each parish celebrates Mass, the main rites of the Mass—the responses, prayers, and actions—always remain the same.

The Liturgy of the Word

God speaks to us today.
We listen and respond to God's word.

The First Reading from the Bible
We sit and listen as the reader reads from the Old Testament or from the Acts of the Apostles. The reader concludes, "The word of the Lord." We respond,
"Thanks be to God."

The Responsorial Psalm
The song leader leads us in singing a psalm.

The Second Reading from the Bible
The reader reads from the New Testament, but not from the four Gospels. The reader concludes, "The word of the Lord." We respond,
"Thanks be to God."

The Acclamation
We stand to honor Christ present with us in the Gospel. The song leader leads us in singing **"Alleluia, Alleluia, Alleluia"** or another chant during Lent.

The Gospel
The deacon or priest proclaims, "A reading from the holy gospel according to (name of Gospel writer)." We respond,
"Glory to you, O Lord."
He proclaims the Gospel. At the end he says, "The gospel of the Lord." We respond,
"Praise to you, Lord Jesus Christ."

The Homily
We sit. The priest or deacon preaches the homily. He helps the whole community understand the word of God spoken to us in the readings.

The Profession of Faith
We stand and profess our faith. We pray the Nicene Creed together.

The Prayer of the Faithful
The priest leads us in praying for our Church and its leaders, for our country and its leaders, for ourselves and others, for the sick and those who have died. We can respond to each prayer in several ways. One way we respond is,
"Lord, hear our prayer."

290

The Liturgy of the Eucharist

We join with Jesus and the Holy Spirit
to give thanks and praise to God the Father.

The Preparation of the Gifts

We sit as the altar table is prepared and the collection is taken up. We share our blessings with the community of the Church and especially with those in need. The song leader may lead us in singing a song. The gifts of bread and wine are brought to the altar.

The priest lifts up the bread and blesses God for all our gifts. He prays, "Blessed are you, Lord, God of all creation . . ." We respond, **"Blessed be God for ever."**

The priest lifts up the cup of wine and prays, "Blessed are you, Lord, God of all creation . . ." We respond, **"Blessed be God for ever."**

The priest invites us, "Pray, my brothers and sisters, that our sacrifice may be acceptable to God, the almighty Father."

We stand and respond, **"May the Lord accept the sacrifice at your hands for the praise and glory of his name, for our good, and the good of all his Church."**

The Prayer over the Offerings

The priest leads us in praying the Prayer over the Offerings. We respond, **"Amen."**

291

ADDITIONAL SUGGESTIONS:

- Take the children on a visit to the parish church. Show them the things that are used in the celebration of the Mass. Let the children see and touch the vestments, books, and vessels. Allow them to stand at the altar, the ambo, and the celebrant's chair so they can experience the church from that perspective.
- Integrate RCL's *Eucharist* music CD, which contains appropriate songs for each part of the Mass.

ADDITIONAL SUGGESTIONS:

- Explain the prayers, responses, and actions of the Mass so that the children understand what is happening throughout the Mass.
- Review the rites of the Mass in relationship to each other. This will help the children begin to see that all the parts of the Mass fit together as one whole prayer.

Preface

The priest invites us to join in praying the Church's great prayer of praise and thanksgiving to God the Father.

Priest: "The Lord be with you."

Assembly: "And also with you."

Priest: "Lift up your hearts."

Assembly: "We lift them up to the Lord."

Priest: "Let us give thanks to the Lord our God."

Assembly: "It is right to give him thanks and praise."

After the priest sings or prays aloud the preface, we join in acclaiming,

"Holy, holy, holy Lord, God of power and might.
Heaven and earth are full of your glory.
Hosanna in the highest.
Blessed is he who comes in the name of the Lord.
Hosanna in the highest."

The Eucharistic Prayer

The priest leads the assembly in praying the Eucharistic Prayer. We call upon the Holy Spirit to make our gifts of bread and wine holy and that they become the Body and Blood of Jesus. We recall what happened at the Last Supper. The bread and wine become the Body and Blood of the Lord. Jesus is truly and really present under the appearances of bread and wine.

The priest sings or says aloud, "Let us proclaim the mystery of faith." We respond using this or another acclamation used by the Church,

"Christ has died, Christ is risen, Christ will come again."

The priest then prays for the Church. He prays for the living and the dead.

Doxology

The priest concludes the praying of the Eucharistic Prayer. He sings or says aloud,

"Through him, with him, in him, in the unity of the Holy Spirit, all glory and honor is yours, almighty Father, for ever and ever."

We respond by singing, **"Amen."**

292

I AM WITH YOU ALWAYS

The Communion Rite

The Lord's Prayer
The priest invites us to pray the Lord's Prayer together. He says, "Let us pray with confidence to the Father in the words our Savior gave us."

Together with the priest we continue,
"Our Father who art in heaven, hallowed be thy name; thy kingdom come; thy will be done on earth as it is in heaven. Give us this day our daily bread; and forgive us our trespasses as we forgive those who trespass against us; and lead us not into temptation, but deliver us from evil."

The priest continues, "Deliver us, Lord, . . . as we wait in joyful hope for the coming of our Savior Jesus Christ."

Doxology
We end the prayer by praying the acclamation,
"For the kingdom, the power, and the glory are yours, now and for ever."

The Rite of Peace
The priest invites us to share a sign of peace, saying, "The peace of the Lord be with you always." We respond,
"And also with you."
We share a sign of peace.

The Fraction, or the Breaking of the Bread
The priest breaks the host, the consecrated bread. We sing or pray aloud,
"Lamb of God, you take away the sins of the world: have mercy on us. Lamb of God, you take away the sins of the world: have mercy on us. Lamb of God, you take away the sins of the world: grant us peace."

293

RECEIVING HOLY COMMUNION

Review with the children your parish's directions for receiving Holy Communion.

- Reverently walk in procession to the altar, singing the communion song, to receive Holy Communion from the priest, deacon, or the extraordinary minister of Holy Communion.
- You may receive Holy Communion either in your hand or on your tongue.
- The consecrated bread, or host, is offered to you with the words "The body of Christ." You respond, "Amen."
- If you choose to receive Holy Communion in your hand, place one hand underneath the other hand; hold your hand out with palms facing up; bow reverently and receive the consecrated bread in the palm of your hand. Step to the side and briefly stop. Slowly and reverently take the consecrated bread from the palm of your hand and put the consecrated bread in your mouth. Chew and swallow the consecrated bread, the Body of Christ.

- If you choose to receive Holy Communion on your tongue, fold your hands, bow, and open your mouth and put your tongue out to receive the consecrated bread. Chew and swallow the consecrated bread which is the Body of Christ.
- You may also receive the consecrated wine, the Blood of Christ. The cup of consecrated wine will be offered to you with the words "The blood of Christ." You respond, "Amen."
- If you choose to receive the Blood of Christ at Holy Communion, bow and take the cup of consecrated wine firmly in both hands; using both hands, reverently bring the cup to your mouth, take a small sip of the consecrated wine from the cup, and carefully give the cup back, using both hands.
- Reverently return to your place, singing the communion hymn.
- Spend some time in quiet prayer and reflection after the assembly has completed singing the communion procession hymn.

Communion

The priest raises the host and says aloud,
 "This is the Lamb of God who takes away the sins of the world.
 Happy are those who are called to his supper."
We join with him and say,
 "Lord, I am not worthy to receive you, but only say the word and I shall be healed."

The priest receives Communion. Next, the deacon and the extraordinary ministers of Holy Communion and the members of the assembly receive Communion.

The priest, deacon, or extraordinary minister of Holy Communion holds up the host. We bow and the priest, deacon, or extraordinary minister of Holy Communion says, "The body of Christ." We respond, **"Amen."** We then receive the consecrated host in our hand or on our tongue.

If we are to receive the Blood of Christ, the priest, deacon, or extraordinary minister of Holy Communion holds up the cup containing the consecrated wine. We bow and the priest, deacon, or extraordinary minister of Holy Communion says, "The blood of Christ." We respond, **"Amen."** We take the cup in our hands and drink from it.

The Prayer after Communion
We stand as the priest invites us to pray saying, "Let us pray." He prays the Prayer after Communion. We respond, **"Amen."**

294

The Concluding Rites

**We are sent forth to do good works,
praising and blessing the Lord.**

Greeting
We stand. The priest greets us as
we prepare to leave. He says, "The
Lord be with you." We respond,
"And also with you."

Blessing
The priest or deacon may invite us,
"Bow your heads and pray for
God's blessing."
The priest blesses us saying,
"May almighty God bless you,
the Father, and the Son,
and the Holy Spirit."
We respond, **"Amen."**

Dismissal of the People
The priest or deacon sends us
forth, using these or similar words,
"The Mass is ended, go in
peace."
We respond,
"Thanks be to God."

We sing a hymn. The priest and the
deacon kiss the altar. The priest,
deacon, and other ministers bow to
the altar and leave in procession.

The Sacrament of Reconciliation

Individual Rite
Greeting
Scripture Reading
Confession of Sins
and Acceptance of Penance
Act of Contrition
Absolution
Closing Prayer

Communal Rite
Greeting
Scripture Reading
Homily
Examination of Conscience, a
litany of contrition, and the
Lord's Prayer
Individual Confession
and Absolution
Closing Prayer

295

SACRAMENT OF RECONCILIATION

Identify the rite of Reconciliation that the children will be celebrating. Take the children to church to walk them through the rite so they can see where and how they will participate. Show the children where they will sit and where the priest will sit.

TOUR OF THE CHURCH

Use this section in conjunction with the text when the items appear for the first time. Use it independently as a learning session, or integrate its use with the "We Celebrate the Mass" section.

USE OF PHOTOS

Read aloud "Baptismal Font." Then have the children look at the photo of the baptismal font on page 296 of their books and share a description. Invite a volunteer to tell where the baptismal font or baptismal pool is in the church. After a brief sharing, move on to "Assembly" and continue the process.

A Tour of a Church

Some churches are made of stone and some are wooden. Some are big and some are small. One thing they all have in common is that they are places where people worship God.

Baptismal Font

The baptismal font is the pool of water used for Baptism. Water is used to remind us of new life. The tall candle is called the Easter candle. It is lit during Baptism to remind us of Jesus, the Light of the world.

Assembly

The assembly is the people gathered for Mass. The pews are the seats where the people sit.

Crucifix

The crucifix is a sign of Jesus' love for us. You see the crucifix near the altar. Not all crucifixes are the same. This one shows Jesus after he was raised from the dead. The crucifix reminds us that Jesus died and was raised again to new life.

296

Altar

The altar is the table where the Liturgy of the Eucharist is celebrated at Mass. It reminds us of the Last Supper and that Jesus died for us. The altar is also called the Table of the Lord. It is the table from which Jesus shares his Body and Blood with us.

Ambo

The ambo is the special stand or place from where the Scriptures are read during Mass. The lector is the person who reads the first and second readings during Mass. The deacon or priest reads the Gospel.

The Book of the Gospels Lectionary

The Book of the Gospels contains the Gospel readings we listen to at Mass. The first two readings are read from the Lectionary.

Tabernacle

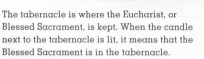

The tabernacle is where the Eucharist, or Blessed Sacrament, is kept. When the candle next to the tabernacle is lit, it means that the Blessed Sacrament is in the tabernacle.

297

VISIT THE CHURCH

Take the children to the church and show them the things that are used in the celebration of the Mass. Let the children again see and touch the vestments, books, vessels, and other items used for the celebration of Mass. Allow the children to stand at the altar, the ambo, and the celebrant's chair so that they can experience the church from that perspective. Remind them to be reverent and respectful during their tour of the church.

Glossary

A

absolution [page 124]
Absolution is the forgiveness of our sins in the sacrament of Reconciliation through the words and actions of the priest.

almighty [page 30]
God alone is almighty. This means that only God has the power to do everything.

almsgiving [page 177]
The word *almsgiving* means "sharing something to help the poor."

ambo [page 57]
The ambo is the place in the church where the word of God is proclaimed.

anoint [page 107]
Anoint means to bless a person with holy oil.

Apostles [page 70]
The Apostles were the disciples who Jesus chose and sent to preach the Gospel to the whole world in his name.

Ascension [page 78]
The Ascension is the return of the Risen Jesus to his Father in heaven forty days after the Resurrection.

assembly [page 131]
The assembly is the people who gather to celebrate the Mass.

B

Baptism [page 106]
Baptism is the sacrament that joins us to Christ and makes us members of the Church. We receive the gift of the Holy Spirit and become adopted sons and daughters of God.

believe [page 14]
To believe in God means to know God and to give ourselves to him with all our heart.

> The words in boldface type are Faith Words in the text.

Bible [page 15]
The Bible is the written word of God. It is the story of God's love for us.

Body of Christ [page 86]
The Church is the Body of Christ. Jesus Christ is the Head of the Church and all the baptized are its members.

Body of Christ [page 148]
The consecrated bread at Mass is the Body of Christ. Through the words of the priest and the power of the Holy Spirit the bread and wine become the Body and Blood of Christ at Mass.

Book of Psalms [page 38]
The Book of Psalms is one of the forty-six books in the Old Testament.

C

Catholics [page 86]
Catholics are followers of Jesus Christ who belong to the Catholic Church.

Church [page 86 and 87]
The Church is the Body of Christ and the new People of God.

commandments [page 174]
Commandments are rules that help us live holy lives.

Communion of Saints [page 86]
The Church is the Communion of Saints. It is the communion of all the faithful followers of Jesus on earth and those who have died.

confession [page 124]
Confession is telling our sins to the bishop or priest by ourselves in the sacrament of Reconciliation.

Confirmation [page 106]
Confirmation is the sacrament in which the gift of the Holy Spirit strengthens us to live our Baptism.

conscience [page 190]
Conscience is a gift from God that helps us to make wise choices.

consequences [page 190]
Consequences are the good or bad things that happen when we make choices.

(298)

contrition [page 124]

Contrition is being truly sorry for our sins.

Covenant [page 46]

The Covenant is God's promise always to love and be kind to his people.

creation [page 30]

Creation is everything that God has made.

Creator [page 30]

God alone is the Creator. God has made everyone and everything out of love and without any help.

crucifix [page 65]

A crucifix is a cross with an image of the body of Jesus on it.

Crucifixion [page 62]

The Crucifixion is the death of Jesus on a cross.

deacon [page 24]

A deacon is a baptized man blessed in the sacrament of Holy Orders to serve the Church and help bishops and priests.

disciples [page 138]

The people who followed Jesus were called his disciples.

Eucharist [page 146]

The Eucharist is the sacrament of the Body and Blood of Jesus Christ.

Eucharistic Prayer [page 147]

The Eucharistic Prayer is the Church's great prayer of thanksgiving that we pray at Mass.

evangelist [page 79]

The word *evangelist* means "one who announces the Gospel."

faith [page 14]

Faith is God's gift that makes us able to believe in him.

fruits of the Holy Spirit [page 161]

The fruits of the Holy Spirit are signs that show we are trying our best to live as children of God.

Gospels [page 70]

The Gospels are the first four books in the New Testament.

grace [page 158]

Grace is the gift of God sharing his life with us. It is also God helping us to make good choices to live as children of God.

Great Commandment [page 166]

The Great Commandment is to love God above all else and to love others as we love ourselves.

hallowed [page 226]

The word *hallowed* means "very holy."

heaven [page 64]

Heaven is living with God and with Mary and all the saints in happiness forever after we die.

holy [page 198]

Holy means sharing in God's life and love.

Holy Communion [page 147]

Holy Communion is receiving the Body and Blood of Christ in the Eucharist.

Holy Spirit [page 24]

The Holy Spirit is the third Person of the Holy Trinity.

Holy Trinity [page 22]

The Holy Trinity is one God in three Persons—God the Father, God the Son, and God the Holy Spirit.

honor [page 158]

To honor someone is to treat them with kindness, respect, and love.

hymns [page 42]

Hymns are songs we use to pray to God.

Jesus Christ [page 46]

Jesus Christ is the Son of God. He is the second Person of the Holy Trinity who became one of us. He is true God and true man.

(299)

Jewish people [page 166]
The Jewish people are the people God chose as his special people in the Old Testament. This is the name of the people to which Jesus belonged.

kingdom of God [page 226]
The kingdom of God is also called the kingdom of heaven.

Last Supper [page 138]
The Last Supper is the special meal that Jesus ate with his disciples on the night before he died.

Liturgy of the Eucharist [page 146]
The Liturgy of the Eucharist is the second main part of the Mass. The Church does what Jesus did at the Last Supper.

Liturgy of the Word [page 130]
The Liturgy of the Word is the first main part of the Mass. God speaks to us through the readings from the Bible.

Lord's Prayer [page 218]
The Lord's Prayer is another name for the Our Father.

M-N

Mass [page 130]
The Mass is the most important celebration of the Church. At Mass we worship God. We listen to God's word. We celebrate and share in the Eucharist.

mercy [page 48]
The word *mercy* means "great kindness."

missionaries [page 169]
Missionaries travel to teach others about Jesus Christ.

mortal sin [page 199]
Mortal sin is serious sin that causes us to lose the gift of sanctifying grace. We must confess mortal sins in the sacrament of Reconciliation.

Nativity [page 47]
The Nativity is the name of the Bible story about the birth of Jesus.

original sin [page 46]
The word *original* means "first." Original sin is the sin of the first humans by which they broke their promises to God.

parable [page 114]
A parable is a story that compares two things. Jesus told parables to help people know and love God better.

parish [page 17]
Our parish is our home in the Catholic Church.

Passover [page 138]
Passover is a holy time of the year for the Jewish people. Jesus celebrated the Last Supper with his disciples during Passover.

penance [page 124]
Penance is a prayer or good deed the priest asks us to say or do in the sacrament of Reconciliation. Doing our penance helps repair, or heal, the harm we have caused by our sins.

Pentecost [page 78]
Pentecost is the day the Holy Spirit came to the disciples of Jesus fifty days after the Resurrection.

prayer [page 210]
Prayer is raising our minds and hearts to God.

prayer of praise [page 38]
A prayer of praise gives honor to God for his great love and kindness.

procession [page 133]
A procession is people prayerfully walking together. Processions are prayers in action.

prophet [page 54]
A prophet in the Bible is a person who God chose to speak in his name.

proverbs [page 182]
Proverbs are short sayings that help us to make wise choices.

psalms [page 38]
Psalms are songs of prayer.

300

Reconciliation [page 122]

Reconciliation is a sacrament that brings God's gifts of mercy and forgiving love into our lives.

Resurrection [page 62]

The Resurrection is God's raising Jesus from the dead to new life.

sacrifice [page 149]

A sacrifice is a gift of great value we give out of love. At Mass we share in the sacrifice of Jesus.

sacramentals [page 101]

Sacramentals are objects and blessings the Church uses to help us worship God.

sacraments [page 98]

The sacraments are the seven signs of God's love for us that Jesus gave the Church. We share in God's love when we celebrate the sacraments.

sanctifying grace [page 198]

Sanctifying grace is the gift of God sharing his life with us.

sanctuary [page 133]

The word *sanctuary* means "holy place." The sanctuary is the place in the church where we see the altar and the ambo.

Savior [pages 62 and 63]

A savior is a person who sets people free. Jesus freed us from sin by dying on the cross. Jesus is the Savior of the world.

sin [page 122]

Sin is freely choosing to do or say something that we know God does not want us to do or say.

Son of God [page 46]

Jesus Christ is the Son of God. He is the second Person of the Trinity who became one of us. Jesus is true God and true man.

soul [page 22]

Our soul is that part of us that lives forever.

Temple in Jerusalem [page 166]

A temple is a building built to honor God. The Jewish people in Jesus' time worshiped God in the Temple in Jerusalem.

temptation [page 228]

Temptation is everything that can lead us away from God's love and from living as children of God.

Ten Commandments [page 174]

The Ten Commandments are the laws that God gave to Moses that teach us to live as God's people.

trespass [page 228]

To trespass means to do or say something that hurts our friendship with God and with other people.

venial sin [page 199]

Venial sin is sin less serious than mortal sin that hurts our relationship with God and other people.

vocation [page 229]

The word *vocation* means "what we are called to do." God calls everyone who is baptized to live as a follower of Jesus.

wise choice [page 182]

A wise choice is a choice that helps us to live as children of God.

works of mercy [page 49]

The works of mercy are ways to be kind and loving to people as Jesus was.

worship [page 98]

Worship means to honor and love God above all else.

301

Index

302

Credits

Guide Credits

Cover Design: Kristy Howard
Cover Illustration: Amy Freeman

Photo and Art Credits

Abbreviated as follows: (bkgd) background; (t) top; (b) bottom; (l) left; (r) right; (c) center.

Page 18 (all), © PhotoDisc; 19 (l), © Tony Freeman/Photoeditinc; 19 (r), © Bill Wittman; 20 (t), © PhotoDisc; 20 (b), © RCL Stock; 21, © Bill Wittman; 22, © Myrleen Ferguson Cate/Photoeditinc; 23, © Jim Cummins/Corbis; 28 (t), © Eyewire; 28 (c), © Punchstock; 28 (c), © Comstock; 28 (b), © Cleo Photography/Index Stock; 29 (t), © Creatas/PictureQuest; 29 (c), © PictureQuest; 29 (c), © Comstock; 29 (b), © Punchstock; 30 (t), © Digitalvision/ Gettyimages; 30 (b), © Corbis; 31, © Myrleen Ferguson Cate/ Photoeditinc; 32, © Sam Martinez/RCL; 46, © Digital Stock; 58, © The Crosiers/Gene Plaisted, OSC; 70, © PictureQuest; 82, 94, © The Crosiers/Gene Plaisted, OSC; 106, Yoshi Miyake; 118, 130, © The Crosiers/Gene Plaisted, OSC; 142, © Cherie Mayman/RCL; 154, © Bill Wittman; 170, © Tony Freeman/Photoeditinc; 182, © The Crosiers/Gene Plaisted, OSC; 194, Yoshi Miyake; 206, © PictureQuest; 218, The Crosiers/Gene Plaisted, OSC; 230, © Anthony Jambor/RCL; 242, © The Crosiers/Gene Plaisted, OSC; 258, © Shannon Stirnweis/Superstock; 270, Gary Torissi; 282, © The Crosiers/Gene Plaisted, OSC; 294, Mari Goering; 306, © Image Farm; 318, © Digital Stock; 334, © Ariel Skelley/Corbis; 346, Gary Torissi; 358, © Myrleen Ferguson Cate/Photoeditinc; 374, © Anthony Jambor/RCL; 378, © The Crosiers/Gene Plaisted, OSC; 388, © SuperStock, Inc.; 394, 406, © The Crosiers/Gene Plaisted, OSC; 416, © Bill Wittman.

Footnotes

Teaching Others to Pray
Page 22
1. Cf. *John* 17:4.

Chapter 1
Page 47
1. Cf. *Catechism of the Catholic Church* 1229; *Christus Dominus:* Decree on the Pastoral Office of Bishops in the Church 14.

Chapter 2
Page 59
1. General Catechetical Directory (1971) 41; cf.r. *Eph* 2:18.
2. Cf. General Catechetical Directory (1971) 41.

Chapter 5
Page 95
1. Cf. *Catechesi Tradendae:* On Catechesis in Our Time 20b.

Chapter 7
Page 119
1. *John* 1:14.

Chapter 8
Page 130
1. Cf. *Mt* 28:9, 16–17; *Lk* 24:15, 36; *Jn* 20:14, 17, 19, 26; 21:4.
Page 131
1. Cf. MPD 9.

Chapter 9
Page 142
1. Cf. *Dei Verbum:* The Dogmatic Constitution on Divine Revelation 7a.
2. Cf. *Dei Verbum:* The Dogmatic Constitution on Divine Revelation 8 and *Catechism of the Catholic Church* 774–776.
Page 143
1. Cf. *Ad gentes:* The Decree of the Church's Missionary Activity 13a.
2. Cf. *Catechism of the Catholic Church* 150 and 176.

Chapter 10
Page 155
1. As has been stated in chapter 1 or this part in "The transmission of Revelation by the Church, the work of the Holy Spirit" and in part II, chapter 1 in "The ecclesial nature of the Gospel message." Cf. *Evangelii nuntiandi:* On Evangelization in the Modern World 60 which speaks of the ecclesial nature of any evangelizing activity.

Chapter 11
Page 170
1. Secret prayer of the 9th Sunday after Pentecost.

Chapter 13
Page 195
1. Cf. *Romans* 10:17; *Lumen gentium:* The Dogmatic Constitution on the Church (LG) 16 and *Ad gentes:* The Decree of the Church's Missionary Activity 7; cf. *Catechism of the Catholic Church* 846–848.
2. Cf. *Ad gentes:* The Decree of the Church's Missionary Activity 13a.

Chapter 14
Page 206
1. Cf. *Lumen gentium:* The Dogmatic Constitution on the Church 11.
Page 207
1. *Evangelii Nuntiandi:* On Evangelization in the Modern World 26.

Chapter 16
Page 231
1. Cf. *Lumen gentium:* The Dogmatic Constitution on the Church 11; cf. *Apostolicam Actuositatem:* Decree on the Apostolate of the Laity 11; *Familiaris consortio:* On the Family 49.
2. Cf. *Gaudium et Spes:* The Pastoral Constitution on the Church in the Modern World 52; FC 37a.

Chapter 17
Page 242
1. *Acts* 20:7
Page 243
1. *Catechism of the Catholic Church* 1211.
2. *Lumen gentium:* The Dogmatic Constitution on the Church 11.

Chapter 19
Page 271
1. JW: *Justice in the World*, II, The Gospel Message and the Mission of the Church, The Saving Justice of God Through Christ.

Chapter 23
Page 319
1. *Libertatis Conscientia:* Congregation for the Doctrine of the Faith, Instruction 72.

Chapter 25
Page 347
1. Cf. General Catechetical Directory (1971) 10 and 22.

Chapter 26
Page 359
1. *Rite of Christian Initiation of Adults* 25 and 188–191.
2. Cf. *Catechism of the Catholic Church* 2761.

Ordinary Time
Page 375
1. *Sacrosanctum Concilium:* The Constitution on the Sacred Liturgy 104; cf. *Sacrosanctum Concilium:* The Constitution on the Sacred Liturgy 108, 111.

Advent
Page 379
1. Cf. *Rev* 22:17.

Holy Week
Page 407
1. Cf. *Maxima Redemptionis Nostrae Mysteria;* St. Augustine, *Epistolas* 55, 24, PL, 35, 215.

Easter
Page 417
1. Cf. *Roman Missal*, Easter Vigil, 53; *Roman Missal*, Ritual Masses, 3, Baptism.